The Politics of Antipolitics

the
POLITICS
of
ANTIPOLITICS

The Military in Latin America

Edited by Brian Loveman and Thomas M. Davies, Jr.

UNIVERSITY OF NEBRASKA PRESS • LINCOLN AND LONDON

This book is dedicated
to
Bernard J. Loveman
and
Thomas M. and *Faith Arnold Davies*

Acknowledgments for permission to reprint copyrighted material appear on p. 307.

322.509

P 75

UNP

94365

First Bison Book printing: 1978

Most recent printing indicated by first digit below:

3   4   5   6   7   8   9   10

Library of Congress Cataloging in Publication Data
Main entry under title:

The Politics of antipolitics.

    1. Latin America—Armed Forces. 2. Sociology,
Military—Latin America. 3. Latin America—Politics
and government. I. Loveman, Brian. II. Davies,
Thomas M.
UA602.3.P64   322'.5'098   77-25256
ISBN 0–8032–0954–1
ISBN 0–8032–7900–0 pbk.

Contents

Preface

When we set out several years ago to prepare an interdisciplinary graduate seminar on the military and politics in Latin America, we found that the available materials were widely dispersed among journal articles, country monographs, government documents, personal memoirs, and military journals in Spanish, Portuguese and English, as well as several well-known books written in the period 1960–74 (particularly the pioneering efforts of Edwin Lieuwen and John J. Johnson). We also found several anthologies on the military in Latin America and the Third World, but none of these had attempted to bring together these diverse Latin American and United States sources nor had there any attempt to compile a reader on military politics in a representative selection of Latin American countries.

This book seeks to fill that void and, in so doing, to provide a volume which will be of use in a variety of courses on Latin America, inter-American affairs, and the role of the military in Third World nations. The central theme of the book is the underlying similarities in outlook, ideology, and practice of military governments in Latin America. Combining historical, thematic, and case-study approaches, the volume traces the origins of these similarities—which we term "antipolitics"—back to the Hispanic political tradition and follows the development of military antipolitics through the century and one-half of Latin American independence.

Focusing on five Latin American nations—Argentina, Bolivia, Brazil, Chile and Peru—we begin with a theoretical essay on antipolitics and then treat, in turn, the age of the caudillos, the creation of modern military establishments through European military training missions, the role of the military from 1919–45, the United States and military antipolitics in the twentieth century, particularly after World War II, and the policy consequences of military rule in the five countries. We have also included a section of speeches and documents by military leaders where the military is allowed to "speak for itself."

We have tried to treat these themes in a logical historical sequence and have sought to achieve continuity through our introductory essays to each section of readings as well as by treating the same five nations for each historical period and each thematic focus. We chose these particular countries after a great deal of consideration and for a variety of reasons including, of course, the availability of materials from which to select. The historical role of the military in the nations that we have chosen ranges from the Bolivian and Peruvian cases of almost constant direct intervention into politics to (with exceptions) the less

ix

overtly political behavior of the Chilean military. The countries themselves range from the poorest to the wealthiest, from those with significant Indian and black populations to those with predominantly European or mestizo populations. Lack of appropriate published and documentary materials forced us, regretfully, to exclude case studies of the Central American republics. We have omitted Cuba and Mexico because in our opinion the unique revolutionary conditions in both led to the emergence of quite different political-military relationships.

In order to avoid excessive length, we were forced to omit all but a few of the footnotes which appeared in the original essays, leaving a few descriptive notes and adding several editors' notes for purposes of clarity. Moreover, we have edited all the essays, some quite heavily, but have always sought to retain the tone and thrust of the original. The spelling, punctuation, and capitalization of reprinted articles have been regularized, and ellipses indicate our own deletions of material.

No book of this nature can ever be completed without the aid and assistance of a great many people. In our case, we are particularly indebted to the students in our graduate seminar. Through their incisive analyses of the military phenomenon and their constant questioning of previous theories and positions, they helped us to rethink and refocus many of our ideas. Thus, to Michael T. Argüello, Mary Berson, Jo Della-Giustina, Penny Hill, Robert Kagon, Steve Kantes, Jim Kennedy, John Mahedy, Fabio Martínez, Gary Page, Marco Antonio Rodríguez, Gloria Stone, Duane Thornton, and Rob Valentine we offer our thanks.

Various Latin American and United States colleagues also contributed their time and knowledge. Foremost among them are Julio Cotler, Frederick M. Nunn, and Víctor Villanueva who cooperated with us in revising and updating several of his essays. Davies's father-in-law, General (r) José Monzón Linares of the Peruvian Guardia Civil, through his vast knowledge of military affairs and language contributed much to the various translations. We alone, of course, are responsible for any errors of fact or interpretation.

Cecilia Ubilla translated the speeches by Humberto Castello Branco and Ernesto Geisel, and Marion Leitner patiently typed and retyped what must have seemed to be an endless number of revisions.

Finally, we owe a large debt of gratitude to our wives, Sharon Loveman and Tita Monzón de Davies, for their support and encouragement, and to our children, Taryn, Mara, and Carly Loveman and Jennifer Davies.

1
Military Rule and the Latin American Tradition

The Politics of Antipolitics

Military leaders successful in anticolonial wars founded the Spanish American republics in the early nineteenth century. Military elites were also responsible for the creation of the Brazilian Republic in the late nineteenth century. In the 1960s and 1970s professional military officers in Latin America scanned the panorama of Latin American history and blamed the ineptitude and corruption of civilian politicians as well as the imported institutions of liberal democracy for the wretched conditions in Latin America. In much of Latin America, professional military officers concluded that only an end to "politics" and the establishment of long-term military rule could provide the basis for modernization, economic development, and political stability. This determination, strengthened by events in Brazil after 1964, led to explicitly antipolitical military regimes in most of Latin America.

Military antipolitics originated both in military understanding of Latin American history and military assessment of the Latin American dilemma in the mid-twentieth century. Throughout most of the nineteenth century "politics," that is, conflict among personalist factions and, later, political parties, over ideological formulas and the spoils of rule, submerged most of the Latin American nations in bloody civil strife. In the late nineteenth and early twentieth centuries, however, military leaders sought to end the chaos and impose stability and order amid the social conflict and dislocation caused by the process of modernization. "Politics," including the demagogic appeals by civilian politicians to the emerging proletariat, promoted class conflict and instability which "forced" sectors of the military to intervene to restore order and cleanse the body politic of political corruption.

The years following World War I witnessed not only the failure of civilian experiments with political democracy, but also the collapse of the Latin American export economies, a collapse which demonstrated to many military officers the folly of total dependence on foreign capitalists. When the military leaders again intervened in the 1920s and 1930s to restore order and deal with the problems that civilians refused or were unable to resolve, they pointed to civilian bungling, ineptitude, and corruption as the primary motivating factors in their decision.

3

4

THE POLITICS OF ANTIPOLITICS

In Chile in 1924, one civilian minister was told:

Even though you now represent to us the most disgusting element in our country—
politicians—all that is corrupt, the dismal factional disputes, depravity and im-
moralities, in other words, the causes of our national degeneration, we recognize that
you, despite the fact that you must defend sinecures, hand out public jobs, support
avaricious ambitions, that you are one of the few honest politicians.[1]

Three years earlier, a statement signed by seventeen Peruvian army officers
contained the following words:

Comrades:
For some time now, since politics infiltrated the army, we military officers have been
serving as steppingstones for unscrupulous politicians. They use our services, and then
they promote us. This must stop. Promotions must be based upon professional competence and not on political activity. . . . We [must] assume the reins of government of the
country in order to root out political influence, the worst of all plagues, and we shall
shape Peru's destiny with our own hands and our own initiative. . . . Our fatherland
suffers daily from the partisan struggles of politicians who care nothing for the development and progress of the nation. It is our task to normalize the institutional life of the
country. . . . The army, drawn from all social classes of the nation, must intervene
directly in the management of the affairs of state.[2]

As the twentieth century wore on, the hopes of career military officers for
modernization and industrialization were increasingly frustrated. The attitudes
and aspirations imparted by the European training missions that professionalized many Latin American military establishments in the late nineteenth
century conflicted with the obvious inability of Latin American civilians to
create viable institutions for directing national development. Thus, while many
young military officers retained kinship and class ties to the traditional elites,
they harbored an ever growing disdain for civilian politicians and for politics in
general.

One widely held assumption of Latin American military officers, and one
also shared by many conservative civilian groups, was that ''politics'' was
largely responsible for the poverty, instability, and economic backwardness of
their nations. This assumption was not new, nor did it originate in all cases
within military circles, but the depolitization of ''politics'' and the establishment of an administrative regime to forge an organic, hierarchically structured
polity provided a crucial ideological link between civilian propertied interests
and military modernizers.

Acceptance of this ideology of antipolitics also entailed the denial of the
legitimacy of labor protest, strikes, political party claims of representing
diverse interests, and, more generally, of opposition to government authority,
policies, and programs. Order, obedience, authority, and stability—cherished
values of the Hispanic socioeconomic elites—not only dovetailed neatly with

the spirit of military training, but also provided easy rationalizations for military rule. With slight alteration, these values and assumptions formed the ideological core of military antipolitics and military rule in the 1970s.

Latin American Antecedents of Antipolitics

Widespread instability and economic deterioration in early nineteenth-century Latin America contrasted markedly with the special case of Chile, where, after 1833, an institutional predecessor of military antipolitics provided the basis for economic expansion, territorial aggrandizement, and regime stability. Thus, the legal and political practices introduced in Chile during those years are useful benchmarks for the organizational assumptions of antipolitics, the political practices of antipolitics, and, from the perspective of conservative civilians and military leaders intent on "modernization," the economic successes of anti-politics.

The Chilean Constitution of 1833 concentrated authority in an all-powerful executive, the president, who was permitted to serve two five-year terms. The legislative branch was subordinate to the executive. For example, when the legislature was in recess (most of the time), the president could declare a state of siege in any part of the country, thereby suspending constitutional government in that region. The administrative officers in each province and department (*intendentes* and *gobernadores*) were named directly by the president as his "natural and immediate agents." Thus, the constitution made operative the organizational premises of antipolitics: (1) centralization of authority; (2) hierarchical rule through administrative (nonparliamentary) agencies at the provincial and local levels; (3) a "flexible" constitution, that is a constitution that offered little effective constraint on the exercise of governmental authority; and (4) official recognition of governance through a state of siege.

These assumptions about the structure and scope of governmental authority were combined with political practices that epitomized the ideological commitment to antipolitics: (1) systematic persecution of opposition elements, including the press; (2) pragmatic repression of the regime's opponents expressing overt resistance to official policy or programs; and (3) nonrecognition of the legitimacy of active opposition or of political bargaining, negotiation, or compromise.

Repudiating the liberal principles used to justify the Latin American independence movements, the leaders of Chile's autocratic republic made no pretense of accepting a noninterventionist state mediating among conflicting pluralist interests. The Chilean state, following the classic Hispanic tradition, sought to impose order, direct and regulate economic enterprise, and maintain the "proper" relationships among the elements of an organically conceived society. These basic tenets concerning the role of government authority and the state apparatus were perhaps best summed up by Diego Portales, founder of the Chilean autocratic regime: "One can never understand lawyers: and, ¡Carajo! what use are constitutions and bits of paper unless to remedy an evil that one knows to exist or is about to exist . . . ? An accursed law, then, [if it] prevents the government from going ahead freely at the opportune moment."[3]

The principles and practices of Chile's autocratic republic—an interventionist, centralized state; a flexible, "suspendable" constitution allowing for government through state of siege at executive discretion; intolerance of opposition; repression of opponents of the regime; and maintenance of order, which is understood to include hierarchical social and class relationships—provided the ideological underpinnings for Latin America's first successful experiment with a deliberate policy of economic expansion founded upon international commerce, foreign capital, and stimulation of the nation's primary sectors, mining and agriculture.

From 1830 to 1860, in sharp contrast to the economies of most of Latin America, Chile's economy grew and prospered. Agricultural output increased, new roads were constructed, and foreign trade mushroomed. American and European entrepreneurs brought modern transport and navigation systems to Chile, which contributed, in part, to the notable expansion in the mining sector. Precepts of liberal economic doctrine, particularly free trade, dominated economic policy, thereby encouraging imports at the same time that Chilean wheat found its way to California markets. Antipolitics produced both stability and economic growth.

The Spread of Antipolitics

In the late nineteenth century, the social and economic implications of positivism offered a philosophical rationale for authoritarian governments' efforts to stimulate economic modernization. The main features of the Chilean autocratic republic were increasingly evident in Mexico, Guatemala, and across much of South America. As with Chile in the years 1830–60, the combination of authoritarian rule, pragmatic (nonideological) repression, and Hispanic capitalism[4] in an international economy demanding Latin America's primary products produced stability and economic growth. Antipolitics worked—for those who ruled. It produced stability, concentrated the benefits of economic growth in the hands of a small elite, and forced the emerging urban and industrial working classes and the rural poor to bear the costs of "development."

The United States and Antipolitics in Latin America

Then came the Mexican Revolution, the Russian Revolution, and World War I, all of which contributed to a general questioning of traditional values and governmental systems and to the emergence of new concepts about societal relationships. Civilization came to mean democracy, and Latin American elites wanted to be included in the civilized world. Unfortunately, democracy did not work very well, certainly not as well as antipolitics. Democracy, after all, required the tolerance of opposition, placed constraints on executive authority, meant mobilization of the rural and urban poor, and entailed demands for income redistribution. The potential threats to the existing order contained in liberal democracy, and after World War I, Marxism, concerned United States policy makers as much as Latin American elites. Foreshadowing the military assistance programs of the Alliance for Progress years, the United States began to create military constabularies whose leaders (for example, Rafael Trujillo in the Dominican Republic and Anastasio Somoza in Nicaragua) recognized the viability of a new version of antipolitics founded on the coercive force of professional military establishments.

On the other hand, the professional military created by United States intervention or earlier German and French military missions posed a contradiction as nationalist sentiments and the desire for economic development aroused both admiration and hostility toward Western European and American ideology and society. Eventually, however, these military officers devised a developmental orientation highly consistent with the Latin American tradition, with the added touch of assigning the predominant governmental role to the military itself. Patriotism, nationalism, self-sacrifice, and absolute commitment to the national welfare and security distinguished military officers, in their own opinion, from the self-seeking, venal civilian politicians, who served special interests rather than those of the nation. The perfection of antipolitics required nonpolitical leadership and the negation of partisan strife. It required, in fact, the military.

Economic Development as a Military Mission

Speaking to the Argentine Círculo Militar in 1926, Colonel Luis Vicat told his colleagues:

The real meaning of national defense is vast and complex; it can be defined by saying that it includes all those activities and security measures necessary to assure the tranquillity, prosperity, and independence of a nation, as well as rapid victory in case of conflict.[5]

Fifty years later, the notion that economic development is synonymous with national defense and national security, that is, a military mission, was widely held by Latin American military officers. One of the theoreticians of the Brazilian Revolution of 1964 contends:

At the beginning of the century it was enough to maintain armed forces capable of ensuring the integrity of national boundaries and overcoming the military might of possible enemies. But this idea has [now] been replaced by another, which recognizes that national security includes everything that in one way or another affects the life of the nation.[6]

That this concept was hardly novel in Brazil can be seen in a statement made in 1952 by one of the founders of Brazil's Superior War College (ESG): "National security lies in the battle for production, in the tranquillity of the population, and in the provision of stability and a reasonable standard of living."[7]

Increasingly, there seemed to be a common assumption among military officers that only through an end to "politics" and the imposition of military rule could any developmental mission be accomplished. Officers no longer intervened merely to restore order or to act as caretakers; in the 1960s and 1970s they adopted a revised version of antipolitics to justify military rule.

Counterrevolution and Antipolitics

The internal rationale for military antipolitics was also heavily influenced by the United States's response to revolutionary change in Cuba. Convinced that communism flourished where people lived in poverty, the United States committed itself to an Alliance for Progress for Latin America. This so-called alliance featured economic and military assistance programs designed both to induce economic growth and to support, finance, and "advise" Latin American civic action and counterinsurgency programs designed to combat those forces which opposed incumbent regimes.

Summing up the objectives of American assistance programs to Latin America, former Secretary of Defense Robert McNamara declared in 1967:

The specific objectives of military assistance are the development of Latin American forces capable of maintaining internal security against threats of violence and subversion, whether Communist-inspired and supported or "home grown"; encouraging the armed forces to support and strengthen democratic institutions and to undertake civic action projects which both contribute to the social and economic development of the country and bring the armed forces and civilian populace closer together. . . .[8]

Despite McNamara's reassertion of the Kennedy administration's thesis that Latin American armed forces would support and strengthen democratic institu-

Military Rule and the Latin American Tradition

TABLE 1

UNITED STATES MILITARY ASSISTANCE FUNDS FOR CIVIC
ACTION PROGRAMS, FISCAL YEAR 1962 THROUGH FISCAL YEAR 1966

(In Thousands of Dollars)

	Fiscal Year 1962	Fiscal Year 1963	Fiscal Year 1964	Fiscal Year 1965	Fiscal Year 1966
Latin America					
Argentina	——	——	298	1,253	539
Bolivia	——	1,817	397	239	114
Brazil	2,200	2,156	2,097	2,386	1,961
Chile	860	2,019	1,279	391	634
Colombia	——	1,488	1,655	550	696
Costa Rica	——	——	222	13	*
Dominican Republic	——	596	59	64	122
Ecuador	1,500	323	709	476	104
El Salvador	——	534	145	99	65
Guatemala	——	863	567	133	343
Honduras	——	84	20	240	71
Mexico	——	——	——	8	20
Nicaragua	——	59	——	3	
Panama	——	——	2	44	22
Paraguay	——	840	1,111	596	576
Peru	1,135	2,794	1,271	2,411	2,871
Uruguay		546	431	286	103
Venezuela	——	——	23	47	59
Region†	——	——	——	——	72
Area total	5,695	14,119	10,286	9,239	8,372

NOTE: Fiscal year 1962 was the first year that civic action assistance was so identified in MAP.
Fiscal year 1967 is estimated to have a worldwide total of $11,810.
* Less than $500.
† Probably refers to funds not dedicated to a particular country but to region "overhead."

tions, by 1967 it had already become evident that the Alliance for Progress's
counterrevolutionary inspiration intensified the contempt of the military's
"new professionals" for civilian politicians. Furthermore, the failure of the
United States to distinguish clearly between "Communist" and "homegrown"
insurgents fit neatly with the Hispanic tradition of antipolitics in dealing with
opponents of the regime.

Still, some military officers were uneasy about the "new professionalism"
that cast military officers in the role of the only force capable of resolving
national problems in a disinterested and patriotic fashion. This uneasiness
resulted from the lack of a systematic ideological and doctrinal rationale for
prolonged military rule. Gradually this void was filled by the emergence of

specialized military universities that not only developed an appropriate rationale for military rule, but also took it upon themselves to train civilians as administrators in the antipolitical military state.

Prototypical Institutions of the New Professionalism of Military Antipolitics: CAEM (Peru) and ESG (Brazil)

In the 1970s, military antipolitics became a predominant political form in Latin America. No longer did military officers feel obliged to insist that intervention in politics was temporary or even undesirable. To a great extent, the openly political ambitions and activities of military elites stemmed from a new emphasis in professional training that provided a rationale for and a stimulus to the creation of military governments as instruments of development.

Prototypical in this respect were the Center for Advanced Military Studies (Centro de Altos Estudios Militares—CAEM) in Peru and the Superior War School (Escola Superior de Guerra—ESG) in Brazil. Interestingly, the military governments in Peru and Brazil, led chiefly by graduates or instructors from these institutions (and also assisted by civilian graduates) have been seen as both "rightist" (Brazil) and "leftist" (Peru) because of the policies and programs adopted in their countries. In fact, however, the basic paradigm of both regimes, "military antipolitics," is consistent with either modernizing populism (Peru) or modernizing capitalism (Brazil).

Historical and environmental factors greatly influenced the particulars of public policy under the new military regimes. Where quasifeudal land tenure systems, ethnic and cultural diversity, and relatively weak industrial economies existed, efforts to modernize through antipolitics appeared to be reformist, populist, or even "leftist." In nations with more developed capitalist economies, or more militant and well-organized labor movements, military antipolitics seemed more reactionary. In either case, law and order, restraints on autonomous popular mobilization, press censorship, restrictions on civil liberties, and intolerance of opposition underlie apparent differences among the military regimes.

While some have labeled the orientation of these institutions the "new professionalism,"[9] neither their orientations nor their attitudes are, in fact, new. Rather, the explicit concern with internal security, economic development, and social services; the ineptitude of civilian politicians; and the inadequacy of politics is the result of an amalgamation of traditional Hispanic antipolitics with the influences of military professionalization from 1880–1930, the Cold War ambience, the United States-influenced counterinsurgency and Alliance for Progress programs, and, importantly, the doctrinal justification for military rule contained in the CAEM, ESG-type military educational experience. But even this doctrinal justification, including the expansion of the concept of national security to encompass all those political, economic, and social conditions that affect the power of a nation, was merely an elaboration upon the sentiments of Latin American military officers in the early twentieth century (see the remarks of Colonel Luis Vicat cited above).

The educational experience at CAEM, for example, reinforced the long-held disdain and contempt that officers felt for civilian politicians and for "politics." Since the civilian governments had failed to stimulate development, it followed therefore that they were responsible for all of Peru's social and economic ills. Moreover, since the civilians who had governed Peru belonged to the traditional elites representing agro-commercial interests, the military's anticivilian orientation coincided nicely with leftist critiques of the Peruvian landed oligarchy. The military saw itself as being patriotic, self-sacrificing, and dedicated to national—not class—interests, unlike the self-interested civilians.

Thus, the Peruvian military was "leftist." Yet the basic assumptions about the role of the state, the nature of authority, and the uses of constitutions bore a much greater resemblance to Diego Portales than to Karl Marx. The military's mission, to provide internal security, required that the state have "freedom of action and the necessary resources to achieve social well-being. . . . [The state must have] the authority to adopt measures considered necessary for achieving its objectives. . . . The state is supreme within its territory."[10] If the Peruvian officers disliked their dependence upon the United States and seemed to attack certain sectors of the private economy, the philosophical basis of these measures reached back to colonial Hispanic capitalism, not to Marxism. CAEM merely provided a modern rationale for antipolitics under military direction.

In Brazil, a larger and much more industralized society than Peru, the socioeconomic dilemmas of political leadership by the military were even more complex. Political experience under civilian regimes had been more varied and the failure of liberalism and populism more recent and more directly menacing to the military. Thus, the Brazilian variant of antipolitics included rabid anti-Marxism. Yet, allowing for Brazil's somewhat unique history in Latin America, the basic assumptions of rule held by the ESG graduates were quite familiar: the need to centralize authority, the intolerance of opposition, the contempt for civilian politics and politicians, the refusal to be constrained by constitutional limits, the propensity to govern by decree, and the censorship or closure of opposition mass media.[11]

Brazilian practice added a relatively new element to antipolitics (an element anticipated by George Orwell): government use of torture and terror as a routine instrument of rule. Variants on the Brazilian version of antipolitics, notably after 1973 in both Chile and Uruguay, have incorporated terror into the arsenal of the public policy instruments of Latin American antipolitics.

Policy Consequences of Military Antipolitics

The assumptions of antipolitics allow for a great diversity of policy initiatives by military rulers. Antipolitics is committed neither to capitalism nor to socialism. It is antiliberal and anti-Marxist. It assumes repression of opposition, silencing or censoring of the media, and subordinating the labor movement to the objectives of the regime. It does not willingly tolerate strikes by workers nor the pretensions to aristocratic privilege by traditional elites. It seeks order and progress; the latter assumed contingent upon the former. It places high priority on economic growth and is usually little concerned with income distribution except insofar as worker or white-collar discontent leads to protest and disorder. It can pragmatically emphasize either concessions or repression in obtaining its objectives.

Military antipolitics adds several elements to those general characteristics: military leadership, a more evident linkage between the state and coercion, a more insistent demand for order and respect for hierarchy, a less tolerant attitude toward opposition, and an outright rejection of "politics," which is perceived as being the source of underdevelopment, corruption, and evil.[12]

Thus, whether military antipolitics includes programs for land reform or industrialization, expanded public health services, urban housing, or new educational facilities, the other policies of antipolitics tend to be shared. And above all, military antipolitics produces a regime of masters and "proles," of rulers and the ruled. Sometimes the masters use torture and other forms of repression to enforce their will and maintain their power; sometimes prosperity permits the use of more pleasant instruments of persuasion. Nevertheless, the military version of antipolitics remains tied to the Portalian notion that: "The stick and the cake, justly and opportunely administered, are the specifics with which any nation can be cured, however inveterate its bad habits may be."[13]

Notes

1. Raúl Aldunate Phillips, *Ruido de sables* (Santiago de Chile: Escuela Lito-Tipográfica, "La Gratitud Nacional," n.d.), p. 87.

2. Quoted in Víctor Villanueva, *Ejército peruano: del caudillaje anárquico al militarismo reformista* (Lima: Librería-Editorial Juan Mejía Baca, 1973), p. 177. The emphasis is in the original.

3. Simon Collier, *Ideas and Politics of Chilean Independence, 1808–1833* (Cambridge: Cambridge University Press, 1967), p. 345.

4. In contrast to the European liberal tradition of laissez faire capitalism, Hispanic capitalism views private enterprise as a concession of the state. Thus, in the Hispanic system, monopoly is not the end product of capitalist development, but rather the starting point of private enterprise. The old slave monopoly, or *asiento*, of colonial days

and the various concessionary monopolies, or *estancos*, of the republican period are merely two examples of this system.

5. Luis Vicat, "El desarrollo industrial como empresa militar," in Jorge Álvarez, ed., *Ejército y revolución industrial* (Buenos Aires: Talleres Gráficos Verdad, 1964), p. 25.

6. Quoted in Víctor Villanueva, *El CAEM y la revolución de la fuerza armada* (Lima: Instituto de Estudios Peruanos, 1972), p. 233.

7. Quoted in ibid.

8. U.S., Congress, House, *Foreign Assistance and Related Agencies Appropriations for 1967, Hearing before a Subcommittee of the Committee on Appropriations,* 89th Cong., 1967, 1, pp. 605–6.

9. For a discussion of "new professionalism," see: Alfred Stepan, "The New Professionalism of Internal Warfare and Military Role Expansion," in Alfred Stepan, ed., *Authoritarian Brazil: Origins, Policies, and Failures* (New Haven: Yale University Press, 1973), pp. 47–65.

10. Villanueva, *CAEM*, p. 156.

11. Stepan, "New Professionalism," p. 55.

12. It must be noted that there remain military officers who wish to return to a narrower professional role. Important divisions within the Latin American officer corps developed (in each of the countries upon which we focus in this book) precisely over the desirability of prolonged military rule or even military intervention. Yet in the 1970s the officers who desired an end to military rule or a return to anything approximating liberal domestic politics were clearly out of step with the dominant doctrines in the military academies and the reality of the Latin American scene.

13. Collier, *Ideas and Politics of Chilean Independence*, p. 359.

Charles D. Corbett

Politics and Professionalism: The South American Military

The concepts of militarism and professionalism are central to our perceptions of the Latin American military. The persistence of the former and the failure of recognized gains in professionalism to stem it have puzzled academicians and policy makers. The classic examples of militarism resided in the historical alliances in many European countries between the officer corps—comprised of second sons of the aristocracy, who frequently practiced the profession of arms as an honorific occupation—and the traditional ruling classes. The officer corps formed an interest group dedicated to the support of the existing system. Its salient characteristics were "a domination of the military man over the civilian, an undue preponderance of military demands, an emphasis on military considerations, spirit, ideals, and scales of value" and "an attitude toward public affairs which conceives of war and the preparation for war as the chief instruments of foreign policy and the highest forms of public service."

The classic maneuver to break up this alliance and remove the military from the political equation—or at least limit its influence drastically—was "professionalization." Officership was made a full-time paid profession, requiring long years of specialized preparation for advancement through a rigidly bureaucratized system. The structural location of the military within the society was fixed within the long traditions of civil control, and its role was defined as an apolitical one. Except for the deep-rooted martial spirit that persists in modern-day Paraguay, the reflections of old-world militarism that were evident in the postindependence period have long since disappeared in South America.

Civil wars were endemic following independence, but the region has been characterized by its generally peaceful international relations. Recent research tends to undermine the image of a regionwide nineteenth-century alliance between the oligarchy and the military, and certainly the various officer corps have in this century been largely middle-class bodies. (Indeed the intensive socialization process of the career system, described later, brings into question the weight assigned in the past to class analysis as a technique in studying military institutional change.) A neomilitarist predilection for the frequent use of military power to dominate domestic processes, on the other hand, has

14

endured, despite the advent of conditions that saw the demise of militarism in "Western" experience elsewhere.

Because they are based on "Western" experiences, Samuel Huntington's distinguishing characteristics of the military professional—expertise, responsibility, and corporateness—are helpful but not sufficient to define professionalism in the Latin American context. In the first instance, the controlled application of violence is singled out as the peculiar skill of the officer; that this be utilized only for socially approved purposes is the imperative of the second; and the bureaucratized, hierarchical, and socially delimited nature of the military institution contributes to the third.

An astute analyst of civil-military relations in Latin America has posited these requirements for a professional army: (1) the specific duty to act as guarantor of the state's security against foreign aggression; (2) the inculcation of strict patterns of authority, with emphasis on the necessity for discipline and obedience within a hierarchically organized command system; (3) formal training for officership; (4) institutionalization of a military career, with a regular salary and a clearly defined pattern of promotion and advancement within the organization, based on the universal criteria of ability and achievement.

Both sets of requirements presuppose a narrow, functional area of expertise for the officer and sharply limit the military institution's role in society to the primary socially acceptable use of violence, that is, security against overt aggression.

General Benjamín Rattenbach, an Argentine military sociologist, differentiates between "organic" and "vocational" aspects of professionalism. The first signifies placing the military career on a stable basis through the satisfaction of two conditions: education of career officers in a formal school system; and promulgation of laws that assure regularized and fair promotions, assignments, retirements, and administrative actions. The second requires that the officer dedicate full time to his profession. General Rattenbach agrees that *apoliticismo* has not followed from professionalization but argues that the phenomena are independent in the Latin American context and likely to remain so:

The old European professionalism could create a theory of conduct appropriate to its ends—*apoliticismo*—that worked well for its environment of developed political culture. Among us it did not work, and we now know why. Consequently we must create a new theory more appropriate to our environment that takes into account the logical and very real relations between politics and the armed forces so that they cease being constant factors of perturbation and assist the country to achieve development and greatness. In other words, we have to define anew the role of these forces in the breast of the society, differentiating it from the European or North American *schema* and molding it to the reality of nations under development. Thus, for example, one could say that they have for a current mission in such countries not only that of exterior defense and internal security, but also that of contributing to the development of the nation in the economic and social aspects as well as the cultural and political. They are not indifferent to any of these aspects, feeling as they do that they are integral components of the society.

That the armed forces not only are "not indifferent" to these aspects, but are increasingly determined to play an institutional role in national development in its broadest terms, is indicated by the officer-led "revolutions" since 1964 in South American countries.

The Career System and Formation of Political Elites

What comprises the "armed forces"? Do they include all of the institutions that society arms for its order and security? In Panama or Nicaragua where the National Guard provides police services as well as guaranteeing territorial integrity and defense against external aggression, the entity is easily definable. In Argentina and Brazil, these functions are differentiated in complex structures. Specially designed organizations are charged with customs and border patrol duties, provincial and federal police jurisdictions are carefully defined, and *internal* defense roles of *military* forces are amorphous, whereas their classic mission of defense against external threats is clear and universally accepted. If we accept the "armed forces" as comprising all of society's armed institutions and the "military forces" as being those concerned primarily with external defense, there are still gray areas in the definitions. The air force most closely fits the "military" definition, but the coast guard functions of the navies and the territorial defense missions of all armies distort the distinctions in their case.

Obviously there is no single voice of the "armed forces" in those countries where the coercive forces of the state are complexly organized. However, little practical difficulty is encountered—no matter what the theoretical problem—in delimiting that sector of the "armed forces" in the larger South American countries that has been directly involved in national politics since World War II.

First, one can say that the armies predominate in political activity. Only a handful of officers from the navy have held important political posts, and since the air forces became separate after World War II, only Bolivia has had a chief executive from that service. Second, only the officer corps participates actively in the political game. Enlisted men have not achieved important political influence, and although there have been attempts (for example, in Venezuela and Brazil) by politicians to manipulate them, the rank and file generally have followed the orders of their officers in political fights. Third, only field grade officers of the line, of the "combat arms," play important political roles. Junior line officers, lawyers, doctors, veterinarians, finance officers, quartermasters, and maintenance officers do not figure in political councils. And in rather a marked change from the past, retired officers are generally out of the picture unless they maintain strong contacts within the active establishment.

Usually a small group within the larger body of command corps officers makes the decision on whether the army will play a hand in any given situation. Exercise of the coup option requires only the ability to mobilize the support necessary for a temporary power advantage. The hierarchical nature of the institution and the pattern of loyalty established by the annual reshuffling of general officers will normally give the command group that power. Ensuing decisions are infinitely more complex, and participation in the deliberative process much more broadly based. Coups may in some cases still be personalist (as in Bolivia in 1964 and 1969), but the consequences are institutional concerns. The capability to move the government apparatus, and through it the society, in a desired direction depends on the accrual of broad support from the field grade command corps officers. The mobilization and maintenance of this support calls for widespread contacts on the part of the leaders and the careful manipulation of many control mechanisms in a highly sensitive and rank-conscious organization. As will be demonstrated, officer corps have become increasingly heterogeneous in viewpoints, and failure in this intrainstitutional political task leads to a countercoup by a group that more nearly reflects institutional sentiments.

The mobilization, by a military junta, of institutional support for political programs is complicated not only by the variety of views within the officer corps, but by the nature of the career system. Popular perceptions notwithstanding, that system is geared to the production of military professionals who, in their formative years, do not conceive of the presidency as the capstone to a military career.

In South American armies all members of the command corps are graduates of the military academy. There are no career line officers from any other source. Branches (cavalry, infantry, artillery) are chosen early, usually during the first year of the four-year course, and form the basis for lifelong association. Technical officers (quartermaster [*intendencia*] and ordnance [*material de guerra*]) also attend the academies, but their training is differentiated from that of the line cadets after the first year and the associations are not nearly as close. Academy life is rigorous, with every aspect of the daily routine carefully structured and controlled. Only the cream of the officer corps is selected to command and administer the academies, and great attention is devoted to the top priority task of character formation. All academies have a mixture of civilian and military *profesores*; some of the former are tenured professors, others are part-time instructors from national or private universities. Tradition is carefully nurtured.

The *subteniente* [second lieutenant] receives his ceremonial saber, usually from the president, at elaborate graduation ceremonies, and goes off to join a regiment. Officers with a high class standing get a choice of the more desirable units—but all are committed to several years of duty with troop units after commissioning. Discipline is rigid within the officer complement; the colonel's whim is absolute law, and in isolated areas the society approaches that of a "total institution." Near the cities life is less confining, but the colonel will still take an interest in the *subteniente*'s social life and overall behavior, and he must have the permission of higher authority to marry. After four years he is promoted to *teniente* [lieutenant], and sometime during the next couple of years he will attend a six- to eight-month course at an *Escuela de Aplicación* to sharpen his talents in his combat specialty and broaden his capabilities as a company officer. Promotion to captain will come at about his eighth year, and he will probably return to an advanced course at his branch school.

The overriding imperative now is to get into the command and general staff course and gain the coveted title of *diplomado de estado mayor* (general staff officer), which opens the road to positions in the higher headquarters and eventual promotion to colonel. Attendance may be by application or selection, but in either case it involves months of intensive preparation for the qualifying examinations, which cover a dismayingly broad range of academic and military subjects. Once accepted, he faces one to three years of intensely competitive study, with underachievers being dropped from the course at the end of each year. In addition to military organization, administration and tactics—generally keyed to the division level—he will study theories of revolutionary warfare, psychology, sociology, economics, political theory, and massive doses of military history.

He will hear the views of the army's "intellectuals," those senior officers who by reason of their positions or reputations have come to be looked upon as spokesmen for the institution. He will also hear a variety of civilian speakers, and the "academic" side of his education will be in the hands of civilian professors. The course will include tours of his country's strategically important locations, and a trip abroad that frequently incorporates a tour of the United States.

Those officers who survive the full course and become general staff officers find new opportunities open to them as planning or action officers on the general staff of the army or in important territorial headquarters as instructors or directors in the school system and as commanders of battalions and groups.

Graduation from the general staff course marks a kind of watershed in the officer's orientation. Up to this point (and for a few years afterward), he has seen himself first and foremost as a military professional, schooled intensively in the military arts and sciences. He takes his profession seriously, assiduously follows developments in organization, tactics, and weaponry in other parts of the world, and in many cases writes and publishes on military-related topics. He chafes at the obsolescence of his equipment and the lack of money for maneuvers and compensates with intellectual activity and meticulous, detailed planning for any conceivable contingency.

The core of his curriculum in the command and general staff course is directly related to improving traditional military skills in the management of violence on a large scale and over great distances. If he is sent to a U.S. school during these years his course will concentrate almost entirely on military techniques and will stress the personal satisfaction to be gained out of becoming proficient at them.

There is a distinct "professional" air about any gathering of South American officers at the *jefe* level (majors and lieutenant colonels), and they feel not in the least intimidated in any professional conversation with a U.S. counterpart by the latter's combat experience in two or perhaps even three wars. Among officers from Argentina, Brazil, Chile, and Peru there is a noticeable flavor of superiority in another sense. Their training and the high degree of institutional socialization involved cause them to look upon the military officer as a superior being. In the officer's view, his calling and its high purpose set him aside from other men and lend to his actions an unselfish aura that is uncharacteristic of his environment, where opportunism is the norm among politicians, lawyers, businessmen, and other professionals.

Most of those selected for promotion to colonel, after about twenty years' service, will attend a one-year higher military studies course devoted to national problems and goals at the broadest level, which considers all the dynamic forces of the society—military, political, economic, sociological, and psychological. The product of these courses is usually a national strategy paper advocating general plans and guidelines for reaching the goals agreed upon in seminar sessions. The small student body includes important civilians from government and the professions, and lecturers from government, industry, and the academic community address the students. Graduates will fill key staff and command positions and form probably the most influential element of the military political constituency. These are the officers whose support is essential to the stability and success of any military government.

The point at which liaisons are established between officers and important civilian elements varies by country and is always changing. Schools at the war college level obviously are important to this cross-fertilization process. Alfred Stepan has identified, by profession or occupational grouping, civilian students at the Brazilian Superior War School (Escola Superior de Guerra) over a number of years, and the range is surprising. By 1966 some 599 officer graduates had been complemented by 224 students from private industry and commerce, 297 from high levels of government, 39 congressmen, 23 judges, and 107 from the professions. Luigi Einaudi says that civilian attendance at the Peruvian Center of Higher Military Studies became routine in the 1960s, and that 16 of the 43 students in the 1971 course were civilians. In Bolivia, the normal course complement is about half officers and half civilians; through 1967, 93 officers and 58 civilians had graduated. In 1970, the National War School class in Paraguay counted a senator and a congressman among its 14 students.

The Argentine army war college (Escuela de Altos Estudios) does not admit civilian students, but they are traditionally in a majority at the National War College. The 1971 class counted twenty-seven students from ministries and state enterprises, eight from private industry, four from police and paramilitary units, one university professor, and eleven officers. Venezuela's new war college (Instituto de Altos Estudios de la Defensa Nacional) counted eleven civilians from government ministries and state enterprises among the thirty-one students in its first class, which got under way in January 1972. The "colonel's courses" in Colombia and Chile are designed primarily to qualify officers for promotion to general, although some government functionaries do attend the latter.

Other links are established by territorial commanders and their staffs with local political leaders, and the common practice of appointing military governors, mayors, and police chiefs (interventors) in times of crisis and civil strife acquaints a wide number of officers with political figures from the civilian side. The large military household staffs that surround most Latin American presidents (the Casa Militar) afford many rising officers an opportunity to get to know important political figures. Traditional family alignments and associations also influence the political contacts and orientation of officers.

Expanded Security Doctrines

Once the officer's professional or military-oriented education is rounded out by graduation from the general staff course and he finds himself involved in larger issues, he becomes concerned about the anomalies of his profession in a region that has had a minimum of international conflict. In the absence of a serious, short-range external threat, he frequently universalizes the communist threat to the "Western, Christian" world and posits a role for his country in countering it. Military interpretations of the local manifestations of that threat, and considerations of the nature of the military response, have led in recent years to a redefinition and great expansion of the concept of national security. The salient characteristic is a nexus of security and economic development that transcends the definitions of national security policy generally ascribed to by other Western countries. Brazilian writer and military critic Vicente Barreto complains that the amplification of concepts of national security has given the military carte blanche to intervene against internal enemies or against anything that contributes or could contribute to the weakening of the nation. The nature of the threats to national security [is] thus subject to the absolute judgment of the formulator of the doctrine. The expanded concept of national security subordinates each and every social activity to its criteria. National security comprehends not only the military protection of the nation, but principally all manifestations of national life, whether in political, economic, social, or cultural areas.

The significant fact of recent years has been the general change in emphasis from classic "military" concerns, which encompass the first three in the list, to the last one, which is in its essence political.

As a key element in the professionalization process in Argentina, Brazil, and Peru, the war colleges have served to institutionalize this concern, formulate doctrine, and prepare cadres to carry out the perceived military tasks in the developmental process, including political tasks.

Two issues raised by the expanded national security concepts predominate in school discussions and condition policy recommendations: the politics of development and the military role in the process. There is almost unanimous agreement on the existence of a nexus between economic development and national security, but there are deep divisions within the various officer corps over specific policies and goals. Two important schools of thought can be identified. Both have nationalist overtones and elitist proclivities, and demarcations are not always sharply defined; in any given country it might be difficult to classify General A or General B in either category. However, the differences are real and will probably intensify during the decade, and an attempt at defining them even in a general manner is worthwhile. Rubrics and labels are misleading, but necessary. For lack of better terms we could call one school "liberal-internationalist" and the other "authoritarian-nationalist."

Officers identified with the first have a commitment to democratic forms, but are not averse to a period of tutelary rule by the military. Mobilization politics is seen as ruinous. The role of the armed forces during the tutelary period is complex, but emphasis remains strong on classic "territorial security" concerns, force modernization, and increased professionalism. Interest in industrialization centers on its importance to national mobilization and its contributions to the attainment of true sovereignty through strong, autosufficient security forces. There is a strong concern for "situational" security policy in the regional context for the short term and in the world context for the longer view. The primary security threat is seen as internal subversion aided and abetted by the world communist movement, and close ties with the United States and other Western countries form a necessary component of the response. There is no deep objection to state enterprises and state control of certain sectors, but private enterprise remains the driving force of the economy, and foreign investment is viewed as essential.

The "authoritarian nationalists" hold that development means much more

22
THE POLITICS OF ANTIPOLITICS

than the old liberal goal of economic growth. Important elements believe sweeping structural revisions of existing socioeconomic patterns are required. The old liberal political philosophy, with its concern for abstractions like liberty and democracy, has proved unable to put together and sustain a development program. An alternative to a Cuba-style revolution must be found in each country, and it must fit that country's unique traditions and imperatives. The internal enemy is frequently pictured as that sector of society allied with foreign and international markets. Continuing nineteenth-century integration of domestic economies with the international economic and monetary systems is viewed as detrimental to the development process; arguments for free trade and the international division of labor are specious ploys to permit continuation of what is seen as a steadily declining relationship between the industrialized center and the raw material-producing periphery. The external enemy is identified as economic imperialism. Its steady penetration and influence undermine national sovereignty in the political sphere as well as the economic (for example, when attempts are made to subordinate national decisions to global objectives of great-power strategy, such as sanctions against Cuba, the Latin American nuclear free zone, the Inter-American Peace Force).

Insurgency and subversion are seen by the authoritarian nationalists as the effects of underdevelopment; national security demands development, and it is therefore an implied mission of the armed forces. The latter are truly national institutions, in touch with all sectors of society and represented in the farthest reaches of the national territory. They are able to coordinate conflicting interests and distribute the inevitable sacrifices of the development process equitably, since they are above narrow sectoral interests. An indeterminate period of military rule is necessary for the transformation of society. Old liberal distinctions between civil and military government are no longer relevant; the distinctions now are between sectors of the society that support national development and those that would maintain the status quo.

Reprinted and edited from *Orbis*, a journal of world affairs, published by the Foreign Policy Research Institute, 26 (winter 1973), pp. 927–51.

2
Antecedents of Military Antipolitics

Instability, Violence, and the Age of the Caudillos

The roots of the antipolitical military regimes of the 1960s and 1970s stretch far back into Iberian and colonial Latin American history. There exist a plethora of theories about and explanations for the form of Spanish colonial government and for the rise of the caudillos in the nineteenth century. One of the most popular, particularly as developed by Américo Castro, holds that the Spanish, and consequently the republican, mentality was decisively shaped by the *Reconquista* experience: El Cid and the warrior priest. Others have pointed to the institutional contributions of the highly developed Amerindian civilizations and particularly to the submissiveness of the lower orders present in Aztec and Inca cultures. Still others explain the rise of the caudillos and the political chaos of the nineteenth century in terms of the heritage from the Spanish conquistadores.[1]

More important for the study of antipolitics, however, is the approach adopted by Professor Richard W. Morse in his classic essay "Toward a Theory of Spanish American Government."[2] Morse points to the dualism and philosophical polarization present in Spanish thought. On the one hand, there was the medieval Thomistic philosophy embodied in the *Siete Partidas* (the basic source of Spanish law during this period) and practiced by Queen Isabella. The *Siete Partidas*, according to Morse, "assumed the nuclear element of society to be, not Lockean atomistic man, but religious societal man: man with a salvable soul (that is, in relationship with God) and man in a station of life (that is, having mutual obligations with fellow humans, determinable by principles of Christian justice). The ruler, though not procedurally responsible to the people or the estates, was bound through his conscience to be the instrument of God's immutable, publicly ascertainable law."[3]

Isabella's husband, Ferdinand, on the other hand, by virtue of the nature of the Aragon Empire, with such diverse components as the Balearic Islands, Sardinia, Sicily, and Naples, was forced to adopt a strikingly different political philosophy for his regime. As Morse notes:

Ferdinand was committed to the shifting, amoral statecraft of competing Christian princes in maintenance and expansion of a domain which, within its Christian context, was diversely composed. Ferdinand ruled under transitional conditions which precluded

25

resorting for authority to Isabella's Thomistic sanction or to statist apologetics. Managing with sheer personal verve and cunning, he was, in the fullest sense, Machiavellian.[4]

Thus, Spanish colonial government had from the outset a "dual heritage: medieval and Renaissance, Thomistic and Machiavellian." The role of the king in this colonial system was crucial, for he was the ultimate unifying symbol. As Morse states:

The king, even though he might be an inarticulate near-imbecile like Charles II, was symbolic throughout his realm as the guarantor of status. In Thomistic idiom, all parts of the society were ordered to the whole as the imperfect to the perfect. This ordering, inherently the responsibility of the whole multitude, devolved upon the king as a public person acting in their behalf, for the task of ordering to a given end fell to the agent best placed and fitted for the specific function.[5]

The stated objectives of this system—order, obedience (both to God and king), authority, and stability—are in many respects identical to those of the caudillos and of the later military regimes. However, the system was fragile, relying almost entirely for its continuance on subject loyalty to the crown.

Napoleon Bonaparte's invasion of Spain in 1808, the placing of his brother Joseph on the throne, and the subsequent criollo revolts in the colonies all had the effect of destroying the delicate political equilibrium. Gone was the supreme moral force provided by the crown, and the subsequent power struggles that emerged represented efforts to find a new basis for political order. For a time, the great liberators such as Simón Bolívar and José de San Martín served as surrogate kings, but with the end of the wars, the liberators either retired from the political arena or were forcibly ejected.

In the early nineteenth century, criollo leaders attempted to rule by applying the new, alien concepts of constitutionalism and liberalism, but they failed to stem the tide of personalism and localism which swept the land. "With the breakdown of the moral authority of the crown, lawlessness became widespread and was overcome not necessarily by a substitute moral authority, but rather by the personal magnetism of a given charismatic leader. Personalism rather than principle tended to prevail."[6]

Argentina's first president, Bernardino Rivadavia summed this up best when he wrote in 1830:

In my opinion what retards regular and stable advance in those republics stems from the vacillations and doubts that deprive all institutions of that moral force which is indispensable to them and can be given only by conviction and decision. It is evident to me, and would be easy to demonstrate, that the upheavals of our country spring much more immediately from lack of public spirit and of cooperation among responsible men in sustaining order and laws than from attacks of ungovernable, ambitious persons without merit or fitness and of indolent coveters.[7]

This leadership crisis was further compounded when most upper-class criollos also withdrew from the active direction of their newly created nations and returned to their great landed estates. The absence of these men created a tremendous vacuum, not only political but also military and moral as well. The old Thomistic order was truncated and replaced by a new order ruled not by statesmen or professional soldiers, but by prototypical Machiavellian leaders—the caudillos. For fifty years, the caudillos, with varying degrees of success, attempted to fill the vacuum caused by the lack of effective, legitimate political institutions—an attempt which invites comparison with today's military antipoliticians.

The nineteenth-century caudillo, whether Juan Manuel de Rosas, in Argentina, Ramón Castilla, in Peru, or Andrés de Santa Cruz, in Bolivia, had much in common with twentieth-century military elites, despite a lack of professional credentials. Neither the caudillo nor today's professional soldier is committed to political movements or interests based on traditional ideological questions of liberal or conservative, left or right. Both caudillos and professional soldiers usually justify their rule in nationalist terms of saving and maintaining the fatherland, although this appears more frequently among the latter than the former. Neither the caudillo nor today's professional soldier tolerates dissent, much less formal opposition, and both react quickly to stifle it. Finally, both the caudillo and the professional soldier employ force as the basis for their political rule.

But there are important differences as well. The professional soldier stresses military education, strict obedience to a hierarchical authority, and submission of personal desires to the well-being of the military institution and the nation. The caudillo, on the other hand, was highly individualistic and hated all laws and authority except his own. The professional soldier, then, adopts many of the precepts of the Thomistic tradition, while the caudillo opts instead for an extreme form of atomism.

The adjectives employed to describe the caudillo are as varied as they are colorful: crude, vulgar, barbaric, cruel, daring, sadistic, strong, fearless, and illiterate. As Domingo Sarmiento noted about the Argentine caudillo Juan Facundo Quiroga, his was a type of "primitive barbarism" which knew no bounds or restraints. The caudillo relied not only upon force to maintain his power, but also, more importantly, on his charisma and his unfailing ability to dominate those around him.

In contrast to the nationalistic professional soldier, most caudillos were committed only to a locality or a region. They possessed a limited sense of nationalism, and when a caudillo did become president of his nation, he still thought in regional terms, often seeking to dominate only the capital city. He ruled the remainder of his country through a rather loose alliance with other regional caudillos or *caciques*. As Hugh Hamill puts it: "Given geographic isolation and the vastness of the region, the scattered power nuclei, controlled by *caciques*, were fundamental to the emergence of a national caudillo. Whereas a *cacique* is a ruler among men, a caudillo is a ruler among *caciques*."[8] The success of his rule depended upon personalism and charisma, not on institutions. Thus, there was little or no institutional development in the period, be it in the civilian political arena or in the military sector.

During the Wars of Independence, the officer corps were drawn principally from the upper classes. After the wars they withdrew and were replaced by men of much lower social status for whom, in the words of Edwin Lieuwen, "'an army career provided the opportunity to break through the arbitrary restrictions of the old social order, to shoot one's way into a share of the power, wealth, and social prestige enjoyed by the landed oligarchy and the church hierarchy.'"[9] Thus the upper classes lost effective control over the military establishments which, in conjunction with regional civilian caudillos, became the arbiters in what amounted to a political system of chaos.

These so-called national armies had almost nothing in common with today's Latin American military establishments. The officers and men alike were ill trained and poorly equipped. As John Johnson has noted, the service academies which did exist were poorly organized, and attendance was not a prerequisite for professional advancement. Moreover, neither the cadets in the academies nor the enlisted men in the ranks were taught any skill that might be of use in national development, despite the fact that the various militaries consumed over half of their nations' yearly budgets.[10] In addition to being poorly trained and equipped, the enlisted men never felt part of a nation or a national institution. What loyalty they did feel was to their commander, who in turn was loyal only to himself or to another caudillo.

Although the creation of the Latin American nations was to a large extent a military achievement, in many cases it was only through the ventures of nationalistic caudillos that the territorial units of Latin America were forged and maintained against European as well as Latin American enemies. As the age of caudillos gave way to that of civilian politics, the successors of the caudillos— the professional military—often saw in the venality and incapacity of civilian elites a betrayal of nations which the military had founded.

In contrast, these modern-day military officers view with respect the regimes of the great caudillos in their nations' past. Not only did the caudillos shape and defend the fatherland, but they also did it with firmness (even violence) and with dedication. They alone prevented the national disintegration which would have resulted from "politics." In short, they successfully applied the politics of antipolitics and in so doing served as vital links between traditional Hispanic politics and the antipolitical military regimes of today.

One of the best known and most successful of all Latin American caudillos was the Argentine strongman Juan Manuel de Rosas. Breaking with his family at an early age, Rosas went to the interior, where he soon gained fame for his daring and skill as a gaucho. He became wealthy in cattle ranching and later expanded into the complementary businesses of salt and slaughter houses. In 1829, he was appointed governor of Buenos Aires province and charged with ending the chaos created by the politicians of the legislature. His solution was as efficient as it was prototypical of *caudillismo*—the carrot or the stick. Rosas totally dominated Buenos Aires province but allowed the regional caudillos to retain control of their respective provinces in return for their absolute loyalty to him. Recalcitrant caudillos were dealt with quickly and severely.

In the early years of his rule, Rosas was enormously popular with all strata of the population. The upper-class ranchers supported him because he had restored internal order and because he emphasized the cattle industry in his economic policies. The lower classes admired his prowess as a gaucho and responded to his tremendous charisma. In 1832, Rosas stepped down as governor and went south with his army to fight the Indians. He succeeded in pushing them almost to Patagonia, thereby adding to his reputation as a fierce warrior. He increased his support among the great ranchers (*estancieros*) by distributing to them the newly opened Indian lands.

The period 1832–35 saw Argentina slip back into the chaos that had been characteristic of "politics" before. Finally, in 1835, after much pleading and a rigged plebiscite, Rosas agreed to accept the governorship again. He quickly reestablished internal order, whipped the regional caudillos back into line, and repressed all opposition. Rosas tolerated no dissent, and those who dared challenge him were either jailed, exiled, or killed, while thousands more fled into voluntary exile. Even the Catholic church was brought into line and forced to hang Rosas's portrait next to the altars in the churches. His was a regime of terror and personalist rule. Argentina was not a true nation, rather a series of provinces held together by the power and charisma of the dictator. Still, it did survive as an entity as it might not have under the rule of "politics."

Rosas sought to rule his neighbors as he did his gauchos. He refused to accept the independence of Uruguay or even of Paraguay and was constantly meddling in the internal affairs of the former. He declared war on his Bolivian counterpart Andrés de Santa Cruz in 1837 in an effort to prevent Santa Cruz from uniting Bolivia and Peru into a strong confederation. He also successfully defended his regime and Argentina from attack by Europeans. In 1838, the French captured Martín García Island and instituted a blockade which lasted until 1840. In 1845, the French returned, this time with the British, and blockaded the entire Río de la Plata estuary. Although the blockades caused severe economic dislocations in Argentina, Rosas held out and forced the two powers to withdraw by 1848.

In 1851, Rosas sought to renew his pact with the regional caudillos, but this time his long-time supporter Justo José Urquiza, the strongman of Entre Ríos province, declared against him. Urquiza succeeded in winning over the other caudillos, in addition to getting support from both Uruguay and Brazil, and defeated Rosas's army in 1852.

Rosas had ruled for almost a quarter of a century, but his sudden defeat is indicative of the fragility of the caudillo system. Nevertheless, Rosas did establish internal order (despite the high social and political costs), and he did defend the nation against both South American and European challengers. In contrast to the weak, corrupt, and inept civilian regimes which followed, the nationalism of the Rosas regime was viewed favorably by subsequent military officers.

In Peru, one finds much the same political situation in the years following independence as that which existed in Argentina. In 1826, Simón Bolívar departed Peru, leaving behind a constitution and a caretaker government headed by Andrés de Santa Cruz. Both were overthrown in 1827, and for the next seventeen years Peru was in almost constant chaos. The principals were military caudillos, veterans of the independence wars, who traded the presidency back and forth by means of *golpes* and counter *golpes*.

Finally, in 1845, Ramón Castilla assumed the presidency for the first time (he served two terms, 1845–51 and 1855–60) and initiated an era of economic prosperity, military preparedness, and political order. He was so successful that he ranks first in the pantheon of Peruvian heroes and is revered by the military today for his honesty, patriotism, and firm commitment to national defense.

Castilla was a mestizo with relatively unsophisticated manners, and this contributed to his popularity with the lower classes. Like most caudillos, he had led an active and eventful life, serving on both sides in the Wars of Independence, being captured and taken to Buenos Aires, escaping and walking back to Peru across South America. He was daring, resourceful, and charismatic.

Upon taking office he faced the monumental task of restoring internal order, both politically and militarily. He quickly suppressed the bandit bands which had flourished between Lima and Callao and on the coastal highway to the north. He ended the political strife between Liberals and Conservatives by using both but joining neither. He used the revenues from guano exploitation to promote business and regularize the economy and the civil service, thereby inaugurating an era of unprecedented prosperity. He built the first railroad in South America, wrote the Constitution of 1860, which lasted for sixty years (longer than any other before or since), and sought to instill a new patriotism in the young nation. Like Rosas, Castilla used the carrot-and-stick technique with opponents, but he did so in a much less violent fashion. He neither executed nor jailed his enemies; rather he sent them into exile with the understanding that they could return under very favorable circumstances anytime they decided to cooperate. In this way he avoided making any really dangerous enemies.

Finally, he subdued the various regional military leaders and centralized the military command structure.

More than anyone else in the nineteenth century, Castilla was responsible for the creation of a national military force, stating that: "Our military forces are not the instrument of tyranny or the enemies of society. . . . Imbued with a sense of the importance of their noble destiny, they are the conservers of the public tranquillity, the custodians of external and internal peace, and the loyal defenders of the constitution and the laws."[11]

Castilla greatly increased the size of the army, reopened the military academy, and purchased modern armaments. He also concentrated on improving and expanding the navy and built it into the most powerful naval force on the west coast of South America. His long-remembered thesis was that if Chile bought one ship, Peru should buy two. The fact that a civilian president, Manuel Pardo, canceled an order for two warships, which were subsequently purchased and used by Chile in the War of the Pacific (1879–83), provided added weight to Castilla's judgment, a judgment which has become an almost religious principle among today's professional soldiers in Peru.

Castilla is also remembered for his success in foreign affairs and in defense of the national boundaries. He was among the leaders of the opposition to the abortive attempt by Spain to retake Ecuador in 1845. He was also an outspoken critic of the United States's aggression against Mexico, and he sought to create a united Latin American front against the Colossus of the North. In 1859, Castilla attacked Guayaquil, Ecuador, in retaliation for the Ecuadorian government's attempt to placate European creditors by ceding them land claimed by Peru.

Finally, in 1865, Castilla, though no longer president, was the first to denounce the Vivanco-Pareja Treaty between Spain and Peru as being insulting to the national honor. The treaty was aimed at ending Spanish occupation of Peru's principal guano deposits on the Chincha Islands, which had been seized by the Spanish fleet some months earlier. What incensed Castilla was that Peru agreed to pay not only Spanish claims dating back to the War for Independence, but also the cost of the Spanish occupation of the Chinchas.

Thus, from a military point of view, Castilla stands as one of the greatest leaders in Peruvian history. He established internal order, brought about economic prosperity, enlarged and improved the armed forces, assumed a leadership role for Peru in foreign affairs (including challenging the United States), and vigorously defended the national boundaries against both South American and European opponents. If one compares Castilla with subsequent civilian presidents, both in the nineteenth and twentieth centuries, one might conclude, as have thousands of Peruvian military officers, that what Peru needs is not civilian "politics," but the antipolitics of Ramón Castilla.

Bolivia suffered a bewildering succession of caudillo presidents in the nineteenth century, a situation which continued to plague her in the twentieth. As with Castilla in Peru, however, one caudillo, Andrés de Santa Cruz, stands above all in terms of leadership and national vision. Born in 1794, Santa Cruz, like Castilla, was a mestizo and initially fought with the royalist forces in the Wars for Independence, later joining the rebels. Santa Cruz was an outstanding military commander, who quickly gained the attention of Simón Bolívar. In 1826, Bolívar appointed him provisional president of Peru, but he was overthrown one year later. He went to Bolivia, where he assumed the presidency in 1829 and held it until 1839.

It is generally agreed that Santa Cruz was the best president that Bolivia has ever had. His ten-year term was not only one of the few stable periods in Bolivian history, but also was characterized by its economic productivity. Santa Cruz was an honest and capable administrator who sought to complete the nation-building task begun by Antonio José de Sucre.

He first established internal order by ending the incessant feuding between factions in the military and in the civilian political arena. He organized the Bolivian national army and the national police force—the *Carabineros*. He founded trade and art schools, as well as the two major universities, in La Paz and Cochabamba. Moreover, he reorganized the judiciary, improved the economic state of the nation, and took the first steps to alleviate the educational and economic plight of the great mass of illiterate, non-Spanish-speaking Indians.

His fatal flaw was one common to many caudillos of the age—an all-consuming ambition, which in his case took the form of redrawing the map of South America. His dream was to combine Peru and Bolivia into one great nation ruled by himself, and he did in fact succeed in creating the Peru-Bolivian Confederation, which lasted from 1836 to 1839. Such a confederation, however logical from either an economic or geographic standpoint, upset the balance of power in South America, and thus provoked the wrath of Rosas, in Argentina, and Diego Portales, in Chile.

Defeated in battle in 1839, Santa Cruz returned to Bolivia, where he was deposed as president and sent into exile. Though he failed in his grand scheme of confederation, Santa Cruz deserves credit for having organized the various components of the Bolivian state. To present-day Bolivians, the ambitions, dreams, and deeds of Santa Cruz compare favorably to the tragicomedy of Bolivian politics in the twentieth century. And like their counterparts in Argentina and Peru, Bolivian military officers look back on their great caudillo with pride and admiration.

The nineteenth-century political experiences of both Brazil and Chile stand in sharp contrast to those of Argentina, Peru, and Bolivia. Unlike the Spanish American republics, Brazil was spared the violence, bloodshed, political chaos, and economic dislocation of a struggle for independence. Instead, Emperor Pedro I abdicated in favor of his son, and the transition was a smooth one. From 1831 to 1889, Pedro II ruled Brazil peacefully, and therefore the Brazilian military establishment developed out of a totally different milieu.

As outlined in the Introductory Essay, the age of the caudillo was extremely short lived in Chile, being replaced after 1830 with a highly centralized, autocratic republic which maintained internal order and greatly expanded the economy of the nation, but which tolerated no opposition or dissent. Thus, Chile also avoided the economic and political chaos associated with the age of the caudillos.

In most of Latin America, the age of *caudillismo* gradually came to an end after 1870. National economies demanded national policy making. National policy making implied effective national leadership, which in many cases meant the dominance of a truly national caudillo like Porfirio Díaz, in Mexico. In other cases, such as Chile and Argentina, national political institutions developed which allowed legal transfers of power and implementation of public policy through national administrative agencies.

A key to the formation of real nation states was the emergence of national military institutions. Control of national politics required the reorganization, modernization, and professionalization of the national military establishments, which in turn meant the destruction of the old regional and personalist armies. This professionalization process did not mark an end to the military as political elites, but rather to the formation of a new national military-political elite to replace the regionalistic caudillo commanders. Latin America and Latin American military officers in particular had begun the slow road back to what Morse has called the Thomistic tradition, a road which was to culminate in the military antipolitics of the 1960s and 1970s.

Notes

1. For a succinct discussion of these and other causal factors, see the Introduction by Hugh M. Hamill, Jr., in his *Dictatorship in Spanish America* (New York: Alfred A. Knopf, 1965), pp. 3–25.

2. Originally published in the *Journal of the History of Ideas*, 15 (1954): 71–93, the essay was reprinted in abridged form in Hamill, *Dictatorship*, pp. 52–68. All citations are from the latter.

3. Morse, "Toward a Theory," pp. 53–54.

4. Ibid., pp. 54–55.

5. Ibid., p. 56.

6. Hamill, *Dictatorship*, p. 21.

7. Quoted in Morse, "Toward a Theory," p. 60.

8. Hamill, *Dictatorship*, p. 11.

34

THE POLITICS OF ANTIPOLITICS

9. Edwin Lieuwen, *Arms and Politics in Latin America*, rev. ed. (New York: Frederick A. Praeger, 1961), pp. 19–20.

10. John J. Johnson, *The Military and Society in Latin America* (Stanford, Calif.: Stanford University Press, 1964), pp. 50, 53.

11. Quoted in Fredrick B. Pike, *The Modern History of Peru* (New York: Frederick A. Praeger, 1967), p. 92.

The Latin American Nation State and the Creation of Professional Military Establishments

One of the great illusions in post-World War II thought on Latin American development was the hope that the Latin American military establishments would be professionalized, thereby ending their periodic intervention into national politics. North American observers in particular equated military professionalism and professionalization with apolitical military establishments. In practice, however, military professionalization in the Latin American milieu actually accelerated institutional and officer involvement in the political arena.

This result surprised many North American and European specialists on Latin America. To a great extent, their surprise stemmed from a misreading of the history of Latin American military professionalization during the latter part of the nineteenth and early part of the twentieth centuries, as well as the quality and direction of this professionalization after World War II. In contrast to what North Americans expected, the introduction of professional training, organization, and staffing of Latin American military establishments by European training missions led to the creation of political as well as military elites. Indeed, key political actors in the first three decades of the twentieth century were graduates of the German or French military professionalization programs or later of the programs run by German-trained Chilean personnel. Examples are Carlos Ibáñez in Chile, José F. Uriburu in Argentina, Luis M. Sánchez Cerro in Peru, and Leitão de Carvalho in Brazil.

In the first selection of part 2, Frederick Nunn presents an overview of the effects of European military training missions in Latin America around the turn of the century. Nunn concludes that ''the overriding impact of fifty years of European military training or orientation on Latin American armies was to stimulate rather than lessen political interest and to motivate elitist professional army officers to assume responsibility for the conduct of national affairs.''

Marvin Goldwert's discussion of the rise of modern militarism in Argentina supports many of Nunn's generalizations concerning the effects of professionalization while at the same time providing a historical background to the role of the military in Argentine politics. As Goldwert notes: ''For those who

35

believe that military professionalization is an antidote to militarism, the Argentine case offers serious doubts."

In the third selection, Warren Schiff analyzes the influence of the German training missions and war industry on Argentina, including the military socialization of José F. Uriburu, who led a successful military coup in 1930. Uriburu's career—a top graduate of the Argentine War Academy in 1902, service with the Imperial Guard in Germany, and director of the War Academy from 1907–13—made him a model professional officer and a highly political one. As Schiff concludes, the German military instructors left a deep impression on the increasingly influential officer corps, an impression which hardly depoliticized the Argentine military.

Frederick Nunn reviews the "Prussianization" of the Chilean army. In Chile, the German military mission actually participated in the Chilean Civil War of 1891, helping to oust constitutionally elected president José Manuel Balmaceda. As in Argentina, the products of German professionalization programs (men such as Carlos Ibáñez, Juan Pablo Bennett, Marmaduke Grove, and Bartolomé Blanche) were hardly apolitical and significantly influenced Chilean national politics in the 1920s and later.

As in Chile, the beginnings of military professionalization in Peru followed Chile's victory against Peru and Bolivia in the War of the Pacific (1879–83). Former Peruvian army officer Víctor Villanueva describes late nineteenth-century developments in Peru, the role of the French military mission in professionalizing the Peruvian military, and the impact of professionalization on the political activities of army officers.

Bolivian military professionalization in the early twentieth century had the benefit of both French and German training missions. The documents transcribed and edited from the State Department Serial File on Bolivia make clear how the German military mission, and particularly its leader Major Hans Kundt, affected Bolivian national politics. From 1912 into the 1930s, with only brief absences from Bolivia, Major Kundt, whose official charge was to professionalize the Bolivian armed forces, became the arbiter of Bolivian politics.

In Brazil, the influence of European military training missions before World War II was slight. Nevertheless, the move toward professionalization of the Brazilian military played a significant political role in the late nineteenth and early twentieth centuries. As in Argentina, Chile, Peru, and Bolivia, professionalization in Brazil, as William Dudley points out, meant the development of a politicized, anticivilian military elite anxious to "cleanse" the Brazilian polity and lead Brazil to continental hegemony.

After World War I, both France and the United States gained military and commercial footholds in Brazil through their military training missions. The documents transcribed from the Serial File on Brazil reveal not only the thrust of United States policy toward military professionalization in Brazil, but also the decade-long internal debate in Brazil before the arrival of the French army mission in 1919 and the United States naval mission in 1922.

Taken together, these descriptions and analyses of military professionalization in Latin America in the late nineteenth and early twentieth centuries suggest that, instead of creating an apolitical military, professionalization actually produced a politicized officer corps, with its own ideology of modernization, industrialization, corporate elitism, nationalism, and antipolitics.

Frederick M. Nunn

An Overview of the European Military Missions in Latin America

The presence of military organizations in Latin American politics is a reality of the twentieth century just as it was of the past. Scholars are in unison on this point but disagree on the reasons for the behavior and political outlook of twentieth century political officers. Obviously "changing times," nationalism, and middle-class origins of officers are insufficient causes for the nationalist, reformist-authoritarian strain of contemporary military attitudes in Latin America.

One of the most important causes for the development of contemporary Latin American military attitudes toward state, nation, and society is the creation of a professional army officers corps undertaken late in the last century and early in this century by the more advanced countries and by some of the lesser republics as well. Military professionalization was undertaken in Latin America for a variety of reasons, depending on time and place. In those countries where pre-World War II professionalization was guided by Europeans—French and Germans, chiefly—it resulted in the creation of a powerful political interest group. That group, the officers corps, completed the laying of the foundations for professional militarism. And professional militarism in Latin American countries where French and German officers served wears the indelible stamp of their presence. It is the purpose of this essay to point out the significance of that presence.

For some time now we have assumed that military professionalization did not achieve the desired results—that is, depoliticization—in Latin America because of such endemic factors as fiscal problems, weak economies, political conflict, and social change. But endemic factors may be the least important reason for the failure of professionalization to preclude political activities by the military in Latin America. The overriding impact of fifty years of European military training or orientation on Latin American armies was to stimulate rather than lessen political interest and to motivate elitist, professional army officers to assume responsibility for the conduct of national affairs. This is by no means a monocausal interpretation; it is, rather, an additional explanation for military interest in Latin American politics.

Abstention from politics, then, did not result from professional training. What did develop first was a state that can be called military professionalism, and more. For the end of military professionalism—expertise, corporateness or

38

sense of career, and responsibility—in Latin America during the age of modernization was professional militarism: a set of attitudes that may result in the resort to political action in an attempt to find solutions for social and economic distresses by methods based on a military ethos.

A careful historical examination of the professional armies selected by Latin American military leaders and statesmen to be models for their own armies indicates that they in fact were highly political. The French and German armies were highly political, not in the sense that they intervened in the affairs of the state time and time again, but in the sense that they were professions, corporate entities, immune in theory but not in practice from civilian meddling. And they were loyal to the state and the nation more than to a specific government or administration. They were vital and potent ingredients of the political process in France and Germany at the same time they were involved in the training of Latin America's armies.

Although the histories of the German and French armies from 1871 to 1914, and then from 1918 to about 1940, are those of a high degree of professionalism, they are also histories in which partisan political issues were of vital importance to the military profession per se. To review the Dreyfus Affair, the Catholic-Radical-Masonic conflict, and the catastrophe of 1914–15 in France, or the German army and the empire, . . . and the rise of Nazism would be redundant here. History has yet to record more politicized armies than those of pre-World War II France and Germany.

It can be tentatively posited that Latin Americans who learned their military science in the classroom, in war games, and on maneuvers learned other things from their mentors. If the French and Germans were exemplary in a professional way, they cannot have been less exemplary in an extraprofessional way.

European military influences—professional and extraprofessional—were most keenly felt in South America, where the military buildup was a facet of traditional international rivalries on the one hand and a component of the overall modernization process on the other between 1890 and 1940. By 1914 German missions and individual instructors were training the armies of Argentina, Bolivia, and Chile. Chileans, who had studied under the retired German Captain Emil Körner (who rose to the rank of general in Chile) and his cohorts, in turn laid the foundations for the modern armies of Colombia, Ecuador, and El Salvador. Cadets and young officers from Central America, Venezuela, and Paraguay studied in Santiago. German-trained Argentines were prominent in that country's army by 1914, and students from Bolivia, Paraguay, and Peru came to study in Buenos Aires. Colonel Hans Kundt, probably the best known of all German officers in Latin America, put in several fruitful years prior to 1914 at the military school in La Paz, Bolivia. He would later prepare and lead that country's army to disaster in the Chaco War.

The Peruvian army was under French influence through a series of missions from 1896 until 1940, except for the 1914–18 interim. And, in 1919, a French mission led by General Maurice Gamelin, later chief of the French general staff, was contracted by Brazil. With the exception of those of the countries in the Caribbean area under heavy United States influence, no Latin American army was without an attachment to French or German (and in certain specialized fields, Spanish, Swiss, or Italian) influence during the half century before World War II.

In those countries most heavily influenced by French or German military training the armies were intensely political, in a professional sense and for professional reasons, as early as 1920 and by no later than 1930. Added to the incredible difficulties of shattered economies, disrupted commercial patterns, political disharmony, and social ferment in the interwar years was the rise of the professional military as a political interest group. By the end of 1930, Argentina, Brazil, and Peru were under army-led or created regimes. Chile was entering its sixth year of military-influenced rule. Bolivia was girding for war; so was the French-trained Paraguayan army.

The integrity of the profession and professional expertise were supposed to have been guaranteed through professionalization by consent of civilian authority, but they were not. Thus, members of the professional officer corps in Argentina, Bolivia, Brazil, Chile, Paraguay, and Peru blamed social disorder, economic collapse, and professional shortcomings on civilians and their politics long before the Cold War, Castro, and Che Guevara. And in doing so, they often displayed attitudes assimilated from France and Germany.

Having been Europeanized, they aped their mentors by holding themselves above the rest of society and by considering themselves superior to their non-Europeanized commanders. They were, they believed, models of modernity and members of a truly national institution. We know this is true in Argentina, Brazil, Chile, and Peru. As junior officers in these countries rose to positions of influence, they naturally favored alternate political systems of organizations that might guarantee them the prerequisites for professional progress.

In Chile and Brazil, European orientation had both similar and diverse results. First, French or German training tended to solidify the profession but did not make it monolithic by any means. Second, political motivation and action were tempered to the point where the status of the profession became both causal and inhibitive to flagrant overthrow of a fragile civilian regime or system. Third, both armies were led by elitist officers who believed they represented the only true national institutions—impartial, apolitical (nonpartisan), pure, and morally superior to civilian interest groups. Fourth, virtually all professional shortcomings were blamed on civilians; the "impotent" Old Republic in Brazil and the "irresponsible" Parliamentary Republic in Chile.

Fifth, Franco-German professional "differences of opinion" kept political action from taking on a personalist tone: in Chile the appeal of *Ibañismo* was more pronounced among civilians than among military men; in Brazil the officer class spawned no *manda chuva* [military caudillo] after the demise of Marshal Hermes in 1923. There are civilian "corollaries" to each of these assumptions, which should not be overlooked in an overall assessment of civil-military relations.

Among the major Latin American nations (excluding Mexico), Brazil and Chile are among the few held up as exemplary in the field of civil-military relations. Not until 1964 did the Brazilian armed forces, led by the army, actually overthrow a government with the idea of holding on to power. Even then the maintenance of power was debated fiercely within the services for some months. Since 1932 the Chilean army has refrained from such conduct until 1973, and except for isolated movements in 1935, 1938, 1939, 1945–46, 1953–55, and 1969, it has stayed "in the barracks." Here one might tentatively posit that professionalization achieved its objective purposes at least until 1964 in Brazil and until 1973 in Chile. Obviously, the existence or lack of strong national civilian political or socioeconomic groups is significant. But the fact remains that owing heavily to European training and orientation, the armies of these two nations became more capable of being intensely political for professional reasons. The nature of their political action was molded by environment as well, but their propensity for it was, and is, an inheritance based on their early twentieth-century experiences.

This is also the case in Argentina and Peru; but inherited and environmental factors vary, despite apparent similarities. German military training in Argentina, like Chile, was a pre-1914 phenomenon, but there the army was successful in eventually casting off the stigma of Germany's defeat by virtue of having asserted earlier that it was quite capable of continuing the professionalization process on its own. Also, the favored position of the army under Gen. Julio A. Roca (president, 1880–86, 1898–1904), then its politicization at the hands of Hipólito Irigoyen (president, 1916–22, 1928–30), was unequaled at the time in South America.

Argentines perpetuated the outlook of the pre-World War I German officer class themselves, and in a roughly similar milieu. Like their counterparts in Brazil, Chile, and Peru, Argentine military elitists were highly critical of civilian politics, particularly during the Radical Era (1916–30). Unlike their counterparts, the Argentine army officers functioned within a cult of personalism, exaggerated by then extant Latin American professional military standards and akin to personalism à la Seeckt and Hindenberg. Generals Agustin P. Justo and José F. Uriburu represented the polarities of military factionalism in the interwar years. Uriburu represented the continuation of

German military orientation fused with chauvinistic Argentine and Fascist-elitist ideas. Justo associated himself with the antipersonalist Radical faction. Despite factionalism, though, the military attitude toward civilian politics retained an authoritarian, elitist character in Argentina from World War I through and beyond the Perón years (1943–55).

As early as 1900, war minister Gen. Pablo Riccheri established limitations on foreign (German) penetration of the Argentine army by stating that the army would not copy any European military organization but would instead adapt what best suited its needs. Argentina, he reasoned, was not European, but American. Nevertheless, until 1914, German officers were in charge of the Escuela Superior de Guerra and trained all Argentine staff officers. Instruction, education, tactics, and strategy were German oriented, whereas for fortification techniques, the artillery and engineers depended more heavily on post-1871 French concepts. By 1914, Argentina's staff school instructors and administrators were strident Germanophiles. During this period, the German theory of all-out offense became the principal doctrine of the Argentine army. This, when coupled with professional attitudes toward military needs, soon took the form of army demands made in public for a national program to support mass mobilization (with two fronts always in mind!). When war appeared improbable from 1904 on, this philosophy became a demand for industrialization and economic development, not for the sake of making war but as a prerequisite to overall national greatness.

At the beginning of the twentieth century, Peru, like Argentina and Brazil, was an unintegrated nation. Geographically and socially, Peru was divided, and from the earliest stages of French military indoctrination, the army officer corps looked upon itself as the agency most capable of bringing the country together.

After the War of the Pacific (1879–84) Peru was not only lacking integration and unity, but it was in political and economic collapse. Chile had eclipsed Peru as the leading Pacific power of the continent and had begun the military reform program under German leadership in order to maintain that position "by reason or force"—the motto on the Chilean escutcheon.

Peru's contracting of a mission in 1896, like Argentina's resort to German training, was primarily in response to the Chilean military buildup. The Peruvian government, however, did not look to Germany for assistance, but to France. France had suffered defeat at the hands of the Germans, to be sure, but the reorganization of the French army in the 1880s impressed the decision makers in Lima. Furthermore, the French army, owing to a large number of Catholic and Monarchist officers, was removed (or so it appeared) from politics. French expertise in fortification, frontier defense, and military engineering appealed to Lima. Forswearing any military designs on lost territory, Peru sought to apply French defensive doctrines to her own situation. In 1896, Capt. Paul Clément was appointed a colonel in the Peruvian army and took up his duties as instructor, inspector, and reorganizer. Some seventy-five French officers served in Peru between Clément's arrival and 1940. Until the 1920s, the French had great freedom in reorganizing the Peruvian army, but, as with the Germans in Argentina, held no command positions.

One of the first things Clément called for was a rigid promotion system that would allow only academy graduates to rise above the rank of *subteniente* (second lieutenant). This became law in 1899, but, unfortunately for discipline, was not rigidly applied. Other French-inspired proposals, dating in many cases from 1899, presaged by a half century proposals emanating from the now twenty-three-year-old, elite Centro de Altos Estudios Militares (CAEM). In his report of 1899, for example, Clément noted that frontiers must be accessible from the capital in time of peace as well as war, that internal lines of communication would aid the development of national unity as well as defense. He further stated that regionalism necessitated a flexibility in training, armament, tactics, and strategy, and that the officer class should seek close association with civilians. These are themes reiterated time and again in this century.

Clément also suggested that staff officers serving in the provinces should study the history, economy, politics, and society of their region in order to know all possible in case an emergency arose. "Peru has not one topographic map," he wrote, "not even of the area surrounding Lima. . . . It will be the army's job to supply one." Just above his signature to the seventy-five-page 1899 report are the words, "Throughout the country, one can sense the desire to see the army move ahead along the road to progress and obtain the prestige that corresponds to the military profession." For nearly forty years, Peruvian cadets, staff aspirants, and colonels who attended special advanced courses (which ultimately evolved into CAEM) had a steady dose of such heady stuff.

Neither Clément nor those who came after him were able to make the army immune to political issues and pressures. But because of their pervasive influence there existed no apparent divisions within the officer corps on professional issues, save those emanating from the old versus the young rivalry.

Unlike their Brazilian counterparts, however, Peruvian political officers (Col. Luis Sánchez Cerro, for example) appealed in a personalistic way to civilians as well as army officers. This lasted well into the second half of the twentieth century. Nevertheless, French emphasis on territorial unification and the awareness of having to deal with a large aboriginal population, based on French experiences in Africa and Indochina . . . laid groundwork for the emergence of the technocratic nation builders of the 1960s. In an article published in 1933, Lt. Col. Manuel Moria wrote of the *misión civilizadora* of the army in Peru, where nationhood had yet to flourish. Transportation, communications, education and health programs for Indian conscripts, patriotism, discipline, and national economic development could all be provided by army service and supervised by the officer corps, he concluded.

Early in this century, therefore, Peruvian army officers saw themselves as nation builders in a backward and divided land. Based on published materials in military journals and given the emphasis on French training, it is possible to trace the origins of the present Peruvian *mentalidad militar* ascribed by Víctor Villanueva to French influences. Army officers today readily cite the French emphasis on communications in remote areas, frontier defense, and flexible organization in the provinces as contributory to the assumption of political responsibility. CAEM, which since 1950 has turned out a number of "intellectual officers," is a direct result of French emphasis on continued education for high-ranking officers.

Examined together, Argentina and Peru appear superficially dissimilar rather than similar. But in more detail, the similarities are evident. First, personalism continued in both armies despite professionalization and because of early politicization. In both countries the "military modernization" issue was hotly debated in civilian circles, and much published material exists that is highly critical of the alleged need for a modern military: defense of the profession by civilians did not go unrewarded in times of national crisis.

Second, both Peru and Argentina originally sought European missions out of fear—Chile being the immediate danger, so they thought, from about 1885 until 1905. Once the heavy emphasis on war subsided, though, the profession did not wither. Instead, in both countries the professional army became a political pressure group with its own mission: national integration, education, nationalization of indigenous and immigrant conscripts, and overseer of internal economic development.

Third, the army became hostile to the civilian center-left. In Argentina, some professional officers blamed the Radicals for the lack of military progress towards professionalism, but others were coopted by that party. The end result was the smashing of traditional civilian institutions, perhaps beyond repair. The disenchantment with *Peronismo*-labor politics is a continuance of this attitude in Argentina. In Peru, the army became anti-Aprista, primarily as Luigi Einaudi says, "based on the perception of APRA as 'another unreliable civilian political entity,' " and because of Aprista attempts to subvert military discipline. Finally, the status of the profession tempered political activities less in Argentina and Peru than in Brazil and Chile, as long as European influences were prevalent. As with Brazil and Chile, these conclusions do not stand alone and cannot be separated entirely from civilian influences.

Because of the nature of civilian politics, and owing to the socioeconomic dilemma, European-trained Argentines and Peruvians did become political, but apparently less for professional reasons than in Brazil and Chile, until World War II. This may be because of politicization and the fact that civilians sought out military allies and promised them much more in Argentina and Peru than they did in Brazil and Chile. Professional training by Europeans plus the environmental factors helped to make involvement of the profession more a constant in Argentina and Peru than in Brazil and Chile.

The Argentine, Brazilian, Chilean, and Peruvian officers who spent time in France or Germany, and Spain and Italy also, after academy and staff training at home, rose to elite status rapidly upon their return. Uriburu, Klinger, Leitão de Carvalho, the Chileans Bartolomé Blanche and Marmaduke Grove, and Luis Sánchez Cerro owed much to their French and German training.

Marshal José Felix Estigarribia of Paraguay, who directed the Chaco campaign for his country, had studied in Chile and in France at the Ecole Supérieure. Without a doubt his French staff training made him a national figure in remote, backward Paraguay.

In summary, nearly all armies in Latin America were influenced in some ways by European training in the first half of this century. Six of South America's ten countries (Bolivia and Paraguay in addition to those treated herein) had significant military missions or instructors. In Argentina, Brazil, Chile, and Peru the contracting of French or German missions was part of the overall modernization process, continental power politics, and military rivalry. War-making potential was minimal, nevertheless, with the exception of the Bolivia-Paraguay conflict. But the European impact on military activities in other spheres was great. Military professionalism in a developing Latin America was also affected by civilian meddling, financial limitations, human resources, and political instability; but the concept of professional integrity and status was very real. The concept stimulated, rather than precluded, political action in the manner called professional militarism.

Reprinted and edited from "Effects of European Military Training in Latin America: The Origins and Nature of Professional Militarism in Argentina, Brazil, Chile and Peru, 1890–1940," *Military Affairs* 39 (February 1975), pp. 1–7.

Marvin Goldwert

The Rise of Modern
Militarism in Argentina

The striking characteristic of modern Argentine militarism is that it evolved in
one of the most highly professionalized armies in Latin America. For those who
believe that military professionalization is an antidote to militarism, the Argentine case offers serious doubts. By professionalization is meant the formation of
a technically trained army officer corps comprised of paid career men dedicated
solely to professional matters. This objective necessitated the establishment of
academies for advanced training in modern methods and weaponry, along with
the adoption of objective criteria for promotion based on merit and seniority.
Paradoxically, professionalization in Argentina, with its emphasis on strict
subordination to civilian authority and dedication to military matters alone,
proved to be a necessary condition for the rise of modern militarism.

The process of military professionalization began with President Domingo F.
Sarmiento, who in 1869 established the Colegio Militar to train officers for the
Argentine army. Sarmiento looked to the formation of a professional army as
the answer to the improvised gaucho militias of provincial caudillos who had
spread havoc in Argentina during the long conflict between the port and the
province of Buenos Aires. After this conflict ended in 1880 with the federaliza-
tion of the city of Buenos Aires, the national army began to play a new role in
Argentine history. It became the praetorian guard of an all-powerful president
representing the landed oligarchy. From 1880 to 1886, President Julio A. Roca
established the *unicato*, the one-man rule of the president, largely through the
use of an army now well equipped with the new Remington rifle and capable of
swift transport on recently constructed railroads. Using the power or the threat
of army intervention, Roca transformed the once powerful provincial governors
into docile instruments of the president. Through these governors, in turn, and
the Ministry of the Interior, charged with electoral supervision, Roca controlled
elections to the congress. Thus it was that the armed forces, the provinces, and
the legislature, were all subordinated to the *unicato*.

While Roca was converting the army into a tool of the president he also
pressed for military professionalization in the late nineteenth and early twentieth centuries. His protegé, General Pablo R. Riccheri, was also a major figure
in transforming the ''Old Army'' into the ''New Army.'' What had been an

46

ill-disciplined cavalry force of impressed soldiers led by amateur officers became a conscript army with modern arms and a professional officer corps. According to military historians, the "three basic columns" which served as the foundation of the "New Army" were the modernization of weaponry and war material, the establishment of the Escuela Superior de Guerra, and the law of obligatory military service.

In 1884, during his first administration, Roca converted the Argentine general staff from a simple bureau for the transmission of orders into a major institution intended to prepare the nation for war. During the 1890s, Riccheri headed an armaments commission in Europe which purchased modern German weaponry on a large scale for the Argentine army. Both developments led to the creation of a war academy to train general staff officers in new military methods and weaponry. In 1899, Roca, then in his second term (1898–1904), engaged the first German training mission to organize such an academy on the Prussian model. On January 29, 1900, the Escuela Superior de Guerra was created by general order of the Ministry of War. One year later, the famous law no. 4031, sponsored by Minister of War Riccheri, established obligatory military service in Argentina.

Military professionalization was destined to have a profound impact on the course of Argentine political history. Professionalization heightened the corporate consciousness of the army officer corps, especially its determination to acquire and maintain autonomy on vital matters such as promotion. By 1910, the criterion for promotion had shifted from political or presidential favoritism to mastery of the techniques of modern warfare. Officers of the "Old Army" were being retired in large numbers to enforce the new criterion. A related development was the shift in the control of promotions from the presidency to the professional army, represented by a Tribunal de Clasificación. The tribunal was comprised of commanders of army divisions headed by the highest-ranking general. This shift meant that able officers could rise in the profession and acquire military prestige apart from that formerly bestowed by the president. In other words, a peacetime military establishment had become the first institution of state to escape the shadow of presidentialism. Should the presidency falter in a grave crisis and the state cease to operate, as happened in 1930, the army officer corps was prepared to provide not only the force but also the leadership needed to define political change.

Reprinted and edited from *Hispanic American Historical Review* 48 no. 2 (May 1968), pp. 189–205.

Warren Schiff

The Influence of the German Armed Forces and War Industry on Argentina, 1880-1914

Discreet German participation in the Argentine arms trade dated back to the beginning of Argentina's nationhood. Paraguay's army, then Argentina's foe, introduced Krupp cannons into the Plata region during the Paraguayan War, between 1865 and 1870. Argentina, with a typical deep suspicion of Chile's intentions, orderd her first Krupp cannons in 1873 under the cloak, just as typically, of an officially inspired press silence.

Soon, prospering but unstable Argentina became increasingly interested in adopting German military methods as well. Her government shared the worldwide respect for German military successes. It felt itself beset by the increasingly German-oriented Chilean army. And it was anxious to use growing quantities of modern German weaponry effectively. In addition, Argentina and Germany shared not only the experiences of a recent national unification and a common European tradition, but also those of authoritarian governmental structures, domination by elites, and a desire for rapid economic modernization. On the other hand, the German government became aware that it had to balance its interests in Argentina against those in Chile.

Reflecting the close link between the purchase of modern weaponry and the adoption of modern training methods, Argentina established military institutes and sought the advice of a few German and other European military technicians while General Julio A. Roca was serving his first presidency between 1880 and 1886. An admirer of the German military establishment and a man of arrogant and martial airs, Roca, for years to come, served as one of his nation's most influential advisers on matters of national defense. Soon a handful of German specialists proved their competence and began to rise to key line positions in the Argentine army.

By 1894, the Argentine government had become sufficiently concerned about the possibility of a violent confrontation with Chile to request special credit for military defense in an urgent congressional session which was kept so secret that the press was prohibited from alluding to it under penalty of the immediate suppression of any offending newspaper. At a time when Chile seemed bent on upsetting the South American balance of power, the conservative newspaper *La Nación* observed how Germany's efficient army was worth its immense cost. It was indeed a tense year, as Chilean reconnoitering parties began to violate Argentinian territory. They included several Germans, who claimed to be astronomers but were really preparing strategic maps for Chile.

Germany's military influence continued to grow despite worry over the effects of the heavy arms expenditures, which could be only partially disguised, on Argentina's budget and credit rating. At one point a number of applications by German officers for service in Argentina had to be temporarily rejected because of budgetary difficulties. Nevertheless, a German military orientation became pronounced during Roca's second presidency between 1898 and 1904. Chile, after all, had been enlarging her contingent of German officers since 1895 and seemed to be preparing for war against Argentina.

Argentina's military leadership determined to provide greater homogeneity, training in modern warfare, and an efficient organization for its own army. Reform measures seemed all the more urgent when Argentina, following Chile, adopted a system of compulsory military service. But unhappily, even the German-inspired Argentine general staff found it almost impossible to handle the frequently inept, overly large, and miscellaneous officer corps. Some of its members had been trained along traditional lines with an adherence to ancient and rigid Spanish regulations. Others followed gaucho guerrilla tactics. Still others had been trained in a number of European countries, in each of which they had been taught to believe that that country's system was the most effective. Many of them, especially political appointees, were hardly trained at all. Roca and his military entourage concluded that a powerful, centralizing war academy would remedy these conditions. It was to be directed and staffed by distinguished military specialists from Germany, the exclusive model country, and serve also as a training institution for senior and general staff officers. An alternate measure, the formation of an Italian Legion, which was supported by members of the growing Italian colony, had to be dropped by Roca in the face of protests by both the Italian government and Chile's Italians.

Official consideration of a German-dominated war academy turned out to be highly controversial. Sharp nationalistic opposition forced Roca to reduce to a mere handful the number of German officers to be invited. Certain misgivings of the nationalists were not entirely unjustified, as at least some German officers appeared to be more concerned with their rank and status in Argentina than they were with their salary. Important newspapers spearheaded the opposition to the War Academy. *La Nación* questioned the need for specialists, feeling that firmness and energy by the military leadership might suffice to shape a well-trained and disciplined army. It worried that the war minister would become a puppet of foreigners and observed that the "Prussianization mania" had reaped the Chileans little but headaches. And only months before the War Academy's inauguration in 1900, *La Prensa* still persisted in its own line of

50

criticism by expressing dissatisfaction with the new institution's curriculum and admission requirements.

Under the circumstances, the War Academy's first director had to be both an effective military planner and a skillful diplomat, requirements that were not fully met by General Alfredo Arent, a former German general staff officer and decorated veteran of the Franco-Prussian War. A competent military man, Arent was also loquacious, politically naive, and vindictive. The latter characteristics not merely curtailed his personal effectiveness, but almost ruined the German military program as well. Arent began by offending Argentine political sensibilities with some comments made during a speech at the War Academy's inaugural ceremony. Somewhat later his overeagerness probably delayed rather than expedited the program for training Argentine officers with the German army. Arent's personal relationship with War Minister Pablo Riccheri was stormy to the extent that Arent repeatedly asked Roca to intervene against this member of Roca's own cabinet.

Another quarrel finally sealed Arent's fate. In 1899, Arent invited his friend Major Rolo von Kornatzki to accompany him to Argentina. Kornatzki had pleaded with Arent to extract him from an unpleasant assignment in Germany, which he had received for having married a Jewess. In Argentina, Mrs. Kornatzki's driving ambition, glamorous appearance, unpopular opinions, and distinguished friends quickly stirred the resentments of Mrs. Arent and other members of the rather parochial-minded German colony in Buenos Aires. Before long, Arent tried and failed to persuade Kornatzki to cancel his contract, then denounced his former friend in his confidential annual report to the war minister. His report was leaked, in turn, to *La Prensa*, whose editors used this new opportunity to hold the German military system up to popular scrutiny by printing it. In view of the subsequent general publicity, the general was induced, within less than a month, to leave Argentina on a temporary basis. But after an Argentine military investigating commission exonerated Kornatzki publicly, the German emperor personally barred Arent's return to Argentina.

Arent, who was now succeeded by Argentine officers, had already managed to pattern the infant War Academy after its prestigious counterpart in Berlin. This standard was modified from time to time, but never abandoned. As planned, the institution gradually extended its influence over the officer corps. Being well acquainted with his own country's concept of a nation in arms, Arent had also furnished important recommendations for the implementation of the new law of obligatory military service. Among the most urgent goals that the general had set himself at the War Academy were the formation of a competent general staff and the inauguration of thorough combat training, with an emphasis on joint maneuvers by large bodies of troops to be drawn from several branches of the army, who would copy the training exercises of elite model units.

The German military advisers or instructors who worked with and succeeded Arent performed their tasks on the basis of reasonably consistent attitudes on ethical values, pedagogy, military organization, and politics. These could be generally traced back to the precepts of a nation in arms and the spirit of a close identification between a people and its army. With this motivation, German officers on assignment with the Argentine army galvanized reforms in military legislation, organization, and methods of instruction. Their efforts evoked ideological support from within the Argentine officer corps. In 1909, for example, an Argentine general arranged that a captain who had served with the German army for two years address a select and receptive circle of officers. The captain eulogized the German army and presented an idealized image of it as a body of thinking and well-trained soldiers. This was meant to counteract the impression of the German army as a giant war machine bent on conquest. More concretely, the exacting German officers were resolved to inculcate in their students and disciples the severe principles of constant professional dedication and unity, obedience, simplicity, efficient flexibility, and personal discipline.

Articulate, pragmatic, and gregarious José F. Uriburu, the War Academy's director between 1907 and 1913, and, ironically, subsequent president of Argentina by virtue of a military coup d'etat, emerged as a key figure among the often younger and "progressive" officers who were eager to implement German military doctrine. Born in 1868 into an aristocratic family, he early chose a military career, but developed a political consciousness as well. Soon he joined the type of officers' lodge that was to affect Argentine politics significantly in later years, in this case the idealistic Lodge of the Thirty-Three, which backed largely middle-class-inspired revolutionary activities in 1890. Like a number of his fellow conspirators, he quickly rose to military prominence as a stringent advocate of the army's modernization, which he came to equate with Germanizing. In 1902 he was one of the first graduates of the War Academy, with top honors. Anticipating the introduction of a formal Argentine-German exchange program, the then Major Uriburu thereupon served a lengthy tour of duty with the artillery section of the German Imperial Guard, and personally impressed Emperor William II.

Employing the maxim of the concurrence of military axioms, Uriburu consciously related military pedagogy to discipline: "The War Academy is not destined to supply incoherent knowledge," he noted, "quite the contrary, it is planned that the instruction in each new field of studies be based on previously understood and well-assimilated principles."

Beyond this, German-type military training suggested to some the standard of a truly national army in the role of a great civilizing instrument. It transformed uneducated and uncultured draftees into literate and articulate citizens, who were aware of their moral and social obligations and who recognized the necessities of hygiene and a healthy way of life. Such men would eventually be able to improve their standards of living. An overall achievement of such goals, it was hoped, would lead to a final recognition by citizen soldiers that nothing could be accomplished anywhere, from school to factory, without recognizing that an individual sense of discipline must prevail in even instinctive social relationships. Particularly in the field of politics, far from implanting militarism, a German-trained army would intervene in the affairs of government only as a stabilizing element in order to safeguard the honor, liberty, and prestige of Argentina's republican institutions.

A rationale was likewise developed to justify Argentine receptiveness to German instruction. It was intimated that, since certain national characteristics of South American countries resembled those of France and Italy, some of the more dissimilar German perspectives and institutions should complement those prevalent in Argentina. A blind imitation of German practices could be avoided easily. It was pointed out in this connection that, in contrast to the highly centralized Argentine military organization, the powerful German general staff enjoyed virtual autonomy and that the German high command and general military administration were decentralized. Especially German military pedagogues, it was also noted, emphasized not specific doctrines but only the acceptance of a fundamental sense of duty and basic education or training. Finally, the German officers themselves taught that, rapid movement by railroad notwithstanding, the advent of weapons of great destructive capacity had placed the individual soldier in greater isolation in any case and had forced him to become more self-reliant.

Defenders of German influence denied that an acceptance of certain German ideas or methods degraded Argentina's national heritage because, after all, Argentina had been affected by the European tradition throughout her history. Even if one did admit that an exclusive imitation of German methods offended Argentina's self-esteem, a Germanophile like Uriburu pointed out, then it was precisely by such emulation that Argentina could catch up most quickly with the more advanced European nations.

Argentina's top command wished to assure, at minimum expense, the long-range survival of its modern training system. But it preferred to be more careful than the Chileans had been to avoid the army's domination by a haughty coterie of foreign advisers. In 1906, with this end in mind and after initial German, as well as Argentinian, misgivings had been overcome, it was decided, ironically, to imitate still another Chilean experiment by assigning Argentinian officers for training in Germany. They were to gradually supplement and, perhaps, eventually replace the approximately thirty German officers who taught in Argentina between 1900 and 1914. The fact that an impressive number of the from one to five dozen annual trainees later reached top command positions in the army bears testimony to the program's success. In 1908, the German officers who served at the War Academy gained, at least temporarily, a controlling voice in the decision-making process for officer promotions to senior ranks. In addition, Uriburu involved himself and his institute energetically in the selection of Argentine officers for training in Germany.

German and other foreign armaments interests pursued their intrigues within the Argentine government to the eve of World War I. While the often unemotional Germans were, as before, more respected than loved, German military instructors and German-trained Argentine officers in key commands were gradually succeeding in shaping a relatively more cohesive, better disciplined, and somewhat less rebellion-prone officer corps at the head of a more modern and better-equipped national army. Even in the face of persistent Argentine nationalistic assertiveness, close relations continued to be nurtured between the aristocratic German officer corps and Argentine commanders tied to the landed elite, like Uriburu. Capable young officers from middle-class backgrounds, who tended to benefit generally from the new German-inspired emphasis on professional ability, were given new opportunities for promotion as a result of the military reform legislation that had been initiated by Uriburu. Furthermore, in line with German suggestions, more emphasis had been placed on practical training.

Only months before the German advisers took their final leave in order to fight for their own country, German military and naval interests were represented through a distinguished ''unofficial'' visitor to Argentina. He was Prince Henry, the emperor's brother and a top commander in the German navy. Prince Henry bore witness to another at least tentative German accomplishment when, in the company of Uriburu, he reviewed troops en route to large-scale military maneuvers.

With the encouragement of members of the Argentine government and officer corps, increasing German weapons sales had helped to bring about a significant German participation in the molding of a modern Argentine army. In the forefront of those who opposed this type of German penetration had been nationalists, traditionalists, pacifists, and a number of supporters of other foreign interests and tendencies. In response, the German government, armed forces, and war industry, at the turn of the century, began to defend their new and growing vested interests with determination. On the whole, activities related to the sale of weapons and warships had a largely passing but corrosive impact on Argentina, a nation in search of a strong sense of national cohesion. But the teachings of the German military instructors, controversial as they had been, left a deep impression in the increasingly influential officer corps. They had, therefore, contributed to the forging of Argentina's national heritage.

Reprinted and edited from *Hispanic American Historical Review* 52 no. 3 (August 1972), pp. 436–55.

Selected Documents on Military Professionalization in Bolivia

This is a letter written by the U.S. diplomatic mission in Bolivia.

January 24, 1913

To the Honorable
The Secretary of State,
Washington.

Sir:

I have the honor to refer to Department's Instruction No. 76, dated October 10, and to my despatch No. 200 of December 10, 1912.

On the subject matter of the said instructions I had yesterday a very interesting and satisfactory conference with the Minister of War who was not only very willing to give me all the information I desired, but expressed pleasure to see for the first time that our Government shows some interest in·the Military affairs of Bolivia and South America.

The present German Military Commission was engaged in 1910 under contract for a period of three years beginning January 1, 1911. The method of its selection was the Bolivian Government made a formal request of the German Government for such a commission. The German Government recommended Colonel Hans Kundt as the Chief of the Commission who was accepted by the Bolivian Government and has proved to be a most excellent selection. The Chief was authorized to choose his staff which is composed of four captains, one each for the Military College, the Artillery, the Infantry and Cavalry and eight Sergeants. The head of the Commission, who has been made Major-General of the Bolivian Army, receives a monthly salary of 2000 marks and in addition a residence, light for the same, servants and two horses. The monthly salaries of the others are as follows: Captain of Artillery, 1416 marks, the other three captains, 1250 marks each and the eight sergeants 300 marks each.

The Military Commission is in full charge of the Army.

It has done very good work considering the material it has had to work with and the conditions. It is said by those competent to express such an opinion that the Bolivian Army has the highest standard and is the most efficient in proportion to its size of any Army of South America.

The influence of the German Commission has been and is very considerable and extends into commercial and social circles. An instance of that is that it has induced the Bolivian Government to buy in Germany within the last year nearly $500,000 of army material and supplies—clothing, shoes, saddles, harness, etc.

It seems to me that it has been a great oversight on our part to permit such European Commissions to come to these South American Countries. Such a policy has caused us to suffer greatly in both prestige and commerce and has held back our forming a closer union and more friendly relations with these valuable countries. I hope our Government has at last recognized our mistaken policy and has decided to make a change.

I have the honor to be, Sir,

> Your obedient servant,

SOURCE: United States Department of State, Serials File on Bolivia, 1910–29, Records relating to the Internal Affairs of Bolivia, National Archives, 824.20/3.

This is a letter from Jesse S. Cottrell, a U.S. diplomatic representative in Bolivia to the secretary of state.

June 1, 1925.

No. 721

The Honorable
> The Secretary of State,
> > Washington.

Sir:

I have the honor to report that the rumors which have for sometime prevailed in Bolivia that General Hans Kundt, the German Chief of Staff of the Bolivian Army, would resign reached a definite status May 27th, when the General submitted his resignation to President Saavedra, asking that he might be released at once and return to his native country. His resignation was promptly declined.

General Kundt stated in his brief renunciation of his charge that the local press had made references reflecting upon his personal dignity. He referred to brief editorial comments in the opposition press which insinuated that General Kundt was being overpaid for his services.

The President in declining the resignation paid General Kundt a high tribute and stated that his salary had not in fact been sufficient and that had the treasury of the country permitted he would have been paid more. He also assured General Kundt that he had the confidence of the Government and that he would, when he did retire, receive a pension whereby he could pass his old age in his native land in comfort and peace. The President incidentally mercilessly excoriated those who have made critical references to General Kundt. Spanish and translated copies of the resignation and the reply of the President are attached.

General Kundt came to Bolivia in 1912, the head of the German Military Commission of sixteen. He was given the rank of colonel in the Bolivian Army and remained here until Germany started the World War. He returned to Germany with the entire commission except Sergeant Kutzner, who remained on account of his age. Of the fifteen German soldiers who went home and entered the Army, only three survived, General Kundt, who during the World War was a member of General Ludenberg's staff, Colonel Fritz Muther, who is now a professor in the "Colegio Militar" (Military College) in La Paz, and an aviator who is an invalid in Germany from permanent injuries received in the service.

Soon after the Armistice and before the Versailles Treaty had been finally terminated, General Kundt managed to leave Europe, came to Buenos Aires and made his way through the interior of the Argentine and Bolivia to La Paz. Under the laws of Bolivia two years' residence in the country is a prerequisite to naturalization. Such is effected by a municipal council or through the Ministry of Colonization. General Kundt was naturalized over night by the La Paz city council on his statement that he had intended during his previous residence to become a Bolivian citizen. He was immediately placed in the station of "el Jefe de Estado Mayor General", or Chief of Staff, on a three year contract at a salary of Bs. 40,000.00 per annum (now about $14,000.00 U.S. Cy.) with a proviso that if killed while in the discharge of his duties his widow would receive Bs. 160,000.00, and at the end of six years if he desired to retire he would receive a pension of "jollification" such as given superannuated Bolivian soldiers, Kundt's pension to be the equivalent of about $300.00 U.S.C., per month.

During the six years he has been here as Chief of Staff, General Kundt has served the Liberal party one year and the Republican party five. He had only limited authority during his year's tenure with the Liberals and it is a recognized fact that had he been in complete control of the Army in 1920, the coup d'etat which placed the Republicans in control of the Government would never have been accomplished.

No sooner had the Republicans come into power than they gave General Kundt absolute authority and control of the Army with orders to keep the Republican party in power. He at once weeded out the "Montesistas" (followers of ex-President Montes, Liberal President), eliminated from "El Colegio Militar" all cadet appointees named during the Liberal regime before they were graduated, lest they would enter the Army and foment Liberal propaganda, and saw to it that no more cadets from families of Liberal persuasion were nominated to the Military College. He gradually dropped from the Army all officers and soldiers of Liberal ideas and began building up an army of 8,000 to 10,000 soldiers of Aymara and Quechua Indians. He established schools in all "quarteles", or barracks, stopped the use of coca and alcohol, provided sustaining food and comfortable quarters, with the result that today Bolivia has the best army in her history,—the first in fact scientifically trained.

That General Kundt desires to leave Bolivia is well recognized. During the six years he has been here he has made investments in Germany and dealt in securities in London until he is recognized as wealthy. His wife and daughter have already left for his home, where he has extensive properties, and now that he is past fifty-five he desires to retire.

Should General Kundt leave, the future welfare of the Republican party would be jeopardized. Several native applicants for his position would appear and a bitter contest would ensue.

It is currently reported that when President Saavedra retires from the executive chair he will immediately thereafter become Minister of War. It is on these conditions, it is understood, that General Kundt would remain. This combination would insure peace in the country, because President Saavedra (by means fair or foul) has made the Republican party the dominant power in Bolivia, with General Kundt meanwhile enabling him to have complete sway by putting down repeated revolutions and building up a well trained army.

General Kundt is an affable and agreeable personality who is very popular with the foreigners of all classes as well as with Bolivians, and withal a soldier at all times.

I have the honor to be, Sir,

    Your obedient servant,

        Jesse S. Cottrell.

SOURCE: United States Department of State, Serial Files on Bolivia, 1910–29, Records relating to the Internal Affairs of Bolivia, National Archives, 824.20/31.

William S. Dudley

Professionalization and the Brazilian Military in the Late Nineteenth Century

Until 1865, the Brazilian army was essentially preprofessional. Its officer recruitment, training, and socialization patterns were based upon the eighteenth-century Portuguese model which had in turn been strongly influenced by Prussian and English standards. A military academy had been founded in 1810, but attendance there was not a prerequisite for success in the traditional cavalry and infantry branches, and the artillery and engineering corps were in their infancy. The conferral of cadet status, based upon a family's military tradition or aristocratic pedigree, gave a young officer preferred status. Sons of the bourgeoisie became eligible for such status in 1820.

After the winning of independence in 1822–23, and the abdication of Dom Pedro I in 1831, the army's prestige fell. Rent with feuds over the type of regime that would replace that monarch, the army was considered unreliable. The regency created a National Guard to restore order, and no move was made to reorganize the army until the late 1830s, after provincial rebellions broke out threatening the unity of the empire. The successful participation of Brazilian cavalry units in the campaign to overthrow Juan Manuel Rosas of Argentina in 1851–52 led to a spurt of reforms in the administrative structure of the army. This victory provided an aura of self-sufficiency that shielded the empire as it matured during fifteen years of prosperity and political consolidation. The Brazilian army immediately prior to the Paraguayan War was still largely based on traditions, organization, and training regulations that dated at least from the Napoleonic Wars, with strong links to the Pomballine period in Portugal, when the last significant military reforms had been carried out.

The Brazilian army awoke to the need for modernization and renewal in the aftermath of the Paraguayan War (1865–70). The country had paid a high price for complete victory over Paraguay. During five years of war, the imperial government had increased the size of its regular army from 18,000 to 60,000 men, proclaimed the need for volunteers, and federalized units of the National Guard. Estimates of the total number of Brazilians who served in Paraguay range up to 111,650. The National Guard had been used as a provincial police force and substitute army during the years 1831–52. There was no army reserve in Brazil at that time. On the other hand, Paraguay had previously prepared for a confrontation against either Brazil or Argentina and began the war with 80,000 men under arms. During the course of the war, Brazilian military pride suffered because of the initial disparity of strength between the opposing sides, reverses during the siege of the Paraguayan fortress of Humaita, shortages of food, and poor generalship.

Far from the front, Rio de Janeiro felt the tremors of battle. There was a loss of political consensus among parliamentary representatives of the landed oligarchy, and the expenses of war threw the nation's economy off balance, rapidly increasing the foreign debt. The demands of the conflict undermined Brazil's traditional social structure by putting freed slaves into uniform, stimulating industrial enterprises, and fostering the growth of the middle class. As a result, Brazilian society during the postwar period became characterized by increasing cultural ferment, polarizing of political attitudes, and a growing feeling that monarchical institutions had become obsolescent. A wave of modernization had begun, and its proponents were members of the intellectual and political avant-garde who favored elimination of slavery and political reforms, if not republicanism. The army officer corps was not isolated from these movements. Progressive officers sought to profit from their wartime experiences by pressing for army reform soon after the war.

It is in the writings of Maj. Antônio de Sena Madureira that the cause of Brazilian army reform was first fully represented. His report appeared in two volumes, the first of which was published in 1874 entitled *Estudo da organisação militar dos principais estados da Europa apresentado ao Ministério da Guerra*. In this work, the author criticized the lack of a standing army in Brazil and made a detailed comparison of the structure of several western European armies. He concluded with suggestions for the reorganization of the Brazilian army. In his eyes, the Paraguayan War was an object lesson for those who through malice or neglect would allow the army to revert to its prewar lassitude. Had the army been more than a skeleton in 1864, " . . . [Paraguayan President Francisco Solano] López would have thought twice before starting the conflict which buried him and his hateful regime." It was alarming to Sena Madureira that so little had been done on behalf of the army since the end of the Paraguayan War. He foresaw that in the future, Brazil would have to "maintain the balance of power in South America just as the United States does in North America." Indeed, he warned that Brazil would be forced to assume this role in order to prevent the United States from usurping it. Brazil had its own "manifest destiny":

Beginning now our country should establish itself to play the role intended for it by Divine Providence which presides over the destinies of all peoples. The military power of Brazil will inevitably result from the power and influence which she exercises even now among her neighbors on the vast South American continent.

The key to this glorious future was the possession of a strong army, but serious defects would have to be eliminated before Brazil could become the overlord of South America. The army needed men of talent, education, and sound morals in the enlisted ranks. They would not be obtained until a broad system of conscription could be enacted, with a minimum of deferments and exemptions. Only then would the detested system of forced recruiting be abolished. Sena Madureira explained that provincial *caudilhos* frequently punished those who opposed them at the polls by forcing them into the army. In his opinion, this showed the abundant disrespect in which the army was commonly held. To make military service more attractive, the author proposed to reduce the enlisted man's obligation from six to three years and to establish an army reserve. These actions would pave the way for the elimination of the National Guard, which had been corrupted after its era of useful service.

The army had been too vulnerable to the whims of politicians. This weakness could be eliminated by modifying the system of peacetime regional commands. As it was, each province had a military commander (*comandante das armas*) who was subordinate to a civilian provincial president. The latter, in turn, owed allegiance to the cabinet of the controlling political party. The abuses of this system could be avoided by altering the boundaries of military districts and by making each area commandant subordinate only to the minister of war. A reduction of the number of civilians employed in the Ministry of War was also needed to help reduce the influence of government patronage in the army.

Sena Madureira argued further that major revisions were needed in army administration, staff structure, and battlefield training. Units then included under vertical administrative organization ought to be integrated horizontally into corps structure to facilitate training, field maneuvers, and mobilization. To upgrade the talents and efficiency of staff officers, he recommended the adoption of the complete Prussian staff organization. Finally, he offered detailed suggestions on battlefield formations for infantry, cavalry, and artillery units so that they could survive the increased destructiveness of modern weapons. The European practice of annual war games should be instituted to improve the skills and raise the morale of officers and enlisted men.

Meanwhile, as Sena Madureira's ideas were being published, modest gains were made in the field of army reform legislation, indicating that the Conservatives were courting the allegiance of the military during the years 1873–75. The two most important bills reflected advances in military education and recruitment. The first established a new course in military engineering as the fifth and final year of an officer's military academy education. Formerly, fifth-year military engineering students had been lumped with civilians in the government-run Escola Central. Under the new law, military engineers were to be segregated with other officer-students in the military academy at the Praia Vermelha. Academic considerations were the primary ones behind this move.

A separation of the two student groups would allow increased specialization in military, as distinct from civil, engineering. Another part of the bill gave a new organization to regimental schools for enlisted men and to preparatory schools for noncommissioned officers. The curricula for these schools were broadened, and courses on mathematics and physical sciences were given increased emphasis at the Military Academy, partly because of spreading enthusiasm for the positivism of Auguste Comte among members of the teaching staff of that school.

During the late 1870s, there arose ample cause for malaise among Brazilian army officers. Officers fresh from the battlefields had voiced their concerns and cabinets had initiated reforms, but their enthusiasm declined as few positive changes were made. In one instance, a two-thirds increase in base pay was debated and approved in 1873, but it was not put into effect until 1887. The lack of governmental action on such a matter could not help but depress military morale.

During the years 1879–86, army officers became increasingly vocal in their demands for parliamentary action on military programs. Spokesmen for the reformers' viewpoint began publication of the military newspaper *O Soldado* in March 1881, changing its title to *Tribuna Militar* three months later. The first issue of *O Soldado* contained a strident statement of purpose: "If the army has the duty of keeping the peace for the empire, then it also has the duty and right to express itself. While the army does not want to arrogate to itself the power that belongs to all Brazilians, it believes that power should be shared by all social classes. The army thus desires to take part in the administration of the state."

Beginning in 1879, Brazilian public life witnessed the intensification of calls for political reform, governmental decentralization, and abolition of slavery voiced by a host of young and eloquent legislators and journalists. Popular enthusiasm for these causes, especially abolition, abounded in the major urban centers, within the intelligentsia, and among the growing industrial and commercial sectors. During the postwar years, the army was increasingly attractive to young men from these middle classes because of the inexpensive technical education provided by the Military Academy. Even when officers came from humble rural families, military socialization led them to adopt attitudes consonant with the technical and institutional aspirations of their corporation.

Military demands for modernization became public in 1881, shortly after the onset of the civilian reform movements. The drive for professionalization, which these demands represented, now began to generate a more intense politicization among the officer corps. The professionalizing goals of the reformers were being met with indifference at the cabinet level by the controlling Liberal party. At the same time, military politicization was stimulated from without by ongoing campaigns for sweeping social reforms, such as abolition, with which many military men sympathized. Finally, army corporateness was strengthened by a series of severe conflicts between the military and cabinets during 1882–84.

The years 1886–89 saw the development within the army of a willingness to confront imperial politicians that had reached a peak unprecedented in fifty years of constitutional monarchy. The immediate event that caused this prolonged crisis was the outbreak of the Cunha Matos-Sena Madureira incident in 1886. The Conservative cabinet led by the Baron of Cotegipe (João Maurício Wanderley) sternly reprimanded two officers who had defended themselves in the press against charges made by government officials with parliamentary immunity. Military men of varying ages and political attitudes closed ranks in defense of their corporation. Marshal Deodoro da Fonseca's refusal to punish Sena Madureira and his subsequent resignation from a high administrative post in Rio Grande do Sul linked that general to the more politicized officers of the middle-echelon and junior officer ranks. From then on he was the acknowledged leader of a politicized officer corps.

By the time Deodoro da Fonseca and Sena Madureira returned to Rio de Janeiro, in January 1887, insubordination had reached into the military academies of Rio de Janeiro and Pôrto Alegre. Some 200 officers met in Rio and approved a motion to empower Marshal Deodoro to make a formal protest to the emperor. The fate of the two officers was now seen as crucial to protecting the honor of "the military class." The garrisons of Pôrto Alegre and other cities voted their support. The officers' determination to fight with new weapons led to the founding of a military club in Rio de Janeiro in May 1887. This event institutionalized military politics in Brazil. From then on, the club became the center of the most politicized elements of the officer corps. From it was launched Marshal Deodoro's unsuccessful campaign for the senate in July 1887; civilian abolitionists and radical officers made common cause as the marshal spoke out for abolition. In November 1887, the Military Club made a formal and public refusal to participate in the pursuit of fugitive slaves.

The "military question" festered throughout the early months of 1887, but the government had begun to appease the military as early as January, when a long-overdue salary increase was approved. This may only have strengthened the military's determination to hold out for a totally favorable solution. The government dismissed the detested Alfredo Chaves as minister of war in February, and the Council of State approved the charter of the Military Club in May. The army demanded not only the retraction of the reprimands given the officers but also the nullification of the regulations they had disobeyed in their resort to the press. The government refused to yield to the last demand until the Viscount of Pelotas warned, on the floor of the Senate, that the army would overthrow the government to attain their goal, if necessary. By this time, civilian republicans had made contact with their military counterparts, but the officers showed they were not yet ready to abandon the monarchy.

The Cotegipe cabinet resigned over the issue of abolition, but it had been severely shaken by the "military question." The next Conservative cabinet passed the long-awaited abolition act and later turned to military legislation. A reorganization bill was passed in August 1888 that reshuffled numbers but made no substantial changes in military organization. The political elite of the empire were still not prepared to take military concerns seriously.

The last imperial cabinet, led by the Viscount of Ouro Preto (Affonso Celso de Assis Figueiredo) representing the Liberal party, showed that they were no more inclined to accept a strengthened military. Ouro Preto tried, however, to keep the army under control. Offering membership in military orders and titles of nobility to many senior officers, he attempted to repay the loyalty of known monarchists among the officer corps. In this, however, he was interfering politically with the army; it was the officer corps as a whole, especially the middle-echelon and junior officers whom he should have wooed. Instead, Ouro Preto managed to alienate them by several unnecessarily harsh acts of discipline that he and his minister of war might better have left for the military to handle in their own way. The return of Marshal Deodoro's Mato Grosso expedition from a useless travail provided freshly discontented members for the Military Club, whose activities were rejuvenated in September 1889 after several months of inactivity.

Finally, in late October and early November, rumors flew about that the government might disband or effectively exile certain units of the army because of their potential for insubordination. Beyond this, it heard that Ouro Preto was rearming the National Guard and police as insurance against the army. Radical officers in the Military Club then joined with civilian republicans in a conspiracy that resulted in the successful coup d'état of November 15.

Conclusions

Military professionalization began in Brazil during the 1870s and 1880s. The level of officer politicization in the army advanced markedly from 1870 to 1889 in three distinct stages, as officers attempted to overcome apparent resistance to professionalizing efforts and combatted governmental interference in professional affairs. From 1870 to 1880, military politics operated at the level of personal influence through which senior officers used ties of long-standing party association to obtain modest reforms. The army suffered losses under Liberal party restraints after 1877. The years 1881–85 mark a rapid transition from personal influence to pressure-group politics, as the older generals disappeared and younger officers more committed to professionalization resorted to political campaigns, military journalism, and finally group meetings to press the government into action. The cases of officer indiscipline, insubordination, and crime that occurred during 1882–84 can be interpreted as a form of military social protest, as well as evidence of institutional weaknesses. Finally, during 1886–89, the escalation of civil-military tensions on the "military question" produced politicization. Politicization moved to the takeover stage as civil-military incidents recurred and the government strengthened countervailing forces to bolster its position against the army. A mature polity of low political culture at mid-century, the empire had faltered under the pressures of war, recovery, and social change. The emperor's declining health and indecisiveness, coupled with the Ouro Preto cabinet's antimilitary policies, created the conditions in which a professionalizing, politicized officer corps felt justified in takeover.

Selected Documents on Military Professionalization in Brazil

This letter was from the U.S. mission in Brazil.

Rio de Janeiro, November 13, 1917.

No. 1052.

To the Honorable
    The Secretary of State,
        Washington, D. C.

Sir:

The Department will have recognized the importance of the information communicated in the Embassy's telegrams of November 9th, 12 Noon, and November 13th, 2 p.m., which reported the possibility of an invitation being extended by the Brazilian Government to the Government of France to send a military mission to this country to instruct in their professional duties the officers and men of the Brazilian Army.

That army undoubtedly is in serious need of instruction. . . . Since the close of the Paraguayan struggle in 1871 they have not participated in a foreign war and their local revolutions have not increased their military experience. Though a certain number of officers have studied in Germany and France where they have been brought into contact with modern military science as it was understood before the present war, the officers corps is not distinguished by many of the qualities and characteristics which the officers corz [*sic*] of other countries possess. In esprit, technical knowledge and general efficiency it is inferior to similar organizations in Argentina and Chile and would be at a disadvantage in a trial of strength. The transportation, commissary and quartermaster departments are notably weak. During the maneuvers last year in the neighborhood of this capital, which terminated the training period of the volunteers, the commissary was so inadequate that unless the young soldiers had been fed from home they would have been short of food. The officers who instructed them proved incompetent and sergeants were obliged to teach their superiors.

... The proposal to invite a foreign mission of instruction is not new. During the visit which Marechal Hermes da Fonseca paid to Germany in 1910, previous to his entrance upon the Presidency of the Republic, a promise was made to the German Government to engage a military mission and when it could not be fulfilled on account of the apprehension that the German influence in southern Brazil would become aggressive if German officers should drill a military contingent from that part of the Republic, a considerable sum was paid as an indemnity. The State of São Paulo, however, has employed a French mission which created a force of State police, the efficiency of which has been proved upon occasions of riots and strikes as well as in the maintenance of order in rural districts.

The Minister of War and the General Staff have been opposed to the employment of Foreign instructors. They do not wish their authority to be lessened nor the impression to be created that they are not competent in professional subjects. They exercise greater influence upon the Senate than upon the Chamber and until the bill relative to a foreign military mission is considered in the upper house, no prophecy can be made as to the probability of its enactment. Public opinion is generally in favor of it but public opinion, as representing the voice of the people, is not sufficiently developed in this country to overcome the opposition of the men in control.

A French military mission would probably accomplish more rapid results than that of any other nationality. The language difficulty would not be an obstacle since educated Brazilians understand French. A similar habit of thought prevails among most Latin nations and Brazil's affection for and familiarity with French ideals has been accentuated by the part which France has played in the war. A portion of the officers who trained the São Paulo State troops and who were recalled when the war began remain available and could enter upon their new duties without loss of time.

The political effect of a French mission, although it would enhance French influence, would be less important than would at first appear because the political role of France in this country is not important. The placing of orders for military materials in French factories as soon as they are reopened would be the obvious gain. Those orders will eventually become extensive and large sums of money will be expended which might otherwise be distributed among the manufacturers of several nations instead of being concentrated in the hands of the French.

... A British naval mission would not only assure the construction in British shipyards of the new units of the Brazilian Navy but would render it impossible for the Bethlehem Steel Company and similar American corporations to secure contracts for arsenals, dockyards and coast defence. Our manufacturers of military material would be entirely shut out and the hopes which they have entertained for some time of obtaining contracts in Brazil would have to be abandoned. The influences which we have recently exerted over the Brazilian Navy were principally due to the effective teaching of Captain Phillip Williams, U.S.N., between 1914 and 1917, in the Naval War College, and to the favorable impressions which the Brazilian Naval Attachés in Washington and the young Brazilian officers who have served on board our battleships, have brought home. The officers who are subjected to American influences are appreciative of them but their authority is not far-reaching. The Minister of Marine and several of the older Admirals whose opinions have weight have either studied in Great Britain or have been attached to naval commissions which have had their headquarters at London or Newcastle during the period the Brazilian ships were under construction. The British men-of-war which have been stationed off this coast and which have frequently visited Brazilian ports have also been instrumental in fixing the idea that the British Navy is supreme. One of to-day's newspapers has published the statement that under his general powers and without waiting for specific authorization by Congress, the Minister of Marine has contracted British officers as naval instructors. This report is by no means necessarily unfounded.

The Embassy cannot believe that the Department will permit a British naval mission to establish itself in Brazil. The political and commercial reasons are so evident that they need not be described at length in this report. I would, however, call attention to the fact that Brazil broke relations with Germany for the alleged reason of following the policy of the United States, but that since she made that declaration a number of her acts would indicate that her sympathy lay with Europe rather than with ourselves. She is preparing to hand over her commercial fleet to France and to invite a French military mission to take charge of her army. If she extends an invitation to a British naval mission her identification with the war will be rather with the Allies of Europe than with the United States and American political influence in Brazil will diminish in proportion as that of France and Great Britian increases. I therefore recommend

a) that the Brazilian Government be immediately sounded as to whether or not it desires an American naval mission; and

b) that a professor for the Naval War College be detailed who will be prepared to discharge his duties when the school reassembles at the beginning of March, 1918.

I have the honor to be, Sir,

Your obedient servant,

Edwin V. Morgan.

SOURCE: United States Department of State, Serials File on Brazil, 1910–29, Records relating to the Internal Affairs of Brazil, National Archives, 832.20/16.

This letter was sent by the U.S. mission in Brazil.

Rio de Janeiro, October 30, 1923

No. 2102

Confidential

The Honorable
 The Secretary of State,
  Washington, D. C.

Sir:

 I have the honor to enclose the original and a translation of two editorials, one from the GAZETA DE NOTICIAS of this city of October 12th, and the other from the JORNAL DO BRASIL of this city of October 19th, relative to the work of the American Naval Mission. The first article was prepared by a Brazilian naval officer attached to the Mission, and is descriptive of some of the results which the Mission has achieved. The second appears to have been written by a less interested author and voices what I believe to be intelligent current opinion regarding the Mission's accomplishments.

 The press report of the recent address of the Secretary of State, in which the purpose of the Mission was described, elicited sufficient attention on the part of the Brazilian Foreign Minister to cause him to instruct Ambassador Alencar to telegraph to the Foreign Office the text of that portion of the address which related thereto. The press has stated that both the New York Evening Post and the London Times have printed editorials deploring the existence of the Mission, and has transmitted telegrams relative to the statements of a Methodist Episcopal clergyman at a recent conference at Lafayette, Indiana. It is regrettable that derogative statements should be circulated by the press as it sets on edge the nerves of the Brazilian Government, which at the present moment is more susceptible than usual to foreign opinion or influences which may tend to disturb Brazil's relations with the Argentine and other South American countries. The success of the Mission is certain to arouse jealousy, and Rear Admiral Vogelgesang is prepared to meet unfavorable criticism from abroad, which will be reflected in Brazil and which however unjustifiable will tend to embarrass the efforts of himself and his associates. In my opinion, the Mission should be allowed to work out its own salvation with as little public notice as possible and that the proverb "the less said the sooner mended" is as applicable in this case as it usually proves to be. The French Military Mission has avoided publicity, and the American Naval Mission will succeed in proportion to the degree in which they avoid drawing upon themselves public attention, however well intentioned may be the friends who desire to commend them. The statement of the Secretary of State should be conclusive in proving that the purpose of the Mission is a pacific one and should be accepted as a complete justification of the object which the American Government had in view in permitting the creation of such a body.

I have the honor to be, Sir,

Your obedient servant,

Edwin V. Morgan.

Enclosures:

SOURCE: United States Department of State, Serials File on Brazil, 1910–29, Records relating to the Internal Affairs of Brazil, National Archives, 832.20/34.

Influence of the North American Naval Mission in the Re-organization of the Brazilian Navy

GAZETTA DE NOTICIAS, Oct. 12, 1923
Rio de Janiero

In spite of the good brains which we have had in our Navy, for various reasons we have not been able to attain the full efficiency and strength to which we aspire and which we should attain in view of the condition of modern navies. We appreciate the cooperation of our predecessors who, by their knowledge, bravery, honor, and ability, made the national name great and famous, in peace as well as in war, for they put into practice many improvements that were in use during their epoch. The astounding progress in the modern elements of combat did not pass unperceived by our modern Navy and by some of the far-sighted statesmen of this generation. At that epoch the naval program of Admiral Julio de Noronha was published and was strongly supported in Congress by the late Dr. Laurindo Pitta and by the Executive Power which was exercised by the venerated Brazilian statesmen, Rodrigues Alves, and Rio Branco.

This program was modified in accordance with the opinion of Admiral Alexandrino de Alencar when he assumed the post of Minister of Marine.

Steadily decreasing in efficiency, our war material almost became obsolete and its renewal was found to be of urgent necessity. We obtained a new squadron without, however, succeeding in obtaining other fundamental bases for a complete naval organization. The great efforts of Admiral Alexandrino de

Alencar, Minister of Marine during several years, are recognized, and many were the new regulations put into effect by this illustrious director of the Navy. The measures which however were adopted were not sufficient because the problem was and remains too complex and burdensome to be solved by the tenacity, dedication, and guidance of a single mentality, who undertakes to reconstruct the naval power of so large a country as ours.

Some of the reports of the Minister of Marine during the present period describe frankly and loyally the state of affairs. Should some careful person analyse the contents of those statements, they will understand the want of resources which cannot continue, if the country is to remain secure and at peace.

Ever since the period when our Navy, in accordance with the epoch, was efficient, a feeling of affectionate sympathy for the powerful American Nation has existed. A statement of the occurrences and reasons which established the strong tie which binds us to the Americans would be very lengthy. A strong and enterprising race is taking its place in the concert of nations and is living up to the ideals of its honorable ancestors—the puritans.

When a keen intelligence founded our Academy of Naval Studies, our confidence for the American Navy was shown in the selection of some of its officers to fill the most important chairs in the Naval War College. And by changing the officers who gave instruction, we became familiar with the choicest elements of the American Navy who brought to us, in addition to their experience and knowledge, the studies and problems which also are under discussion in other war colleges.

This proof of affection and complete confidence is symbolic when in a time of selfishness other countries are trying to conceal the details of the manipulation and preservation of equipment which would be very useful to us. Thus the tie of friendship became closer and there was a strong current of opinion that we should look for guidance and instruction in the teachings of America.

As our war material became visibly useless, that fact became more evident to the officials of the Navy who were under instruction. Then came the European conflagration and with it the proof of the great value of the United States as a World Power, or rather as a real arbiter in the solution of the greatest conflict which ever took place on the face of the globe.

From the brief synopsis above mentioned, without entering into a more ample consideration, one of the reasons can be deducted, which contributed toward our decision that the instruction of our modern organization should be administered by an American Naval Mission.

If the public powers, after examining the general situation, decided to engage a naval mission, it is proper that we should examine the work of the Mission which daily cooperates with us with devotion and sincerity.

Relegating to the second place our analysis of what already existed, we shall state what the Naval Mission has already accomplished in the short space of time it has been in our country. As is already known, after a contract was signed on November 6, 1922, the American Naval Mission arrived on the 21st of December of the same year, directed by Rear Admiral Carl T. Vogelgesang, an officer who is highly thought of in the American Navy, as well as in our Navy, where he has shown his professional culture when he filled the position of professor of Strategy, Naval Tactics, and War Maneuvers in the Naval War College of Brazil. The Mission is composed of 15 officers and sub-officers, specialists in their different spheres. After being received by our Navy with general sympathy and appreciation, and from the first endeavoring to maintain close contact with the different naval administrative organs in order to obtain a full knowledge of local conditions and requirements, the Mission commenced its work in the beginning of January and presented its plan of administration to His Excellency the Minister of Marine. This plan represents the program which the Mission intends to follow. It consists of subdivision of work, rapid and exact knowledge of the requirements of the Navy and the way in which the various problems should be approached.

The officers and sub-officers having been placed in direct contact with the departments to which they belonged, a loyal and effective cooperation was at once established with the American officers who sincerely and honestly proved the justice of the opinion that was current regarding their ability.

SOURCE: *Gazetta de Noticias* (Rio de Janerio) Oct. 12, 1923. Translation by American diplomats in Brazil for the State Department. United States Department of State Serials File on Brazil, 1910–29, 832.20/34.

Frederick M. Nunn

Emil Körner and the Prussianization of the Chilean Army

In 1885 the Chilean government appointed Captain Emil Körner of the Imperial German Army to train its officers. When Körner arrived in Chile he found an experienced officer corps composed of veterans from the War of the Pacific and the Indian campaigns in Araucania. They were men who took pride in being the heirs of Bernardo O'Higgins and Manuel Bulnes, but they had little experience in the rigors of the classroom. Chile wanted a modern professional army; Körner molded one; and when he retired in 1910, he left behind the best-equipped land fighting force and the best-educated officer corps in Latin America. But by the time Körner died, ten years later, that same army found itself enmeshed in politics, a professional organization within an anachronistic political and social order and almost a distinct political institution.

Chile emerged victorious from the War of the Pacific. Established as the dominant state on the Pacific coast of South America, she faced potential enemies on each of her three borders. To the north and northeast, Peru smarted from the loss of Tarapacá, Tacna, and Arica; Bolivia became a landlocked nation with the Chilean annexation of Antofagasta; and across the Andes, Argentina, always suspicious, viewed the territorial cessions with envious concern. Chile's victory in the War of the Pacific merely heightened the need for a modern, powerful fighting machine and for increased sea power.

But South American "power politics" was not the sole reason for the Chilean military buildup of the late nineteenth century. Historians, overemphasizing this factor, may have obscured the true role of the army and (to a lesser extent) the navy in Chilean history. In 1904 a Costa Rican major studying in Santiago cited certain factors, endemic to Chile, which should be carefully considered when viewing the Prussianization of the Chilean army. In the beginning, war created and maintained the national identity, as the Chileans defeated the Spaniards, carried the campaign to Peru, and then eliminated the confederation of Peru and Bolivia in 1837. When Chile's position and integrity were menaced again in 1879, war made her preeminent on the west coast of South America. Despite the relegation of the armed forces to a nonpolitical role after 1831, military might (for external use) was traditional in Chile. During the nineteenth century, Chilean military men had great prestige; they earned it.

. . . Further, by 1885 the existence of a professional, educated army was an established if poorly observed tradition. In 1817 Bernardo O'Higgins founded the Military School, the oldest such national institution in Latin America. However, it did not function effectively during the troubled times between the fall of O'Higgins in 1823 and the Battle of Lircay seven years later, in which the Conservatives defeated the Liberals and assumed complete control of politics.

Diego Portales, the *éminence grise* of Chilean conservatism in the 1830s, undertook to remove the military organization from politics. He purged or exiled officers who had sided with the liberal faction in the civil conflict of 1830 and some Conservatives whose loyalty to the new government of President Joaquín Prieto was questionable. Well aware of the army's potential threat to civilian control of politics, Portales also set up a civil militia as a counterpoise to ambitious officers. While he directed Chilean affairs, the militia performed this function. Portales himself commanded a militia infantry battalion quartered in La Moneda, the presidential palace, and paraded in uniform with the group on festive occasions. After Portales's assassination in 1837 the exclusion of the army from politics continued, except for short-lived revolts in 1851 and 1859. The Military School continued to function, as did the militia.

The forty-year period between the death of Portales and the final confrontation with Peru and Bolivia was one of great progress in Chile. Kept busy externally by the war of 1837–39 and by sporadic Indian uprisings on the southern frontier, the army eschewed political activities. At the end of the War of the Pacific, however, military education was antiquated; organization and ordinances had changed little since the days of O'Higgins; organically, the Chilean army was essentially the same as the forces which had struggled for independence. By 1885, tradition, discipline, and experience were not enough for Chile's needs. The government, therefore, turned for inspiration to Germany, the military titan of Europe.

President Domingo Santa María instructed Guillermo Matta, head of the Chilean legation in Germany, to find a qualified officer who might be engaged as military instructor, and Matta selected Körner. Actually Körner was Matta's second choice, for his first selection, Major Clemens Meckl, had already accepted a position with the Japanese army. In August 1885 Körner agreed "to serve in the Military School . . . as professor in artillery, infantry, cartography, and military history and tactics." The salary agreed upon was 12,000 marks a year, payable in Chilean gold.

Körner assumed his new duties early in 1886, with the rank of lieutenant colonel and the title of instructor and subdirector of the Military School. He immediately began to plan the organization of Chile's own *Kriegsakademie*. The Chilean government officially founded the War Academy on September 9, 1886, only thirteen months after Körner had agreed to serve in Chile.

The government created the academy for the purpose of "elevating, as much as possible, the level of technical and scientific instruction of army officers, in order that they may be able, in case of war, to utilize the advantages of new methods of combat and modern armaments in use today.''

In its first years the War Academy offered a three-year program. The first-year class studied tactics, fortification, cartography, ballistics, military history, geography, military science, inorganic chemistry, physics, a choice of either mathematics or world history, and German. The second-year curriculum consisted of further training in tactics, fortification, cartography, geography, military science, physics, chemistry, mathematics or world history, and German, plus topography and war games. The third year consisted of Chilean military history, war games, Latin American military geography, hygiene, international law, general staff service, either mathematics or world history, and German. The first class (originally limited to fifteen select officers) began its courses on June 15, 1887, under the supervision of the academy's first director, Brigidier General Marco A. Arriagada. After graduation in 1890, five of its members went to Europe for further study.

On January 1, 1891, parliamentary leaders challenged the executive branch and, supported by conservative navy chiefs, pronounced against Santa María's successor, President José Manual Balmaceda. Though the bulk of the army remained loyal to Balmaceda, Körner and his followers did not. Balmaceda formally dismissed Körner from his position, and the German, accompanied by other dissenting officers, sailed north on May 9, 1891, to join the congressional forces in Iquique, the revolutionary capital. According to General Francisco Díaz, Körner fully appreciated that a congressional victory would facilitate the reform of the army and joined the revolutionary forces, not because of political ideas, but to open new military horizons and to lead those who had been his students. In less than six months Körner trained an army of 10,000 officers and troops which ultimately defeated the regular army.

On the cessation of hostilities in 1891 Körner set out to implement Prussianization as he conceived it. The immediate problem facing the victors was what to do with officers of the defeated Balmaceda's army. This problem was resolved in several ways. A decree of September 14, 1891, gave to Colonel Estanislao del Canto, commander in chief of the congressional army, the power to prosecute any officers from captains to generals who had served the Balmaceda government at any time during 1891. That same day Canto named a four-man court martial to try the accused.

Balmacedista officers were divided into four groups: (1) Those who were guilty of nothing more than having served in the army; (2) those accused of war crimes or breaches of civil law; (3) those who had committed war crimes under orders; and (4) those who, failing to appear, were tried in absentia. A second official decree of September 14 stated that only those who had joined the congressional army or who had at least refused to serve under Balmaceda would be allowed to continue in service. In this way, high-ranking Balmacedista officers were to be purged, clearing the path for Körner's Prussianized professionals. In October, 118 Balmacedista captains went on trial for treason by virtue of the fact that they had obeyed commands of a man who had ceased to be president for his violations of the constitution. The accused based their defense on loyalty to the president as commander in chief and on the apolitical nature of the army, established by the constitution, but they were not allowed to testify or to obtain legal advice. All but 2 were removed from service for a period of six years and were denied the right to hold public office as citizens for an equal period. Some who escaped this harsh verdict at first were retried later and found guilty.

At the end of 1891 Brigidier General Emil Körner became chief of the general staff. The following year he returned to his original mission and served as professor of applied tactics and military geography in the War Academy as well as heading the general staff. He filled both positions until April 1894, when he went to Europe to supervise completion and shipment of coastal artillery batteries being built by the Krupp armaments factory in Essen.

Körner returned to Chile in October 1895, resumed his post as chief of staff, and on November 1 was promoted to division general. With him came thirty-six German officers, who were to play key roles in the Prussianization of the Chilean army. Lieutenant Colonel Wilhelm Ekdahl directed the War Academy from 1904 to 1907, after having served on its faculty for nine years. Majors Edward Banza and Carl Zimmermann taught at the War Academy. Captain Günther von Below taught at the Military School, as did Majors Alfred Schönmeyer and Herman von Bieberstein. Three Germans and an Irish colonel, Robert O'Grady, served in the War Ministry's fortification section; two Germans served in the technical section; two served on the Chilean armaments commission and one on the general staff. Two Germans were instructors in ballistics at the artillery school; four served in the Escuela de Clases, an institution for the training of noncommissioned officers. Two had staff positions in provincial garrisons. One German was a member of the presidential cavalry escort; three served in cavalry regiments, four in infantry regiments, three in the artillery, and one in the engineers. Two years later twenty-seven more Germans came to Chile.

As the German officers began to arrive in Chile, the first of many Chilean officers went to Germany for further training. Until the end of World War I these men studied with distinction at Charlottenburg and served with the elite Imperial Guard. After returning to Chile many of these Prussianized Chileans distinguished themselves in military and other government service, becoming the nucleus of a Chilean army elite. Led by General Carlos Ibáñez del Campo (who attended the academy but did not study in Europe), this elite involved the army in politics from 1924 until 1932. All important military positions and many political positions during that time were held by graduates of the War Academy or by Prussianized officers. Prominent among these foreign-trained soldiers were Colonel Arturo Ahumada Bascuñán, General Juan Pablo Bennett Argandoña, General Bartolomé Blanche Espejo, and Colonel Marmaduke Grove Vallejo.

. . . On May 12, 1906, Chile adopted a reform program intended to make the military organization a creole copy of the Imperial German Army. Körner had proposed this reform seven years earlier, but it soon proved disappointing to him and his followers. The administrative reorganization reduced the powers of the inspector general and increased those held by division commanders. This decentralization was supposed to make administration more efficient and flexible but did not. Consequently the administration of the War Ministry was also decentralized and a German-style general staff created for planning and coordination.

The government might create new administrative units on the order of the German army, but it soon found that there were not enough qualified officers to serve as administrators. Divisions functioned with skeleton staffs. Younger officers, lacking experience but pressed into higher administrative ranks, clashed with superiors whom they considered unfit to serve because they lacked German training. The hasty reorganization also created havoc in the War Ministry, for when division commanders found that they could not deal with all problems, they bombarded the ministry with requests for solutions. In the crush to fill all administrative positions, political pressure was used, so that friends of high-ranking civilians or officers got coveted posts, while those without connections did not. In the haste to fill up the skeleton divisions, too many untrained subalterns commanded new, untrained troops. One officer later wrote that the changeover of 1906 was outright adoption when it should have been adaptation and that the government was at fault for basing a peacetime reform on extreme wartime needs, rather than on the country's financial and manpower capabilities.

Twenty years after he had begun the task of Prussianization Körner saw it carried to the extreme in 1906. During the last four years before his retirement in 1910 he was no longer overseer of Prussianization, for the reforms of 1906 had limited his power as inspector general. Nevertheless, he continued to be an influence on the officers who had trained under him or in his system. In his 1908 report to congress he pointed out that politically influential but poorly trained officers in important positions would endanger discipline and morale: "The ease of jumping in rank predisposes the favored one to become restless in a short time, and if his aspirations to be promoted even further are not satisfied, his energy and his enthusiasm diminish, no doubt justifiably."

In 1910 the War Ministry's official report to congress supported Körner's complaint that there were not enough trained and experienced officers to fill posts created by the 1906 reforms. The 1910 report called for changes in the promotion system (which was still based on 1890 legislation) as a solution to the problem of unfit or "political" officers in key positions. Two years later the ministry's report repeated this view and disapproved outright adoption of the German model for Chilean army organization.

Even from the standpoint of the German-trained professional officer the reforms of 1906 were singularly unsuccessful. Despite a superficial glitter, the Chilean army was Prussianized beyond the capacities of the nation and suffered from serious internal problems. From the official point of view these were structural and administrative; as the government, with its anachronistic parliamentary system, creaked on, the complaints of military men became a blend of professional grievances and political interest. Even before Körner retired the army had become a "state within the state."

But German influences did not stop with Chile. They extended to officers of other Latin American armies trained at the Military School at Santiago; and the Chilean army carried "second generation" Prussianization directly to El Salvador, Ecuador, and Colombia. In the latter two cases the Chilean government was motivated by a desire for friends in the power structure of the Pacific coast.

In 1903 the government of El Salvador requested a Chilean military mission to improve army instruction. On September 4 Chile designated Captains Juan Pablo Bennett (as chief) and Francisco Lagreze and Lieutenants Julio Salinas, Armando Llanos, and Carlos Ibáñez to staff the mission. The Chilean mission stayed in El Salvador for six years. At the same time, three Chilean officers were also sent to Ecuador as army instructors, Captain Estanislao García Huidobro and Lieutenants Arturo Montecinos and Luis Negrete. Three Chilean army captains had already been acting as advisers in Ecuador for nearly a year and helped an Ecuadoran officer, Major Luis Cabrera, to write a new military code in 1902. In 1907 General Rafael Reyes, the president of Colombia, reopened the military school, which had been closed during the civil war of 1899–1902 and on six other occasions in the past century. Reyes wanted the Colombian army to be led by apolitical professional officers and chose the Chilean army as his model because of its reputed success with German training. . . .

While some of the Prussianized Chilean army officers went abroad to train other Latin American armies, others stayed home to form pressure groups and influence the Chilean government. The army had long resented meddling politicians, the cumbersome parliamentarism, and the government's inability to find long-range solutions to social and economic problems. This inability forced the army to improvise short-range solutions, as when it used force in putting down numerous strikes during the first twenty years of this century.

In 1907 a group of army officers in Santiago organized a secret lodge, the Liga Militar. Liga members, exasperated at a government which they considered "disorganized and undisciplined," swore under oath "to work for the progress of the army." Their primary objectives were professional—new promotion, salary, and retirement systems for army officers—and the Liga undoubtedly owed its creation to the effects of Prussianization, especially the reforms of 1906. According to a contemporary member of Chile's officer corps, the Liga blamed civilian political disorganization for the army's problems.

By 1910 the Liga was nationwide. Ramón Barros Luco, who assumed the presidency on the death of Pedro Montt in that year, knew of its existence, but did nothing about it. In the same year the Club Militar opened its doors in Santiago. This national social center for army officers became the seat of Liga activities and made Santiago the preferred location for politically minded officers during the next two decades.

The creation of a modern army in Chile had serious long-range consequences, both professional and national. Prussianization set ambitious professional officers against their superiors, against their incompetent colleagues, and against politicians who meddled in army affairs or who failed to support the military's legislative requests. Prussianization created an army elite which magnified its role in Chilean society and politics during the second decade of this century. The aping of the Prussian army became a curse for government and military alike when officers began to challenge the traditional power structure from 1907 forward. As long as that structure remained outwardly solid the army was kept in its place. But the shattering experiences of 1919 and 1920 ended one chapter in Chilean civil-military relations and prepared for another, even more dramatic—the outright military intervention and domination from 1924 to 1932 by those who had shared in the experience of Prussianization.

Reprinted and edited from *Hispanic American Historical Review* 50 no. 2 (May 1970), pp. 300–322.

Víctor Villanueva

Military Professionalization in Peru

The government of Nicolás de Piérola (1895–99) provided ample opportunities and incentives for the industrialization of the country. New factories and commercial enterprises appeared, mineral production increased, and in 1895, with the opening of an electrified alum plant in Lima, the first industry employing electric power began functioning. But this industrial boom, mineral and commercial, resulted from the introduction of foreign capital which appropriated the principal production sectors, thereby reinforcing the economy's dependence on the export of primary products.

One would presume that accomplishments would not have been achieved if Piérola had not first reorganized the army and then placed it under civilian control. He understood that if the personal ambitions of the men in the barracks were not curbed, the result would be political instability and economic chaos. It was essential to subordinate the military officers [to civilian control] and in order to achieve this, it was also necessary to create new and different attractions, apart from politics.

But returning for a moment to the eighteenth century, the triumph of the French Revolution in Europe made it possible, up to a point, to displace the Spanish nobility in the colonial army and replace them with members of the bourgeoisie who had previously received military training. The new profession, once the exclusive property of the aristocracy by virtue of their privileged birth, passed into the hands of those who had some expertise—although the government at first demanded purity of blood (*limpieza de sangre*) [for a man] to be an officer, a requirement which gradually lost its importance.

In Peru, the army was not under the control of a noble class, but rather in the hands of aristocratic caudillos who were dedicated political adventurers, hungry for power, but who lacked basic military skills. It was necessary, therefore, to replace them with true professionals, something which various governments in the nineteenth century had encouraged but at which all had failed. Piérola tried, once more, to resolve this acute problem and to change the soldier into a technician, a true professional who had no desire other than to serve in an institution dedicated to specific tasks such as the defense of the nation, its laws, and its legally constituted government.

In order to attain this end, it was of course necessary to provide the military officer with career stability and to bureaucratize him within a military organization which would require academic studies to enter and within which it would be possible to achieve the highest ranks without recourse to extraprofessional activities.

Piérola adopted two procedures to ensure the complete success of his program. He reduced the regular army to 2,000 men, thereby making any military insurrection almost impossible. The drastic reduction in numbers of regulars decreased even further the possibilities for promotion, a situation which undoubtedly caused widespread discontent. However, the increasing loss of morale which the military was suffering forced them to accept with resignation the new government policies.

During the Piérola administration exports tripled and government revenue doubled. The boom benefited public functionaries, whose salaries were increased between 15 and 50 percent in some cases, but military salaries remained unchanged. Such a situation was accepted by the military with patience and submission, not only for the above-mentioned reasons, but also because of their lack of arms. Moreover, the disastrous loss to Chile in the War of the Pacific [1879–83] still smarted, and civilians eagerly took every opportunity to remind the military of it. The classic haughtiness of the old officer had to yield to the insolence of the upper class.

By the end of the Piérola administration, the military occupied an economic position within the national bureaucracy which was very inferior to what it had been before. Taking the four highest ranks of the judiciary, the administrative bureaucracy, the church, and the military, according to that part of the budget which they each received, we have constructed the following index: clergy 550, judicial and public administration 330, army and navy 212. Ministers of state had an index of 600 and the president of the republic 3,000. This is the period in Peruvian history in which the military officer slipped to his lowest point not only economically but also in terms of his political influence and social position.

Despite owing to Piérola its transformation into a modern institution, it may be these events, and the memory of 1879 and 1895, that have generated the hatred which the military feels for Piérola. Jorge Basadre expressed it this way:

It is possible to state that, consciously or unconsciously, many members of the Peruvian armed forces have a deep hatred for the memory of Piérola, recalling that by accident, without belonging to the military profession, he tried to direct the defense of Lima against the Chilean invasion with dismal results, but that as the head of bands of guerrillas, he successfully faced professional soldiers [the Peruvian military] on March 17, 1895.

In addition to impoverishing the army in a material sense, the victor of 1895 adopted another procedure for removing the military from politics: the reorganization of the institution on a technical basis which would be directed by a military mission contracted in Europe. In 1871, the Prussian army inflicted a serious defeat on the French army, thereby demonstrating the inferior professional quality of the French officers, who were surrounded in the Sudan and forced to surrender. From that moment the Prussian army was considered to be the best in the world. It would have been logical, therefore, for Piérola to choose it as a model for the Peruvian army, particularly if one remembers that Piérola had a German military adviser in the 1895 campaign.

In spite of these reasons, however, Piérola contracted with French officers to reorganize and train the Peruvian military. The motives behind the president's action are unknown. The fact that the Chilean government had hired a military mission in Germany some years before[1] may have been one reason why Piérola did not turn to the same country in search of military assistance. Perhaps, as has been suggested by Klaus Lindenberg, the German government might have refused to lend technical aid to two rival countries at the same time.

The fact that France was a republic and not an empire like the new Germany might have been another motive; perhaps also the fact that France was a Catholic country rather than Lutheran might have had certain influence. One might also point to the activities and probable influence of Auguste Dreyfus, the guano monopolist and probable financier of Piérola in the revolution against Pardo, and also (and why not?) the romantic memory of the French widow who accompanied him during his first revolutionary activities.

It could have been these motives or even others that led Piérola in 1896 to hire a French military mission to direct the restructuring of the Peruvian army. Under the command of Lt. Col. Paul Clément, three captains, one each from the branches of artillery, cavalry, and infantry, arrived in Peru with the new rank of Lt. Col.—Clément now held the rank of colonel. All of them had participated in the colonial campaigns of Tunisia, Algeria, Madagascar, and the Sudan. Moreover, Clément was a staff officer.

These army officers had been shaped professionally during the Third Republic, a time when the bourgeoisie had consolidated its power and had pushed the nobility out of high public office. The nobility sought refuge in the army, in the clergy, in the arts, and in scientific study, that is to say in those activities where it was not necessary to work with one's hands—something considered undignified for persons of their lineage. . . .

Since the French army had been professionalized, some officers did not belong to the nobility, but they also quickly identified with the aristocratic spirit of the institution. An officer who remained aloof from the ideological foundation of the army was an officer who lacked esprit de corps, a black sheep who had no possibility of advancing. And the members of the bourgeoisie who joined the army did not do so for the same reasons as the old nobility. Rather they entered with the desire of making the military a career; they were careerists—what Morris Janowitz calls those military men who join the army with a bureaucratic spirit, as a means of living, a vehicle for economic security, both personal and familial, now and in the future. These officers, then, if they wanted to have a career, had to accommodate themselves to the norms of the institution, including its ideology.

To the traditional military virtues of valor, courage, and honor, the bourgeoisie inculcated in the military new virtues, such as poverty and patriotism, by which they replaced the old loyalty to the monarch with loyalty to and identification with the nation. With these new ideas, the dominant class succeeded in dislodging the military from its previously class-oriented vocation and from its love of power.

As the army was badly paid—France [was] a poor country—poverty was elevated to a military virtue. The military profession, the bourgeoisie said to the officers, does not have profit as its purpose; wealth is the property of the bourgeoisie and therefore contemptible. The bourgeoisie substituted for the old military privileges the "honor of dressing in the military uniform," with certain economic concessions such as the education of the children and dowers for the wives. With the uniform in which they dressed and the honor which it signified, the officer was converted into a "priest of the fatherland," dedicated exclusively to its service, without any interest other than the nation—elements which generated a special mysticism. Imbued in the officer was the desire to be appreciated by posterity, a sentiment lacking in the mercenary, who is only interested in pay.

The French officers were to serve with pleasure in the colonies and enlist with enthusiasm in wars of conquest, even though their salaries were not raised, because such operations provided the opportunity to gain glory and also because they provided a psychological outlet for the loss of power in the Metropolis. The colonial officer acted as an administrator, almost independent of the civilian government of France. The lower-ranking officers had certain autonomy within the colonial division governed by a senior officer. In addition, they wielded power over the indigenous population. These officers "describe in offensive terms the civilian officials and petty politicians, whom they despise. As administrators, they are crude, but they boast of knowing the indigenous population well, of respecting their customs, and of not subjecting them to a given ideology."

Marshall Lyautey, the famous Gallic colonial, wrote in Indochina, in 1882, that he did not aspire to be "more than a warrior, a good cacique . . . a young feudal chieftain."

It was in that period in France that the Dreyfus Affair exploded, a period in which the army openly identified itself with the most reactionary elements in the country. Almost all the officers were anti-Semitic, antiliberal, antirepublican, and proclerical. This feeling of autonomy manifested itself during the affair. Whether Dreyfus was innocent or guilty did not matter; what did matter was that the army had made its decision, and there was no excuse for civilian interference.

After the innocence of Dreyfus had been established and the sentence of the military tribunal annulled, the autonomy of the army was destroyed, and it experienced a crisis. The dower for the wives was abolished, and candidates for the military school of St. Cyr were required to spend a year in the ranks. Moreover, military protocol was modified to give subprefects preference over colonels and prefects preference over generals, minutia that had great importance for military pride. Thus, militarism suffered a serious decline in France as a result of the sacrifice of Dreyfus.

Such was the ideological background of the French officers who arrived in Peru at the end of the last century, with their burden of frustrations ranging from their subordination by the bourgeoisie to their defeat by Prussia and their loss of institutional autonomy. I have presented these details because I deem it important to understand the ideological baggage of those who came to shape professionally the Peruvian military, which had itself suffered similar crises—the defeat by Chile, the loss of political power, and the forced subordination of the military to civilian authority.

The French officers were to influence seriously the minds of their Peruvian colleagues and to collaborate effectively with the governments of the *civilista* aristocracy in the attainment of their political goals. The Gallic officers inculcated their ideology which, in its principal aspects, coincided with that of the earliest Peruvian officers, who were shaped by the Spanish army—monarchist and colonial—since the French army was also colonial and antirepublican at the end of the century.

Owing to these similarities, the intellectual task of the French was an easy one. All they had to do was revive old ideologies and antiquated institutional habits which were perhaps dormant because of military defeats, the indiscriminate recruitment of officers during the war, the loss of prestige suffered by the army in losing the war, and the deplorable economic situation they had been placed in as a result of the fiscal collapse of the nation.

The French mission succeeded in isolating the Peruvian army and reinforced its historic belief that it was an institutional repository of the honor and dignity of the nation, with a monopoly on patriotism. This belief, together with the fact that they dressed in a military uniform, made them see themselves as a superior class. At the same time, the mission lent its influence to maintain the official aloofness from "that dirty thing which is politics," manifested in the army's total contempt for politicians and therefore the entire parliamentary system.[2] In a word, the mission contributed to the depolitization of the army.

In a general way, the Gallic instructors achieved their principal goals. Perhaps they even succeeded in temporarily assuaging the political appetite of the military. However, when the threat of new social upheaval presented itself, the bourgeoisie again called the soldiers out of the barracks to resolve their problems. The evangelization of the army that converted it into "the tutelary institution of the fatherland," came very shortly afterwards. The dominant class elevated the military institution to this level to alienate it from the people so that it would continue to defend the traditional social structure, which was particularly vital in the early years of the century when there was a new wave of working-class activity and organization directed by the anarcho-syndicalists.

The messianic sense acquired by the military officer (or perhaps it was just reinforced) undoubtedly was a direct consequence of bourgeois deification of the army. When the bourgeoisie, terrified of a popular uprising, calls upon the army to silence labor protest and when the military succeeds in bringing peace and tranquility, the Peruvian military officer has to believe that his institution is predestined, if not to win international wars, then at least to triumph in the social arena. That self-confidence has lasted until the present in that the armed forces honestly believe, without doubt, that they possess the capacity to establish harmony between antagonistic classes without eliminating the causes of that antagonism.

French officers continued arriving in Peru in successive missions until 1922. In 1932, French military officers were again hired, this time on an individual basis, but they were withdrawn by their government in 1939 with the outbreak of World War II. In all, more than fifty officers were hired. Most held the rank of general or lieutenant colonel, but there were some lower-ranking officers, generally specialists.

The influence of these officers on the Peruvian army was decisive, as much in professional and technical aspects as in ideology and politics. French influence increased when large numbers of Peruvian officers began studying in French academies. According to as yet unpublished research by Luigi R. Einaudi, between 1916 and 1940, every Peruvian general had spent some time studying in France. By 1950 that figure had dropped to 59 percent and finally to 30 percent in the period 1960–65.

. . . The French military mission began its work in 1897. In April of the following year, the School of Applied Military Science was inaugurated, "destined to improve the professional knowledge of line officers and to pass that knowledge onto bright young men who wish to follow a military career. . . ."

The first goal was transitory and received little attention; at the same time instruction began of the newly accepted students. The first class of six officers graduated in February of 1901. This primitive School of Applied Military Science evolved, changed its name and organization, and became the Chorrillos Military School of today.

The Chorrillos Military School became the alma mater of the Peruvian army. From its founding until the present, 5,144 officers have graduated, including sergeants who enter in the third year of studies. In addition to these, some 807 officers came from the ranks, until, in 1963, it was decreed that the Chorrillos School would be the only source for officer recruitment.

Translated, reprinted, and edited from *Ejército peruano: del caudillaje anárquico al militarismo reformista* (Lima: 1973), pp. 122–33.

Notes

1. See the selection by Nunn earlier in this section. [ED.]

2. During the present century, the armed forces have dissolved the Congress on the following occasions: with Augusto B. Leguía in 1919, with Luis M. Sánchez Cerro in 1930; with Oscar R. Benavides in 1936; with Manuel A. Odría in 1948; and by military coup in 1962 and 1968. In 1963, there was an evident desire to proceed in the same way, but the coup was thwarted by the opposition of President Fernando Belaúnde Terry. In 1914, the coup by Oscar Benavides had as its declared goal the defense of the parliament, but that was not really a military coup, rather it was an oligarchical coup in which the army was used as a mere tool.

3
The Military and
Latin American Politics, 1919-45

Modernization, Instability, and Military Leadership, 1919-45

In the years between the end of World War I and the end of World War II, much of Latin America experienced a period of intensified urbanization and industrialization. These socioeconomic developments were accompanied by hopeful turns toward formal democracy, which were occasionally interrupted by civilian or military dictatorships.

With the onset of the economic depression of the 1930s, even the seemingly most "democratic" Latin American governments saw military elites, by themselves or in alliance with civilian allies, put an end to the post-World War I experiments with liberal democracy. In these years, military elites were still not willing to become permanently involved in "politics," and caretaker regimes or temporary restorationist movements followed coups. Still, divisions were developing within the military establishments themselves over the viability and utility of democratic institutions in Latin America.

Not until two decades after World War II, however, did the military factions committed to long-term military rule emerge triumphant. Nevertheless, in the period 1920–45, military officers attracted to corporate, fascist, or military populist political models temporarily dominated governmental institutions in all five of the countries upon which we focus in this book: Argentina (1930, 1943, 1946); Bolivia (1936–39, 1943–46); Brazil (1937–45); Chile (1927–31); and Peru (1930–39). Whether their programs were rightist or leftist, the military elites usually made antipolitics a basic foundation of their programs. They broke with or subordinated traditional political parties and repressed leftist parties or movements. They sought to administer national policies without the distraction of "politics" or the inconvenience of a tolerated opposition. Ironically, these antipolitical officers often belonged to secret societies or lodges—for example, the Logia General San Martin and the GOU (Grupo de Oficiales Unidos) in Argentina, and the RADEPA (*Razón de Patria*) in Bolivia—which engaged in intrainstitutional politics.

In Argentina, Bolivia, Brazil, Chile, and Peru, the appeals of European corporatism or fascism allowed the nationalist, hierarchical, and antipolitical inclinations of the military elites to combine with conservative or reactionary civilian sectors in new political experiments. Frequently the patronage and

89

partisan politics characteristic of formal democracy were used as a pretext for military intervention. Leading officers blamed civilian politics for the consequences of the economic collapse of the 1930s, as well as for the intromission of party politics into the supposedly sacrosanct realm of military promotions, budget decisions, and military education.

The selection by Robert Potash in this chapter describes an archetypal case of this phenomenon in Argentina, where after more than a half century of legal transfers of government, a military coup in 1930 set the stage for restoration of oligarchic rule and then for the reign of Juan Domingo Perón. Of particular interest are the types of justifications provided by the military officers for their action against President Hipólito Yrigoyen as well as the prominent role of the most highly professionalized military elites in Argentina (including Generals Uriburu and Justo) in the reaction against the results of fourteen years of government by the middle-class Radical party.

Also to be noted are the divisions within the military professional elites over the proper role of the military in politics and the substantive character of public policy once the military found itself in control. Clearly, civilian political cleavages had affected the Argentine military establishment, as officers, like civilians, were divided over the policies of the Radical politicians, economic nationalism, populism or oligarchic restoration, and the Argentine constitution itself. Professionalization had done much to improve the Argentine military, but it also made politics and public policy an intimate concern of the professional officer corps. The eventual emergence of Juan Perón as a military populist with a highly political antipolitical appeal was a product of the events of the 1930s in Argentina.

In Bolivia, the tutor of military professionalization, Hans Kundt, led Bolivian soldiers in the disastrous Chaco War against Paraguay. From this debacle came a new military elite which blamed civilian corruption and ineptitude for their losses on the battlefield. While Bolivia never really experienced, even in limited form, the formal democratic experiments of Argentina, Brazil, or Chile, the military reaction to civilian ineptitude spawned nationalist military lodges (RADEPA), military "socialists," such as Toro and Busch, and alliances with fascistlike civilian movements including the MNR, which later carried out the Bolivian National Revolution of 1952. These Bolivian movements shared with Uriburu, Castillo, and Perón of Argentina the anticivilian, hierarchical, nationalist, and "integralist" orientations antithetical to the liberal democratic beliefs of the post-Versailles world. The essays by Herbert Klein and William Brill describe the Toro and Busch governments in the late 1930s and events leading up to the Revolution of 1952.

Likewise in Brazil, the 1930s saw an end to an era of liberal democratic experiments. Getulio Vargas in alliance with modernizing elements of the armed forces (including the *tenentes*) and civilian industrial interests took power with a military movement and sought to forge a truly national political regime in a Brazil still dominated by local and regional notables with private armed retainers or state militia. The article by Ronald Schneider describes the coming to power of Vargas. Despite the fact that Vargas himself was a civilian leader, it is clear that military political thinking and military support formed the foundation for the Vargas experiment in Brazil.

In Chile, military antipolitics dominated the years 1924–32. From 1932 until 1973, no successful military coup interrupted the evolution of Chilean formal democracy. Frederick Nunn analyzes the background and consequences of the ''honorable mission'' of the armed forces in Chile in the period 1924–32. The lack of successful military movements in Chile from 1932 until the coup which overthrew President Salvador Allende in 1973, however, does not mean that the Chilean military was completely devoid of antipolitical officers, as periodic military protests or ''strikes'' from the late 1930s onward made clear.

In Peru, a civilian dictator, Augusto B. Leguía, ruled from 1919–30 with the complete support of the armed forces. The role of the military in the Leguía administration and in the numerous coups and countercoups until 1945 is dealt with by Víctor Villanueva. As with the German advisers in Bolivia, officers of the French military mission in Peru played a significant role in post-World War I Peruvian politics.

In 1930, one of the officers trained by the French, Lt. Col. Luís M. Sánchez Cerro, led a successful revolt against Leguía. Owing to divisions within the military establishment, Sánchez Cerro was first elected head of the military junta and later, by popular vote, president of the republic. Sánchez Cerro allied himself with the traditional landed oligarchy against the center-left reformist elements in the Alianza Popular Revolucionaria Americana (APRA) party led by Víctor Raúl Haya de la Torre.

Sánchez Cerro's regime was characterized by extreme violence, including the bloody Trujillo massacre of July 1932 and two assassination attempts against his person (the one of April 1933 being successful).

General Oscar R. Benavides, who had led a coup in 1914 and served briefly as president, assumed power and sought to end the bloodshed and establish internal order. He first tried to achieve this through a policy of liberalization and traditional politics (that is, maintaining the Constituent Congress and calling for presidential elections in 1936). When this policy failed, he resorted to antipolitics, which in the Peruvian case meant annulling the elections of 1936, dissolving the Congress, and repressing political parties, both rightist and leftist.

It is also in this period (1936–39) that the influence of fascism began to spread among the Peruvian officer corps and among certain civilian elites who were closely allied with the military. The new ideology seemingly offered a panacea for ending the chaos and bloodshed which many officers blamed on civilian politics.

Robert A. Potash

The Military and
Argentine Politics

Increasing professionalism, even when accompanied by physical growth and expanded budgetary allocations, did not necessarily make for greater unity, contentment, and morale within the Argentine officer corps. Quite the contrary, a series of strains developed in the 1920s between rival groups of officers and between parts of the corps and the governing authorities. These strains were all related in one way or another to the rise of Hipólito Yrigoyen and the Unión Cívica Radical (Radical party) to political power. The process of professionalization had coincided with, and to some extent was a response to, the efforts of the Radical party to gain access to power for its growing number of middle-class adherents. From its founding in 1891, the party had been frustrated by electoral fraud from legally achieving its goals; and under Yrigoyen's leadership it had demanded electoral reform, while engaging in a series of conspiracies and revolts. These culminated in the unsuccessful revolution of February 1905, in which numerous officers took part even at risk to their professional careers. Partly in reaction to their involvement, the revised military statute enacted later that year restated the standing regulations prohibiting officers who held troop commands or any assignment under War Ministry control from participating directly or indirectly in politics, even by exercise of the franchise, and warned that "military men who do not comply with [these] prescriptions . . . will be punished for disobedience."

Such regulations did not prevent individual officers from joining the Radical cause, and even General Ricchieri, who as war minister in 1901 had authored the original prohibition on political activity by troop commanders, is said to have offered support in 1909, when serving as a field commander, in Yrigoyen's struggle for electoral reform. Conspiratorial activity involving civilians and military men continued, but no new uprising took place. The guarantees of electoral reform offered to the Radicals in 1910 by the newly elected Conservative president, Roque Sáenz Peña, initiated instead a peaceful process of change that culminated in the election of Yrigoyen to the presidency in 1916.

The calm with which the military accepted the peaceful revolution inherent in the Radicals' rise to national power was subsequently disturbed by the policies of the new administration. The military apparently had little criticism of the international policies of Yrigoyen, especially of his determination not to break relations with Germany in World War I. On the domestic scene, however, the numerous provincial interventions had definite repercussions. Yrigoyen justified the interventions as a means of extending the honesty of the ballot to provincial government and of ending political corruption, a policy of atonement for past wrongs that he liked to call *reparación política*. But these interventions made extensive use of the army to maintain order, and critics noted that the diversion of army units to police duties seriously interfered with the training of conscripts. Moreover, the use of military forces to enable Radical party provincial politicians to take over the offices of rival political groups must have been disturbing to those officers who thought of their mission in professional military terms.

In applying the concept of *reparación* to the army itself, Yrigoyen also aroused resentment in the professional-minded officers who regarded military regulations as sacrosanct, or at least not to be disregarded at the whim of the civil authority. The president, for his part, quite naturally wanted to reward those men whose military careers had suffered because of involvement in the "cause." Acting through a civilian minister of war—in itself a break with the usual practice of appointing a high-ranking officer—Yrigoyen passed over officers eligible for promotion in favor of ex-revolutionaries and issued decrees altering the rank lists, promoting retired officers, and granting pensions regardless of the stipulations of existing law and regulations. The alienation of many officers was increased by a 1921 legislative proposal, whose enactment President Yrigoyen urged, declaring that participation in the Radical revolts of 1890, 1893, and 1905 constituted service to the nation. This bill proposed the reincorporation into the retired list and the granting of retirement benefits for those ex-officers who had been dropped from military service, and one-grade promotions for all those now on the retired list who had been passed over because of their involvement in the revolts. Although the beneficiaries of the bill, after its enactment in modified form in 1923, proved to be relatively few, this attempt to reward personnel who, to paraphrase the words of the bill's author, placed civic obligations above military duty, was an assault on the consciences of those who had remained loyal to that duty. In arguing that there were "primordial obligations to country and constitution far superior to all military regulations," Yrigoyen's supporters unwittingly offered a rationalization for future military uprisings, of which they were to be the first victims. The tragedy was that in looking backward and trying to redress past inequities, Yrigoyen was helping to undermine the none-too-strong tradition of military aloofness from politics and to weaken the sense of unity in the officer corps.

Indeed that unity all but disappeared in the 1920s as differences between officers hardened and factionalism grew. Evidence of this was the organization in 1921 of a secret society of officers alienated by the administration's handling of military matters. This society originated in a merging of two groups of officers, one a group of captains largely from the cavalry, the other, field grade officers of various services. The society took the name Logia General San Martín and eventually comprised some 300 officers, or about one-fifth of the total line officer strength.

A recent study of the Logia ascribes its formation to five basic factors: the toleration shown by the War Ministry to politically minded officers who used their positions to campaign for public office or to generate support for Yrigoyen; favoritism and arbitrariness in the handling of promotions; the development of deficiencies in the training of conscripts; the failure of the administration to act on army requests for adequate arms and equipment; and a general deterioration of discipline within the army that was reflected in enlisted and noncommissioned ranks as well as among the officers.

To these essentially professional concerns leading to the creation of the Logia must be added the apprehension with which certain officers viewed the spread of left-wing activities in Argentina. Still fresh in mind was the week-long breakdown of order in Buenos Aires in January 1919, the so-called *Semana Trágica*, when a minor labor dispute gave rise to bloody clashes with the authorities, mob violence, and what some regarded as an abortive attempt at social revolution. The subsequent discovery that soldiers and noncommissioned officers in at least two garrisons had been forming "soviets" exerted a direct influence on several of the officers, who two years later took the initiative in forming the Logia General San Martín. The Logia's members looked on the organization, therefore, not only as an instrument for correcting professional ills but also as a means of pressuring the government to be less tolerant of the political left. . . .

The appointment of Agustín Justo as Alvear's minister of war in 1922 was a victory for the Logia but no less so for the persistence of factionalism. The gulf between officers who had been critical of Yrigoyen's military measures and those who had profited from them grew wider than ever, the major difference being that it was the former critics who were now the ones to enjoy positions of power. Logia members received many key assignments, including chief of the war ministry secretariat, chief of the president's military household (Casa Militar), and director of the military and war academies. Moreover, the promotion list for superior officers, which the outgoing administration in its final weeks had submitted to the Senate, was recalled before it could be approved, and a new one was prepared.

The Logia members waged relentless war against those officers who in their view were engaged in political activity. Not only did they secure an official decree calling for enforcement of the statutory prohibition on such activity, but they resorted to ostracism of officers who continued to violate it. The leaders of the Logia devised what they termed a blacklist of such officers and called on their members to refrain from any personal contact with those blacklisted except as required by acts of the service. The Logia's existence as a formal organization ended early in 1926. A majority of its governing committee had reached the conclusion that its mission was accomplished, and to prevent its being used for personal ambitions, they moved to dissolve it, a step that was supported by the bulk of the membership. Nevertheless, the procedures used by the Logia in its five years of existence had not eliminated factions in the officer corps. Among some of the former *"logistas"* there was built up a special bond that was to manifest itself in the politics of the future, while on the part of those who had suffered from the Logia, a determination developed to seek revenge against Logia members.

. . . The inauguration in October 1928 of Hipólito Yrigoyen marked the return to the presidency of a charismatic leader, the most popular figure in Argentine history before Perón. Neither the limited achievements of Yrigoyen's first administration (1916–22) nor his six years out of office had dislodged him from the special place he enjoyed in the hearts of average Argentines. Unlike other leaders with mass followings, Yrigoyen was neither a spellbinder nor a crowd-pleaser. Indeed, he had rarely appeared in public and had carefully avoided making speeches, even during the recent electoral campaign. His strength lay rather in his personal persuasiveness, in his ability to convince those who came into direct contact with him to accept his leadership. Strong-willed, tenacious, a firm believer in his own historic mission to redeem the downtrodden, Yrigoyen projected at once a sincerity of purpose and a weight of authority that was difficult to resist. Reinforcing his appeal was the air of mystery he maintained about himself and the austerity of his private life. Even while serving in high office he avoided ceremony as much as possible and continued the ascetic life that had been his norm for the past half century. In his predilection for conversing in low tones in shaded rooms, his preference for wearing dark, nondescript suits, and his reluctance to pose for photographs, he revealed the continuing effects of his early career as a political conspirator. . . .

The Yrigoyen administration's handling of the military construction and armaments program in its first eight months in office was the source of considerable dissatisfaction within military circles. At the close of July 1929 the U.S. ambassador, in a message devoted to analyzing the general situation observed, "The officers of the Army and the Navy are said to be generally disgruntled with the Government because work has stopped, through failure to make payments, on barracks and many other improvements undertaken by sanction of the previous Government."

The military malaise that developed under the Yrigoyen administration had other roots than its mishandling of the capital outlay program. Much more serious from the viewpoint of the ordinary officer was the display of political favoritism in the treatment of military personnel. This favoritism took various forms: the reincorporation into the officer corps of personnel long since discharged with full credit for serving the intervening years; retroactive promotion of retired officers, contrary to explicit provisions of the military laws, with the right to collect the differential in retirement pay; and alteration in the date-of-rank of favored active-duty officers, giving them greater seniority than their contemporaries and consequently an advantage for promotion. . . .

President Yrigoyen's role in the promotion process and in other personnel decisions was not a passive one. He felt free to request changes in the lists submitted by army promotion boards, and he ordered additional promotions in response to personal appeals by individual officers. Indeed, his propensity to respond generously to individuals seeking changes in status introduced a chaotic note in personnel administration. As *La Prensa* observed in July 1930: "It is well known today in the entire national administration, even in the navy and especially in the army, that the military man or his relatives who can secure access to the president of the nation gets everything he wants, even if it is unjust or illegal." . . .

Early in the new administration, officers who were identified with the Logia or with the outgoing war minister, General Justo, were relieved of their posts and placed in an unassigned status (*disponibilidad*). This status, which some officers endured for more than a year, resulted in enforced idleness, as well as loss of the supplementary pay that went with specific assignments. Eventually many of these officers were given assignments, but others preferred to ask for retirement. Among the latter was Colonel Luis García, onetime head of the Logia and former director of the Colegio Militar, who used his retired status to fire salvo after salvo at the War Ministry from the editorial columns of the conservative Buenos Aires daily, *La Nación*. His 137 articles, published from mid-July 1929 to September 5, 1930, spelled out in convincing detail the administration's military mismanagement, seeking thereby to undermine officer corps loyalty.

Working toward the same end was General José F. Uriburu, whose retirement from active duty in May 1929 freed him of inhibitions against participating in a conspiracy. In December 1927, when approached by young nationalists to consider a military movement that would prevent the return of Yrigoyen, his reply is said to have been, "Aren't you forgetting that I am an officer on active duty?" Now, on the occasion of his retirement, he made plain his hostility to the Yrigoyen government in a speech that denounced its influence on the army. After noting that an armed force is a reflection of the nation, having the same virtues and defects, he observed:

The weaknesses of command, which in themselves are usually an expression of the decadence of character, take on a catastrophic aspect the moment that the political power undermines its innards, by destroying through favor or threat what is most respectable in the soul of the officer: his disinterestedness. And it can be asserted without fear of error that from the very moment this sentiment begins to weaken, intrigue and base servility substitute for the common ideal of serving the country with disinterest.

. . . As the Argentine winter of 1930 set in, the administration of the aging president was being buffeted from all sides. Within his own party, disillusioned elements questioned his leadership and that of the men who surrounded him, but Yrigoyen made no move to change either his style or his advisers. Instead, he contented himself with criticism of the critics, including intemperate remarks about the role of foreigners and young people in the party. Outside the party, the barrage of criticism reached unprecedented heights. In the latter part of August, with reports that Yrigoyen was planning to intervene in Entre Ríos province, the atmosphere became explosive. Leaders of all opposition parties called on the president to change his course. A series of mass meetings sought to mobilize public opinion against the administration, while certain political figures on the right began conspiring with army officers. The stage was being set for the military intervention of September 6. . . .

General Uriburu's assumption of power in September 1930 as president of the provisional government marked the beginning of a seventeen-month period of de facto rule. In its own day and ever since, the Uriburu government has been described variously as a military regime, a civil-military government, and a personalist dictatorship. The confusion in terminology derives from the contradictory makeup of the regime. To understand its true character and the place of the military in it, it is necessary to examine the persons who made up the administration, the procedures by which it governed, the groups that supported it, and finally the policies it pursued. . . .

The Uriburu regime rested primarily on the support of the armed forces, which, as we shall see, was not unqualified; on the support of vociferous nationalist groups, including the paramilitary Legíon Cívica Argentina (Argentine Civic Legion) described below; and on certain provincial political organizations, of which the Conservative Party of Buenos Aires was the most important. At the very beginning of his administration, however, as a result of the euphoria produced by the very success of revolution and by the pledges given to respect the constitution and work for national harmony, General Uriburu enjoyed the support, or at least the goodwill, of much broader sectors of Argentine opinion. Not only were the political parties that had worked to bring on the revolution, notably the Independent Socialists of the Federal Capital, the Democrats of Córdoba (a conservative group), and the Anti-Personalista Radicals, prepared to cooperate with the government, but parties that had opposed military intervention, the old-line Socialists and Progressive Democrats, showed a willingness to go along with the regime. Even an important sector of the divided labor movement made a public declaration of support.

Had the revolutionary government been content to serve simply in a caretaker capacity while preparing the country for early general elections, these various groups would have supported it in this task. But Uriburu's determination, publicly acknowledged early in October, to promote a series of constitutional reforms that would, among other things, alter the existing electoral and representation system, precipitated a process of political alienation. To the natural and open opposition of the Radicals was added the tacit opposition of several of the parties that had opposed the Radicals. In the absence of any public enthusiasm for his reforms, Uriburu's support was eventually narrowed to the military, the nationalists, and small conservative groups.

Military support for the Uriburu government, while sufficient to enable Uriburu to stay in power for a year and a half, was not unconditional. He had to contend not only with the threat of officers still loyal to Yrigoyen, but also with the influence and ambitions of General Justo and his supporters, who disagreed with Uriburu on the goals of the revolution. . . .

Although the Uriburu administration was able to conduct its economic policies with relatively little concern for military reactions, its political policies involved it in a dialogue with armed forces officers. The war and navy ministers were the normal channels of communication, but President Uriburu frequently spoke before military audiences to build support for his policies. Paradoxically, some of his most important political announcements were made in speeches at military installations, where politics was supposed to be regarded as a threat to morale and unity.

General Uriburu's political objective, as has already been noted, was the adoption of constitutional changes that would, in his view, prevent a repetition of an Yrigoyen-type government. While some of these changes embodied long-standing proposals to strengthen the legislative and judicial branches in relation to the executive and to shore up provincial autonomy against domination from the center, the heart of the proposed reform was alteration of the existing system of universal manhood suffrage and geographical representation. Never spelled out in detail, the proposals aimed at some sort of restricted vote and direct representation of functional groups. . . .

The Uriburu government did use its decree powers, however, to make one far-reaching innovation, the creation of the Escuela Superior Técnica, the technological counterpart of the War Academy. This institution, replacing the advanced course given at the Colegio Militar, trained military engineers and was the logical corollary of the efforts already under way to develop an armaments industry, including the production of aircraft. Under its first director, Lieutenant Colonel Manuel Savio, the Escuela Superior Técnica was to become the center for studying technical problems related to heavy industry development and the promoter of economic nationalist doctrines within the army.

The impact of the Uriburu era on the Argentine army of course transcended questions of size, promotions, training, and regulations to affect the very morale and outlook of the officer corps. Professional values tended to be subordinated to political issues, and what had once been regarded as beyond their competence became matters of daily discussion. The harmful effects on professional standards were evident even to officers who had supported the revolution. Writing in April 1931, Captain Perón observed to Lieutenant Colonel Sarobe, then far removed from the Argentine scene:

I think this revolution has done great harm to the officer cadre. It will be necessary for the men who govern in the future to return things to their place. There is no other solution than to multiply the tasks. The year 1932 at the least ought to be for officers in general a year of extraordinary work of every sort; only in this way can we avoid the harm produced in the army by idleness, backbiting, and politics. Every officer will have to be kept busy in professional tasks from reveille to retreat. Otherwise this will go from bad to worse.

. . . Deterioration of discipline and intensification of rivalries within the officer corps were the inevitable consequence of the September revolution. Another result was an increased disdain for civilians and civilian politicians. Uriburu's speeches to his comrades-in-arms repeatedly denigrated politicians and inculcated the view that patriotism was somehow the monopoly of the armed forces or of special groups like the Legión Cívica. How many officers were persuaded of this view cannot be determined, but it seems likely that a good many junior officers accepted as their own the scornful attitudes of their commander in chief.

The damage inflicted on Argentine society by the revolution worked two ways. On the one hand, it made many officers unwilling to accept completely the idea that political party activity is normal and essential in a democratic society. On the other hand, it lowered civilian confidence in the armed forces as a national institution above politics and spread skepticism about its aims. As Alfredo Colmo put it, "The army will have difficulty, henceforth, in convincing anyone that it is the patrimony of the entire country, that alien passions are not playing in it nor self-centered or irresponsible elements meddling in it. It will have to work to recover its prestige and good name."

An enormous burden was thus thrust upon the Justo administration when it took control in 1932, a burden that its very pursuit of power had helped to create. Not only did it have to cope with the alienation of the Radicals and face the economic and social problems of the deepening depression, but it had to work out, in an atmosphere of considerable distrust, a viable relationship between the army and a goodly part of Argentine society. . . .

From the very beginning of his administration President Justo was extremely sensitive to the problem of military support. The bulk of the officer corps, he was well aware, was politically neutral. However, there were two potential sources of danger: on the one hand, those officers who belonged to, or sympathized with, the Radical party and who subscribed to its view that the Justo government was illegitimate in its origin; and at the other extreme, and bitterly hostile to the Radicals, the authoritarian-minded officers who had been close to Uriburu and who after the latter's death developed the myth that Justo had betrayed the ideals of the September revolution.

Justo's response to the problem was a mixture of measures designed to reduce the likelihood of further alienation of officers while safeguarding him against the subversive activities of unreconstructed elements. Perhaps his shrewdest move was the appointment of Manuel Rodríguez to the War Ministry. As already noted, Rodríguez was a prestigious officer known for his deep commitment to professional standards. As minister of war, Rodríguez undertook to isolate the military from politics and to restore the discipline that had been shattered by the events of 1930–31. For one thing, he deliberately intensified the daily training schedules so as to leave little time for other activities. For another, he constantly emphasized the concept of professionalism and the primacy of military duty over other considerations. The sincerity with which General Rodríguez was able to proclaim these values undoubtedly helped maintain the loyalty of the bulk of the officer corps.

To protect his government against the politically minded officers, however, President Justo employed other means. A surveillance system was developed that included monitoring long-distance telephone calls placed through Buenos Aires and maintaining a close watch on contacts between officers and politicians. With information supplied by military intelligence personnel and by the Federal Capital Police, Justo was in a position to deal quietly with would-be conspirators, in some cases transferring them to innocuous positions, in other cases using the promise of promotion to wean them away from their allies. Arrest and retirement, however, were the usual penalties for those active-duty military personnel who carried their opposition into the open.

Justo much preferred to use indirect methods for thwarting military opposition. This is seen in the promotion of superior officers. In the list he submitted to the Senate in July 1932, the first to be approved since 1928, the grade of colonel was requested for forty-three officers, including Uriburistas and Radicals as well as members of the "Justo group." There is some reason for believing, moreover, that the president tried to exploit the mutual hostility of Radical and Uriburista officers as a means of keeping both in check. His overtures to the former through a proposed amnesty for pro-Radical officers penalized by the Uriburu regime and his concession to the former Uriburistas in not shutting down the paramilitary Legión Cívica support such an interpretation. The discontent of both groups persisted, but neither was able by itself to upset Justo's position.

The most determined efforts to overthrow him in the first two years of the administration came from the Radical side. A small group of officers and noncommissioned officers, of whom Lieutenant Colonel Atilio Cattáneo was the driving spirit, tried to organize a civil-military revolution in conjunction with leaders of the Radical party. Opposition from the Alvear wing of the party and rivalries among the military and civilian elements pledged to take part plagued the effort, as Cattáneo's memoirs attest. The first attempt, which was to consist of coordinated uprisings in the capital and several provinces, never came off because an accidental explosion a week before the planned day in December 1932 alerted the authorities and resulted in Cattáneo's arrest.

A few weeks later two Radical officers tried, unsuccessfully, to raise a regiment in Concordia, Entre Ríos, but the next major effort was scheduled to coincide with the holding of the Radical party's national convention in Santa Fe, in December 1933. This time the authorities knew the timing of the uprisings in advance, although not exactly where they would take place. Waiters on the river vessel that carried Radical party members to Santa Fe had been replaced by police agents, and on the basis of their reports, the president and his advisers waited up on the night of December 28–29 for the blows to strike. The main fighting took place in Santa Fe and Corrientes, with other disturbances in Buenos Aires province, but federal forces were easily able to restore order. A nationwide state of siege was proclaimed, and President Justo now took advantage of the situation to crack down on the entire Radical party, arresting Alvear and other moderate leaders who wanted a return to electoral politics, as well as those who frankly favored revolutionary methods.

With the failure of the 1933 movement, conspiratorial activity among the pro-Radical officers was confined to a few diehards. The party itself, recognizing the impossibility of regaining power by force, decided, despite vigorous internal dissent, to resume contesting elections in 1935. Thereafter, its contacts with the military were designed primarily to persuade the officer corps that a Radical victory at the polls would not threaten their careers. . . .

By 1937, President Justo had gained sufficient control of the political process to rig the election for his successor without fear of military intervention. Radical appeals for the army to supervise the balloting received no visible response from the officer corps, which obeyed Justo's injunction, repeated at the annual armed forces dinner on July 6, to stay clear of politics. The politically minded nationalist officers, who had as little use for the official candidate as they did for his Radical opponent, were in no position to act. Instead, they decided to await Justo's exit from office before making a new attempt to take power.

The willingness of the officer corps as a whole to leave politics to the president was undoubtedly influenced by their approval of Justo's handling of military affairs. Under his administration the modernization of the armed forces, which had been interrupted after 1928, was renewed and outlays of funds for military purposes reached unprecedented heights. . . .

The support given the Justo administration by the armed forces obscured but did not prevent the intensification of nationalistic sentiment in the officer corps and of the accompanying belief that the military should play a larger role in shaping public policy. Evidence of this trend may be seen in articles published in semiofficial and official military organs during and after the Justo era. Although the views expressed were those of individual authors, it is evident that the military men who edited the *Revista Militar* and the *Revista de Informaciones* were not opposed to having such views associated with the military establishment. A favorite theme of these articles was the great destiny that awaited Argentina and the need for the nation to prepare for an important future international role. Typical of this view was the flat assertion of a military engineer, Major Ricardo Maraimbo, that "the Argentine Republic ought to be and must be a great world power." The preparation that he and like-minded fellow officers proposed included nationalization of foreign investment, promotion of industrial self-sufficiency, intensification of patriotic sentiment through the repudiation of "utopian, internationalist, pacifist, and exotic ideas," and a substantial strengthening of the peacetime army. . . .

Not content with setting forth general goals, some officers insisted on the army's right to a major voice in foreign policy decisions. Colonel Carlos Gómez repeatedly advocated that the general staff chiefs participate in a national defense council concerned not just with defense plans but with the entire process of international relations. With reference to bordering countries, he specifically claimed the right for the military to say "With this neighbor we ought to be friends or allies; with this other it does not matter whether we are." Strategic considerations alone, he felt, should determine the nature of Argentina's relations with her South American neighbors.

From the belief that the military had a natural right to determine foreign decisions, it was no great jump to the conclusion that this competence extended also to the domestic field. Civilian nationalists like the poet Leopoldo Lugones had long been advocating military influence in domestic matters, of course, and had seen their ideas translated into approximate reality during the Uriburu interlude.

As the Justo administration came to an end, the gap was widening between the official view of the army's role and that held by an indeterminate but increasing number of individual officers. Officially, the army was depicted as an institution without interests apart from those of the nation, one that accepted subordination to the constituted authorities, one that contributed to the general progress of the republic. Justo's first war minister had once summed this up by stating to the Congress that he was "a representative of the interests of the nation in the War Department, and not the representative of the interests of the army.'' But even though General Rodríguez had spoken of the army as ''a weapon to be used by the civilians who have responsibility for the governments of the nation,'' military skepticism about the ability of such civilians to conduct its affairs was very much alive at the time the fraudulently elected Ortiz-Castillo government took power. The six years of the Justo administration had postponed, not resolved, the delicate question of the place of the military in the political process. . . .

The Army in Power, 1943–44

The substitution of military for civilian government [again] in June 1943 took place under conditions quite distinct from those prevailing at the time of the first takeover thirteen years before. Missing was the atmosphere of public excitement that had preceded the Uriburu-led coup, an atmosphere deliberately fomented by Yrigoyen's opponents. The June uprisings, in contrast, came as a surprise to the general public and even to those politicians who were aware of the widespread discontent within the officer corps. The politicians were anticipating a move in September, not in June.

Still, it would be erroneous to claim that the military acted without regard for the civilian sector, or indeed without encouragement from it. The officers shared the universal concern over President Castillo's electoral plans even while they disagreed among themselves on the wisdom of his foreign policies. Moreover, the belief that it was their responsibility to take action was strengthened by their increasing contacts with political leaders, especially those of the Radical party. Without this stimulus, it is questionable whether the liberal, pro-Allied sector of the army would have risen, and without their participation the movement could not have succeeded. The inability of the nationalist sector to mount a successful coup by itself had been demonstrated time and time again in previous years.

In acting to oust the Castillo government, the military was responding to a harsh axiom of Argentine politics: that no constitutional authority is strong enough to prevent a determined president from imposing his will, even if this involves violation of the laws and the constitution itself; and that only the withdrawal of military support can call a halt to such an administration. With his control over the Senate, Dr. Castillo could be unconcerned about impeachment proceedings, and he had shown by his continued extension of the state of siege his determination to ignore hostile opinion. The belief that it was up to the military to intervene was by no means limited to military circles; many civilians would have agreed with General Rawson when he told his comrades-in-arms: "When the nation, as a result of bad rulers, is put into a situation where there are no constitutional solutions, [the military] has a duty to fulfill: to put the nation in order." But here was the rub. Could an officer corps as deeply divided as that which existed in 1943 "put the nation in order"?

Adapted from Chaps. 1, 2, 3, 4, and 8 of *The Army and Politics in Argentina, 1928–45: Yrigoyen to Perón*, by Robert A. Potash, with the permission of the publishers, Stanford University Press (January 1977), © 1969 by the Board of Trustees of the Leland Stanford Junior University. Footnotes are omitted.

William H. Brill

An Overview of the Bolivian Military in National Politics to 1952

The armed forces in Bolivia have a long history of political involvement. It was the military that carved the republic out of the remnants of the Spanish empire and provided it with its early leaders. Unlike the revolutionary army of North America, which willingly laid down its arms and surrendered its power to well-developed civilian institutions, the Bolivian military assumed both by intent and by default the proportions of a ruling institution. Along with the church, the military became the bastion of conservatism and assured the landowning and merchant class that the revolution would not go beyond the achievement of independence.

With the decline of the powers of the church in the late nineteenth century, the military came to wield even greater power; it was limited only by the advent of the liberal movement of the early twentieth century. But even during this era, the military continued to exert a powerful influence on Bolivian politics and was always a force to consider. After senior officers had opposed the take-over of the government by the Republicans in 1920, [Bautista] Saavedra, the new president, felt it necessary to organize his own army, the Guardia Republicana (Republican Guard), and to remove the firing pins from the rifles issued to regular army soldiers stationed near the capital city of La Paz. And in an effort to block the political artery that led from the top of the armed forces to the presidency, a former German military adviser, Hans Kundt, was made chief of the general staff. Although respected as a military officer, the fact that Kundt was a German also recommended him, for it precluded his ever taking over the government.

The working relationship that had been crudely and imperfectly fashioned between the military and civilian leaders in the early part of the twentieth century broke apart under the impact of the Chaco War. This bitter, agonizing experience was a defeat not only for the German-trained Bolivian Army—but also for the entire nation. As Robert Alexander has pointed out, "the four-year conflict with Paraguay from 1932 to 1936 disorganized the economy, discredited the army, spread new ideas among the urban workers and miners, and sowed discontent among the intelligentsia."

The social disorganization which followed the Chaco War led to the formation of new political parties. In 1937, the Falange Socialista Boliviana (Bolivian Socialist Falange, or FSB) was created, patterned after Franco's falange in Spain, and in 1940 a Marxist-oriented Partido de la Izquierda Revolucionaria (Party of the Revolutionary Left, or PIR) was formed, along with a Trotskyite Partido Obrero Revolucionario (Revolutionary Workers party, or POR). It was not until 1941 that the most important party of all was born—the Movimiento Nacionalista Revolucionario.

To its founders, such as Víctor Paz Estenssoro, Hernán Siles Suazo, José Cuadros Quiroga, and Augusto Céspedes, the MNR was intended to be something more than a "party" in the traditional Bolivian sense. According to Céspedes, and explicit in the name of the organization, the MNR was to be a "movement"—a broadly based structure that linked miners, peasants, and middle-class intellectuals under a banner that was revolutionary and nationalistic and thus against the members of the established oligarchy, such as the large landowners and the foreign mine owners. Although never able to fashion a definitive ideology, the MNR did ultimately translate the symbols of nationalism and revolution into a program which called for the nationalization of the mines, land reform, and universal suffrage and education.

In the years that the new political parties were forming, the military was far from idle politically. Shaken, bitter, and humiliated at its defeat by the lightly regarded Paraguayans, it promptly elevated a series of military officers to the presidency of Bolivia. A few of these men proved to be adventuresome. Colonel David Toro, for example, nationalized Standard Oil, established the first Ministry of Labor, and initiated some workers' legislation. But his otherwise casual approach to the presidency, characterized by heavy drinking and other festivities in the palace, led to his downfall, and he was succeeded by Colonel Germán Busch. Busch intensified Toro's liberal political policies. Before his death in 1939, he established a federation of miners and even encouraged the formation of trade unions.

At the same time that the military was maneuvering on the national level, another force was at work within the institution. This was the RADEPA (Razón de Patria), a secret society formed by young officers in the prison camps of Paraguay during the Chaco War. Sworn to secrecy and vowing to save Bolivia, these officers in the years following the Chaco War slowly moved up through the ranks of the Bolivian army. Some of them were sent to Germany and Italy, where their need for pride and identity was fully exploited by their hosts—even to the point of granting the Bolivians audiences with Der Führer and Benito Mussolini. Upon their return, these officers, by now majors, joined their RADEPA brothers and for the first time became an active force in the military.

It was the RADEPA that opened the dialogue between the MNR and the army. The year was 1943. The popular Busch had been succeeded by General

Carlos Quintanilla and then by General Enrique Peñaranda, an honest, simple man by all accounts, who had gained the presidency by a popular election in 1940. Once in power, Peñaranda was beset by falling tin prices and trouble in the mines. In December 1942, government troops fired on rebellious miners at the huge mining complex of Catavi, and the MNR made the ensuing massacre its rallying cry. At the same time, RADEPA leaders were charging the government with corruption and with mismanagement of Bolivia's natural resources. Advocating a strong, authoritarian government, RADEPA gained the support of the young officers and began casting about for a revolutionary ally. According to one of the founders of RADEPA, the leadership of the society made contact with all the major political parties of the day after deciding that they needed a ''political base.'' At one point, the RADEPA leaders even thought of trying to make the Marxist-oriented PIR more nationalistic but rejected the idea in favor of the MNR. Whether the MNR was selected simply because of its growing political strength or whether there was a perceived ideological similarity is difficult to say. Both the MNR and the RADEPA have been charged with fascist leanings during this period, and both have denied it.

In any case, the year 1943 brought the RADEPA and the MNR to power after a bloodless coup against the feeble Peñaranda. Gualberto Villarroel, a young major and member of the RADEPA, was made president, and Víctor Paz Estenssoro, the MNR leader, became minister of finance.

The Villarroel regime lasted a little more than two years. During this time several opposition leaders were murdered, the United States charged the coup with being fascist-inspired and withheld recognition for six months, and the MNR and the army frequently found themselves at odds. But despite the friction and the intense opposition to the regime, this brief period allowed the MNR to consolidate its support. Trade unions were formed, and Villarroel and his ministers called and attended a national Indian congress. Moreover, the Villarroel government gave the MNR its first experience with power, and it was during this period, it should be noted, that the MNR and the army first took each other's measure.

The circumstances of the fall of Villarroel are shrouded in mystery. Both the army and the MNR charge each other with betraying the president. The MNR cites the failure of the army to defend Villarroel against the mob that dragged him from his office in the palace and hanged him from a lamppost; and the army charges that the MNR cut the telephone lines to the palace. In any case, Villarroel is something of a hero to each of his former supporters. According to Colonel Ponce, a RADEPA leader who talked to Villarroel hours before his murder, the president ''preferred to be dead rather than misunderstood'' and refused to issue orders for the army to take action against the mob. The MNR, for its part, made a monument out of the lamppost upon which Villarroel was hanged.

With the end of Villarroel, the army and the MNR parted. It was to be six years before they were to meet again—this time in mortal combat. In the interim, the MNR suffered the fate of the opposition in Bolivia, while the army, purged of the RADEPA, backed the new government which was headed first by Enrique Hertzog and then by Mamerto Urriolagoitia.

Reprinted and edited from *Military Intervention in Bolivia: The Overthrow of Paz Estenssoro and the MNR* (Washington: Institute for Comparative Study of Political Systems, 1967), pp. 5–9.

Herbert S. Klein

The Military and Bolivian Politics after the Chaco War

More than once during the twentieth century, radical army officers in Latin America have seized the reins of government and attempted to reform the national socioeconomic structure by authoritarian rule. Few such men, however, have equaled the naïveté or achieved the revolutionary mystique of Colonel Germán Busch, president and dictator of Bolivia from 1937 to 1939. Following the government of Colonel David Toro, who had attempted to establish a union of radical officers and reformist civilian parties, Busch tried to carry this "military socialist" movement to completion through the establishment of a partyless dictatorship. Though his attempt at radical change led to frustration, the political movements which flourished under his regime and the legislation which his government carried to completion created a crucial background for the rise of revolutionary parties after the defeat of the "military socialist" experiment.

The future dictator of Bolivia was born in the lowland province of Santa Cruz in March 1904 to a German physician who had married a Bolivian. Unlike his European-educated father, Germán Busch felt little inclination toward the liberal professions, and in 1922 he entered the Colegio Militar. Graduating in 1927, he was appointed to the general staff in 1929 and became a close associate of David Toro, the most brilliant and politically astute of the younger officers. Although Busch himself at this time seems to have been apathetic toward politics, his association with Toro led to his removal from the general staff in the revolution of 1930. For the next several years Busch carried out important geographical survey work in the Gran Chaco, for which he was highly honored. At the outbreak of the Chaco War he was given a front-line position and greatly distinguished himself in the difficult battle of Boquerón. Impetuous and intelligent, he was a rarity in the slack and corrupt Bolivian officer corps. He thus rose rapidly in the front-line command. A full lieutenant at the opening of hostilities, he had risen to the rank of lieutenant colonel by the end of the war.

Through his prominent leadership in several important engagements and especially in the last great defensive operation at Villa Montes, Busch also achieved national prominence. With few real heroes on whom to bestow their adoration, the Bolivian public especially adulated this seemingly shy but

109

effective military commander. As was also to be expected, this previously apolitical officer began to become ever more involved in the political machinations of the army itself. Although at the beginning of the war members of the officer corps were largely subservient to civilian authority, by the time peace came again they found themselves in open conflict with their civilian superiors. Because of his prominence as a well-known field officer, Busch played a leading role in the overthrow of President Daniel Salamanca in 1934 and was rewarded by his fellow conspirators with important staff positions. By 1935 Busch was able to consolidate his growing power and popularity by capturing the top army command itself, when he became chief of the general staff and active head of the La Paz garrison. It was from this position that he began to negotiate with the new political forces of protest and reform unleashed by the war to which he felt a strong affinity.

On May 17, 1936, the younger officer veterans following Germán Busch and the younger moderate leftist civilian elements under the leadership of men such as Carlos Montenegro and Enrique Baldivieso successfully overthrew the caretaker civilian government of Tejada Sorzano and established a joint civilian-military junta to rule in its place. Despite his crucial role in the revolt, Busch still felt himself to be unsophisticated in political matters and called upon David Toro to assume the leadership of the government. Toro was not a committed revolutionary, and, according to his own account, he was unaware of the *golpe* before its occurrence. But he was a sophisticated politician, nevertheless, fully sensitive to the new tone of national political life. Therefore, he gave his government the name of "military socialism" and initiated a host of social reforms, including the establishment of Bolivia's first Ministry of Labor.

Despite the bewildering outpouring of reform legislation and the president's constant discourses on social justice, Busch began to grow discontented with Toro's methods and results. When the civilian members of the coalition began struggling for power, Busch, in a fit of pique, decided to remove them from the government. Without the prior knowledge of Toro, he dissolved the junta and remade it into an all-military regime. This move apparently produced few results, however, and he offered his resignation to Toro as a vote of no confidence in the government. While Toro was able to prevent Busch from withdrawing, he was forced to act at once in an effort to produce results. Toro seized upon a long-standing dispute with the Standard Oil Company, terminated it abruptly, and on March 17, 1937 seized all of the company's Bolivian holdings and equipment.

Even this radical act did not satisfy Busch for long, and he was soon calling not only for immediate revolutionary results, but for a moral rejuvenation as well. The everlasting political compromises of the pragmatic Toro seemed to him to be leading nowhere. Busch wanted a reawakened "New Bolivia," and despite the concrete, if hesitant, advances made by Toro, he wanted more visible change. On July 13, 1937 he announced to Toro that the president no longer had the army's support and demanded his resignation. Toro was forced into exile, and Busch announced the formation of a new government under his own direction.

Although Busch was a major national hero and had strong ties to the veterans' movement, he was an unknown political quantity to the nation at large. The labor movement and most of the left moderates as well as radicals had benefited greatly under the Toro regime. They feared that Busch would destroy the experiment in military socialism and would return the government to the traditional political forces. The rightist press, for its part, reinforced this assumption by hailing the coming of Busch as a major renunciation by the army of Toro's "socialist" policies.

At the start Busch did little to clarify the situation, for he seemed to have been confused about his own reform plans. In his first public pronouncement to the nation he indicated that the previous regime had strayed from the principles of the May 17th Revolution, which had brought Toro to power, and that the army was therefore forced to take direct control again over the movement of "national regeneration." One of the prime aims of the May 17th movement, he declared, had been to end the class struggle between capital and labor and to replace it with harmonious national cooperation. He guaranteed that his government "would maintain public order [and] respect private property legally acquired." These vague statements gave no indication of the real attitude of the new government, and Busch's next major address to the nation did nothing to clarify the situation. In a long autobiographical discourse he talked of his own modesty and patriotism and of the need for all to work for national progress and stabilization.

While showing a strong conservative tendency in the economic sphere, the Busch regime began to assume the more radical attitude of the Toro government in the political area. In August the civil registers were opened to inscribe voters for the elections of the constitutional convention which Toro had been planning. The new government put into operation the Toro plans for some type of corporate representation and announced that the veteran's Legión de Ex-Combatientes and the national labor Confederación Sindical de Trabajadores de Bolivia could take part both in the registration and in all later political acts with the same status as political parties. Another major opening toward the left occurred when the government gave permission for Bolivia's leading leftist intellectual, Tristán Marof (Gustavo A. Navarro), to return from exile for the first time since 1927.

The March 1938 convention elections were the first in which the new postwar political forces were able to express their power. Endorsing Busch as their candidate for constitutional president, the labor, veterans, moderate, and even radical leftist movements temporarily banded together into an electoral alliance. Faced by Busch's support of this movement, most of the traditional parties withdrew from the contest, and the resulting election was a landslide for the new postwar forces.

Thus when the constitutional convention opened in May 1938, the *Generación del Chaco* found itself with a national platform for the first time. As the nation had had no legislature for three years, the convention dominated the national scene and became the debating ground for the major political ideologies which had invaded the restless generation. Reflecting these new ideas were a group of radical deputies, most of whom were new political figures and some hardened Marxist labor leaders. Opposed by the traditional political parties, these new men dominated the convention and forced the reluctant conservatives to abolish the classical Constitution of 1880. Rejecting the liberal doctrines of laissez faire, limited government which had influenced the nation's constitutions since the founding of the republic, the convention adopted the revolutionary concept of "social constitutionalism." The radical majority eliminated the safeguards which had confined the national government to a passive role of protecting property rights and individual liberties and wrote into the constitution a new "social" concept of government. The central authority was now given a positive role in providing for the social and economic welfare of all its citizens, and the thesis of the inviolability of private property was greatly modified. Property was no longer to be considered a natural right existing prior to the state, but a derivative right granted by the state only so long as it fulfilled a "social function."

The new Constitution of 1938 formally proclaimed the rights of labor and the governmental responsibility for matters such as social security, minimum wages, full employment, and social justice for all classes and races. While these provisions were revolutionary enough, the extreme left of the convention, or the "labor sector" as it was called, even attempted to have full-scale land reform and the abolition of peonage (*pongueaje*) written into the constitution. Under the leadership of Víctor Paz Estenssoro these radicals also proposed government domination of the great tin industry through control of the companies' foreign exchange earnings. Though these proposals were defeated after bitter debates, they nevertheless had their first national hearing and provided the platform for future radical action in these areas.

At the same time the traditional political forces of the nation underwent a profound change when it was learned that Bautista Saavedra had died in exile. The death of this last of the great prewar political caudillos ended the pattern of traditional political organization. An astute politician who had maintained a delicate balance between the traditional political parties and the new postwar groupings, Saavedra had even changed the name of his party to include the word "socialist." Adopting the language of Marx, he had held his party together in the postwar era through a temporary alliance with the younger military to establish the Toro government. While retaining the leadership of the prewar generations, he had appealed to the postwar youth so successfully that time and again Busch had been forced to exile him lest he overthrow the government. The only prewar leader capable of bridging the gap of generations, Saavedra was irreplaceable. His death accelerated the drift away from the center on the part of the new and traditional political groupings.

A few days after Saavedra's death, news began to circulate of a unity move among the traditional forces who were attempting to create a Concordancia, as they called it, among the three great rivals of the past: the Liberal party, the Genuine Republican party, and the Republican Socialist party. The stated object of the front was to prepare for the coming May congressional elections, to promote the return of the army to its professional services, and to call for the dissolution of the elected congress of 1938–39.

The signing of the Concordancia pact was a major turning point in Bolivian political history, for it brought to an end the political system which had been created in the aftermath of the War of the Pacific in the 1880s and which had characterized national life ever since. This carefully constructed system was based on intraclass parties struggling over forms of liberal government and *personalismo*. Dissident leaders such as Saavedra or Siles might temporarily appeal to the middle and lower classes for support, but they usually operated within the same socioeconomic class as their opponents. The Concordancia represented an abandonment of this system and its sterile debates over the issues of federalism, corruption, and personalities and substituted a comprehensive defense of the oligarchy and its power against the rising tide of radical reform. The traditional parties, their power at its nadir, now recognized their inability to command a national following. Denied access to the forum of Congress and participation in cabinets, they had no concrete base from which to operate. In the years after 1936, party discipline had cracked as leading party members joined the government on an individual basis and broke their traditional party ties. Without the discipline of a continually operative congressional delegation the national committees seemed incapable of preserving their strength. Therefore, though the signers of the Concordancia pact seemed to imply that this was a temporary electoral expedient, the giant parties of prewar days were dead, and the Concordancia was to endure in various forms for a long time to come. It was the inevitable response to the need of the upper classes for a united political front to represent and defend their interests since the old system could no longer exercise the desired control over national politics.

Faced with grave charges of government misconduct on a large scale, without adequate support from the disorganized ranks of the moderate left, and believing that his "reforms" were producing few results, Busch decided that purifications and rejuvenation were needed. With elections only a few weeks away, he declared on April 24, 1939, to the surprise of the entire nation, that he was establishing a dictatorship.

The manifesto which Busch issued in defense of his act was a curiously revealing psychological document. He began by describing the long years of selfless service he had given to the nation, including the supreme test of war. He, too, had felt along with his fellow veterans the need for a "patriotic resurgence," for a "profound renovation" and "purification of the national soul." Even the public administration reflected moral degeneration, he charged. . . . Public and private immorality, he declared self-righteously, "had converted themselves into a chronic sickness." Alluding to the demands of the Concordancia for an end to military rule, he attacked those who wanted to divide the army from the people and accused them of waging fratricidal war. The army was still vitally needed, he said, for Bolivia was passing through a political, moral, and economic crisis.

In the face of this "crisis" Busch declared that he could not remain impassive but must react in an energetic fashion:

With the same faith, with the same spirit of sacrifice with which I defended Bolivia in the times of battle, offering my life at each and every moment, I want to undertake a new campaign which will save this decaying nation. Beginning today I am initiating an energetic and disciplined government, convinced that this is the only road which will permit the invigoration of the republic, in the internal and the international area. The country needs order, work, and morale to fulfill its destiny.

A flood of decrees followed the announcement of the dictatorship. The coming Congress was suspended, and the new elections were cancelled. Although the 1938 constitution was declared to be still in effect, the government now arrogated to itself the right of legislation and proposed to rule through executive decree. A host of laws defining morality in government and business also came forth from the presidential office, as Busch tried to legislate away that moral decay which he believed was rotting the foundations of the nation. Among the many actions of the dictatorship was a new education code, which provided for major changes in the nation's school system and increased government control.

The most important development in the field of social legislation, however, was the signing into law of the first national labor code on May 24. Of prime importance as an enduring and revolutionary piece of legislation, the Código del Trabajo, or the Código Busch as it soon came to be called, was a major victory for Bolivian labor and the culmination of long years of agitation for major social legislation. One of the few successful and permanent reforms of the Busch regime, the Código Busch was actually the work of Waldo Álvarez, the first minister of labor. Embodying early drafts by Álvarez and later elaborations by local directors of the Ministry of Labor, this 122-article code included a wealth of concrete benefits to Bolivia's laboring classes. It provided for government protection of labor contracts, job security, annual paid vacations, accident compensation, the closed shop, and collective bargaining. Entire chapters were devoted to the problems of the cottage industries, domestic laborers, *engage* (hiring out of labor contracts for work away from homes), and apprenticeship contracts, all major problems in underdeveloped Bolivia.

Despite the profound importance of the Código Busch another action of the government soon dominated the thoughts of the nation. On June 7 Busch ended a long and complicated dispute with the tin industry over the special wartime taxes and controls over foreign earnings which the government was still exercising. Taking up the rejected plank of the radical deputies in the 1938 convention, Busch decreed that henceforth all the tin companies would be required to turn over all of their foreign gold earnings to the government. Busch decided to adopt for a revolutionary slogan the issue of "economic' independence," much as Toro had used his decree for the nationalization of petroleum. Accordingly, he rescued from oblivion the project for *divisas* of 100 percent and proclaimed it to the nation.

The terms of this potentially revolutionary decree provided that the mine owners had to turn over to the Central Bank all earnings (*divisas*) resulting from the total gross sale of their tin exportations before they could receive a customs-house permit allowing them to export their minerals. Article 38 of the decree provided that

all passive resistance to the fulfillment of the present decree law: sabotage, lockout, restriction of labors, and any direct or indirect measures which try to disturb the progress of the mines in their normal operation, will be considered as a crime of high treason against the nation [that is, subject to the death penalty], and its administrators, directors, and counselors will be judged summarily, . . . [with the possible penalty as well] of an intervention on the part of the state in the management of the guilty enterprise or enterprises.

In short, Busch threatened death and confiscation to all those who should attempt to impede the operation of the law by stopping production of minerals.

In a national radio address on June 10 Busch explained the full implications of the decree. He stated that its basic aim was to ensure the nation's economic independence and to promote cooperatives and small- and medium-sized producers in the mining industry, then dominated by the "Big Three" giants: Patiño, Hochschild, and Aramayo. Proudly he proclaimed that this law, "for the first time in Bolivia, established a system of defense of the national wealth." He justified it by reference to the 1938 Constitution, which permitted state intervention in the national economic processes. He claimed that this type of intervention was now practiced by nearly every nation in the world, including the United States under the New Deal of Franklin D. Roosevelt, and he denied that it would destroy private property or confiscate the mining utilities. The decree, he insisted, did not prevent private exploitation of minerals, but only maintained the rights of the state to intervene and "avoid the flight of capital and the impoverishment of the nation." By the terms of the decree, the state promised to pay the miners at the legal rate of exchange in bolivianos for half of their gold earnings and to allow them the full use of the other half under certain controls. As for profits, the state would permit mining companies to export 5 percent in gold certificates to pay interest on stock to foreign investors. Finally, the Central Bank was handling the whole affair, and Busch promised that representatives from the mining industry itself would sit on its board of directors.

Busch ended this broadcast to the nation by shifting from the defensive to the offensive. For too long, he said, the state had been poor, despite the wealth of the mining industry, and now this imbalance would be corrected. The nation's sacrifices in the Chaco, he declared, demanded a new era which would make Bolivia a wealthy nation. He appealed to his fellow military men and his fellow veterans to remember that the Great Marshal of Ayacucho had charged his successors "to defend Bolivia regardless of all the dangers."

Although decrees spouted from the presidential palace, they produced few reactions and fewer results. Even Busch eventually had to realize that he was neither solving problems nor changing the moral climate. He had mistaken a single popular manifestation for a great emotional resurgence in his favor. A lonely figure, without organized political or military support or a fixed ideology of his own and completely dependent on the old oligarchy even to carry on routine administration, Busch sensed the utter folly of his own quixotic and romantic dreams. On the evening of August 23 he committed suicide.

With the death of Busch the experiment in radical military government was at an end. General Quintanilla as head of the army had little difficulty in creating a conservative military regime with the backing of the Concordancia. This rapid overthrow of the military socialist regime gave the radical left an opening to charge the oligarchy with assassinating Busch. These charges are unfounded. Not only does the testimony of witnesses prove the thesis of suicide, but a careful reading of the public utterances of Busch will lead to the same conclusion. More than anything else his speeches reveal the psychological destruction of his driving personality in the last months of his government. His impassioned, rambling, and self-defensive public declarations reveal his distorted, romanticized view of public affairs and his growing awareness of this distortion, which finally overpowered him.

While the death of Busch brought a temporary halt in the army's experiment with political reform, the period of military socialism had lasting effects. It was the source of inspiration for the Villarroel regime of 1944, and, even more important, it marked the dramatic end of a major era in Bolivian political history. With the creation of the Concordancia in 1939 came the formal recognition that the great period of the traditional political party system had ended. From 1880 to the Chaco War this party system had dominated the nation, and until the formation of the Concordancia the traditional political leaders refused to believe in its destruction. At that time, however, the oligarchy finally brought home to them their weakness and forced them to forget their historic differences and unite self-consciously to defend their class interests.

The era of military socialism also stimulated the postwar moderate reform movement which produced the Partido Socialista under Toro, various factions of the Republican Socialists, and Independent Socialist groups. But the attempts of these civilian reformers had failed, largely because of the hostility of Busch. In the resulting collapse of the moderates, prewar radicals such as José Antonio Arze, Tristán Marof, Fernando Siñani, and others captured the student and previously apolitical labor movement and in the last days of the Busch regime came the first tentative steps in the organization of the powerful Partido Izquierda Revolucionaria.

With the traditional parties forced to renounce compromise and the extreme left gaining powerful student and working-class support for the first time, the collapse of the experiment of military socialism marked the end of national consensus and the beginning of uncompromising class conflict in Bolivia. This new type of political warfare would ultimately lead to the Bolivian National Revolution of April 1952.

Reprinted and edited from "Germán Busch and the Era of 'Military Socialism' in Bolivia," *Hispanic American Historical Review* 47 no. 2 (May 1967), pp. 166–84.

Ronald M. Schneider

The Military and Brazilian Politics to World War II

Since the establishment of the republic, there have been very few periods in Brazilian history that have not been marked either by military revolts or by heavy armed forces tutelage of the government. In the recurrent struggle between legalism and political activism within the Brazilian military, the latter has long been substantially stronger than depicted by most historians and many contemporary observers. Neglect of this fundamental fact and the corresponding overemphasis of the role of civilian politicians and political movements have distorted interpretations of Brazilian political development. While a series of civilians from São Paulo did govern the country with reasonable security after the initial years of military domination under Marshals Deodoro and Floriano, two of these three presidents faced military crises that in the context of the times posed threats to their continuance in office. Prudente de Morais (1894–98) was plagued by dissatisfaction over his handling of the Canudos "insurgency" problem and in November 1897 was saved from assassination by a veteran of that campaign only because War Minister Machado Bittencourt sacrificed his own life to save the president. Following Campos Salles's quite peaceful term (1898–1902), Rodrigues Alves survived the November 1904 revolt of the Military School at the midpoint of his administration. The first *mineiro* president, Afonso Pena (1906–09), died in office of a "moral traumatism" soon after being thwarted in his preferences for a civilian as his successor and being forced to accept the candidacy of War Minister Hermes da Fonseca. Nilo Peçanha's year in office was little more than an opportunity to preside over the marshal's election, and Hermes himself was barely settled in the presidency when the naval revolt of 1910 broke out. His regime was also plagued by protracted insurgency in the northeast and south by dissident politicians. The latter problem extended into the term of Wenceslau Braz (1914–18), who otherwise enjoyed stability, although the nation's political king-maker, Senator Pinheiro Machado, was murdered (to the ill-concealed satisfaction of some officers). The military's involvement in World War I temporarily reduced its political interference and left Braz a good bit freer than he might otherwise have been.

Military involvement in politics resurged during the interwar period.

118

Epitácio Pessoa (1919–22) was involved in rather constant friction with the armed forces because of his insistence on appointing civilians to head the war and navy ministries. By the last year of his term a grave military question had arisen as the army, behind Marshal Hermes da Fonseca, adamantly opposed the choice of Arthur Bernardes as president for the 1922–26 term. Indeed, the entire decade of the 1920s was one of repeated military uprisings, culminating in the successful 1930 Revolution. [Gertúlio] Vargas himself, although heavily backed by, and to a considerable degree dependent upon, the armed forces, faced civil war in 1932 and a communist revolt in 1935, in both of which movements regular army elements were involved, before staging his own dictatorial coup in 1937. Like Wenceslau Braz, a quarter of a century earlier, Vargas also benefited from the military's concern with its wartime obligations. But with the end of World War II, Vargas was unceremoniously removed from office by the armed forces.

The transition from dictatorship to a constitutional, competitive regime after 1945 did not place undue strains upon the political process shaped by Vargas, at least so long as it received predominantly support rather than demands from the armed forces. Subsequently, however, the problems of aftermath politics in a period of emerging populism and resurgent traditional clientelism, aggravated by dislocations caused by the external influence of postwar international adjustments, gave rise to increasing tensions and a "revolution of rising frustrations." Under these conditions, Vargas's return to power through popular elections took place in 1950, only to encounter the full brunt of the participation crisis. Governing within the constraints of a constitutional system that had been consciously devised to thwart a president who might try to operate in his old style, Vargas found his tried-and-true techniques of manipulation and conciliation inadequate. His response involved a shriller demagoguery and intensified exploitation of nationalism rather than evolving a more serviceable substitute political style. In this situation, the majority of the officer corps withdrew their support from his regime.

Thus, the military's repeated intervention in the political arena in the postwar era had behind it a substantial tradition. Indeed, the relative political peace under Juscelino Kubitschek (January 1956–January 1961) was as long a recess from major political-military crisis as the republic had yet witnessed. When Kubitschek turned over the presidential office at the end of his full term to an elected successor in a climate of normalcy, he was accomplishing something achieved only by three previous civilian presidents (Campos Salles, Rodrigues Alves, and Wenceslau Braz). Moreover, three governments fell by force in the single constitutional term between [Eurico Gaspar] Dutra and Kubitschek, while the five-year presidential period after Kubitschek saw the emergence and decline of three distinct regimes in a process of nearly continual crises that interred the old pattern of civil-military relations and brought the armed forces back to the direct exercise of power they had experienced in the infant years of the republic.

In a very similar sense to the continuity of *tenentismo* (the political militance of the junior officers entering the service after World War I) and even of the *tenentes* themselves from the 1920s through the 1960s, *Florianismo* in the form of advocacy of military rule as practiced by Marshal Floriano [Peixote], spanned the 1890s to the early 1920s. First with the "Consolidator of the Republic" himself, then through the political career and presidency of his aide and favorite nephew, Marshal Hermes da Fonseca (1910–14), and finally with the bridge between *Florianismo* and *tenentismo* in the form of the 1921–22 campaign of the Military Club against the government under Hermes's leadership, this interventionist current left its impact on the military generation born after the establishment of the republic. Thus, if events before 1910 were just faint memories to the senior officers of the early 1960s, the same was not true of the Hermes da Fonseca administration and the period of World War I. For with few exceptions, the generals of the post-Vargas era were already cadets at this time, enrolled in military preparatory school (Colegio Militar) if not already in the academy (Escola Militar). Hence, for example, the naval revolt that broke out after Hermes's inauguration appears to have left an imprint that disposed them to react strongly to the navy insubordination in March, 1964.

While the earlier military interventions and revolts were part of the armed forces' historical memory, the developments of the 1920s were directly related—through the Revolution of 1930, the 1937 coup, and the ouster of Vargas in 1945—to the developments of the 1954–64 decade.

Throughout this period, military figures were actively involved in the political life of the states, albeit more often behind the scenes than in the spotlight. In point of fact, between 1900 and 1930 the Brazilian armed forces were an even more active factor in the politics of the nation than were their Argentine counterparts—conventional wisdom to the contrary. The Brazilian armed forces differed from the Latin American norm during the first three decades of the twentieth century more as a result of the nature of the Brazilian political system as a whole than in terms of their own particular characteristics as an institution. As the system underwent a process of change, so did the military subsystem, in response to many of the same dynamic factors.

With the beginning of the political decay and institutional deterioration of the Old Republic at the end of World War I, the military was at the center of every crisis. The increasing division within the armed forces along generational lines, which placed them on both sides of the conflict between the established order and the forces of change, nourished a continued belief, strongest within the military but accepted by much of the public, that it was national rather than institutional interests or personal ambitions that motivated their political actions, and to a considerable degree this was true. As their predecessors were the midwives of the republic in 1889, the younger officers—those emerging from the Military School toward the end of the war and after—were its gravediggers.

By 1928, the republican regime in its nearly four decades of existence had reached the same point of deterioration, and the oligarchic system a parallel degree of political decay, as had been the case with the empire in the mid-1880s. Institutions and processes that might have been suitable for the first years of republican self-government had failed to evolve beyond an amalgam with traditional practices carried over from the monarchy. Indeed, they became entrenched through the federal government's willingness to let state power structures alone as long as they cooperated in Congress and created no undue difficulty over presidential succession. The electoral process was highly fraudulent; national parties were nonexistent; and protests against the inequities of the established order were increasingly met with repression rather than compromise and evolutionary reform. The federal executive, while frequently arbitrary, often lacked the compensatory merit of strength and effectiveness. The political representatives of the patriarchal and "oligarchic" regime could not point with pride to outstanding accomplishments to justify their continued stewardship of the nation. Or rather, when they sought to do so, they were convincing only to themselves, while appearing hypocritical and self-seeking to an increasing proportion of the politically conscious public.

As long as elections might lead to change, there was no strong popular base for revolution. But the people were aware that never in the history of the republic had the government's candidate lost. Moreover, only on two widely separated occasions had the electorate been given even the shadow of a real choice rather than just an opportunity to ratify the decision of the powerful state machines (and this only when the bargaining process among the president and the governors of São Paulo, Minas Gerais, and Rio Grande do Sul had broken down). Indeed, to all intents and purposes, the selection of São Paulo's governor for the 1926–30 presidential term had taken place in 1919, when the election of Epitácio Pessoa to the presidency was understood within the political class as a temporary "emergency" interruption of the pattern of São Paulo-Minas Gerais alternation, which would give the young state executive four more years to mature. In this context, the presidential succession of 1930 turned out to be the last chance for the old republican system to demonstrate significant flexibility or adaptability. But the course of events from late 1928 on demonstrated that Brazil's political crisis was one both of men and of institutions.

The core of the revolutionary movement that eventually triumphed in October 1930 was composed of the *tenentes*, who had gained conspiratorial experience as well as a degree of popular renown during the four years of their armed struggle against the government of Arthur da Silva Bernardes (1922–26). During 1928–29, they were able to win additional adherents to their cause within the officer corps, exploiting the growing dissatisfaction with the regime's policies. The successful revolution became possible only after they formed an alliance with a broad coalition of political forces possessing a significant power base in the key states, but their proselyting and infiltration of military units throughout the country were essential to the achievement of this purpose. Indeed, without the assurance of widespread military adhesions, the generally cautious political leaders would not have risked a revolutionary venture, particularly the coldly calculating Gertúlio Vargas, in whose name the 1930 revolt was ultimately launched and who had delayed his commitment until the movement was far advanced.

Tenentismo paralleled in many respects the postivistic republicanism of the young officers in the last decade of the empire. On the intellectual side, its origins can be found in the Military Academy, reopened in 1911–12 at Realengo after being closed in the wake of the 1904 cadet revolt. There during World War I such future leaders as Eduardo Gomes, Luís Carlos Prestes, Siqueira Campos, Oswaldo Cordeiro de Farias, Stenio Caio de Albuquerque Lima, and Ciro do Espirito Santo Cardoso (to name but one group among several who maintained a significant exchange of ideas) studied and lamented a "Brazil laden with problems, beneath the weight of the crisis and in the hands of politicians [who are] inept as well as unscrupulous and instruments of oligarchies." The leaders of the academy made a conscious effort to keep the education essentially technical rather than highly theoretical, with a taste of the humanities, or at least of positivist philosophy, as had been the case at the old academy at Praia Vermelha during the years when its instructors were still the disciples of Benjamin Constant. The goal was to develop competent professional soldiers, well disciplined and obedient to constituted authority. This orientation was successful with many. But in light of the lower-middle-class origin of a large proportion of the young officers, the example of their superiors' often mixing in politics, the siren call of renewed *Florianismo* through the person of Hermes de Fonseca, and the magnitude of national problems (contrasted with the "selfish" interests of the "boss"-dominated political system), it is not surprising that a significant minority questioned the military's institutional role as a support of the established order.

The militants of both the legalist and reformist theses were greatly outnumbered at the time (as they would be three decades later) by the vast majority of officers for whom the two sides of the nation's motto, "Order and Progress," had equal importance. Since the 1891 Constitution enjoined the armed forces on the one hand to be "essentially obedient, within the limits of the law" to the president, but on the other hand declared them "obligated to support the constitutional institutions," it virtually consecrated ambivalence in ambiguous situations when the threat to the constitution's integrity appeared to come from the executive. Moreover, the increased emphasis upon study and training advocated so vigorously by the champions of professionalism and embodied in the 1920 military regulations, along with the arrival in the same year of a French training mission, which was destined to have a heavy impact upon the army's mentality, appears to have made young officers more aware of national problems than before. Growing numbers came to believe: "On the national scale, the army, and only the army, was the organized force which could be placed at the service of democratic ideals and popular demands, against the interests of the bosses and oligarchies which increasingly aggravated the burdensome conditions of survival for the unprivileged."

The spread of this reformist-activist sentiment among the military coincided with the increasing alienation of urban progressive groups who found the establishment unresponsive to their demand for a significant voice in policy making and not at all disposed to yield to demands for any type of reform, including that of the electoral system. As had been the case forty years earlier, nearly all of the preconditions for revolution existed. Dissension within the political elite over presidential succession combined with the impact of the world economic crisis made the regime vulnerable and provided additional impetus to the formation of a revolutionary coalition capable of overthrowing the established order.

The successful revolutionary movement of 1930 was a heterogeneous amalgam of groups desiring sweeping political changes if not a new social order, with elements, which although violently opposed to the incumbent administration and the president's hand-picked successor, were devoid of any wish for more than modest political and administrative reforms. In both its civilian and military components—each crucial to its success—the revolutionary coalition was essentially, indeed almost exclusively, bourgeois in nature. The Communists, considering the October 1930 revolt to be narrowly concerned with regional rivalries within the existing system, refused to participate or support it—a fact that was to have significant implications for the postrevolution political struggles.

Presidential succession was the issue that coalesced the fragmented opposition forces into a single movement cohesive insofar as its immediate objective—attainment of power—was concerned. In 1929, the world market crisis combined with a record coffee harvest to thwart government price-support policies and trigger an economic recession. Elements linked to industry, finance, commerce, and services began to react strongly against economic policies favoring export-oriented agricultural producers. Against this background, an unusually strong opposition coalition was forged to contest the 1930 presidential election. When outgoing President Washington Luis, of São Paulo, broke with tradition and sought to impose another *Paulista* as the official candidate, Minas Gerais political leaders threw their support to the "Liberal Alliance" slate headed by Getúlio Vargas, the governor of Rio Grande do Sul.

Júlio Prestes was announced the winner, but the Liberal Alliance refused to accept the allegedly fraudulent results and launched a revolt in October 1930. Alarmed at the prospect of civil war and impressed with the visible decay of the old regime in the face of this challenge, the high command of the armed forces, after a good deal of maneuvering by generals with key commands, stepped in and forced the president to resign in favor of a junta, which it was hoped by some participants might prove a viable alternative to the revolutionary forces.

Vargas became provisional chief executive at the head of a very heterogeneous movement. Although the *tenentes* and some "young Turk" politicians desired a real social revolution, they lacked any coherent plan; other groups wished only to correct the evident deficiencies of the old political system. They agreed only upon a new electoral code incorporating the secret ballot, proportional representation, a system of electoral courts, and extension of the franchise to include women. Following an unsuccessful "Constitutionalist" revolt centered in São Paulo in July 1932, a constituent assembly was elected and in 1934 conferred a four-year presidential term upon Vargas. During this time both the communists and the local fascists (known as Integralists), thriving in a situation where less ideological parties failed to take root, sought Vargas's overthrow by violent means. In November 1937, Vargas staged a coup with the acquiescence of the armed forces' leaders, assuming dictatorial powers and decreeing a semicorporate "New State" (*Estado Nôvo*). By absorbing into his regime important elements of the dominant state machines, he was able to bend the existing political system to his wishes and adapt it to his needs. Thus, he was able to govern without a formal party structure while maneuvering to neutralize critical military elements.

Vargas's fifteen-year stay in power, although interrupting Brazil's tradition of constitutional government, helped to break the hold of the traditional elite groups and brought new elements into the political arena. Moreover, Vargas gave impetus to social and economic developments that subsequently tended to give a broader base to Brazilian experiments with representative regimes in the 1946–64 period. Yet more than anything else the *Estado Nôvo* reinforced authoritarian tendencies and corporatist structures which proved barriers to the development of a pluralist system.

Reprinted and edited from *The Political System of Brazil: Emergence of a Modernizing Authoritarian Regime, 1964–1970* (New York: Columbia University Press, 1971), pp. 37–48 by permission of the publisher and the author.

Frederick M. Nunn

The Military in Chilean Politics, 1924-32

Prior to 1973, political orientation and motivation of Chilean army officers in the twentieth century was generally confined to the 1924–32 period. During those eight years the military functioned as a politically deliberative body in four distinct ways. First, in September 1924 the actions of junior and middle-grade officers caused President Arturo Alessandri Palma to resign his office, whereupon a junta composed of two generals and an admiral assumed executive functions. Four months later, in January 1925, a coup led by the progenitors of the 1924 movement deposed the junta and recalled Alessandri, allowing him to serve out the remaining few months of his five-year term.

Second, during the two tense years that followed, the army, under the control of a clique of colonels, steadily increased its influence in national politics while observing constitutional procedure. From the pose of an obedient, objectively controlled military organization the Chilean army moved to a position of dominance. It was the army which provided impetus for civilians to write a new constitution in 1925. In September 1925 the recalled Alessandri resigned his office a second time because of military pressure. His elected successor fared no better and by early 1927 was a pawn in the struggle between reform-minded military men and recalcitrant and antimilitarist political leaders. The army's insistence on full exercise of constitutionally provided executive powers forced him to resign. When he did so, it was only a matter of weeks before the military reform leader Colonel Carlos Ibáñez del Campo became president, the first military man to occupy the presidential chair in three-quarters of a century.

Third, Ibáñez and his civilian and military supporters governed Chile for four years, until July 1931. Applying the socioeconomic reforms called for in the new constitution, Ibáñez paid only lip service to civil liberties and democratic procedures of governance embodied in the same document. He was not a true dictator, but a rigid authoritarian, elevated to power constitutionally, who had grave doubts about traditional liberal democracy and constitutionalism.

Fourth, after the fall of Ibáñez in 1931 army officers continued to engage in intrigue and plotting for nearly fifteen months. In this last period the prestige of the armed forces suffered greatly. Plotting and effecting the overthrow of three administrations within three months in 1932 assumed an almost Parnassian

125

quality and showed little orientation toward national issues at stake during the previous three epochs.

It is in the second of these clearly delineated periods that an aberrant civil military relationship came to fruition. In the 1925–27 period the leaders of the Chilean state within the state were not concerned with the classic freedom from budgetary powers of parliament or with the refusal to accept democratic controls. Their concern hinged upon a refusal to accept what they considered to be an outmoded form of democracy per se. They adopted such a stance in order to see to it that a new form of democracy be realized in state and society. More than a mere withdrawal of "the most vital military matters" from all civilian controls, Chilean political officers desired to alter the very basis of those controls by changing the form of civilian administration. They partially achieved this in September 1924 when Alessandri agreed (temporarily) to designate only military men as war and navy ministers.

These politicomilitary aspirants adhered to no ideology; as politicomilitary participants they had no programmatic approach to reform. They paid prime allegiance to Chile not to the parliamentary system of government or its adherents; not to Alessandri, its leading foe or his civilian colleagues; not to any political party or coalition, social sector or economic group. In word and action they paid allegiance to the nation.

Only twenty-five years earlier the Republic of Chile was the supreme military and naval power on the Pacific coast of South America. Economically, the country was in the midst of a nitrate boom brought about by the successful termination of the War of the Pacific against Peru and Bolivia (1879–83). Socially and politically, Chile was stable, its homogeneous society being remarkably free from immobility (by Latin American standards) and its politics modeled after those of Great Britain in a pseudoparliamentary regime.

Within a quarter of a century, however, Chile fell under the influence of army leaders who looked with distaste on politics, believed that serious social problems were going unattended, and who realized that the effects of the post-World War I recession had ruined their country's economy. Chilean politics encased in parliamentarism did not prove representative of society in a changing Chile. The country was on the threshold of social change being brought about by urbanization and increasing personnel changes at all levels of government. "Middle-class" and provincial elements were important in politics, but their voices were those of the minority until 1924. The army identified more with new social and political elements than it did with those of the past, but this did not necessarily mean that it would serve their interests.

Chile's crisis of the 1920s was essentially one of leadership. The Chilean advocates of change—who held that government action and/or constitutional reform were necessary for social and economic modernization—were a divided lot. The "social reform" parties, the Radicals and Democrats, were not at all committed to sweeping constitutional reforms proposed by the man they helped elect president in 1920. That man, Alessandri, fervently worked for a return to the presidential system (or at least an executive-legislative equilibrium) through constitutional reform as the way to provide necessary leadership and solutions for national problems. For the first four years of his presidency he failed.

Finally a ray of hope met Alessandri's gaze. In March 1924 he arranged for army officers to oversee congressional elections in certain key districts. It was this maneuver which enabled him to establish a shaky coalition majority in both houses of Congress. The 1924 elections so compromised the army that it was unable to dissociate itself from politics for over eight years. Nevertheless, it was not until early 1925 that the army became a disciplined and united political force.

Involvement of the army in the crucial March elections brought cries of intervention from all quarters. The conservative opposition to Alessandri (composed of Conservatives and many Liberals) accused the army of intervention. Even Alessandri's cohorts were uneasy about military collaboration. When Congress failed to act on Alessandri's legislative proposals the army, already torn between old and new leaders, reacted. In September 1924 Alessandri left office because of the pressure exerted on him by both elements, and military rule was imposed on Chile. But the high command's answer to Chile's crisis (the provisional junta) was unsatisfactory to those junior- and middle-grade officers who had initiated the pressure tactics on Alessandri and Congress in September.

By January 1925 Chile's new army leaders took the initiative themselves. Led by the Comité Revolucionario (headed by Lieutenant Colonel Carlos Ibáñez del Campo and Lieutenant Colonel Marmaduke Grove Vallejo) they overthrew the interim government headed by General Luis Altamirano. Ibáñez, a cavalry officer, and Grove, an artillery officer were long-time friends and former colleagues in the Academia de Guerra, Chile's army staff school. The clique of elite officers responsible for important political decisions in the 1925–27 period and during the subsequent presidency of Ibáñez (1927–31) were all products of the "Generation of 1912–14," the last class to enter and leave the Academia prior to the outbreak of World War I. While bent on recalling Alessandri, they let it be known that the army would, by no means, allow a restoration of traditional parliamentary politics. Ibáñez became war minister on January 23 and did not relinquish the post until 1927 when he rose to the Interior Ministry.

The coup met with little opposition except for objections from the conservative anti-Alessandri Consejo Naval, Chile's admiralty, based in Valparaíso. Once this opposition was overcome, however, nothing stood in the way of the president's return.

The next step in ensuring that the army would have its way was the creation of a transition government to administer Chile until Alessandri returned. The transition government was a junta hand picked by Ibáñez and his collaborators. From his desk in the War Ministry, Ibáñez began acting a king-maker's role even before Alessandri arrived home. He was aided by Grove and another long-time friend and Academia cavalry colleague, Colonel Bartolomé Blanche Espejo, the subsecretary of war. In the hiatus between January 23 and March 20, when Alessandri arrived in Santiago, Ibáñez made several moves designed to strengthen his grip on the army; hence the army's position as a political force.

To preclude intra-army rivalries he transferred loyal cavalry elements from the provinces into Santiago and gave Blanche a free hand to deal with recalcitrant infantry officers who, particularly, objected to the new influence of the cavalry. He transferred the rural carabineros from the Interior Ministry and brought them under control of the War Ministry to eliminate the possibility of any armed conflict between them and the army. Included in all transfers and shifts were key promotions or assignment for Ibáñista officers.

Army influence in restored politics was evident from the outset. Fearing a civilian reaction to military intervention, Ibáñez bluntly let Alessandri know that he owed his reinstatement to the army Comité as much, or more, than to civilian resistance to the Altamirano government. In short, the army still eschewed actual political control, but demanded its just due for allowing Alessandri to finish his term in office.

Alessandri had struggled with Congress since 1920 for constitutional reform to provide a balance between the executive and legislative branches, to reform the Chilean fiscal system, separate church and state, and establish a governmental role in the labor and welfare fields. He realized these goals with the promulgation of a new constitution on September 18, 1925, but not without considerable help from the army. Though written by civilians, it is doubtful that the Constitution of 1925 would have become a reality without military pressure. It is doubtful if that military pressure could have been applied had Ibáñez and the new leaders not taken an adamant stand on the need for reform.

Doubtless Chile would have been provided with a new constitution at this time in its history. The precise time, manner, and form of this provision, however, was dependent on the politics of the army, specifically the politics of the war minister Ibáñez.

Ibáñez and Alessandri clashed numerous times during the winter of 1925, during and after the constitution-making process. In May and June the nitrate port of Iquique was convulsed by continuous labor agitation. Ibáñez ordered carabineros to forcibly break up demonstrations in which the red flag was shown and refused to rescind the order when ordered to do so by Alessandri. Ibáñez received numerous telegrams congratulating him for maintaining order and discipline, but Alessandri accused him of aiding the forces of reaction and violating civil liberties. When demonstrations turned to violence, Alessandri ordered General Florentino de la Guarda, commandant of the First Division, to crush resistance to the government and placed the provinces of Antofagasta and Tarapacá under a state of siege and martial law. Guarda carried out his order to the letter and tried all agitators as "communist revolutionaries." Concomitantly, rumors circulated in Santiago that Ibáñez had political ambitions. These rumors were summarized ably in official despatches written by United States Ambassador William Miller Collier. Alessandri's enforced reliance on the army as an internal police force and rumors of a political future for the army's chieftain led to an Alessandri-Ibáñez estrangement and made the army even more a political force.

On September 29 a group of party and independent leaders presented Ibáñez with a petition requesting his declaration of intent. Ibáñez accepted the petition and declared his candidacy. The next day the cabinet resigned en masse, a customary act when a minister of state became a candidate. But the war minister's name was missing from the list of resignations. When Alessandri demanded his resignation, Ibáñez refused in an open letter to the president published October 1. Referring to himself as "chief of the revolution," he stated that his tenure in the cabinet was vital to the maintenance of public order. He then informed Alessandri that as the only cabinet member in service his signature had to appear on any executive decree. Alessandri's response to this was his own resignation and transfer of the government to Luis Barros Borgoño.

The obdurate stand of Ibáñez in the face of Alessandri's demand for his resignation has been interpreted as evidence of his own presidential ambitions. Whatever his personal ambitions may have been at this point, they were frustrated.

Reaction to the Ibáñez-Alessandri showdown came from both the military and the civilian realm. An ill-conceived putsch attempt of October 3 failed to restore Alessandri, but some of the political leaders who petitioned Ibáñez on September 29 now expressed doubts about his motives. Further, there was military pressure exerted on him to bow out of the incipient presidential contest in favor of a civilian unity candidate. Admiral Juan Schroeders, director general of the navy, and Inspector General Navarrete both urged him to do so. Just four days after Alessandri resigned, party leaders agreed to support a colorless aristocrat, Emiliano Figueroa Larraín of the Democratic Liberal party. Ibáñez promptly withdrew his candidacy, so did the Radical Quezada.

The Rise of Ibáñez, October 1925–February 1927

Clearly, the impact of the military on Chilean internal affairs depended on the actions of Ibáñez. Equally clearly, the political effectiveness of Ibáñez and his cohorts depended on their control (or lack of control) of the army. Ibáñez's ambivalence during October reflected the delicate politicomilitary position into which the perhaps over hasty "acquiescence to a presidential draft" had temporarily lodged him. He stated that Figueroa was a reactionary. When José Santos Salas announced as a candidate of the Republican Social Union of Chilean Wage-Earners (*Unión Republicana de Asalariados de Chile*, or USRACH), Ibáñez supported him. Then he changed his mind on Figueroa; finally he called for postponement—but not cancellation—of the elections. The elections were held as scheduled, with Figueroa the victor.

Congressional elections, held a month later, resulted in gains for the reform parties, the Radicals and Democrats; but the new leaders of Congress showed no immediate willingness to yield to presidential prerogatives established in the new constitution, and President Figueroa showed a similar lack of will to exercise them. This dual unwillingness to adjust lasted throughout 1926 and served to renew military doubts about the viability of Chilean liberal democracy.

That this attitude became dominant in the army, and then the navy, can be seen in the gradual reestablishment of Ibáñez's strong position during 1926. From the nadir of October 1925, Chile's war minister rose to a new zenith by February 1927. Figueroa retained him in the cabinet, for it was apparent that he was less a threat if kept inside the government. The state and the state within remained in conjunction once normal constitutional processes were restored and extraordinary conditions ceased to be. Because of this, military influence continued to grow.

Politics drifted to the right during 1926, but it was not until April that Ibáñez showed his obdurate side again. On April 16 he addressed the Chamber of Deputies, whose presiding officer, Conservative Rafael Luis Gumucio, the editor of *El Diario Ilustrado*, was an outspoken critic of the army since the overthrow of 1925 and opposed the new constitution. Ibáñez debunked charges that there was new plotting in the army and defended the army's (and his) actions since 1924. He said that military men were concerned about the nation's postwar difficulties and characterized the army's role since September 1924 as one of a national institution which acted for the good of the country, not for any single political faction. He reminded the deputies of the army's role in securing legislation long stalled in Congress and in the constitution-making process. The war minister concluded by stating that if Congress could not carry on the work begun by the military, the military might be forced to assume the burden.

The April 16 confrontation did nothing to bring about executive-legislative harmony; if anything, it exacerbated an already existing conflict. During the Chilean winter of 1926 the Alessandri-Congress impasse of 1920–24 was replayed with new personnel. Administration spokesmen were heckled in the Senate and chamber, and Radicals and Conservatives refused to compromise with the executive branch on any major items of legislation. Meanwhile, Chile's economic situation continued to deteriorate. By the time Congress adjourned for the September 18 independence festivities, the Radicals led by Senate president Enrique Oyarzún and party president Pedro Aguirre Cerda had broken all relations with the administration. The Radical party, receptive to social and economic reform, would not support measures introduced by an administration it considered reactionary and would not cooperate with it even in the face of growing pressure from Ibáñez.

Ibáñez accused the chamber and the Senate of irresponsibility and lack of concern for national needs. These, he claimed, made the people susceptible to extreme leftist propaganda. He closed by challenging the right of senators and deputies to criticize the army, in or out of congressional session. In late October 1926, Chilean politics entered a new crisis stage.

For six weeks Chilean politics remained static, and relations between Ibáñez and the parliament continued strained. On November 13, Chile's emerging strong man tried a new tactic; he demanded that the cabinet be reconstituted because it had proved powerless to cope with Congress, unable to realize its reform programs, and incompetent in dealing with the communist menace. Ibáñez turned his attention temporarily from the legislative to the executive branch. The cabinet resigned en masse on November 14; Ibáñez resigned in a separate document, but in his quest for a successor Figueroa met with no success. So solid was Ibáñez's position by this time that no officer would accept the War portfolio. A new cabinet (with Ibáñez retaining his post) was sworn in on November 18. At this point, the traditional Chilean civil-military relationship inverted.

Carlos Ibáñez del Campo attained an "unassailable position" in November 1926, a position which allowed him a free hand to represent the interests of the state within the state and of the tight clique of staff officers who had aligned themselves with him in January 1925 before the civil authorities of Chile. This "unassailable position" was enhanced in January 1927 when leaders of a new naval reform movement appealed to him for support. When Ibáñez feigned ignorance of the navy affair, the new interior minister, Manuel Rivas Vicuña, resigned in disgust. On February 9, 1927, President Figueroa appointed Ibáñez interior minister and allowed him to form a new cabinet.

In February 1927 the Chilean state within the state ceased to be, for its leader had become a political figure with civil authority. Within two months of his appointment to the Interior Ministry Ibáñez became vice-president when Figueroa took a leave of absence for "personal reasons." On May 5 Figueroa officially resigned, and on May 22 Ibáñez was elected to the presidency. The Chilean army elite, whose advocacy of social, political, and economic reform and whose hostility toward traditional liberal democracy were first made obvious in the crisis of 1924 and the overthrow of 1925, had succeeded in

132

imposing its version of reform and democracy on the state. Once this was done military influence continued, to be sure, but in a slightly less obvious manner until the desperate days of 1931–32.

No valid appraisal of modern Chilean democracy can be made without bearing in mind the impact of the military on the internal affairs of Chile from 1924 to 1932. No valid appraisal of that octennium can be made unless the 1925–27 period is understood, for it was in that period that the Chilean army figuratively marched the nation toward reform and provided the necessary national leadership to do so.

Reprinted and edited from "A Latin American State Within the State: The Politics of the Chilean Army, 1924–1927," *The Americas* 27 (July 1970), pp. 40–55.

Víctor Villanueva

The Military in Peruvian Politics, 1919-45

In 1919, Augusto B. Leguía launched his campaign for the presidency against Antero Aspíllaga, a large landholder from the north who was backed by outgoing president José Pardo and the Civilista party. The Pardo administration, however, had lost a great deal of prestige due to its bloody repression of the general strike, which had been called to demand an eight-hour day. Moreover, the traditional oligarchy was in decline, with the general populace completely opposed to it, and Leguía easily won the army-supervised elections. It was rumored that the government would refuse to accept the election results, so Leguía immediately began to conspire.

He searched for a "man on horseback," making offers to various officers with all the savoir faire he had learned from his years of business experience. Finally, he obtained the support of an officer of the Palace Guard who promised to open the doors of the National Palace at an opportune moment.

The army had seen Leguía win at the ballot box, but more importantly they had seen Pardo cut the military's share of the national budget from 25.21 percent in 1915 to 17.87 percent in 1919. Thus, they quickly decided to support Leguía, who wielded a chauvinistic slogan: "Recover the Bluff of Arica," which Peru was forced to surrender to Chile in the War of the Pacific.

In the early morning hours of July 4, 1919, the Lima garrison revolted, arrested President Pardo, and put Leguía into power. Leguía entered the palace accompanied by the legendary Andrés Cáceres, symbol of the resistance against the Chilean invasion and principal guarantor of Leguía's future military policy—the recuperation of Tacna and Arica.

Despite the fact that he was a civilian, Leguía quite frankly initiated a new militarist and dictatorial period in Peru, a period that had its antecedents in the insurrection of February 4, 1914. Now the term *militarism* referred not only to specific military governments but also to military influence in a nation's politics and to the use of the military as a tool for capturing and maintaining power.

Leguía gained the presidency by means of a military coup. He had himself reelected twice without any popular backing, relying instead on the exclusive support of the armed forces, and succeeded in remaining in power against the popular will for eleven years (the *Oncenio*). The Leguía government paid very

133

little attention to the army as an institution, but it did obtain the individual support of many officers, due principally to the concessions and gifts provided them. Military discipline kept the remainder in line. By carefully selecting loyal officers and giving them key posts, Leguía was able to elude all kinds of dangers and even to control the discontent within the army's own ranks. . . .

As a means of rewarding the sergeants who took part in the July 4 coup, Leguía promoted them to officers, thereby violating the Promotions Law. He did the same for all the officers who had participated in the barracks revolt. The process of demoralization of the army, begun by Benavides in 1914, was accelerated by Leguía's 1919 action. The illegal promotions caused a profound disquiet among military officers. Those who had been so promoted were nicknamed "horse thieves" and were looked down upon, but since they enjoyed official approval, those officers continued their careers undaunted. Not a few achieved high rank in the officer corps, and a few even succeeded in donning the embroidered uniform of a general.

Leguía then was responsible for reimplementing the system of paying for political favors with military promotions, a throwback to the previous century. A popular joke held that military officers were like gasoline—sold by the gallon. The loss of prestige engendered by this caustic joke lasted for a very long time. The army, made up of true professionals, was contaminated by the "horse thieves," who, since they were regime men, were given the highest positions. The other officers, either through discipline or prudence, obeyed these new officers, thereby giving the impression that the entire army supported the Leguía regime, which quickly changed into a dictatorship. Many officers, who had never had much moral stature, accommodated themselves easily to the system of offering their political allegiance to the dictator in return for being favored in the promotion lists. The sops to the "cooperative" officers also took other forms such as "educational trips to Europe" for undeserving men and salary increases and corresponding perquisites in a period characterized by fiscal penury. Moreover, in addition to military backing, Leguía enjoyed the decided approval of United States imperialism, which provided him with numerous loans.

In spite of the unconditional allegiance which the army gave to the dictator, it received very little in return, except for the gratuities offered to selected military personnel. Indeed, Leguía even tried to diminish the importance of the army. In order to create a military equilibrium and counterbalance the army, Leguía organized the Guardia Civil [Civil Guard], granting to the officers of the new institution the same prerogatives, remuneration, and even the same uniforms as army officers. The Guardia Civil even succeeded for a time in having more regular troops than the standing army.

It seems that the military officers of that period were not concerned with the state of the army. They received promotions and stipends, and they did not ask for more. Leguía neither acquired new armaments nor increased the size of the army nor tried to reorganize and modernize it. When Leguía came to power he found a military budget which absorbed 17.87 percent of the national budget. In the first year, he abruptly increased it to 22.1 percent but then steadily decreased it to 17.59 percent by 1930, the year he was overthrown. The budget of the Ministry of Government and Police, on the other hand, rose from 807,234 Peruvian pounds in 1919 to 2,090,896 pounds in 1930, a threefold increase.

Leguía did more for the navy than he did for the army, acquiring four submarines. He also supported the air force, purchasing a number of planes and founding the Palmas Aviation School. Leguía named his son Juan Leguía to be commander of the air force, with the rank of colonel even though his only qualifications were his relationship to the president and the possession of a private pilot's license from England.

Though Leguía was not a military caudillo, militarism dominated the period. The army principally, but also the other military services, acquired great political importance, with the opinions of high-ranking officers carrying more weight than those of a senator or minister. Nevertheless, that was the period in which they invented or reactivated the slogan: ''The military should not intervene in politics.'' The intention was not to remove officers from politics, but rather, since it was now ''illegal'' to play politics inside the army, to give those officers loyal to the regime a better opportunity to impose their will.

It was said, as it always has been, that an officer was playing politics when he uttered one critical word against the government. On the other hand, he was applauded for attending ''official receptions'' in order to praise whatever action the government had taken. Thus, eulogizing what the government had done was not ''playing politics,'' according to that curious regime logic.

To maintain his regime, Leguía depended on the continued support of the military and the availability of foreign loans, the combination of which created a false impression of internal tranquillity and economic prosperity. The economic crisis of 1929, however, decisively brought to a close the ''Leguía Century'' which had lasted eleven years. The leader of the revolt was Lieutenant Colonel Luis M. Sánchez Cerro, a man with a reputation for both bravery and conspiracies and a captive of the intellectual bourgeoisie of the provinces. He was the commander of a sapper battalion in Arequipa, and that became the core of the military uprising.

Once the Arequipa revolt was known, the government adopted the necessary measures to put it down; but the economic crisis had undermined the regime, and the army found itself morally defenseless, with its high command in crisis because of the prolonged support it had lent to the dictatorship. In addition, popular pressure against the regime was mounting and antiregime propaganda by the oligarchy became insistent.

At the beginning, Sánchez Cerro enjoyed authentic popular support and the unanimous backing of the citizenry. Of a decidedly mestizo background, in fact a *cholo*, the insurrectionist of Arequipa could have become a true caudillo by virtue of his great charisma, his personal valor, and the fervor he was able to awaken in the masses; but he lacked political experience, he lacked a coherent ideology, and he fell victim to vanity.

An analogous thing happened to Luis Carlos Prestes in Brazil. The "Knight of Hope," who roamed all over Brazil fighting against the regular army and defeating it in more than one hundred battles over a two-year period, never found the road to attainment of his ideals. But then it is necessary to put that into proper perspective. Prestes, an army captain, was a legitimate *tenente*, a member of the *tenentismo* movement, an expression of Brazilian militarism, yes, but a progressive militarism which arose in defense of the people's rights. Prestes was the heir of Marshall Hermes de Fonseca, who had tried to stop the army from shooting at the population of Pernambuco. [See selection on Brazil in this section, pp. 118–124].

Sánchez Cerro, on the other hand, lacked the democratic "pedigree" of which one could be proud. His predecessors had only fought for their own interests at the beginning and for the interests of the oligarchy afterwards; his successors did not do anything except shoot at the populace until a new type of militarism arose in Peru in 1962.

During the Sánchez Cerro period, militaristic attitudes proliferated to the extent that they assumed the characteristics of an epidemic. In the lapse of one month, six military uprisings broke out. At one point there was a government in Lima and another in Arequipa, and five different juntas followed in quick succession. The period compared favorably with the most tumultuous times of the past century.

Sánchez Cerro was elected president and took office on December 8, 1931. Though he failed to remain in power (he was assassinated in 1933), he did succeed in consolidating a third period of militarism in Peru. Except for a brief period ruled by a civilian-led junta, military regimes controlled the destinies of the nation throughout the 1930s. From 1948 to 1956, there was another military dictatorship, and the two administrations of Manuel Prado (1939–45, 1956–62) were contrary to the popular will, being maintained only by the armed forces. In 1962, a new military junta ruled for one year, and in 1968 the armed forces returned to power and have ruled to the present [1978].

With the death of Sánchez Cerro, the oligarchy, terrified of the social struggle which threatened their interests and powerless to take power on their own, prudently pulled back and gave power to another general [who] hopefully would know how to defend their interests and continue the struggle against APRA, the political party most hated and feared by the oligarchy, which was not aware of, or perhaps did not believe in, the venality of its leaders.

The oligarchy did not realize that through the use of bribes, it could have converted the APRA movement into the best tool for defending the bourgeoisie, as Manuel Prado succeeded in doing some years later.

With the body of the tyrant still warm, the Constituent Assembly elected General Oscar R. Benavides, then inspector general of national defense, as president of the republic to finish Sánchez Cerro's term. The election violated the newly promulgated Constitution of 1933, which prohibited, in Article 137, the election as president of "a member of the armed forces on active duty." But the infringement of the constitution mattered little to them. Stopping the enemy was the primary concern; putting a halt to the social revolution they saw coming was basic. And Benavides was chosen for the task because of the qualities he had already demonstrated in the pro-oligarchy coup of 1914. Moreover, his background was completely acceptable.

In 1936, Sánchez Cerro's term ran out, and Benavides was supposed to step down. He called for elections and proposed the candidacy of Jorge Prado for president—as he had done years before with Javier Prado and would do later with Manuel Prado, whom he finally succeeded in putting in power. The Aprista party, incapable of launching a revolution and legally prevented from running their own candidate, threw its support to Dr. Luis Antonio Eguiguren, an honest and upright, but very conservative, lawyer.

As the election returns came in, the bourgeoisie viewed with dread the victory of the Aprista candidate. Benavides, in a totally dictatorial decision, ordered the Congress to annul the elections in as much as Eguiguren's victory was due to Aprista votes, that is to say, votes of an "international party" which was prevented by the constitution from taking part in politics. Benavides also ordered the Congress, whose legal term had likewise ended, to recess and delegate all legislative powers to the president.

Benavides first used these new powers to name three vice-presidents: General Ernesto Montagne as first vice-president, General Antonio Rodríguez as second vice-president, and General Federico Hurtado as third vice-president. Benavides had become an all-powerful dictator, and the most curious thing is that his dictatorship was "constitutional" and "legal" in that it had been approved by the Congress which, at least in theory, represented the will of the people. The armed forces not only accepted passively the trampling of democracy and the violation of the constitution; they went even further and congratulated the dictator on his actions and promised him their complete support.

The military dictatorship continued along the road of oppression and bloodshed. To the end of improving on the means of repression, Benavides contracted a fascist Italian police mission which brought and implemented the most modern systems of repression and torture. He created the Assault Battalion, a motorized unit which specialized in breaking up demonstrations, equipped specially for its mission, and assigned its command to several civilian politicians.

The campaign of Nazification of the army was effectively carried out. Magazines in Spanish, seemingly technical in nature but full of political propaganda, circulated freely. The military services adopted German techniques, and Hitler's rantings were well received within the army, which had always been inclined to applaud certain types of attitudes, particularly when they were backed up with brilliant and spectacular military deeds.

Benavides approved of this campaign of penetration and pushed it throughout the country. The principal newspapers of the capital, although they were enemies of the regime, played the same game. Carleton Beals lists the headlines of one Lima daily to show how it exalted the totalitarian powers and eulogized their activities. Beals also details the diverse activities of Nazi-fascist penetration in the Benavides dictatorship.

At the same time, APRA, realizing that it could not come to power by means of a popular uprising, turned to the army as a possible vehicle for achieving power. The first officer they approached was General Antonio Rodríguez, second vice-president and minister of government in the Benavides administration. Convinced he was the "chosen man" to lead the country out of oppression, Rodríguez and a few friends revolted in the early hours of February 19, 1939, taking advantage of the absence of the president, who was on board a navy ship taking a pleasure cruise off the coast. The conspirators captured the National Palace, something which was relatively easy because of Rodríguez's high position. They then obtained the support of the Guardia Republicana [Republican Guard], which in turn captured the Lima penitentiary and freed all the political prisoners. But then all action ceased.

The movement, well-planned from a political point of view, was not equally well-planned militarily. The conspirators remained in the palace without taking any further action until the Assault Battalion arrived and killed Rodríguez with a burst of machine-gun fire. The other officers did not know what to do; they were incapable of taking any action at all. The Aprista party, which according to the agreed-upon plan should have taken to the streets as soon as the palace was captured, likewise did nothing. The "popular support" offered by APRA never materialized.

From that moment, when they persuaded General Rodríguez to revolt, the Apristas have continued to interact with military officers. The antimilitarist party that APRA originally was henceforth had to praise the generals, apparently submit itself to their will, and approve of army intervention in politics. APRA has openly urged the armed forces to leave their barracks and take power, many times begging that they do so "in defense of the constitution." Aprista newspapers, pamphlets, and speeches are full of such calls.

Thus, the militarism that had long counted on the complacency and tolerance of the oligarchy, then on the consent of the rich bourgeoisie, henceforth could count on the support and cooperation of a party which called itself "antimilitarist" and "of Marxist extraction," and which was popularly based even though it was directed by a sector of the petit bourgeoisie.

Benavides was president on three occasions: in 1914, when he took power by force; in 1933, when the Congress gave it to him; and in 1936, when that same Congress extended his term. In none of these cases was he elected by the people, nor did he ever enjoy any popular support. Benavides never counted on any party to back him nor did he try to organize one. It was enough that the armed forces supported him, together with his own background and experience as a dictator.

These were the times in which Hitler and Mussolini shone like stars of the first magnitude in the world arena. These were the times in which a Peruvian author wrote: "We are walking triumphantly on top of the decaying body of the god of liberty." These were the times in which dictatorship was considered to be the best system of government ever invented by man and democracy only an obstacle to the progress of civilization. To imitate those men of the Old World was the dream of all the apprentice dictators of Latin America.

But Benavides demonstrated that he was not an apprentice; his period of apprenticeship had already passed. He was a man of his time, a dictator in every sense of the word. He was also the last great man of Peruvian militarism.

Despite the fact he was a military man and had governed with the exclusive support of the armed forces, Benavides reduced military expenditures during his administration from 24.11 percent of the national budget to 21 percent, increasing instead expenditures on public works and social programs.

However, there were several reasons why the military dictator did not give much importance to the armed forces. Not one of the Aprista conspiracies against his government ever crystallized; all were smothered at the outset, so he never had to call upon the armed forces. In order to sustain his slogan of "Order, Peace, and Work," in order to put down uprisings, and in order to uncover conspiracies, Benavides never had to go beyond the police, particularly the investigative police and his own well-paid secret police. The armed forces served only as guarantors of the stability of the dictatorship, not as an active instrument of repression.

The recurrence of militarism in Peru with the coup of Sánchez Cerro and its consolidation under Benavides were not isolated incidents in Latin America. On the contrary, they constituted what we might say was characteristic of the period. During these years, there were only four countries ruled by popularly elected civilians: Colombia, Uruguay, Chile, and Costa Rica.

Europe was dominated by Hitler, Mussolini, Franco, and Salazar—four dictators backed by their respective armed forces. The dictatorship of Stalin in the Soviet Union completes the picture of an epoch that was characterized by the crisis of bourgeois democracy on a worldwide scale.

In 1939, Manuel Prado became president of the republic. APRA came out of hiding, the Aprista prisoners were set free, and there was a type of undeclared amnesty. It was not what APRA wanted, however, for semilegality hardly suited them. Prado did not fulfill his part of the political bargain, and APRA moved into open opposition and subsequently back into hiding.

The Prado government was constitutional in origin, but it lost its claim to constitutionality by violating statutory guarantees. The armed forces, in obedience to that same constitution, had to defend the government. It is said that the Prado government was oligarchical and consequently the military supported the oligarchy. This is true, but it is also true that the army, according to the constitution, does not question, it only obeys. It could also be said that if the oligarchy is in power that the armed forces are not responsible, but rather the people who elected it. Nevertheless, the army did uphold that tyrannical regime.

On the one hand, the armed forces were accused of collaboration with tyranny, and, on the other, they were urged to revolt. APRA did both at once. In some clandestine publications, APRA invoked the constitution and reminded the armed forces, with frequent insistency, of their duty to respect the constitution. In other flyers and broadsides, APRA blamed the armed forces for the state of the country. At the same time, Apristas sought contacts with high military officers and tried to conspire for the overthrow of the Prado regime. Those same officers, however, were satisfied with the government and invoked the classic slogan used when they want to remain passive: "We do not get involved in politics."

The Aprista party held a leadership convention in 1942 and among other things issued a "Political Declaration," which held that the Prado regime was carrying out "an antidemocratic policy of persecution of APRA and a policy of denying citizen rights." The party also issued a call to the armed forces to come out in defense of the constitution, an action which "would not constitute subversion of the public order, but rather would mean the preservation of constitutional order and of the democratic norms of the nation which every Peruvian has the civic duty to respect and defend."

But the ranking officers of the armed forces remained deaf to Aprista demands. Only when the party shared power in 1945 did those same officers declare their long-standing sympathy for *Aprismo*. It should be noted, and many observers have already written on the subject, that this phenomenon is common in Latin America. The high command of the armed forces always identifies with the oligarchy that governs their respective nations, while the younger officers, on the other hand, try to get closer to the people and support them in their struggle for social change.

At any rate, the armed forces are constantly pressured by the bourgeoisie to leave their barracks and intervene in the political process of the country. The Aprista party, representing the petit bourgeoisie, acted the same way with the two military strata: officers and enlisted men, and within the first, senior and junior officers. To the first they talked about the necessity of respecting the constitution, of returning to the democratic course, and of fighting against communism, which is to say they emphasized conservative positions.

To the younger officers and to the enlisted men, the Apristas spoke of establishing social justice, of the great changes needed by the country, and of the destruction of the oligarchy. The Aprista preachings had a greater impact among the junior officers than on the senior ones. In addition, the Apristas knew of the honesty of the younger officers, so they talked to them of the fatherland, not of the party, of the people and not of *Aprismo*. What APRA wanted was to take power, but they wanted someone else to do it for them. Therefore, they encouraged the militaristic attitudes of the army. . . .

At the beginning of 1945, the end of the Axis Powers was in sight, the fall of German Nazism and of Mussolini's fascism was imminent. The fervent admirers of those ideas in Peru were crestfallen. The generals who before had had no objections to heaping praise on the totalitarian dictators now preferred to turn their attention to the Allied officers and speak of the advantages of democracy, including in that term, the Red Army which had succeeded in resisting Hitler's army.

Translated, reprinted, and edited from *El militarismo en el Perú* (Lima: T. Scheuch, 1962), pp. 52–107. Víctor Villanueva slightly revised this article in September 1976 for publication in this volume.

4
The United States and
Latin American Military Politics

The United States and Military Politics in Latin America

After World War II, the United States sought to incorporate Latin American military establishments into the Western defense alliances against the expansion of international socialism. The Río Pact of 1945 bound Latin American nations, at least formally, to a collective security arrangement explicitly oriented against "Communist" intervention. But just as only Brazil had actually sent armed forces to fight against the Axis Powers in World War II, only Colombia participated in the war to "contain Communism" in Korea. Thus, the Latin American military establishments remained largely without a serious professional mission to perform in regard to defending their nations against external threats. Then came the Cuban Revolution. On January 27, 1959, shortly after the victory of Fidel Castro over Fulgencio Batista's dictatorship, Ernesto "Che" Guevara outlined the implications of the Cuban Revolution for the rest of Latin America:

The example of our revolution for Latin America and the lessons it implies have destroyed all the cafe theories; we have shown that a small group of resolute men supported by the people and not afraid to die if necessary can take on a disciplined regular army and completely defeat it. This is the basic lesson. There is another, which our brothers in Latin America in economically the same position agriculturally as ourselves should take up, and that is there must be an agrarian revolution and fighting in the countryside and the mountains. The revolution must be taken from there to the cities.
. . .

It did not matter that Batista's army was hardly disciplined or that Fidel's *guerrilleros* never "completely defeated" a regular army in pitched battle. The Cuban experience was to provide an inspiration to Latin American revolutionaries such as Chilean presidential candidate Salvador Allende, who proclaimed in 1960:

Cuba's fate resembles that of all Latin American countries. They are all underdeveloped—producers of raw materials and importers of industrial products. In all these countries, imperialism has deformed the economy, made big profits, and established its political influence. The Cuban Revolution is a national revolution, but it is also a revolution of the whole of Latin America. It has shown the way for the liberation of all our peoples.

If many on the political left saw Cuba as a hope for the future, policy makers in the United States and traditional power holders in Latin America came more and more to fear the spread of the Cuban Revolution or its principles to the rest of Latin America. Furthermore, the fate of the Cuban officer corps was not lost on the military establishments in the rest of the hemisphere.

From 1961 onward, the United States, in cooperation with Latin American governments and military elites, organized a counterthrust to the Cuban Revolution: the "Alliance for Progress." The Alliance, however, came more and more to be an alliance between United States policy makers and Latin American counterrevolutionaries and military elites.

During 1962 and 1963, the United States expanded its counterinsurgency programs and training capabilities. These included the army's special forces, the Southern Command in the Panama Canal Zone, and the center at Fort Bragg, North Carolina. The Agency for International Development (AID) established the Inter-American Police Academy in the Canal Zone in 1962. From 1962–68, United States military missions provided training, support, and personnel to assist Latin American regimes in the destruction of guerrilla movements and other opposition (at times even banditry) to incumbent governments. These combined United States-local military efforts were overwhelmingly successful, culminating in 1967 with the deaths of Che Guevara and his guerrilla band in Bolivia.

The training received by Latin American military officers and police officials as part of the counterinsurgency programs had more than simple technical substance and implications. This training not only prepared officers to lead troops against insurgents, but also led them to ask questions about why such operations were necessary in their countries. The answers to these questions involved complex relationships among (1) international communism, (2) Cuba, (3) the lack of economic development in their countries, and (4) the ineptitude and corruption of civilian politicians.

In the United States there were some policy makers who resisted the United States role in fomenting counterrevolution and military rule in Latin America. Despite such objections, however, the United States role in assisting, training, and buttressing military expansion and rule in Latin America continued, as evidenced by the selection which describes the activities of the United States Army School of the Americas. By 1975, over 70,000 Latin Americans had been trained in the United States, in the Canal Zone, or in various Latin American countries by United States military instructors. In 1972, a highly sophisticated theoretical formulation of the United States view toward stability operations (as elaborated by Raymond Barrett) made clear the United States support for military rule in Latin America.

In this context, Latin American leftists and reformers became increasingly aware of the United States role in maintaining dictatorship or military rule. The selection by John Saxe-Fernández analyzes the motivation and implications of these United States policies, especially with regard to the Central American nations.

U.S. Army School of the Americas

U.S. military missions were established in Latin America during World War II to perform two primary functions—to serve as a liaison between the Latin American and U.S. military establishments and to offer training to members of the Latin American armed forces.

Although the military missions are relatively new, the concept of collective security which they embody dates back to 1815 when the idea was first advanced by Simón Bolívar. Not until 1936, however, was the concept adopted in principle by all American republics. By 1941, as a direct result of Nazi-Fascist activity in the hemisphere, U.S. army missions had been established in every capital of Latin America.

Once established, the missions noted the lack of training capability in various Latin American countries. A number of the missions requested that Latin American military and paramilitary personnel be allowed to attend Canal Zone service schools, which had been functioning to train U.S. personnel stationed in the zone. Thus, between 1943 and 1945, a total of 423 Latin Americans from eleven nations acquired skills as motor mechanics, radio operators, clerks, and food service specialists.

Schools Consolidated

When the war ended, the missions continued to send students for schooling and plans were formulated for a Latin American-oriented, U.S.-administered training center. In 1946, the Latin American Training Center was established at Fort Amador in the Canal Zone to centralize administrative tasks involved in training the increasing number of Latin Americans attending U.S. service schools located throughout the zone. This arrangement continued until 1 February 1949, at which time all Canal Zone service schools were consolidated and moved to Fort Gulick.

A former antiaircraft post situated five miles inland from the Atlantic entrance to the canal, the post is named in honor of Major General John W. Gulick, late chief of coast artillery. Designated the U.S. Army Caribbean

148

School, the institution continued to exist primarily for the training of U.S. troops. The graduates of 1949 included 743 North Americans and 195 Latin Americans.

A reduction in U.S. troop strength in the Canal Zone beginning in 1949 was coupled with an increased demand by Latin American governments for schooling. This resulted in changes in the student body so that, by 1954, a majority of the school's students were Latin American. By 1956, all English instruction was eliminated, and the school's mission became directed almost entirely toward Latin America. In 1963, the name of the school was changed to U.S. Army School of the Americas.

Although North Americans are, for the most part, unfamiliar with the school, it has become well known and highly respected among the military establishments throughout Latin America. Those who have attended as students or rendered service as guest instructors enjoy added prestige as a result of their association with the institution.

Four Instructional Departments

The school now consists of three principal staff elements and four instructional departments. Administrative requirements, curriculum coordination, course scheduling, logistic support, and maintenance functions are centralized and directed from the staff level. This permits the four instructional departments to concentrate on academic matters.

The school conducts forty-two separate courses, some of which are offered as many as three times a year. During the past fiscal year, approximately 1,600 officers, cadets, and enlisted men attended sixty-seven courses.

One of the four instructional elements—the Department of Command—offers courses exclusively to higher level commanders and staff officers. The department's command and general staff course is a forty-week course patterned after the command and general staff course offered at Fort Leavenworth, Kansas.

Indicative of rising Latin American interest in management instruction is the preparation of two management courses for presentation in fiscal year 1971.

The Department of Combat Operations offers instruction to officers, cadets, and enlisted personnel. Two courses in irregular warfare are aimed principally at junior officers, with the varied terrain of the Canal Zone providing an ideal training environment. Because of the strong correlation between irregular warfare and the welfare of the populace, these courses emphasize civic action to include practical work in rural Panamanian villages.

This department also offers courses to cadets from military academies of eleven nations. Cadet courses range from three to forty weeks in duration. The forty-week basic officer qualification course completes the cadets' preofficer training. Cadets are taught leadership roles for units assigned to irregular warfare, jungle operations, and combat engineer missions. The cadets receive marksmanship and mechanical training with assorted light weapons and are thoroughly trained in tactical operations. Assaults, ambushes, and patrols are carried out both day and night in the thick, insect-infested, obstacle-ridden rain forests bordering the Panama Canal.

The cadets also study engineering techniques such as well drilling and bridge construction. These subjects complement instruction on civic action theory and will enable the cadets to play a role in the development programs undertaken by the military forces in their home countries.

Cadets studying at the school for eighteen weeks or longer complete a week-long maneuver known as the *Balboa Crossing*, in which they trek across the isthmus from Pacific to Atlantic shores on a simulated search-and-destroy mission, putting into practice what they have learned about guerrilla warfare and jungle living. The expert infantryman badge test highlights the forty-week cadet course. During current year 1969, forty-eight cadets took the examination, and four passed. This was a good percentage for this most rigorous of all U.S. army qualification tests. Cadets currently account for a third of the school's total number of graduates.

Practical Instruction

The two remaining instructional departments are Technical Operations and Support Operations. Emphasis throughout the courses of these departments is on practical instruction. Technical Operations contains communications, engineer, and maintenance instructional groups. Support Operations consists of medical, military intelligence, military police, and supply instructional elements. Courses taught by these departments are primarily intended for specialists and enlisted men, although officers also attend a number of courses.

In many Latin American nations, the armed services are one of the few institutions adequately trained, equipped, and disciplined to provide skilled technicians for the civilian economy. The school has emphasized training in technical skills for civic action programs. Over the past five years, the number of graduates from courses with direct application to programs that enhance national development exceeds 2,250, or 30 percent of the students during that period. Twenty-three of the school's forty-two courses, or slightly more than half the curriculum, fall into this category, providing training as heavy construction equipment operators, well-drilling specialists, radio repairmen, basic medical technicians, and water purification specialists.

Since 1966, the school has sponsored annually a week-long civic action seminar attended by officers of at least a dozen nations. The findings are published and distributed to agencies throughout the Americas. The school's civic action instruction stresses the pragmatic approach, opposes "give-away" programs, and emphasizes the joint nature of successful civic action activities. This includes the recipients' participation in the planning, as well as the actual work, involved in the project.

The Jungle Operations Training Center, located at Fort Sherman across the Panama Canal from Fort Gulick, presents a block of instruction in jungle warfare to Vietnam-bound U.S. personnel. The same subject matter is taught by the school to Latin Americans. An average of 180 students from the school go through the rugged course twice a year. Cadets who attend the school for ten weeks or longer and officers attending irregular warfare courses receive this training.

The school is presently staffed by approximately 60 officers and 130 enlisted men, most of whom are bilingual. The school not only caters to students of the Americas but is staffed by instructors from all sections of the hemisphere as well. Guest instructors normally serve for a period of one year. Most of these are former students and, in many cases, honor graduates of the courses they attended. More than 300 instructors have served with the school in a guest capacity, carrying instructional loads equal to those of their U.S. counterparts. Ranks of the present group of 30 guest instructors range from corporal to lieutenant colonel.

The school does not attempt to compete with the fifteen specialized service schools in the United States from which it draws its curriculum. Since English is not a prerequisite for attendance, the target group of students includes most of the military personnel in Spanish-speaking Latin America. Instructional standards are kept high, but the failure rate is only slightly more than 1 percent.

Special efforts are made to keep instruction current. Translation of U.S. army field and technical manuals has, therefore, become a major extrainstructional undertaking at the school, which is responsible for translating all academic material. Some 25,000 to 30,000 pages of instructional material are translated annually into Spanish.

In virtually all courses, students receive classes in methods of instruction to enable them to impart their newly acquired skills to fellow nationals upon return to their home countries. In this sense, the 25,000 Latin American graduates of the school represent but a portion of the actual number of persons reached by the school. Venezuela's Military Academy was originally staffed by nearly 100 graduates of the Latin American Training Center. Similarly, the Peruvian Armed Forces Motor Mechanics School was founded by early graduates of the center.

During the past decade, Latin American graduates have increased from an annual average of 1,000 in 1959 to some 1,600 today. The 350 students who attend the school at any one time represent all Latin American nations, with the exception of Costa Rica, Cuba, Haiti, and Mexico. No one particular nation receives special attention, although a number of countries send a relatively small number of students. Brazil, Argentina, and Chile, for example, have sophisticated military education systems and do not rely as heavily on the school as do other countries.

As for the future, the school may play an even greater role in the educating of Latin American military personnel. In a recommendation to President Richard M. Nixon after his mid-1969 tour through Latin America, Governor Nelson A. Rockefeller said:

In view of the growing subversion against citizens and the rapidly expanding population, it is essential that the training programs which bring military and police personnel from other hemisphere nations to the U.S. and to training centers in Panama be continued and strengthened.

Rockefeller's proposals were not limited to purely military considerations. The report also dealt with

the new type of military man [who] is coming to the fore and often becoming a major force for constructive social change. Unlike older generations of conservative colonels and generals who represented the landowners and fought reforms, the new officers come largely from the working class families. Increasingly, their concern and dedication is to the eradication of poverty and improvement of the lot of the oppressed.

The School of the Americas is playing a significant part in educating and training manpower for the defense and the development of the region.

Reprinted and edited from *Military Review* 50 no. 4 (April 1970), pp. 88–93.

Raymond J. Barrett

The Development Process and Stability Operations

The development process itself is highly destabilizing. Development means change and adjustment, often painful. Thus, the development process is unsettling, fraught with difficulties, and laden with potential violence.

These considerations are important to the U.S. army and to the United States generally. One of the army's three missions is labeled "Stability Operations." This mission is designed to prevent, deter, or counter destabilizing violence that threatens important interests of the United States. The means to carry out this mission are described by the army as "internal development and internal defense." More broadly, the United States still needs a way to deal with episodes of violence or instability. As our policies and public opinion evolve, the United States is less likely to intervene in such situations. But there are still those that could be very worrisome in terms of important U.S. interests. And we still need to be sure that such situations do not get out of hand.

In the context of the destabilizing nature of the development process, the concepts of stability operations, internal development, and internal defense are ticklish indeed. In fact, the idea of *stability* operations may well be misleading. The basic situation is not stability interrupted by occasional violence, but, rather, continuous change and adjustment, constantly threatening to deteriorate into instability or violence. Stability, at least as we tend to conceive it, is short-lived or absent. Instability, actual or potential, is the dominant condition.

Vulnerability is an integral part of the development process. Development means change, and change means that things are going to be different. To the degree that change is resisted, violence is also a possibility, if not a likelihood. The problem, then, is how to channel change in [a] constructive fashion while trying to avoid excessively disruptive instability or violence. The emphasis needs to be on the uncertainties, the likelihood of discontent and potential disruption, and the difficulties of keeping change in constructive channels.

These characteristics of the development process have many important implications for the army's stability operations mission and for the content and tone of our concepts of internal development and internal defense. They also have a significant impact on U.S. understanding of violence and instability in the world and on U.S. policy toward these problems. To pinpoint these

153

implications, it is necessary to analyze the disruptive nature of the development process.

Perhaps it is best to stress first that the development process cannot be stopped or deterred. The aspirations for a better life imbue all parts of the world. The striving for economic and social betterment is intense and likely to grow more so in the foreseeable future. In short, our problem in understanding and living with the development process is real and will not go away. Our only realistic choice is to try to cope with the turbulence of social, economic, political, and psychological change.

Development is disruptive in many ways. One of its most crucial impacts is on the basic question of viable government. Why do the processes and institutions of government seem so fragile in developing countries? Because development means challenge to or displacement of ruling elites. We are so used to our form of government that we overlook how unstable democracy is when examined dispassionately. Our peaceful transfer of power is based on the awareness that the "outs" and the "ins" will ultimately shift places; it, therefore, behooves the "ins" to treat the "outs" with the same kind of respect and consideration they will need once they are the "outs."

This experience, this awareness, is not yet a reality in developing countries. Much more real is the contest of aspirations. In important measure, development means realizing some of the aspirations of significant portions of the populace. However, aspirations for a better way of life can only be satisfied if groups not among the existing elites get some say over matters affecting them. This, in turn, means some challenge to or displacement of the existing ruling elites.

Effective labor unions, for instance, challenge or reduce the power previously held by businessmen; agrarian reform reduces the economic, social, and political dominance of the landed aristocracy. To the degree that others achieve some control over their destinies, the ruling elites are no longer masters of society or government to the extent that they had been. Their power to rule is threatened or diminished.

Obviously, this sort of change has an important impact not only on the attitudes, but on the realities of power. Certainly, it is not surprising that this displacement, even though seemingly modest, is seldom easy and often resisted. Equally, it is not surprising that this change has sometimes been attended by violence, either by way of revolt or by attempts at repression.

In similar fashion, the creation of viable political institutions in developing countries is understandably difficult. Only recently, as our institutions have been challenged by dissidents, has it become clearer to most Americans that institutions reflect political realities and not vice versa. Political institutions in developing countries reflect, as we have just noted, a real and fundamental conflict of interest in the society. The ruling elites understandably tend to resist change, even evolutionary change. They are largely satisfied with things as they are because they are benefiting. Even preliminary or partial change is resisted because of its ultimate implications.

Looked at from the narrow viewpoint of the ruling elite, any concession is the opening wedge to a process that will eventually displace them. And they are right, from their point of view. This is a point often overlooked by outsiders, such as ourselves, who view development as inherently equitable and desirable. The ultimate result of the development process, if it is to proceed at all, is substantial lessening of the power of the ruling elite.

A change in institutions is, or foreshadows, a change in political power. The threat to the ruling elite is thus fundamental in their eyes, and they will resist altering the institutions. In fact, they are likely to feel themselves increasingly insecure as the aspirations of others become clearer, whether the latter's hopes are realized or not. Similarly, the ruling elites may well become increasingly adamant as they perceive the likely dimensions of the changes being sought. This phenomenon is an important factor in the oft-noted and apparently irrational resistance to seemingly modest or moderate change in political institutions in developing nations.

On the other hand, those groups seeking fulfillment of their aspirations are likely to become increasingly insistent. The apparent intransigence of the ruling elites raises questions regarding the equity and validity of existing political institutions. Not only do they react against the restraints of the ruling elites, but their desires for change tend to become increasingly specific. Even more broadly, these groups tend to seek not only an effective role in decisions regarding their particular interest, but also in the general concerns of the society and government. If the realization of their aspirations is delayed, as it often is, they are likely to become increasingly frustrated and amenable to violent solutions.

Both sets of attitudes and behavior are quite understandable. But they are not conducive to the development of viable political institutions. Nor are they likely to produce the attitudes of cooperation and mutual accommodation essential to evolutionary political development.

Another destabilizing feature of development is the competition for resources and status that is involved. To some degree, development generally increases the resources available in a society. But under the best of circumstances, the total resources are limited and not adequate to meet all the pressing needs.

The ruling elites are likely to resent, and probably to resist, the increasing claims by other groups against the resources they have long controlled. Yet aspirations in the society can only be satisfied in two ways: either resources must be diverted from those controlled by the ruling elites; or the new resources generated, primarily from the assets of the elites, must be allocated almost entirely to meet unfulfilled aspirations. In either case, the ruling elites are likely to feel deprived and resentful, quite possibly to the point of active resistance.

A typical example is agrarian reform. To meet peasant aspirations, there must be land distribution at the expense of the landed elite. Or productivity must be increased to provide the means to absorb the agricultural labor as it becomes surplus or disenchanted. This situation has created an acute dilemma in virtually every developing nation. It has been attended by great frustration, resistance, and often violence. Few, if any, developing nations have solved it without great social dislocation and violence. It is still unsolved in many countries and remains a difficult and disruptive problem.

The allocation of resources often comes down to a question of money. To the ruling elite, additional expenditures for development programs mean increased taxes, or, in other words, a requisition of some of their resources, seemingly for the benefit of others. Aspirant groups, on the other hand, want to have extensive development programs as a means to improve their status. Because of the potential benefits to them and their own limited resources, these groups will not be particularly troubled by the thought of increased taxes. In addition to the actual redistribution of resources, this situation strongly reinforces the conflicting attitudes among social groupings and the consequent destabilizing effects.

The changes that development involves also challenge cultural beliefs and patterns. This observation, of course, has often been made. However, cultural patterns tend to reflect the economic and social arrangements through which the society operates. Much of the cultural conditioning is not consciously perceived, and, to this degree, threatened change is more likely to elicit irrational response. In short, it is worth noting that cultural patterns add an important element of rigidity that increases the potential for frustration and resultant violence and instability in development.

Development is destabilizing in another direction because change tends to foster many economic and social inequities. Education, for instance, is clearly of basic importance to increase the number and variety of trained personnel, without which development cannot proceed. But it has become quite apparent that education is not an unmixed blessing. If appropriate jobs do not increase in proportion to the output of educated people, frustration and disruption are highly likely to result.

With all the uncertainties and delays in the development process, keeping opportunity and training in parallel is all but impossible. Consequently, the phenomenon of the frustrated intellectual has become a common characteristic of the development process. In addition to his own frustration, he serves as a catalyst for the discontent of others, thus increasing the potential for instability or violence.

The development of an education system can have other disruptive effects, often extending far out into the society. For instance, a broad and vigorous increase in elementary education is an essential step in almost any development program. The disruptive effects of even so beneficial and necessary an effort as this can be illustrated by outlining what actually happened in one case.

In one country, children had to be gathered from considerable distances because of the rural population patterns. Many of the new elementary schools, therefore, had to provide boarding facilities. Thus, in addition to the normal school plant, such facilities as dormitories, meals, dining halls, and medical care had to be included. One immediate practical consequence was a marked increase in the operating costs of the educational system. There were also important social and cultural impacts on the students living in this new manner. There were even significant nutritional and health consequences because of the improved dietary and medical care.

Another important change was the removal of these students from the extended family. In many cases, they had been part of the family's labor supply. To enable the families to survive economically, compensatory assistance had to be provided. This again increased the operating costs of the educational system. It also made an important change in the extended family system by introducing cash income to what had been an almost entirely subsistence economic and social arrangement.

The cultural conditioning of both the families and the students was also greatly altered by this removal of younger members during their formative stages. The amount of change involved in this one instance is obvious. In the aggregate, the disruptive potential of changes such as these is profound, and sometimes their impact can be enormous.

Change is usually inequitable, and this, too, is disruptive. The ruling elites because of their already well-established position will benefit, or appear to benefit, from almost any development program. Certainly, those groups in favor with the regime in power are likely to do better than others. Inevitably, some groups benefit more than others from development programs. Similarly, various groups will feel, rightly or wrongly, that others have received greater benefits than they have. Either way, dissatisfaction and the potentials for disruption are increased.

Furthermore, if a change of regime should take place, the situation can be appreciably worsened. Often, those entering the ruling elites are not only anxious to get in on the benefits, they also take punitive action against those who had formerly benefited. A debilitating sequence of reprisals and resentment can easily be set in train. Feelings of inequity are easily aroused in the atmosphere of aspirations and frustration that is the essence of the development process. Again, the potentials for violence and instability are enormous.

In closing this review of some of the particularly destabilizing features of the development process, it is probably prudent to make clear that this analysis focuses on the problems. Social, economic, and political development is clearly essential to achieve the world of free and independent nations that we and most people seek. And beneficial development does take place in a multitude of ways. If anything, there is a tendency, looking at the long, hard way to go, to discount how much real progress has been made. We are concerned here to identify better the difficulties in development so that we can better help the process.

The destabilizing nature of the development process has many practical implications for the concepts of internal defense and internal development. One that should be prominent is the attitude of mind in approaching questions of internal defense. The idea of "stability" can be seriously misleading. Stability in the sense of law and order is but a limited part of the picture. Development is a disruptive process and one that continually threatens to get out of bounds. In fact, it almost certainly will get out of bounds occasionally. The disruptive potentials are so constant and considerable as to be almost certain to produce some episodes of violence.

The only realistic concept is probably one of minimizing overt violence and trying to prevent it from becoming so excessive as to disrupt development itself. In fact, fully "peaceful change" may often be impossible. A more realistic concept may be "largely nonviolent change."

Our doctrine should be written in these terms. It is not at present. The considerations should be clearly and pervasively written into our doctrine, training, programs, and procedures. The fragile and disruptive nature of development should suffuse our own doctrine.

It is important to be careful in identifying violence. We must distinguish between the type of disorder and instability that is a function of national growth and that in which violence is fomented or exploited in ways inimical to economic, social, and political development. To oppose all instances of instability or disorder is impossible. To try to do so is likely to make the eventual instability or violence far more disruptive.

History suggests that it is not possible to entirely deprive people of the use of force for social change. Repressive action can force the pressures for change outside legal or acceptable channels and into subversion. In some cases, a certain amount of potential or actual violence may be necessary to obtain political, economic, or social change toward equitable development. The history of the United States, from the American Revolution to the civil rights protests of recent years, is replete with examples of this phenomenon. The practical need is not only to be aware of the constant potential for violence, but to discriminate carefully in assessing the nature of episodes of violence when they occur.

The United States, as a matter of policy, does not regard every situation of instability or disorder and violence as a threat to U.S. interests. The United

States would usually prefer basic changes in a society to be evolutionary rather than revolutionary. But we acknowledge that the development process is generally accompanied by unrest, upheaval, and violence. In fact, U.S. policy explicitly notes that, in some cases, the forces making for instability and political upheaval may contribute, in the long run, to achieving objectives deserving U.S. encouragement and support.

The primary U.S. goal is to enable the changes inherent in the development process to take place in as orderly a manner as possible and without outside interference. The under secretary of state for political affairs made these points explicit in saying: "What we must guard against is disruptive change, change which results in instability and violence."

This discriminating and realistic approach should also be explicitly incorporated in army and other U.S. doctrine and programs. It is not there now—certainly not in the careful and forceful way that it should be. An understanding and candid evaluation of violence, when it does occur, is fundamental to any program of internal defense.

Also essential is a pragmatic attitude toward the political process in developing countries. For one thing, it is understandable why political developments so often tend toward confrontation. At work are real conflicts of interests as resources, status, and governing power are being changed. The issues often are stark, and the questions raised for the participants are traumatic. Discussions understandably tend to be emotional and dogmatic. The tone of debate and the political process are thus extreme. Counsels of calm and compromise, typical of more developed societies, hardly accord with the realities.

The political process in developing countries also reflects the high premium on unity and a sense of nationhood. These concepts provide a broader context to try to contain and channel some of the aspirations and discontents. The result can often be a nationalistic assertiveness, pride, and sense of independence. Stimulating a feeling of common purpose serves a positive and well-nigh essential psychological role in the development process. Similarly, developing countries often adopt a distinctly neutralist stance in the world or simply avoid involvement in many international questions. Again, this behavior tends to mitigate the disruptive potentials by at least reducing the possibilities of additional destructive elements from outside.

We sometimes find this type of behavior exasperating. Often, we feel these attitudes counterproductive in terms of what we believe to be in the best interests of a particular society. Perhaps we should recall our own history. George Washington and the Founding Fathers devoted a great deal of their efforts to nurturing the fragile, newly born United States of America and the development of a sense of U.S. identity. They also maneuvered very adroitly to reduce or avoid entanglements with the great powers of the day, who were far from prepared to leave the new republic alone. The United States developed a fetish of neutrality, and Americans were very brash and assertive about their talents and destinies.

All of these are features of most of today's developing countries. The historical persistence of this type of behavior suggests that it is an inherent characteristic of the development process. It behooves us, therefore, to show sympathy and understanding and to use our common historical antecedents as positive assets in U.S. relations with the presently developing countries.

An important element in the character of political institutions in a developing nation is the desirability of muting changes. Multiparty democracy institutionalizes antagonisms and change. Having in mind the sharply contending forces in developing society and the consequent potentials for violence, it probably asks too much of human beings to expect regular and peaceful changes in the ruling power. One-party regimes thus seem to reflect important forces at work on the political institution building process. The preference for one-party states in most developing countries should, by now, have suggested to us that this is a possible corollary of the development process.

On the record, there is often considerable variety of viewpoint in one-party regimes. A good case can often be made that the reasonable aspirations of the people are being met and the quality of life improved. At the same time, this type of institution helps channel the inherent differences and offers a better framework for unity and a wider sense of common purpose. We do not have to endorse any and all one-party regimes. Some are clearly oppressive. But we do have to understand the legitimacy of this approach to political institutions and be prepared to work with it.

What is probably most important regarding political institutions in developing countries is how they handle change. There is no general formula. But, obviously, the more rigid the system the more likely destabilizing violence will be. Similarly, the sharper and the more emotionally that change is structured in the system, the more chance for disruption. Nor is emphasis in local institutions enough to defuse the dangers. Cooperatives, committees, labor unions, and similar organizations can be used to focus on specific problems, but only within fairly narrow limits. Issues soon become national because the underlying aspirations are general in nature. Tangible benefits from the governing process are essential. The most critical need is institutions that are clearly seen to be equitable and effective.

The nature of political institutions also has an important bearing on the types of organizations feasible for internal defense. Our doctrine talks a great deal about nation building, interagency coordination, and even such specific entities as National Command Centers, Area Command Centers, and advisory committees, etc. Our relatively sophisticated prescriptions assume a unity of purpose and institutional viability that may well be lacking in a developing society. In the area of institutions, our doctrine should be made a good deal more qualified and tentative.

In similar fashion, our internal development concepts need to be more fully caveated. The disruptive nature of the development process itself means that economic and social improvements by themselves are not likely to prevent violence and destruction, particularly in the earlier stages of development.

Most developing countries, despite earnest and often extensive development programs, have experienced violence in greater or lesser degree. The record of recent decades suggests this corollary, one we have been slow to appreciate fully. Violent destruction seems to be reduced only when economic and social development are thoroughly taking hold and become generalized during the period in the development process that has been labeled the takeoff stage. Our internal development concepts must make explicit an awareness that potential and actual violence must be taken into account realistically.

One particularly sensitive consideration is the dual nature of programs for improved communications between populace and government. We are fond of advocating such devices. They can provide strength against subversion. But they can also foster or strengthen discontent by stimulating awareness and focussing aspirations. They also offer a lucrative target for exploitation by malcontents, and, if captured by such forces, greatly increase the likelihood of instability. The key requirement, which we should feature in our approach, is that the rate of increase in the sense of popular participation and improvement must exceed the rate of increase in manifest discontent.

The real and constant possibility of violence means an ever present threat of destructive insurgency. Realistically, therefore, if development is to proceed toward realizable goals, an essential element is a carefully trained internal security establishment.

Reprinted and edited from *Military Review* 50 no. 2 (November 1972), pp. 58–68.

John Saxe-Fernández

A Latin American Perspective on the Latin American Military and Pax Americana

North American Military Policy in Latin America

North American military policy has undergone a noticeable change in the sixties. It is divided into two periods: one from 1942 to 1960, in which a series of measures to guarantee the defense of the continent against any external aggression are established, and another since 1960, which emphasizes programs of internal repression and civic military action.

I. During the Second World War, the United States Congress granted a help of $400 million worth of equipment to the Latin American military establishments. In 1942 all the Latin American nations agreed to cooperate with the United States when, in a declaration issued in Rio de Janeiro, they stated that any act of aggression from a non-American state to any American nation would be considered as an aggression to all the countries under the agreement. At the end of the war, this structure was perpetuated in the Chapultepec Act (1945), which was later incorporated in the 1947 Rio de Janeiro Treaty. From 1952 on, military assistance to Latin America was considerably increased under the Mutual Security Act of 1951.

Under the Mutual Security Act, a variety of terms and conditions had to be met before the Latin American nations could "benefit" from military assistance. Two of the basic requirements to obtain funds were: (a) subscription to bilateral treaties, and (b) authorization to establish American military missions.

II. In the early sixties, North American civil and military strategists realized that the Soviet Union was not threatening the Latin American continent with a massive attack. As [Harold] Hovey comments, "The policy of getting ready for the external defense of the hemisphere, typified by the Pact of Rio de Janeiro and indicated by the nature of North American military assistance, seemed to imply preparations for a non-existent threat." On the other hand, the Soviet Union's development of intercontinental missiles and nuclear weapons made obvious the uselessness of Latin American armies in the eventuality of a Third World War.

UNITED STATES MILITARY AID TO LATIN AMERICA, 1952–61

Fiscal Year	Amount (In dollars)
1952	200,000
1953	11,200,000
1954	34,500,000
1955	31,800,000
1956	30,400,000
1957	43,900,000
1958	47,900,000
1959	54,000,000
1960	53,700,000
1961	91,600,000

SOURCE: Remarks by Senator Gruening in Senate Debate, August 21, 1962. Reported in *Congressional Record*, p. 14414.

The attention of the strategists was concentrated on the "wars of national liberation," which stirred the so-called underdeveloped world. The Cuban Revolution finally shattered the nervous system of imperial United States. As an answer, the previous policy of "external defense" was abandoned in favor of policies of "internal security," which include the immediate military preparation to fight against any type of subversion. The era of "counterinsurgency" began, a prophylactic military term equivalent to "counterrevolution." As a part of such a strategy the Alliance for Progress program was initiated. This program, together with those of civic military action, tends to create antisubversive "prophylactic belts." Brigadier General Enemark expressed this idea before the American Senate Foreign Relations Committee:

The role of Latin American security forces (not only the police but also the Army) is of a basic importance. In order for the Alliance for Progress to have any chance of success, the governments must have enough power to control subversion, prevent terrorism, and eliminate flows of violence which may reach unmanageable proportions.

In the beginning of the Alliance for Progress era, Latin American armed forces began to receive the explicit approval of the American Congress. In 1961, a study mission sent by the American Senate, after a tour of Latin America, advised the American government to "take a more favorable attitude toward the military groups in most Latin American countries. . . . We are convinced that the military are not only the sole forces of stabilization, but they also promote democratic institutions and progressive changes of a socioeconomic nature." After Kennedy's assassination, Assistant Secretary of State Thomas Mann saw to it that such opinions reached the American executive power.

With the exception of naval defense programs, military assistance to Latin America is concentrated on internal security and civic military action projects. To implement these programs, higher budgets were promoted, adequate training and equipment provided, and military bureaucracies reorganized:

A. *Budget*. When counterinsurgency and civic action programs were established early in 1960, United States military assistance to Latin America doubled. It is estimated that in the decade of the fifties the yearly average of United States military assistance to Latin America was $35 million, while for the years 1960 to 1965, the annual average was over $70 million.

B. *Equipment and training* are being provided according to the new strategic requirements. The so-called School of the Americas in the Canal Zone has trained over 16,000 Latin American students in counterinsurgency and civic action. According to the annual report of the United States Defense Department, "the emphasis of the training has been given to counterinsurgency. . . . The courses and operations of counterinsurgency . . . were started in July 1961, and they take place four times a year." As of 1964, from a total of 16,343 Latin American students trained, 8,154 were Central Americans. By countries the distribution was as follows:

Country	Number
Costa Rica	1,639
El Salvador	358
Guatemala	958
Honduras	810
Nicaragua	2,969
Panama	1,420
Total for Central America	8,154
Total for Latin America	16,343

C. *Bureaucracy*. The Latin American armed forces leadership is trained at the Army Special Warfare Center at Fort Bragg, North Carolina. This training center is under the United States Continental Army Command (CONARC) supervision. Its purpose is to conduct the training of the "special forces," psychological warfare, and counterinsurgency units. The courses and training received by the Latin American personnel were described by Assistant Secretary of State Edwin M. Martin. The training program includes subjects such as "riot control, counter-guerrilla operations and tactics, intelligence and counter-intelligence, and other subjects which will contribute to the maintenance of public order, and the support of Constitutional Governments."

The counterinsurgency and civic action blueprint has been extended to every aspect of the program of military aid to Latin America. William S. Gaud, administrator for the International Development Agency (AID) said recently at

The United States and Latin American Military Politics

a press conference: "That program—of military aid—is directed towards training for internal security and Civic Action." Lincoln Gordon, former assistant secretary for inter-American affairs, maintains that the "Latin American Armed Forces are developing an increasing capacity to face any threat to their internal security."

COUNTERINSURGENCY AND CIVIC ACTION
ORGANIZATIONAL MODEL FOR TRAINING

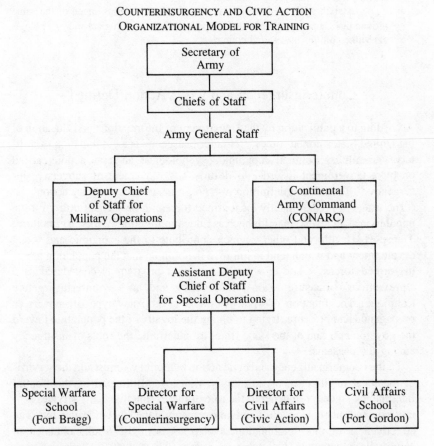

SOURCE: United States Department of the Army, Organizations for Counterinsurgency and Civic Action (Civil Affairs School, Fort Gordon, Ga., 1964).

D. *The Heirs of Camelot.* After the "Camelot debacle" (a U.S. government project in Latin America in which many U.S. social scientists became involved) a series of projects covering the same grounds was initiated:

　　1. *Project Role* "is studying the changing roles of indigenous military establishments."

2. *Project Resettle* "is probing the problems of agrarian colonization in cooperation with the Peruvian government."
3. *Project Simpático* "is an effort in Colombia to analyze military civic action programs and their effect on the attitudes of people."
4. *Project Secure* "is a study of internal security problems such as riot control."
5. *Project Numismatics* "is an analysis of the strategic and tactical factors underlying military counterinsurgency operations."
6. ". . . A sixth study—whose title is classified—is covering much of the same ground that Camelot set out to do: 'to explore major sociological and psychological vulnerabilities in selected countries. . . .' "

Counterinsurgency and Civic Action Defined

According to a publication by the Department of Information and Education of the United States armed forces, "counterinsurgency is a combination of military, paramilitary, political, economic, psychological, and civic actions carried on by a Government in order to destroy any movement of subversive insurgency." The official definition of "programs of civic military action" is: "The usage of predominantly local armed forces, in projects of utility for the population at all levels, in fields such as Education, Public Works, Agriculture, Transport, Health, and others, which contribute to the economic and social development and which tend to improve the opinion that the population has of the armed forces." The civic military action program is considered as a "preventive" measure against insurgency and as a counterinsurgency technique. The function of civic action is to stop any type of subversive propaganda and pressure, trying to obtain the loyalty of the population toward the government, and at the same time, to undermine the roots of insurgency among the peasants.

To the counterinsurgency and civic action blueprint we must add the services of the local intelligence organizations, trained and directed by the Central Intelligency Agency. In general, the role of these "intelligence" services is to infiltrate and sabotage revolutionary movements at the level of leadership. The effectiveness of this combination is obvious from the results obtained in Venezuela, Guatemala, Colombia, and Peru, where guerrilla activities have been controlled and the guerrilla leaders systematically eliminated.

The consequences of this kind of military assistance on the political structure of Latin America have no precedents. The traditionally weak civil political structures, as opposed to the military, are reduced to virtual impotence. The impact of those kinds of programs on the poor and underdeveloped countries of Central America is still greater. John D. Powell shows how military aid has given to every member of the National Guard of Nicaragua, under the leadership of "Tachito" Somoza, an average of $930 worth of equipment and training in order to impose their power and to lead violent actions over a population whose annual income per capita is $205. In the case of Guatemala, the "military aid" has provided the average soldier with a power worth $538 (in equipment and training) to exert violence over the average Guatemalan, whose annual income is $185.

A parallel between the rationalizations under which *caudillismo* was nurtured and the slogans behind counterinsurgency and civic action programs is not difficult to visualize. The ideology for *caudillismo* was provided by nineteenth-century European positivism under the motto *Orden y Progreso* (Order and Progress). The rationalization for today's version of *caudillismo* is provided by North American militarism. Instead of *orden* we have counterinsurgency, and *progreso* is translated as civic military action.

U.S. MILITARY ASSISTANCE TO CENTRAL AMERICA

Country	Cumulative U.S. military aid, 1950–62 (Thousand dollars)	Cumulative U.S. military aid per member of armed forces (In dollars, July, 1962)
Nicaragua	3,813	930
El Salvador	1,136	169
Honduras	2,324	529
Guatemala	4,311	538
Panama	929	n.a.
Costa Rica	832	n.a.

SOURCES: Agency for International Development, U.S. Foreign Assistance, July 1, 1945 to June 30, 1962. Statistics and Reports division, AID, Washington, D.C., 1961. See also John Duncan Powell, "Military Assistance and Militarism in Latin America," *The Western Political Quarterly*, V. 18, June, 1965.

The basic deficiency of *caudillismo* and its incorporation into counterinsurgency and civic action programs is that it fails to provide the necessary democratic institutional mechanisms through which socioeconomic conflicts could be released. If a political catastrophe is to be avoided in the face of intensified economic stress and . . . demographic pressure, different interest groups (including labor unions, the intelligentsia, and peasant organizations) must be given proper institutional channels to express their tensions and demands. Gino Germani and Kalman Silvert maintain that "the military will be reduced to their barracks and their professional functions alone only when Latin American countries develop sufficiently complicated power structures and a society sufficiently flexible and integrated . . . when socioeconomic conflicts have found institutionalized expression within a common framework of shared norms." While agreeing with these authors, we must also add that current emphasis on militaristic solutions and increased military intervention in civilian affairs tend to inhibit the growth of efficient political systems. This tendency is observed not only in the banana republics but also in Latin America's biggest nations. A typical case is the recent militarization of Brazil, where the armed forces took over the executive, legislative, and judiciary powers at the municipal, state, and federal levels; militarized the labor unions; wiped out political parties; and made a mockery of all democratic institutions. In Argentina (and, with few exceptions, in the rest of Latin America) a similar situation prevails. A good share of responsibility for this condition has to be assigned to North American military policies. They inflate military power. While the counterinsurgency program trains and arms the Latin American armies, increasing their superiority over the average citizen in any situation of physical conflict, civic action provides an ideological frame which justifies and encourages military intervention in situations which would normally be under civilian control:

If "civic action" would mean tractors *instead of* tanks, encouragement of civic action could be justified even if there are doubts as to whether the military is the best and most economical agency to conduct such operations. But if we must insist that civic action must not detract from military capabilities—and the U.S. Congress has made this stipulation with the U.S. military's concurrence—then civic action is likely to mean tractors *in addition* to tanks.

To their image as the champions of anticommunism, the Latin American military have added that of economic messiahs. In fact, contemporary Latin American militarism is ideologically directed against both "Communist infiltration" and "civilian inefficiency." All military takeovers occurring between 1960 and 1965 were rationalized thusly.

Civilians are incapable of: (a) controlling communist infiltration, and (b) solving economic problems. This attitude is exemplified by the remarks two Chilean military officers made after attending a joint inter-American military maneuver: "[our] foreign colleagues seemed more convinced that it was their mission to save the hemisphere not only from the Communists but also from the Civilians."

The exuberant power gained by Latin American armed forces in the last five years seems to be placing them as a determining factor in political, economic, and even social events. It seems as if the increase in their power is reaching the takeoff stage, at which they generate their own power, with a high degree of autonomy from their respective political systems and an equally high degree of dependence on their foreign benefactors.

The growing militarism generated not only by the programs previously described but also by the explicitly favorable attitude of the United States toward military regimes is insulting to all Latin American countries. Senator Wayne Morse, alarmed by these tendencies, declared the following, when the

The United States and Latin American Military Politics

1967 program for military aid was being discussed:

The mild attitude of the United States towards the military establishments in Latin America has contributed to deny Argentina a Constitutional government. The example set by the United States by extending the economic and military aid to the staffs of the Dominican Republic, Guatemala, Honduras, Ecuador, and El Salvador, contributed to the gestation of Castelo Branco's coup d'etat in Brazil. Moreover, when we decided almost automatically to approve of such a regime and to offer it great amounts of money as aid, we encouraged the Argentinian military to overthrow their government. . . . All our reasonings that our military aid tends to teach the civilian groups to control the military have been completely contradicted by such events. The situation was deplorable enough when these coups used to happen in the small Central American republics. Now they have spread to Brazil and Argentina.

The Washington decision makers should be reminded that the periods of unprecedented *orden* and notable *progreso* provided by the caudillos were followed by national political cataclysms:

Thirty years of Díaz's "prosperity" were followed by nearly twenty years of civil war. Thirty years of Gómez's "prosperity" were followed successively by a period that came seriously close to civil war . . . and an extended period of violence. . . . The demise of Trujillo after twenty years of uninterrupted "peace" and "economic development" has left the Dominican Republic ripe for civil war. . . . No North American needs to be told what followed the prosperity of the Batista regime in Cuba.

What ought to concern us is what will follow Central American *Orden y Progreso* as well as Castelo Branco's and Costa e Silva's prosperity in Brazil and General Onganía's peace and tranquillity in Argentina. We are acutely aware of the Vietnamese nightmare, with its napalm conflagrations and human tragedy. After the Dominican affair we know that if something goes wrong in Brazil or Argentina—or for that matter in any Latin American republic—we can no longer assume immunity from American infantrymen and the latest Phantom jets. The Vietnamese experience is therefore more than an irritating irrelevancy for inter-American affairs.

Reprinted and edited from "The Central American Defense Council and Pax Americana," in Irving L. Horowitz et al., eds., *Latin American Radicalism: A Documentary Report on Left and Nationalist Movements* (New York: Random House, Vintage Books, 1969), pp. 75–101.

5
The Military Speaks for Itself

Military Spokesmen for Military Rule

In the years following the Cuban Revolution, the military antipolitics which dominated Latin America took on distinctive policy agendas from country to country. Differing policy emphases flowed from national political legacies as varied as *Peronismo* in Argentina and the Peruvian military's seeming commitment to destroy the vestiges of neofeudalism in the Peruvian Andes. Despite national idiosyncrasies, however, the following selection of speeches and policy statements by prominent military leaders in Argentina, Bolivia, Brazil, Chile, and Peru make clear an underlying unity of commitment to economic developmentalism and to antipolitics. Whether we turn to Onganía in Argentina, Ovando in Bolivia, or Velasco in Peru, we find civilian corruption, deceit, or even treason blamed for the ills of the Latin American nations. We also hear military officers promising to restore law, order, stability, and social discipline—and to repress opposition elements, whether rightist or leftist—who oppose the military program.

Without ignoring the diversity of viewpoints and ideological orientations within the military establishments of Latin America, we have chosen the selections herein in order to provide: (1) an initial statement by military leaders of the rationale for military rule in each country and (2) an assessment by those responsible for military rule of the evolution of the military regimes and their public policy initiatives. Our choice of speeches or policy statements was also influenced by the peculiarities of each case. In Argentina, Chile, and Peru, where military antipolitics was initially associated with the extended influence of a particular military officer, the choice was relatively easy. In Bolivia, where a succession of military authorities exercised authority after 1964 and military rule was less institutional than in Brazil, we have included selections from three different officers. For Brazil, in contrast, we have included speeches only by the initiator of military rule in 1964 and by the latest (1976) in a line of military-chosen officer-presidents.

Argentina

SPEECH BY PRESIDENT JUAN CARLOS ONGANÍA, 1966

Armed Forces of the Nation:
Again on the eve of the birth date of the Argentine Republic, her men in arms come together around a common table in all the barracks of the country. Once again we come to renew our old bonds of friendship and camaraderie with a profound love for the fatherland overflowing our hearts.

In the past, this great celebration was always an occasion to reaffirm, with simple eloquence, our common ideals and our common profession of service to the country. But never as today have we so profoundly felt the responsibility that the historic national process has conferred upon the armed forces. . . .

The Recent Revolution

A number of serious events led to a deceitful and decadent social situation in which we Argentines witnessed the perversion of everything that in other times had been the source of our pride. It is because of this that the revolutionary action of June 28, 1966, finds its irrefutable principles in the defense of the essential values of the republic and in the removal of those causes [of the decadent social situation thus] opening a hopeful future for the tenacity and imagination of our people. In this way 1816 and 1966, so distant in time, merge into the same revolutionary significance, with transcendental aims.

Argentina has completed a historic cycle. In the future, no one will be able to excuse his aberrancy by appealing to the legacy of some anonymous past which [once] existed. Our political and institutional resources have been exhausted. The time has come to live to our fullest capacity and to create a new nation for ourselves and for our posterity. The future will be the inexorable result of the common efforts of all of today's Argentines.

The armed forces have been the instrument of the Argentine Revolution and because of that our celebration is filled with a sense of history and responsibility. We feel as never before the essence of the *patria* overflowing our spirits because the determination of her future has coincided with the strict fulfillment of our mission.

Institutionally fixed within Argentine society, the armed forces actively participate in the national business. Their disciplinary system, which ensures subordination and hierarchical order, does not constitute an inhibition to accepting the consequences that political leadership entails, within the social body of which they form a part. Their profound spiritual constitution, the result of an education which is inspired by our historic roots, confirms the dominance of moral values over material ones and their strict acceptance by the Argentine people.

Contradictions

During the last few years, we have been witnesses to a contradictory process between the conduct of politics and the exigencies of the national reality. With the mechanism for representation damaged, the popular will was rendered impotent and the far-reaching changes so vitally needed became merely wishes. The armed forces constituted the medium of legitimate expression of that popular will which had been isolated through cunning. From that point, this revolutionary unanimity and consent were expressed in our history only when it was necessary to make a decision about the national destiny. . . .

The armed forces have begun the revolutionary process, and it is now up to the government to act to satisfy fully the pressing needs of the country. The cohesion of our institutions, which made this historically important act possible, ought to be our permanent concern because that cohesion is the maximum guarantor of the spirit that gave rise to the republic.

We will protect that unity, avoiding the moral erosion inherent in the exercise of public office, firmly convinced that an authentic and honest administration is the only means of maintaining the support and participation of the citizenry in the governmental endeavor which we are undertaking.

The modern concept of national defense also requires us to adopt a productive and intelligent system of cooperation which will permit the armed forces to overcome [their] . . . financial difficulties and to have at their disposal the means necessary to fulfill their mission. One could not conceive of any military operation without the strict cooperation of the three service branches. Therefore, we should put into professional practice this profound spirit of camaraderie that brings us together today and this unity of purpose that has made possible the legitimate interpretation of the aspirations of the citizenry.

We will integrate ourselves into a solid and efficient military entity, highly qualified to lay out the modern methods and doctrines that will allow us to carry out completely the exigencies of defending the moral and material patrimony of the nation. This contribution to the nation's transformation will be just as important as the other deeds which you have accomplished with decision and discipline, thereby earning you the respect and devotion of our citizens.

On this solemn occasion, I want to express our gratitude to all the sailors, aviators, and soldiers (who) came before us; to our old comrades who contributed their effort to the growth of the spiritual and technical character of the armed forces; to those who made our profession an apostleship of Sanmartinian virtues and bequeathed to us, with the abnegation and sacrifice of their lives, this instrument of order and liberty that has just lent such signal service to the republic; and to all the men of the air, sea, and land who today guard our frontiers and who are present in spirit at this glorious celebration of the birth date of our fatherland.

As president of the nation, I pray that this unity which we reaffirm today will inspire the solidarity of the Argentines and make us deserving of their respect and everlasting gratitude.

Translated and reprinted from *La Prensa* (Buenos Aires), July 7, 1966.

THE ARMED FORCES' DECISION TO ASSUME THE DIRECTION OF THE STATE
1976

Since all constitutional mechanisms have been exhausted and since all possibility of rectifications within the institutional framework has ended and since the impossibility of recovery through normal processes has been irrefutably demonstrated, the armed forces must put an end to the situation which has burdened the nation and compromised its future.

Our people have suffered a new frustration. We have faced a tremendous political vacuum capable of sinking us into anarchy and dissolution. We have also been faced with the national government's inability to call the people together; with the repeated and successive contradictions evidenced by the adoption of all kinds of measures; with the lack of a government-directed strategy to confront subversion; and with the total lack of solutions for the basic problems of the nation which have resulted in the steady increase of extremism; with the total absence of ethical and moral examples which the directors of the state should exhibit; with the manifest irresponsibility in the management of the economy which has exhausted the production apparatus; and with the speculation and the generalized corruption—all of which translates into an irreparable loss of greatness and of faith.

The armed forces have assumed the direction of the state in fulfillment of their unrenounceable obligation. They do so only after calm meditation about the irreparable consequences to the destiny of the nation that would be caused by the adoption of a different stance. This decision is aimed at ending misrule, corruption, and the scourge of subversion, but it is only directed at those who are guilty of crimes or abuse of power. It is a decision for the fatherland and does not suppose, therefore, to discriminate against any civic group or social sector whatever. It rejects, therefore, the disruptive actions of all extremists and the corrupting effect of demagoguery.

During the period which begins today, the armed forces will develop a program governed by clearly defined standards, by internal order and hard work, by the total observance of ethical and moral principles, by justice, and by the integral organization of man and by the respect of his rights and dignity. Thus, the republic will succeed in unifying all Argentines and will achieve the total recuperation of the national sovereignty. . . . To achieve these goals, we call upon all the men and women, without exceptions, who inhabit this land, to join together in a common effort.

Besides those shared aspirations, all the representative sectors of the country ought to feel clearly identified with and committed to the common undertaking that will contribute to the greatness of the fatherland.

This government will never be controlled by special interest groups, nor will it favor any one group. It will be imbued with a profound national spirit and will only respond to the most sacred interests of the nation and of its inhabitants.

Upon incurring such a far-reaching obligation, the armed forces issues a firm summons to the . . . citizenry. In this new stage, there is a battle post for each citizen. The task before us is both arduous and pressing. It will not be free of sacrifices, but it is undertaken with the absolute conviction that this example will be followed from top to bottom and with faith in the future of Argentina.

This process will be conducted with absolute firmness and with a spirit of service. Beginning now, this newly assumed responsibility imposes on the authorities the rigorous task of eradicating, once and for all, the vices which afflict the nation.

To achieve that, we will continue fighting, without quarter, all forms of subversion, both open and clandestine, and will eradicate all forms of demagoguery. We will tolerate neither corruption nor venality in any form or circumstance, or any transgression against the law, or any opposition to the process of restoration which has been initiated.

The armed forces have assumed control of the republic. And we want the entire country to understand the profound and unequivocal meaning of our actions so that the responsibility and the collective efforts accompanying this undertaking, which seeks the common good, will bring about, with the help of God, complete national recovery.

Signed:

Lt. Gen. Jorge Rafael Videla, commander in chief of the army

Adm. Emilio Eduardo Massera, commander in chief of the navy

Brig. Gen. Orlando Ramón Agosti, commander in chief of the air force

Translated and edited from a text of the radio announcement by the three commanding generals of the armed forces (March 25, 1976), published in *La Nacion* (Buenos Aires), March 29, 1976.

A TIME FOR FUNDAMENTAL REORGANIZATION OF THE NATION
SPEECH BY GENERAL JORGE RAFAEL VIDELA
1976

To the people of the Argentine Republic:

The country is passing through one of the most difficult periods in its history. With the country on the point of national disintegration, the intervention of the armed forces was the only possible alternative in the face of the deterioration provoked by misgovernment, corruption, and complacency.

. . . The armed forces, conscious of the fact that the continuation of this process did not offer an acceptable future for the country, put forth the only possible answer to this critical situation. Such a decision, predicated on the mission and the very essence of the military institution, was planned and executed with temperateness, responsibility, firmness, and a balance that has earned the gratitude of the Argentine people.

But it should be abundantly clear that the events which took place on March 24, 1976, represent more than the mere overthrow of a government. On the contrary, they signify the final closing of a historic cycle and the opening of a new one whose fundamental characteristic will be manifested by the reorganization of the nation, a task undertaken with a true spirit of service by the armed forces.

This process of national reorganization will require time and effort; it will require a broad capacity for living together; it will exact from each one his personal quota of sacrifice; and it will necessarily count on the sincere and complete confidence of all Argentines. The attainment of this confidence is, above all else, the most difficult of the endeavors which we have undertaken.

For many years, so many promises have been unfulfilled, so many plans and projects have failed, and so deep has been the national frustration that many of our fellow citizens no longer have faith in the word of their government leaders, even to the point of believing that public employees do not serve the people but only serve themselves. Thus, they were convinced that justice had ceased to exist for the Argentine citizen.

We will begin then by establishing a just order within which it will be incumbent upon each to work and [to] sacrifice; in which the fruits of this effort will be transformed into better living conditions for all; in which the honest and exemplary citizen will find support and encouragement; in which those who violate the law will be severely punished regardless of their rank, their power, or their supposed influence. In this way, the people will regain confidence and faith in those who govern them, and we will have established that point of departure indispensable for confronting the grave crisis which afflicts our country.

It is unnecessary to list the tragic conditions under which the country lives; each inhabitant of the fatherland knows and suffers intensely from them day after day. Nevertheless, it is worthwhile to point out some of the most important components of this situation.

The management of the state had never been so disorderly, directed with inefficiency [because] . . . of general administrative corruption and accommodating demagoguery. For the first time in its history, the nation came to the point of suspending all payments. A vacillating and unrealistic economic leadership carried the country toward recession and the beginnings of unemployment, with its inevitable sequel of anguish and desperation, a condition which we have inherited and which we will seek to alleviate.

The indiscriminate use of violence by all sides engulfed the inhabitants of the nation in an atmosphere of insecurity and overwhelming fear. Finally, institutional stagnation, manifested in the unsuccessful attempts to produce in time the urgent and profound solutions which the country required, led to a total paralysis of the state, with a power vacuum incapable of revitalizing it. . . .

Profoundly respectful of constitutional powers, the natural underpinning of democratic institutions, the armed forces, on repeated occasions, sent clear warnings to the government about the dangers that existed and also about the shortcomings of their senseless acts. Its voice went unheard, and as a consequence not one essential measure was adopted. Therefore, every hope of institutional change was completely dashed. In the face of this dramatic situation, the armed forces assumed control of the national government.

This conscious and responsibly taken action was not motivated by an interest in or a desire for power. It was in response to the demands of an indispensable obligation emanating from the armed forces' specific mission to safeguard the highest interests of the nation.

Faced with that imperative, the armed forces, as an institution, have filled the existing power vacuum and also as an institution, inspired by an authentic spirit of service to the nation, have provided a response to the national crisis by establishing objectives and guidelines for the government to develop. For us, respect for human rights is not only born out of the rule of law and of international declarations, but also it is the result of our profound and Christian belief in the preeminent dignity of man as a fundamental value.

And it is precisely to ensure the just protection of the natural rights of man that we assume the full exercise of authority; not to infringe upon liberty but to reaffirm it; not to twist justice but to impose it. After reestablishing an effective authority, which will be revitalized at all levels, we will turn to the organization of the state, whose performance will be based on the permanence and stability of juridical norms which will guarantee the primacy of law and the observance of it by the governors and governed alike.

. . . Even though the armed forces have suspended all political party activity in order to achieve internal peace, they reiterate their decision to guarantee freedom of opinion in the future to those movements authentically national in expression and [having] a proven spirit of service.

A similar attitude determines our policy in the area of labor relations, directed as much at management as at labor. Both labor and management should confine their activities to defending the legitimate aspirations of their members and avoid intruding into areas foreign to their competence.

Likewise, we trust that both workers and businessmen will be conscious of the sacrifices required in these early days and also of the unavoidable necessity of postponing requests that are just in periods of prosperity but which are unattainable in times of emergency. . . .

This immense task which we have undertaken has only one beneficiary: the Argentine people. All the government measures are aimed both at achieving general well-being through productive labor and at developing a genuine spirit of social justice in order to form a vigorous, organized, and unified society that is spiritually and culturally prepared to forge a better future.

No one should expect immediate solutions or spectacular changes in the present situation. The armed forces are cognizant of the magnitude of the task to be performed: they are aware of the profound problems to be resolved; and they know of the special interests that will oppose them on this road that everyone should travel together. But we have to travel this road with firmness, a firmness that is expressed in our decision to complete the process with a profound love of nation and without concessions to anyone. . . .

Speech by Gen. Jorge Rafael Videla. Translated and edited from *La Nación* (Buenos Aires), April 5, 1976.

Bolivia

JUSTIFICATION OF THE REVOLUTION OF NOVEMBER
SPEECH BY GENERAL ALFREDO OVANDO CANDÍA
1966

Honorable Gentlemen:

At the end of the Chaco War [(1932–35),] the new generation was confronted with the necessity of transforming the traditional society. Today, we again find ourselves obligated to resume that uncompleted task and rectify the errors of those who made a mockery of the Bolivian people's longing for liberation.

When the armed forces of the nation took charge of the government in November 1964, they found the country submerged in a desolate and chaotic situation. Nevertheless, in spite of the errors of the last regime, errors for which they will have to account before this honorable Congress and before future generations, it would be unjust to attribute all the defects of the economic, social, political, and administrative structure of the country to the political system which was ousted in November 1964. In truth, the presence of such a corrupt party at the top level of public life can only be explained in terms of the power vacuum produced in 1952 in the country as a tragic result of circumstances accumulated over decades and as an unequivocal sign of the end of a political era.

All the problems of the past were aggravated by the presence of inept and venal politicians, conspirators for the possession of power. Masters of the art of destruction, they turned out to be incapable of establishing the foundations of the Second Republic called for by the Bolivian Revolution.

Under different banners, power was always highly concentrated in the presidency, to the detriment of the other branches of government, but the despotism of the last twelve years finally transformed the republican system into a type of absolute monarchy with total power and authority. The suffrage that, as in all incipient democracies, did not have the minimum breadth or decorum that is needed to be classified as democratic, was converted into a grotesque parody of universal suffrage, which precluded all citizen participation in the determination of public affairs. In the past there had been problems

181

regarding the length of the presidential term and the pretensions of continuism, but never had the people been so stunned by the institutional means used to maintain the political leaders in power.

The . . . constitution of the state, amended to serve that end, did violence to the constitutional traditions of the country. The cabinets, which in the past had not always been constructive, now were characterized by ineptitude and servility. The all-powerful authority to select government functionaries reached every level to such a degree that the legislative branch, the judicial branch, the local governments, and the rest of the vital organs of the republic lost their institutional integrity, thereby cancelling the principle of separation of powers.

In such a state of disintegration, it was understandable that subservience would be rewarded. How painful it was for the armed forces to see the symbols of Bolívar and Sucre, of Santa Cruz, Ballivián and Linares, of Frías, Campero, Pando and Montes; of Busch and Villarroel in such unworthy hands.

The contradictions between a backward social structure and the political forms of a liberal, representative democracy were evident from the early days of the republic. The effects of that conflict were felt in many ways in the institutional life of the country. Because of that, faced both by the demand for reform and the burden of the decrepit structure, the Revolution of 1952 took place. But since the improvising leaders of the great process either did not know how or did not want to create the new vehicles for structural change, all the evils of the past were accentuated and the virtues of the people ignored.

With the inordinate growth of the executive branch, the legislative branch steadily declined. The parliament lost its majesty and functioned inefficiently. Full of revolutionary verbiage, it never did anything to develop the country. Bolivians were so humiliated that they almost seemed to lose hope of returning to representative democracy. The tribunal of the great legislators of our history surrendered in shame without playing its high and noble institutional role. In truth, very few men dignified the Parliament with their valor in those twelve years. One-partyism suffocated democracy and paralyzed the opposition. The despotism ignored the parliamentary jurisdiction. Never before then had the legislative branch sunk to such abject levels. And what about the judiciary and the municipalities? Justice was replaced with prevarication, and the municipalities, with very few exceptions, were converted into solicitous and inoperative appendages of the central government.

. . . It disturbs us to recall before this assembly such painful events, but in order to analyze the twenty-one month administration, it is necessary to re-member the economic state of the country in 1964. COMIBOL [the Bolivian Mining Corporation], the Central Bank of Bolivia, and the State Petroleum Corporation, to mention only a few of the most important national agencies, were all in a state of bankruptcy.

The process of social disintegration reached a critical point; very few institutions were spared its effects. It is enough to remember how a bureaucratic caste took over the leadership of the nation's labor organizations in order to undermine the principles of authority, democracy, and union independence.

The campesino strife, unleashed by interests of the ruling party, the labor anarchy, the administrative corruption, the incredibly low educational indices, and the growing unemployment and misery of the people were unmistakable signs of the desperate situation that prevailed.

The political parties were almost completely destroyed. Functioning only intermittently, not one party had a significant number of members because terror inhibited the active participation of the citizenry. The majority of the parties suffered both from a lack of organization and a lack of press coverage. Heavily infiltrated by spies, they were subjected to a steady campaign of vilification.

With few exceptions, the private businessmen were victims of extortion. Terrorized by the regime, they barely succeeded in surviving, abandoning all dynamic and creative drive. The muzzled press saw its freedom curtailed by censors.

Education at all levels was left helpless; both teachers and students were treated as enemies by the regime. The universities also existed under tragic circumstances, to oppression was added the burden of financial asphyxia.

Year after year, a growing number of professionals, laborers, and campesinos left the country in search of better living and working conditions. The flight of talent and human capital reached astronomical proportions, but even more serious yet was the flight of material wealth. Since the regime deemed obsequiousness to be one of the highest of ethical norms, intellectual ability was viewed with suspicion, and negativism reached such a point that it was inadvisable to strive for excellence.

This process of disintegration soon affected the ruling group itself; it ceased to be a political party and became instead an instrument of power and oppression. That process culminated in the creation of political fiefdoms located in the federal administration and distributed regionally. In this way, the most extreme forms of pressure were institutionalized. Instead of promoting the national interest through legitimate channels and through the dialogue and analysis that are the essence of democracy, they turned to threats, corruption, sabotage, and direct action which in many cases ended in crimes that went unpunished. . . .

A monstrous apparatus of political repression and demagogic practices, without precedent, was installed, converting the regime, despite its instability, into something seemingly omnipotent. Only a cold analysis of the realities, with an ardent patriotism, permitted the armed forces, seconded by the people, to destroy the artificial base of that regime and make possible again the institutional life of the country through law and progress. The state of our foreign relations was equally bad and, as a consequence, the frequent blunders endangered our national honor.

The spirit of reform which had moved the Bolivian people for decades lost its true significance because of bad leadership. The nation's sovereignty, instead of being strengthened, was compromised by the increasing dependence upon external power groups. Not even the national budget depended upon Bolivians alone. After twelve years, the nationalization of the mines continued to be an empty gesture because it was not complemented by the installation of foundries. The agrarian reform was at a standstill, with no hope of effective progress. The so-called plan for economic diversification never moved beyond talk. Universal suffrage was a myth, and educational reform merely [an unimplemented] law. Per capita income declined from 123 dollars to 97 dollars. Mining exports declined from $120 million to $40 million and more than seven hundred factories closed, thereby decreasing the number of employed persons by 25 percent.

During this period of disintegration, the only organism that maintained a unity of doctrine strengthened by a truly national outlook was the . . . armed forces. The Bolivian military officer possesses neither a reactionary mentality nor a sense of caste. On the contrary, resulting as much from their origin as from their tradition, the armed forces of Bolivia embody the national and democratic essence. This fact allows us to comprehend the need for profound change in the confused world created by the Bolivian Revolution.

Honorable Gentlemen, I must solemnly state before you that the armed forces took power in 1964 to make the Bolivian Revolution a reality and to establish the foundations of the Second Republic. For that reason, we ask that all social groups and institutions work in solidarity for the social and economic development of Bolivia. We want a vigorous union organization which is conscious of its rights and its obligations; we want a youth full of healthy rebellion, optimistic, studious, and honorable; we want the citizenry to act freely and the political parties to be organized on a solid doctrinal base; we want the Christian ideal to light our way and democracy to strengthen our institutions; we want happiness for all; and we want culture and progress to flourish, and our thinkers, artists, workers, and soldiers to make the life of man in our fatherland even more beautiful.

The armed forces believe that the revolution belongs to the people, and because of that we contend that the Bolivian Revolution means the slow and steady liberation of the national economy from its semicolonial dependence upon foreign markets. This means controlling our national resources and marketing and distribution of our products under the conditions most favorable to internal development and to the expansion of Bolivian power. In sum, we seek state planning and dominance in the principal areas of production in order to avoid the excessive concentration of power and the absentee ownership of wealth enjoyed in the past by financial monopolies more powerful than the state. That is the road chosen by the armed forces. That is our philosophy of economic development, of popular action, of national unity, and of national sovereignty.

Bolivia is faced with a social complexity that has erected a multitude of obstacles to her progress. The objective of the Second Republic is to accelerate the social integration now under way, respecting the will of all groups, employing technology to relieve the demographic pressure on the Altiplano, and promoting literacy and culture to the fullest extent for the campesinos. In that way we are proud to declare that the Indian population of our country will achieve undreamed of levels of progress. . . .

Translated, reprinted, and edited from "Informe a la nación por el general Alfredo Ovando Candía, Presidente de la H. Junta Militar dal Gobierno," August 6, 1966, in Guillermo Lora, ed., *Documentos Politicos de Bolivia*, pp. 584–93.

THE MILITARY-CAMPESINO PACT
SPEECH BY JUAN JOSÉ TORRES
1971

Comrades:

It is an enormous satisfaction for me to attend this closing ceremony of the National Assembly of Bolivian Campesino Leaders. I do not wish to make a formal speech nor do I want to refer exclusively to the campesino question. . . .

In addition to considering largely campesino matters, it is necessary to treat national problems as well, above all, those which are related to political problems. The democratic nature of my government has permitted the free interplay of all ideologies and of all union organizations. Very few periods in our history have been characterized by the unrestricted liberties that the Bolivian people enjoy today. But never as today have the uses and abuses of those liberties shown the country the depth of immorality reached by certain political organizations and by certain leaders who have taken over the management of labor unions.

In these times when the country has begun to rebuild for the future by redirecting the National Liberating Revolution toward the paths of the true popular interest, antinational forces, that previously squandered the revolution away by surrendering it to imperialist greed in an infamous alliance with the infantile left, have hypocritically joined with "Johnny-come-latelys" in a pseudorevolutionary cult. The conquerors and the conquered embrace, yesterday's enemies unite, and the extreme left joins the right under a nationalist label, ignoring entirely the most elemental principles of conduct and consequence as if the struggle for power consisted of easy compromise or of the distortion of history.

It has been said that leftist brigandage easily turns to rightist opportunism in order to achieve its ends, at times changing its political color like a chameleon. But at any rate, the extremes always join together when they try to attack a pure and popular administration following a national revolutionary model. The paper anti-imperialists sign a shameful pact with the academicians of surrender. The defenders of human rights have no trepidation in agreeing to a "Holy Truce" with precisely those who trampled on such rights. Those who consider themselves to be true revolutionaries and depositories of purity resort to rhetorical tricks in order to whitewash the pack of lies, scorning as always the opinion of the national majority—silent spectators of the national drama.

. . . It seems that in politics everything goes, at least the criollo exercise of the old Machiavellian adage employed with exemplary skill by those who by accident control the popular assembly, sheltering those whom only yesterday they helped to overthrow. In this same clear and sincere manner, I ask that the workers, the university students, the campesinos, and all the men and women of Bolivia make a frank and honest evaluation of the past and weigh on the scales of justice what my government represents now because of special reasons and historic circumstances.

The position of the government is firm because we are conscious of the role we are required to play in the current historical situation. For that reason we will not fall victim to the simple naïveté of treating our impatience as a political theory, but we will march forward with firmness in order to achieve our liberation and our full sovereignty. We have been and we are enemies of the solutions of pamphleteers that lead to guerrilla adventures, because the results speak for themselves; the revolution should be made with objectivity and not by simple subjective or personal impulses. The revolution is neither a fantasy nor a romantic posture. The revolution is a long and painful undertaking, enriched by daily experience, with both successes and failures.

. . . The forces interested in destroying the unity of the rural workers have launched an active campaign to denigrate the Military-Campesino Pact. The connotations of their attitude are easily discernible. They seek to divide two important forces that make up the revolutionary process in order to weaken the national front and contribute to the return of the oligarchy.

The Military-Campesino Pact must be broadened into a pact in which the revolutionary sectors of the proletariat and of the middle class will join and participate. Only the union of all the progressive sectors will be able to consolidate the united, national, and anti-imperialist front.

Moreover, the work accomplished by the military and the campesinos in the common struggle against those factors that are halting the process in the rural regions, has to be recorded in history as a part of the struggle against underdevelopment, dependence, and misery. This Military-Campesino Pact is neither aggressive nor exclusive. And in no way do I want anyone, through an erroneous interpretation of this pact, to seek to militarize the campesinos. In that sense, I consider inadequate the creation of campesino military schools when what we should try to create are campesino agrarian schools through the effective aid of the armed forces . . . and of the revolutionary government over which I preside.

The Military-Campesino Pact has to be maintained within the context of the national pact which arose on October 7 [the day Torres took power]. The free men of these lands should begin the task of establishing liberty. Those who feel themselves to be responsible people, friends or allies of the process of liberation which Bolivia is experiencing today, should help in the necessary task of organizing the people. But the most important thing is not to organize the people to serve one person but rather to organize the people to serve the people.

Speech by Juan José Torres, February 16, 1971, at the closing ceremony of the National Assembly of Campesino Laborers of Bolivia. Translated, reprinted, and edited from *Chile, Perú, Bolivia: Documentos de tres procesos latinamericanos*. Buenos Aires: Editor de América Latina, S.A., 1972, pp. 17–21.

THE PATH OF DUTY
SPEECH BY HUGO BANZER SUÁREZ
1971

When I spoke at the commencement of the Military College last year, the state of the nation was very different from that of today. The agents of anarchy and extremism were preparing to take the country by storm in order to place it at the service of interests foreign to the fatherland and to destroy our institutions and our cultural heritage.

Those agents were embedded in the government itself and in the state security agencies. With funds from the National Treasury, contributed by all Bolivians who pay taxes, they financed extremist organizations like the so-called People's Assembly, where they replaced the portraits of our heroes and our founding fathers with those of adventurers [like Ernesto "Che" Guevara] who came to our country to kill and to try to impose on us doctrines and systems foreign to our culture. Our glorious tricolor was replaced by another flag which waved over the buildings of the agencies of extremism.

In the university, which should be a temple dedicated to scientific and technological research and to the formation of professionals qualified to direct the development of Bolivia, they paid homage to violence and redirected energies and resources toward the attainment of goals contrary to the highest interests of the fatherland. We have now confirmed that, fortunately, the promoters of disorder were in the minority and that the great majority of the university students, deceived and supplanted by a handful of agitators, only wanted to dedicate themselves to study and research in order to place their energy and knowledge at the service of Bolivia. We will soon fulfill those legitimate and positive aspirations of Bolivian youth.

Similar conditions were causing the paralysis of all creative initiative and the strangulation of the economy and were causing the army of unemployed and desperate to grow enormously. Nevertheless, in the breasts of the armed forces of Bolivia, the sacred fire of love of the fatherland and of dedication to defend it at all costs, was never extinguished.

It was in those critical and difficult hours, in which all appeared lost because of vacillation and weakness, that I had the privilege of delivering the commencement address at this military college. Denouncing, in the name of the armed forces, the intolerable state of affairs, I asserted that the bastard ambitions, the political and administrative corruption, the demagoguery, the lies, the hate, the rancor, and the institutional disorder had come to rot the very heart of the fatherland. We are living, I said, in permanent frustration, and wherever you look, you will see only division.

I added that we had, with a passive and indifferent attitude, been witnesses to the appetites of extranational ideologies. The extreme left and the extreme right had sunk their teeth into the nation's guts, causing the mental subservience of some Bolivians. It was time to put a stop to that national disgrace; it was time that we realized that the fatherland will rise again as the result of . . . peace, . . . labor, and the understanding of the citizens. It was time to put an end to the attitude of those traffickers of foreign ideas, of demagogues who thousands of times had cheated their brothers the campesinos, the miners, the workers, and their fellow citizens. I said this had to be the moment of truth; either we go with the fatherland or against it, respecting the laws or trampling on them, with order or with chaos and anarchy, with sincerity or with fraud and deceit, with peace or with war, with courage or with servility, with honesty or with systematic robbery. That then was the hour of reckoning, and we military men, trustees of the national honor, with the people, ought to have demanded it of those who commanded and governed us.

Those were difficult words to say in those moments in which the dignity of men who were upright and respectful of law and order was at the mercy of veritable hordes of fanatics who were ready to utilize any means to silence criticism and quash any form of opposition to their abuses and misbehavior.

As a dramatic confirmation of the veracity of my judgment, a judgment and belief shared by a majority of the armed forces, they did not delay in taking reprisals against me, seeking to teach the entire [military] institution a lesson through the example made of the commandant of the Military College. First, I was removed from this command, which I served with singular affection and devotion, then retired, and finally forced into exile, which is the cruelest of punishments for an honorable military officer.

But my warning had the effect of alerting the armed forces to the true nature of the regime that oppressed us and to the hidden designs for the destruction of the fatherland and the annihilation of its institutions. . . .

Soon the spark became a firestorm of national fury that swept away forever the agents of extremism and hate, returning to Bolivians their right to liberty, work, peace, and security. The heroic movement of August of this year . . . was begun in this same place, exactly a year ago, in the presence of many of you who attended the commencement exercises and the graduation of new officers in 1970. It was through that opportunity that I had the honor of being selected to plant the seeds of rebellion and to calm the spirits of those who, months later, returned our flag and our sacred symbols to their place of honor on the national altar.

Today the country has returned to normal and . . . to more propitious conditions. With the institutional backing of the armed forces, a solid alliance of civilian political forces has been produced, and large contingents of people are preparing to enter this pact in order to construct, for the first time in Bolivian history, an organization representative of the majority of the Bolivian people.

The mission of the military in Bolivia today, apart from its specific functions of maintaining internal peace and defending the national sovereignty, has been expanded in scope: to be the unifying and cementing factor of the nation. The role that the armed forces played in the patriotic uprising of August has conferred upon them the perfect right of protecting the national institutions and has, in fact, confirmed their status as the vanguard institution [of national development]. . . .

Speech by Hugo Banzer Suárez. Translated, reprinted, and edited from *El Pensamiento del Presidente CNL, Hugo Banzer Suárez* (La Paz: Ministero de Información y Deportes, 1971), pp. 107–112.

Brazil

SPEECH BY HUMBERTO CASTELLO BRANCO
1967

Gentlemen Members of the National Congress:

When I addressed the nation for the first time as president of the republic, I promised all Brazilians that I would relentlessly promote the general welfare. I did not ignore, at that moment, either the responsibility attached to such a gesture, nor the magnitude of the tasks ahead. I was also convinced that the whole nation would respond to my dramatic call to collaborate, even with some sacrifice, in order to resume the development process and to achieve true social justice.

After almost three years, I bring before your Excellencies an account of my government, as a testimony of how much has been demanded from the Brazilian people so that they could regain confidence in the ideals of their government.

There was no break in this process, and the struggle included all areas of activity. The initial steps of the program called for implanting radical structural reforms, a stoical and permanent inflationary decompression, along with the overriding objective of boosting the national economy and revitalizing the country's management.

But no social change can take place without having [an] effect on the balance of political forces. The defects of the infrastructure always incite the former privileged groups to resist the new laws promoting equality; the new institutions still arouse stubborn opposition . . . and the memory of old habits stirs up discontent and regret in a permanent struggle to retake the government.

For that very reason, the rupture of the juridical order existing until March 31, 1964 called for the adoption of certain political measures in order to provide an adequate transition according to the terms and the ideas of the revolution.

I want to emphasize, of course, the application of Articles 7 and 10 of the First Institutional Act, strengthened later by Articles 14 and 15 of Institutional Act number 2.

In the exercise of such prerogatives, some legislative measures were can-

190

celed and the political rights of persons indicated by the members of the National Security Council, were suspended. I repeat, these decrees were political measures of the revolution. They were not inspired by a simplistic whim to punish. On the contrary, a rigorous verification of responsibilities was conducted in every case. And it must be remembered that every revolutionary process presupposes, in its own context, measures of a repressive nature. Very few, however, have proceeded with as much justice and moderation as the March 1964 movement. . . .

Since 1945, the legislation and dynamics of the representative system has deeply misguided and profoundly distorted the will of the people. A multiplicity of parties and the abuse of economic power in the electoral campaigns were two of the basic causes.

. . . In turn, the effects of multipartyism on the administrative life of the country provoked a continuous instability, with the obvious consequences. As an example, let it be remembered that the average term in office for the ministers of state, from 1946 to 1964, did not reach 224 days.

. . . [In this context] it is once more fitting to review the serious weakening of democratic institutions in the phase prior to the revolution. A social and political crisis, which reached unbearable levels, became a factor in the deteriorating internal and external economic situation, then already very critical.

As an unavoidable consequence, there occurred a decline in the efficiency of all aspects of national activity. Confronted with the need to reveal the implications of such a situation in relation to national development, we shall now undertake a brief analysis of the Brazilian situation as of March 1964, focusing especially on the socioeconomic aspects.

Despite the various structural limitations that tended to conspire against self-sustained and rapid development, the Brazilian economy experienced satisfactory performance in the period from World War II to the year 1961, and especially between the years 1947–61. During that period the gross domestic product grew at an average annual rate of 5.8 percent (equivalent to 3 percent per capita). The . . . expansion of the industrial sector through the substitution of domestic products for imported goods was the most important stimulus.

However, this process of development took place against the backdrop of a social and economic structure unfavorable to lasting economic progress. Alongside the rapid growth of the manufacturing sector, the conditions of the agrarian sector—in which more than 50 percent of the national population existed at a low standard of living—remained almost unchanged, victim of the reigning technical backwardness in the rural sector and of the unsatisfactory levels of education, health, and hygiene.

Likewise, an archaic financial structure, highly sensitive to inflationary pressure, persisted along with a lack of basic services (transportation, energy, silos and warehouses, and communications), aggravated over and over by incorrect economic policies. An opportunistic and myopic view of the economic relations of the country with the rest of the world led to neglect of exports, which constituted the main determining element of the external purchasing power of the country. As a consequence, the Brazilian capacity to import stagnated.

Finally, during the entire above-mentioned period, that is, from after the war to 1961, the Brazilian economy developed within an atmosphere of continuous inflation of variable but bearable intensity, to the point of having permitted the satisfactory evolution of the gross domestic product, at least until 1961. In the meantime, the presence of those inflationary pressures, with partial control by government officials, was harmful enough to produce undesirable distortions in the system of relative prices and to give way to speculative activities, one consequence of which was the weakening of the money and capital market and the rates of savings and exports. The extraordinary growth of the Brazilian population and the resulting increase in the demand for new jobs, linked to the vulnerability of the public administration to political pressure, encouraged the transformation of employment in the public sector into "political spoils." This undermined operational efficiency and generated increasing deficits. The consolidated deficits of the government in turn were traditionally financed with currency issues, a source of new inflationary pressures. It ended in a vicious circle. . . .

Starting in 1962, several circumstances tended to increase the government expenses, independent of the comparative increase in the fiscal revenues, with a consequent progressive evolution of deficits in the case of the National Treasury and an increase of the rate of inflation. There were also serious signs of a worsening of the balance of payments situation and the reduction of import capacity. The deficiency of the economic infrastructure became more acute, creating a climate of uncertainty and uneasiness. As a consequence, the level of investments and the growth rate of the economy declined, and the weaknesses of the national economy became more evident.

As a result of all this, increases in the general level of prices, which had reached an average of 15 percent per year between 1941 and 1946 [and] rose to 20 percent in the period from 1951 to 1958, suffered a rapid acceleration starting in 1959. The rate of increase in the cost of living rose in that year to 52 percent in Guanabara, and, after going down in 1960, started rising progressively until reaching 55 percent in 1962 and 81 percent in 1963. In the first quarter of 1964, it reached 25 percent and, given its rate of acceleration, it could have very well reached 150 percent by the end of the year. . . . The social and political atmosphere of the previous administration could not have been more unfavorable; the following factors should be underlined: the constant political tension created by the disharmony between the federal executive on the one hand and the national Congress and the state governments on the other, distrustful of the anticonstitutionalist intentions and desires of the old regime [to maintain itself in power]; a penchant toward state property and control that created a continuous discouragement and threat to private investors; the communist infiltration, generating apprehensions about the overthrow of the social and economic order; the successive paralysis of production by the "strike commands." Not only did urban activities suffer but also investment in farming and cattle raising were discouraged. . . . Political instability and administrative improvisation prevailed, producing a lack of national direction . . . the entrepreneurial classes suffered from a crisis of distrust; the working classes found themselves frustrated because of the impossibility of their realizing the demagogic promises; finally, certain, more restless groups, such as the students, not finding an outlet for their idealistic impulses slipped into the error of subversive solutions. . . .

To summarize, when this government took power, the financial and economic situation was truly gloomy. To the structural deficiencies of the national economy had been added temporary troubles which underscored these [deficiencies], disrupted internal markets, pushed the increase in prices to the verge of extreme inflation, generated a crisis of confidence [and] a slowdown in the flow of investments and in the rate of economic development. [These troubles also] increased the level of unemployment, and, finally, they damaged the country's credit abroad. The most urgent task, therefore, was to contain the extraordinary rise of the general level of prices, to recover the minimum necessary order for the functioning of the national economy, to overcome the crisis of confidence, and to return to the entrepreneurs and to the workers the tranquillity necessary for productive activities. . . .

Reprinted and edited from Mensagem ao Congresso Nacional Remedita pelo Presidente de la República Na Abertura da Sessão Legislativa de 1967 (Message to the National Congress at the Opening of the legislative session of 1967). Translated by Cecilia Ubilla.

SPEECH BY PRESIDENT ERNESTO GEISEL
BEFORE THE BRAZILIAN CABINET
1974

. . . In a previous public statement I have already pointed out that the modernizing Revolution of 1964 bases all of its strategic doctrine on the two pillars of development and security, recognizing, of course, that in essence the first of the two is the dominant one. In more precise terms, one can say that the strategic action of the revolution has been and will continue to be exercised in such a way as to promote for the Brazilian people at all levels, at every stage, the maximum possible development with a minimum of indispensable security.

Likewise, in the area of national security the process is also essentially integrated, since this process is the same as national development, though applied to a more specialized and more restricted area. The minimum of indispensable security results, therefore, from an interaction duly balanced . . . in each of its integrated components.

. . . It is clear that we have received a valuable heritage from the governments of the revolution, which in these last ten years managed to raise Brazil to an outstanding position among the new world powers, with an internal market which places Brazil among the ten largest of the western world, and a gross domestic product, this year, on the order of $66 billion. After a phase of pressing sacrifices, during which combating inflation, remodeling economic institutions, and reestablishing internal credibility became priorities, and, parallel to this, the creation of a climate of order, stability, dedication to work, and faith in the future—we begin to see indications of highly satisfactory performance: rates of growth of actual product, since 1968, between 9 percent and 11.5 percent a year; inflation on the decline and neutralized in regard to its major distortions, because of corrections in monetary policy and the system of minidevaluations; balance of payments surpluses, permitting the accumulation of reserves, [which amounted] in December 1973 to more than $6 billion.

Thanks to the impressive dynamism of the economy under President Medici, the country recorded the highest level of prosperity in modern history, with expectations that per capita income will exceed 600 dollars in 1974.

The great expansion and diversification of our external sector, accomplished in those ten years, increased foreign trade to a value of $12 billion in 1973, which will enable the country to face the most serious challenges of the future confidently.

It is not less certain, however, that the drastic changes which have taken place in the world scene—such as the serious energy crisis, the shortage of basic foods and raw materials in general and the shortage of oil and its by-products in particular; the instability of the international monetary system, already in a painful search for a new order; the inflation which has spread over the entire world at alarming rates; the political and social tensions, aggravated by the ferment of the irresponsible calls to violence, which disturb the life of many nations, in a setting of transition toward the still not well defined new international order—all of these have serious repercussions on the national scene, especially in a year of intense political activity such as 1974. . . .

The great success achieved and the spirit of unity of the governments of the revolution . . . suggest that the major thrusts of government policy be continued.

Continuity, however, does not mean immobility. And if we intend to adapt to those new external circumstances, which represent a serious challenge, we must not only improve the institutional mechanisms for the coordination of development and security policy, but also to take care of new objectives and of new priorities which derive, naturally, from the high level of progress already attained by the country.

. . . In regard to domestic politics, we shall welcome sincere movements toward gradual but sure democratic progress, expanding honest and mutually respectful dialogue and encouraging more participation from responsible elites and from the people in general . . . in order to create a climate of basic consensus and to proceed to the institutionalization of the principles of the Revolution of 1964. I am anxious to see the extraordinary instruments with which the government has armed itself to maintain an atmosphere of security and order which is fundamental for socioeconomic progress, . . . used less frequently [and] . . . made unnecessary by a creative political imagination which will install, at the opportune moment, efficacious safeguards . . . within the constitutional context.

It is evident that this will not solely depend on the federal executive power, since, to a great extent, it calls for the sincere and effective collaboration of the other powers of the nation as well as that of the other government organs in the state and even municipal centers, including conscientious discipline and their own ironing out of difficulties. It will necessarily depend on the spirit of debate of the restless and disoriented minorities, disturbers of the country's life, irresponsible or demagogic, resorting even to deceit, intrigue, or violence—[and their] recognition of the general repudiation [of their doctrines] and the full recognition of today's unquestionable reality: the definitive implantation of our revolutionary doctrine.

One must not accuse this doctrine of being antidemocratic when . . . it is essentially aiming at perfecting, in realistic terms, democratic practices and adapting them in a way better suited to the characteristics of our people and to the current stage of the social and political revolution of the country, yet safe from the attacks—overt or covert—of those who in the name of liberal democracy only wish, in fact, to destroy it or to corrupt it for their own benefit. . . .

Reprinted and edited from *O Estado* (São Paulo), March 20, 1974. Translated by Cecilia Ubilla.

SPEECH BY ERNESTO GEISEL TO MILITARY COMRADES 1976

Gentlemen:

I thank you for the welcome that you have given me at this barracks today, in this garrison of Vila Militar. I thank you for the wishes for my personal happiness proposed in the toast by his Excellency the secretary of the army and answered by all of you.

My visit here today is for me a source of special satisfaction, for it gives me the opportunity to share this day with my highly esteemed army comrades, and, with them, the representatives of the navy and air force.

It is not only the feeling of an old soldier who returns to military life, to the place where he worked and toiled for many years and where, at an early age, he began his education. It is not merely a sharing with his fellow soldiers or [a chance] to exchange impressions, to taste their successes, their aspirations, and the anxiety under which they live. It is not merely the return to this Vila Militar, where I served for many years, in my youth and also as an adult, with energetic professional activity, totally dedicated to the army: it is truly much more than that. It is because, in fact, there is no more appropriate surrounding in which to commemorate our Revolution of 1964 than the site of an army barracks. In fact, the armed forces—and among them the army—played a principal role in the Revolution of 1964, by taking the initiative to combat a situation of anarchy and havoc which was spreading throughout the nation.

And it was the armed forces which, through their efforts, made this revolution successful, gave stability to it, and gave order to the country, an order with which it was possible to ensure the progress that Brazil has enjoyed since 1964. Furthermore, it was the armed forces which confronted and fought the subversive movements. These movements, which aimed at the destruction of our nation, had, to a great extent, been inspired from abroad.

It was also the armed forces which were able to overcome intrigue, lack of understanding, slander, and insults, and made possible—I must repeat—this stability in which we have been living for the last twelve years. And these armed forces are today united, cultivating the ideals of our revolution, wholly fulfilling their constitutional duties, which allow the government favorably and on a large scale to undertake at the present time an evolution [toward progress]. A gradual evolution certainly, aiming at the improvement of our social and political institutions, based on the economic development that we are continuing, despite the critical international situation.

These are, then, the extraordinarily important motives which bring me on this visit here today. Undoubtedly the contacts that I had and my presence here constitute an extraordinary source of encouragement for those who, like me, shoulder an exceptional responsibility in the leadership of the Brazilian nation and who try honestly and with integrity to find the way, or the road that we must take, which will undoubtedly be difficult. . . . It is a path troubled by intrigue, by harmful information, by meddling of all sorts that we must untangle in order to see the true direction that we must follow. . . .

I must also say that I shall carry out this most noble, however difficult, task which has been laid upon my shoulders. I shall comply with my duty with all my strength and using all the means and resources which the government has available. I think that I shall successfully carry out this task. With all the delights and difficulties that government life implies, I still have the zeal and the hope to say sincerely that we shall carry out our task to a successful end—a success which means well-being for the Brazilian people, a success which means the aggrandizement of the Brazilian nation.

My good wishes are expressed in this direction, and I ask you to join me in a toast for the fulfillment of them all.

Reprinted and edited from *Journal do Brasil*, April 1, 1976. Translated by Cecilia Ubilla.

Chile

THE REASONS OF THE JUNTA
1973

In Order of the Day No. 5, the Junta outlines for the public benefit the reasons which moved it to assume control of the country.

The text of the order is as follows:

Order of the Day Number 5

Whereas:

1. The Allende government has exceeded the bounds of legitimacy by violating the fundamental rights of liberty, of speech, and of education; the right to congregate, to strike, and to petition; the right to own property and, in general, the right to a worthy and stable existence;
2. the government has destroyed national unity, encouraged sterile and, in many cases, cruel class wranglings, disdained the invaluable help which every Chilean could give to preserve the country's welfare, and engendered a blind fratricidal struggle based on ideas alien to our national heritage which have been proven false and ineffective;
3. the government has shown itself to be incapable of assuring a peaceful association among Chileans by nonobservance of the common law on many occasions;
4. the government has placed itself outside the law on multiple occasions, resorting to arbitrary, dubious, ill-intentioned, and even flagrantly erroneous interpretations of it, which, for various reasons, have escaped sanction;
5. by the use of subterfuge, which the government was pleased to call *resquicios legales* (legal recourses), some laws have not been promulgated, others have been flouted, and a situation of illegitimacy engendered;
6. the government has repeatedly failed to observe the mutual respect which one power of the state owes to another, disregarding decisions approved by Congress, by the courts of justice and by the comptroller general of the

198

republic, offering unacceptable excuses for so doing or none at all;

7. the supreme authority has deliberately exceeded its attributes . . . gravely compromising the rights and liberties of all;

8. the president himself has been unable to disguise the fact that the exercise of his personal authority is subject to decisions taken by committees of the political parties which support him, impairing the image of maximum authority which the constitution confers upon him;

9. the agricultural, commercial, and industrial economies of the country are in a state either of stagnation or recession and inflation is rampant, but there are no signs whatever that the government is interested in them, except as a mere spectator;

10. anarchy, stifling of liberties, moral and economic chaos, and, as far as the government is concerned, absolute irresponsibility and incapacity have led the country to ruin, preventing it from occupying its proper place among the leading nations of the continent;

11. the foregoing justify our opinion that the internal and external security of the country is in dire peril, that our very existence as an independent state is in danger, and that the continuance in power of the government is fatal to the interest of the republic and the welfare of its people;

12. that, moreover, the foregoing, viewed in the light of our national and historical idiosyncracies, is sufficient to justify our determination to oust an illegitimate, immoral government, no longer representative of national sentiment, in order to avoid the greater evils which threaten the country, there being no other reasonable method holding out promise of success, and it being our objective to reestablish normal economic and social conditions in the country, with peace, tranquillity, and security for all;

13. for the foregoing reasons the armed forces have taken upon themselves the moral duty, which the country imposes upon them, of deposing the government, which, although legitimate in the early exercise of its power, has since fallen into flagrant illegitimacy, assuming power for ourselves only for so long as circumstances so demand and counting on the support of the vast majority, all of which, before God and history, justifies our action; and hence whatever regulations, norms, and instructions we may think fit to lay down for the attainment of our objectives aimed at the common good and the maximum patriotic interest;

14. Consequently, the very legitimacy of the said norms obliges all, and especially those in authority, to abide by them.

Signed: Government Junta of the Armed Forces and Carabineros of Chile.

Santiago, September 11, 1973.

Reprinted and edited from *Three Years of Destruction* ASIMPRES (Chilean Printers Association, n.d.).

This speech was given on the second anniversary of the military coup.

SPEECH BY AUGUSTO PINOCHET UGARTE, 1975

Today Chile commemorates the recent achievement of its national liberation.

Barely two years ago, sombre misgivings filled the air, and the general feeling of anguish knew no bounds. Chilean women instinctively feared the destruction of their homes, realizing the extent to which violence had undermined their children's most elemental safety. Our youth rebelled against the sinister aims and alien ideas of a minority who endeavored to control their consciences and curtail their freedom. When it became evident that the country was in a state of chaos, workmen of all types protested by putting an indefinite stop to their activities.

In this atmosphere, an unsuccessful and corrupt government forfeited its last traces of legitimacy by neglecting its functions as the established authority and, seeking to divide Chileans by means of systematically fomented hatred, prepared a civil war which would have inflicted a death blow to our beloved nation.

Yet the proud, indomitable Chilean spirit rose again with renewed vigor. From the bottom of their hearts our people demanded their liberation, and on a morning such as this, our armed forces and carabineros, in complete unison, and, in fact, representing the last reserve of a juridically organized state, took over the government of the nation.

Our flag once again waved proudly, dignified and victorious, and the date of September 11 took its place among the most glorious periods of our independence.

I shall outline today the task which our government has undertaken. It has not been an easy path to follow, but on this second anniversary we face a nation which lives in peace, order, and respect, after three years of chaos and Marxist-Leninist violence; a nation which threads its way among many stumbling blocks, but is convinced that it advances towards a definite goal; a nation which daily becomes more united, with renewed confidence in its own destiny. What a contrast this is to the desolate picture of a world universally submerged in spiritual oppression, moral confusion, and physical violence!

For this reason, my words this morning are those of a president of the republic who, in spite of fully assessing the difficult situation we still confront, can point with satisfaction to the ground we have already covered and invite the Chilean people to continue treading the path of progress in order and justice.

. . . One of the most difficult aspects in the task of national reconstruction, which directly affects every Chilean, is the socioeconomic field.

For this reason, rather than going into a very detailed and technical account of the matter, I would simply prefer to outline the fundamental objectives pursued by the government and the steps taken to achieve them.

One must not forget that the country's economic and productive systems were so severely damaged, that it is no exaggeration to compare the conditions to those of a war-ridden nation.

All the symptoms for runaway inflation were present. The principal cause of this situation was the unprecedented increase in money issued by the Central Bank in order to pay for the fiscal deficit deriving from the excessive growth of the public sector. To this we must add the large losses suffered by the approximately 500 state enterprises, either seized, requisitioned, or bought by CORFO, [Chilean Development Corporation, created in 1939 by a popular front government] and the combination of immorality and inefficiency with which unemployment was disguised by means of hiring unproductive political activists, all of which was financed by the state.

The situation of the productive sector was chaotic. It is enough to recall that agricultural production had fallen 30 percent, thus forcing the country to multiply its food imports by more than four; in 1973 these ascended to over 600 million U.S. dollars.

. . . Never had we been so dependent or suffered such an economic disaster, which compromised social peace and national security, as through the deliberate action of the worst government in our history; the socialist regime, which had promised so-called economic independence.

The new government's first preoccupation was to take the necessary measures to allay the impending collapse. In order to prevent extreme inflation, fiscal expenditure has been rationalized, taxes have been increased, and the situation of "intervened" [a legal-administrative term in Chile referring to "temporary" government management of a firm] or requisitioned business enterprises has been normalized. On the other hand, we have adopted a strategy of freedom of prices, fixing these only for those essential goods in which there is insufficient competition. In order to correct the crisis in our balance of payments, a policy of liberalization has been adopted for international commerce, and we have effected one of the largest currency devaluations in recent history.

Some of these measures have aroused understandable criticism, but the fact remains that it has been possible to reestablish the normal functioning of a ruined economy, definitely removing the danger of runaway inflation and putting a stop to the existing chaos.

Only then could the present government turn to the deeper and more permanent problems which have affected our economy, to a greater or lesser degree, for over three decades and whose solution is essential for solid future development.

Viewed in perspective, the government's economic and social policy has three main objectives:

The first of these is the rechannelling of our productive resources, that is, their progressive displacement toward those products which can be more efficiently produced.

It seems inconceivable—and unthinkable for the future—that for entire decades, and in benefit of an often artificial and overprotected industry, Chilean agriculture has been neglected, and full use has not been made of the country's mining possibilities. The fact that we possess a comparatively great mining and agricultural potential obliges us to channel our resources preferably in that direction. This does not mean a restriction of our industrial development, but rather its orientation towards fields which seem more advisable, such as agricultural industry, among others.

This by no means implies an artificial manipulation of our economy. On the contrary, only a proper redistribution of our productive resources can do away with this long-standing absurdity and guarantee a rapid, solid, and stable growth.

The socialist trends in our economy during the past decade have provoked the uncontrolled growth of the public sector, so that in 1973, fiscal expenditure was 26 percent of the product, and the state financed 80 percent of investment. The second objective of our economic and social policy is therefore to reduce this public sector.

When we maintain that the state should only retain those productive activities or business enterprises which are of strategic or vital importance for national development and hand over the rest to the responsibility of the private sector, we are by no means minimizing the functions of the state. Precisely because it is the state's supreme obligation to promote the common good, and its mission is so fundamental, it should not be driven to neglect its inherent and irreplaceable duties by performing tasks which can be adequately handled by private citizens. With respect to the state's intervention in the national economy, we are not guided by rigid dogmas. There is no doubt that the modern era requires a state which engages in the active planning and flexible regulation of the economic field, but current factors should indicate how far it can go. What we do proclaim as a fundamental principle, however, is that this intervention should keep its subsidiary character and should not annul or invade the framework of private initiative, for the latter is essential for collective progress in a . . . free economy.

. . . Having detained hyperinflation by means of the initial measures already described and laid the foundations for our economic future, the government has now devoted itself toward controlling inflation, which last April was still very high, with an added deficit of 1 billion U.S. dollars resulting from the low price of copper.

A plan for economic recovery has been devised and put into practice, with the main purpose of defeating inflation. Otherwise we cannot expect the necessary degree of new investment, and what is even worse, the great efforts made by the government, as well as by the country in general, would have been wasted.

. . . However, the application of this plan for economic recovery has meant lowering the income of our countrymen to that which our present economic capacity can really afford.

A great part of the so-called social cost of the economic program is merely the acknowledgement of the effects of the international crisis on the persistently low price of copper. On this account alone each Chilean family receives a monthly average of 105,000 escudos less than during 1970.

This impoverishment of the country, produced by factors which lie beyond our control, has necessarily meant a reduction in consumption, as well as the open manifestation of a higher rate of unemployment, particularly in the great urban centers. You will note that I say "open manifestation of unemployment", because it is common knowledge that in 1973 the enormous existing rate of unemployment was disguised by means of creating useless and unproductive jobs in the public sector, which required constant currency issues.

It is the government's duty to warn the public that as a consequence of the temporary state of economic contraction resulting from the country's straitened circumstances, and from the agreements of CIPEC (copper-producing countries) in order to defend the price of copper in 1975 production will decline approximately 10 percent compared with last year. This should not be disheartening or produce confusion, since it is contemplated in the economic plans and will be recovered in the near future.

To have eluded this "social cost" would have meant once more deceiving the people by allowing them to continue living on false hopes for a time, but within a few months Chile would have faced an even worse social and political situation than that of 1973.

It is far from agreeable for any government to assume the obligation of taking such drastic measures, especially when not personally responsible for the causes involved. But when power has been attained not through one's own will, or personal political ambition but by a moral, historical, and patriotic imperative, the exercise of authority only makes sense in the strict compliance with moral duty. I feel that the reason for the generous support which I, as well as the entire government, am constantly shown throughout the whole country, [is the result of] the people's instinctive conviction that this is the case.

. . . The world beholds today a generalized crisis of the traditional forms of democracy, whose failure and exhaustion, at least as far as Chile is concerned, should be considered definitive.

This situation is particularly favorable for totalitarian regimes of differing ideologies, [having in] common scorn for the spiritual values of mankind, to take advantage of this weakness and seize power.

Those of us who believe that the concept of democracy essentially contains a sense of man's dignity are duty bound to face this problem with decision and resolutely advance towards the creation of a new democracy by means of a new political and institutional regime.

The profound crisis of contemporary democracy finds its deepest cause in the loss of the basic spiritual unity of the peoples of the world. The free play of [opposing ideas] in both the generation and exercise of power offers no major institutional obstacles if at least certain fundamental principles are accepted by the whole community, but when this minimal [consensus] is lost, society can no longer be ruled by the same mechanisms, whose efficiency has been damaged at its source.

The existence and propagation of Leninist-Marxism in the world today represents the destruction of the basic moral foundations from which the Western and Christian civilizations derive. Under the euphemism of alleged "Leninist morals", communism destroys all notion of good and evil, cynically judging acts according to whether or not they are convenient for totalitarian revolution. And thus, in the name of that entirely immoral doctrine, we have witnessed the assassination of millions of beings; the slavery of entire nations; hatred, lies, and slander as an habitual line of conduct; and all kinds of aggression against man, his rights, and liberties. It is evidently impossible to live in democratic harmony with such a doctrine.

Reality has laid bare the inadequacy of the concept of liberty as understood by classic liberalism and has placed us in the position of having to redefine it in its authentic significance. True liberty is not simply each individual's right to do or say as he pleases. Freedom is an innate attribute of man which enables the human being to defend the inviolability of his own conscience, as well as to exercise the right of unconfined choice for himself and his family, free from the oppressive interference of the state. Since liberty derives from man's inherent spirituality and is therefore justified if put to use for his moral and intellectual development, it is unacceptable if employed for the weakening and destruction of those very same values. However, social environment and a correct juridical order require certain restrictions on individual liberties, not only to preserve the personal freedom of others, but for the common good.

Facing today's novel circumstances, it is imperative to react in a vigorous and alert manner. In this day and age, a state's sovereignty not only depends on its territorial integrity, [but] its political, economic, and social organization must also constitute an efficient guarantee against another graver peril: the attempt of international communism, as the instrument of Soviet imperialism, to seize states, infiltrating them from within by means of the local Communist parties, aided by other groups who favor or condescend to Marxism by paving the way or ensuring their [freedom to act].

Direct territorial conquest is thus replaced by the penetration of the vital centers in free countries which naively permit the access of Marxism to the control of labor unions, universities, and the mass media. Even the churches, which by definition should provide the most solid protection against this avalanche, have suffered Marxist infiltration in their ranks.

The world today faces an unprecedented form of war. Communism penetrates society ideologically and at the same time, from its various centers of power, imposes upon democratic governments a line of action which favors its own advancement. The universal character of the Leninist-Marxist revolution fits in perfectly with the imperialistic hegemony of the Soviet geopolitical school.

In this war, nothing can be of greater use to communism than the declaration of ideological neutrality by states which are not yet under its control. How can a state possibly defend itself in an ideological war if it officially declares its neutrality in the ideological field? To this, we must add that communist control of a country not only means the end of all personal liberty and state sovereignty, but, it also involves the destruction of the very essence of nationality. The latter is inadmissible in the name of liberty. The fatherland, with its traditions and historical-cultural identity, cannot be the patrimony of any given generation, for it also belongs to those who built it in the past, and those who have a right to its future inheritance. Nor can any generation so consider itself the sole possessor of its nationality as to feel authorized to destroy it.

Our country temporarily forgot these truths and experienced the bitter consequences. To begin with, communism was allowed direct or indirect control of fundamentally influential media and was given ample facilities for political action and propaganda. Later its vocabulary and ideas were gradually adopted by democratic sectors, who from the habit of dialogue inadvertently became imbued with its myths and slogans. Thus the "noncapitalistic road to development," "community socialism," "Christians for socialism," and other such manifestations appeared, which, when it comes to the definition of their doctrines, were either devoid of meaning or could only answer to Marxist ideology.

It is not surprising then that these sectors never quite realized the virtual suicide they were committing by allowing Marxism access to power when they could have avoided it constitutionally. And not content with this, they officially introduced the most unrestricted ideological pluralism into our constitution, by declaring that to sustain or spread any political idea would not constitute offense. Thus, guerrillas, terrorism, or the organization of paramilitary forces could go unpunished if endowed with the protective cloak of "political ideas."

Now that we have risen from the bottom of the abyss to which this attitude led us, Chile has resolutely proclaimed its nationalistic and Christian definition, by means of a Declaration of Principles, laying down the foundations for the future state which our regime is endeavoring to build, [which will include] a sense of duty to defend our national sovereignty and tradition in a manner suited not only to conditions fifty or one hundred years old, but also to those of the present time.

Not to permit the enemy access to the control of the mass media, universities, or trade unions, does not in any way curtail the legitimate freedom of expression of cultural thought or of labor organization. On the contrary, it implies preserving these from the destruction they would be exposed to if the very forces who intend to annihilate them are allowed to grow freely.

We Chileans have recently had proof of these harsh realities and are firmly determined not to repeat the same mistakes.

The classic concept of punishment is often defied nowadays by the appearance of terrorism, a contemporary iniquity by means of which small minorities commit criminal offenses against innocent people who generally have no connection whatsoever with the objectives of the delinquents. Because of the danger and cruelty involved, society is under the obligation of drastic self-defense, thus giving birth to new restrictive measures in the exercise of personal liberty or lawful rights, in order to reconcile these with the imperative of security which every community justly demands.

The aforementioned is directly related to the problem of human rights, on which I wish to dwell for a moment, since it is still being used all over the world as an instrument to oppose our government and our country. Human rights, in the measure that they are truly such, are universal and inviolable, but they are certainly not unrestricted or of equal hierarchy. As outward manifestations of liberty, they are, without exception, subject to the restrictions imposed upon them by the common good. In this respect, it is curious to observe that those who admit without hesitation that the right to private property is limited by its social function, are often the first to protest the restriction of other rights and liberties, even if also applied for the sake of common good.

Nor are all rights of the same hierarchy. Even among natural rights, some are more fundamentally important than others. They may usually all be exercised simultaneously, but this is impossible when society becomes sick. The latter situation is precisely a symptom of political abnormality requiring an exceptional juridical regime in which the exercise of some rights is limited or can even be suspended in order to ensure the free exercise of other more important ones.

Those who condemn the juridical restrictions essential for the present state of emergency in which we are living should definitely understand the reason why their arguments go against the mature conviction of the Chilean people. The vast majority of our fellow countrymen accept and support these restrictions because they are aware that [such restrictions] are the necessary price to be paid for the peace and social order which make our country a veritable island within a world convulsed by violence, terrorism, and general disorder.

The greatest possible enforcement and highest respect of all human rights implies that these must not be exercised by those individuals who spread doctrines or commit acts which, in fact, seek to abolish them.

. . . If we feel ready today to reduce by one degree the state of siege, it is thanks to the efficient action which the government has taken to dismember organized extremist groups. But while any kind of significant subversive action still exists, whether overt or covert, we are obliged to maintain the necessary restrictions to ensure social peace and prevent the return of chaos.

. . . Chileans:

Soon after our independence, Chile was one of the first countries in the world to abolish slavery. Now our country has broken the chains of totalitarian Marxism, the great twentieth-century slavery, before which so many bow their heads without the courage to defeat it. We are thus once again pioneers in humanity's fight for liberation.

Our victory over communism is especially significant because of the geopolitically strategic importance of our country in the defense and security of the continent, but even more so for its deep spiritual content.

Today Chile will ignite the flame of liberty, as a living symbol of its faith and hope for a world which at present labors in darkness.

As president of Chile, I feel certain that this flame will be lit with the support of the entire Chilean population, whose hearts beat in unison with the highest and purest patriotism.

I devotedly implore Our Holy Lord, with deep humility before the magnitude of our task, never to allow this flame to die down and that Chile may always face, with renewed vigor, the tempests which may arise and keep its patriotic oath of forever being "the tomb of the free or else the shelter against oppression".

Edited from *Chile Lights the Freedom Torch* (Santiago: Editora Nacional Gabriela Mistral, 1975), pp. 1–68.

Peru

MANIFESTO OF THE REVOLUTIONARY GOVERNMENT OF PERU—1968

Upon assuming power in Peru, the armed forces want to make known to the Peruvian people the underlying causes for their far-reaching and historic decision, a decision which marks the beginning of the definitive emancipation of our fatherland.

Powerful economic forces, both national and foreign, in complicity with contemptible Peruvians motivated by [the desire for] unbridled speculation and profit, have monopolized the economic and political power of the nation. These forces have frustrated the people's desire for basic structural reforms by maintaining the existing unjust social and economic order which allows a privileged few to monopolize the national riches, thereby forcing the great majority to suffer economic deprivation inimical to human dignity.

The economic growth rate of the country has been poor, creating a crisis which not only adversely affects the financial condition of the nation, but which also weighs heavily on the great mass of our citizens. The contracts for our natural resources have been ruinous, thereby forcing us into a dependent relationship with the great economic powers, compromising our national sovereignty and dignity, and postponing indefinitely the reforms necessary to overcome our present state of underdevelopment.

Overwhelming personal ambition in the exercise of the responsibilities of the executive and legislative branches in the discharging of public and administrative duties, as well as in other fields of the nation's activities, has produced immoral acts which the public has repudiated. This selfishness has also destroyed public faith and confidence in the government, a confidence which must be restored if the people are to overcome their feeling of frustration and the false conception of government that has come about because of the lack of action and responsiveness on the part of those charged with rectifying this unfortunate situation and with improving Peru's present world image.

In 1963, the Peruvian people went to the polls with a profound democratic faith and voted for the recently ousted regime in the belief that that government's program of reform and revolutionary change would become a reality. Our history will record the overwhelming popular support enjoyed by that now defunct government, as well as the loyal and dedicated cooperation offered by the armed forces, support with which it should have been able to implement its program of action. But instead of dedicating their efforts to finding executive and legislative solutions to the nation's ills, that government's leaders, with other corrupt politicians, scorned the popular will and moved to defend those powerful interest groups which had thwarted the aspirations of the people. They subordinated the collective welfare to their . . . ambition for personal aggrandizement. Proof of this can be seen in the government's lack of direction, its compromises, its immorality, its surrender [of natural resources], its corruption, its improvisation—in the absence of any social sensitivity, characteristics of a government so bad that it should not be allowed to remain in office.

The armed forces have observed with patriotic concern the political, economic, and social crisis which has gripped the nation. The armed forces had hoped that a combination of good judgment and hard work would enable the nation to overcome the crisis and to improve the lot of the people through the democratic process, but that hope too was shattered.

The culmination of all these blunders came with the fraudulent and unbridled use of extraordinary powers which were granted unconstitutionally to the executive. One example was the pseudosolution, a national surrender, in the La Brea y Pariñas affair, a surrender which clearly demonstrated that the moral decline of the nation had reached such . . . extremes as to jeopardize Peru's very future. It was because of this that the armed forces, fulfilling their constitutional obligations, is acting to defend one of Peru's natural sources of wealth, which since it is Peruvian, should be for Peruvians.

As the people come to understand better the revolutionary stance of the armed forces, they will see it as the road to salvation for the republic and the way to move definitively toward the attainment of our national goals.

The action of the Revolutionary Government will be shaped by the necessity of transforming the structure of the state in such a manner as to permit efficient governmental operation; of transforming the social, political, and economic structures of the country; of maintaining a definitively nationalist posture, a clear, independent position internationally, and a firm defense of national sovereignty and dignity; of reestablishing fully the principles of authority, of respect for and obedience to the law, and of the predominance of justice and morality in all areas of national endeavor.

The Revolutionary Government promises that it will respect all the international agreements that Peru has ratified, that it will remain faithful to the principles of our Western, Christian tradition, and that it will encourage foreign investment that subjects itself to the interests and laws of the nation.

The Revolutionary Government, clearly identified as it is with the aspirations of the people, issues a call to work with the armed forces to achieve social justice, dynamic national development, and the reestablishment of those moral values which will assure our fatherland of its greatest destiny.

Reprinted and edited from Peru. Comando Conjunto de la Fuerza Armada, *3 de Octubre de 1968*. *¿Por Qué?* (Lima: n.p., 1968).

This speech was given on the first anniversary of the military takeover in Peru.

SPEECH BY JUAN VELASCO ALVARADO, 1969

Fellow Citizens:

Upon completing the first year of government, I am here tonight, on behalf of the armed forces, not only as the chief of state, but also principally as the chief of the revolution. But this title carries with it a meaning radically different from those of the past. . . . To be chief of the revolution is to be the leader of a team of men who are profoundly identified with the revolutionary spirit of the armed forces, on whose behalf was initiated a year ago the process of transforming our country.

This is not a personalist government. There is no one preordained nor irreplaceable among us; nobody has a monopoly on either wisdom or power. We are a team that is carrying out the revolution that Peru needs, the revolution that others proclaimed, only to betray once they were in power. But we know that this will not be understood by those who in reality are no more than simple *caciques* of a new breed, extremists of personalism, vanity, and political fraud.

During the year that ends today, we have begun the process of national transformation that the armed forces promised the country on October 3, 1968. In this brief period, we have completed an enormous task, but it has only been the beginning of the revolutionary process. There still remains an immense job which will require long years of effort and struggle. We will finish it regardless of the obstacles because that is what the urgent needs of our people demand and because that is what the armed forces committed itself to doing when they assumed the responsibility of governing the country.

Faced with this duty, on whose fulfillment the very destiny of Peru depends, we assign little importance to the selfish cries and false protests of those who always used power for their own profit and benefit. Today there is a chorus of voices, known to everyone, that demands the immediate return to constitutionality, that aspires to encourage a vanity which we do not possess, in order to suggest our sudden retirement and our participation in an electoral contest through which they hope to restore that formal democracy which they debased to the point of converting it into a great hypocrisy—speaking of liberty to a people victimized by exploitation, misery, hunger, corruption, surrender, and venality.

Because of that, I want to repeat that not one of us has political ambitions. We are not interested in competing in the electoral arena. We have not come to play the game of politics. We have come to make a revolution. And, if in order to make it we are required to act politically, we should not be confused with those criollo politicians who did so much damage to the country. . . .

Certainly those people do not want to understand what has happened in Peru, but we are living a *revolution*, and it is time that everyone understood it. Every genuine revolution substitutes one economic, political, and social system for another which is qualitatively different. Just as the French Revolution was not made to shore up the monarchy, ours was not launched to defend the established order in Peru, but rather to alter it fundamentally in all of its essential aspects.

Some people expected very different things and were confident, as had been the custom, that we came to power for the sole purpose of calling elections and returning to them all their privileges. The people who thought that way were and are mistaken. One cannot ask this revolution to respect the institutional norms of the system against which it revolted. This revolution has to create, and is now creating, its own institutional structure. . . . Our proposals have nothing to do with the traditional forms of criollo politics that we have banished forever from Peru.

For that reason, our legitimacy does not come from votes, from the votes of a rotten political system, because that system never acted in defense of the true interests of the Peruvian people. Our legitimacy has its origins in the incontrovertible fact that we are transforming this country, precisely to defend and interpret the interests of that people, who were cheated and sold out with impunity. This is the only legitimacy of an authentic revolution like ours.

Of what value to the true man of the people was the liberty they spoke of and then traded away in the back rooms of the National Palace and the Congress? What did these defenders of formal democracy and constitutional rights ever do to resolve, once and for all, the fundamental problems that afflicted Peru and her people? . . . Where are the profound reforms that they promised so often at election time and then, once in power, whisked out of sight in order to serve the oligarchy? . . .

Nevertheless, do not think we have any interest whatsoever in refuting the charges that are hurled against the revolution. The best defense of the revolution lies in its accomplishments. . . . We do not talk of revolution; we are making one. That is our best justification before Peru and before history. All honorable Peruvians are conscious of the fact that, for the first time, we have begun to attack in toto the fundamental problems of the country.

There is plenary proof of our deeds. There is that handful of far-reaching accomplishments that greatly surpass everything that was achieved by past governments. There is the recovery of our petroleum from the hands of a foreign company which previously, because of bribery or fear, influenced the politicians that governed this country from both the [executive branch] and the Congress. There is the new Agrarian Reform Law that benefits the campesinos and breaks the back of the oligarchy, which until recently was all powerful. There is the General Water Law that at last fulfills the dreams of thousands of farmers whose rights were always trampled upon to benefit the *latifundistas*.

There is the new mining policy which ends the old practices which were prejudicial to the interests of Peru. There is the law which puts a stop to the abusive speculation in lands for urban expansion and which will contribute, in a very important way, to remedying the problem of urban housing. There is the initiation of a policy of state control over the Central Reserve Bank, which now does not represent private interests but the interests of the nation. Finally, there is the new international policy, not of submission but of dignity, whose course is limited solely to the interests of Peru.

All of this, and much more, has been achieved in scarcely one year of government action. There are those who assert that the power of propaganda is very great, and possibly this is so. But no propaganda can erase from the minds of all Peruvians the conviction that this government is doing the things that no other dared to attempt, either because of fear or selfishness. Nevertheless, it is completely understandable that incredulity and skepticism still persist in this country where so often promises were betrayed and where political chicanery was substituted for politics. . . .

We have wanted to do much more than we have done for the good of Peru, but there exist monumental obstacles that the citizenry ought to know about. We found Peru in a profound economic crisis; we did not inherit a bonanza situation. The last administration left an external debt of more than 37 billion soles [more than $860 million]. What great or important thing for our people was done with this immense sum of money? Which great reforms were financed by that enormous debt, which the past government borrowed from other countries? It is necessary to speak plainly: a large part of those 37 billion soles was squandered in the unparalleled corruption that devastated this country during the last regime. Where are those who trafficked in the misery of the poor? It is necessary to make known that some of them escaped justice by taking refuge in the international organizations which they always served with no care for the reputation or the future of their fatherland. The day will come when we will settle accounts with those who betrayed the trust of the people. We have no reason to speak in euphemisms. A revolution implies also a different language without halftones and without subterfuge.

But the limitations that the revolution has to overcome are not based solely on the heavy burden of the huge foreign debt that the last government contracted and that Peru has to repay. There is another very important limitation. The oligarchy that has seen its interests affected by the Agrarian Reform Law is not investing its money in the country. This is the great conspiracy of the economic right, its great antirevolutionary strategy, its great treason to the cause of the Peruvian people. It persists in this manner in order to create a fictitious economic crisis that will endanger the stability of the government. The excuse for not investing is that there does not exist in the country a "climate of confidence." This venal phrase is the refrain, as well as the psychological weapon, that the right uses day after day to cover with a smokescreen its true, antipatriotic intentions.

What type of "confidence" do the great proprietors of wealth demand? A "confidence" that permits them to maintain the luxury and the privileges that are not justified except by the bad habits of inveterate exploiters of the Peruvian people? . . . This type of confidence they are not going to have while we are governing because on this type of confidence are based the injustices that submerged the great majority of our people in misery and exploitation.

But there are conditions of authentic confidence for all those who understand that wealth should also fulfill a constructive social responsibility. There is confidence and government backing for investment that promotes the economic development of the country within a framework of respect for the just expectations of capital and for the legitimate rights of the workers. There is confidence because there is total political stability in the country, because social violence no longer exists, and because the people clearly support this government. . . . There is confidence because private investment enjoys all the guarantees that any modern business requires.

From the beginning, the Revolutionary Government declared its support of and encouragement to private investment, including the foreign investment that complies with the laws of the country. There exist then all the conditions of legitimate confidence that honorable investment requires. Many businessmen now understand this, and there are very clear indications of a new and positive tendency in the investment field. But the oligarchical sectors of national capitalism are plotting against the revolution through their control of the economic apparatus, assisted by an ultra reactionary press. . . . The Peruvian people ought to have a very clear idea of the oligarchy's true economic conspiracy because the revolutionary government will not maintain forever its serene attitude of waiting for these people to recover their sense of reality and abandon their pernicious, anti-Peruvian position.

The immense task of realizing effective changes is being carried out by this government without violence and without bloodshed. Ours is the only revolution that, having succeeded in initiating profound transformations, is executing them peaceably. In other countries, agrarian reforms less advanced than ours cost thousands of lives over years of brutal, fratricidal struggle. Until now, Peru has escaped that fate of blood and death, and we are confident that this will continue to be the case in the future. But we understand that the experience our fatherland is living through today represents a conquest without precedents. Without any doubt, this revolution is a radically new phenomenon; it cannot be understood within traditional models. For that reason, the Peruvian example excites interest, expectation, and admiration in the rest of the world and particularly in our Latin American continent.

. . . There are, to be sure, very powerful forces behind the campaign to confound the ongoing revolution. These forces dictate the course of that propaganda which, on one side, demagogically urges deceitful extremism and, on the other, insinuates that our revolution has entered a mellowing phase. Both antirevolutionary postures have the same source of inspiration—the purses of those who pay for them. These two strategies are clearly perceivable. One of them holds that the revolution has gone too far, too fast. But we will not commit that error. The other antirevolutionary strategy persists in presenting us as a movement overcome by complacency, without energy, and incapable of moving beyond that which we have done. Naturally, to halt the march of a revolution which has only recently begun would be another regrettable error, [one] which we are not going to commit. We know very well that, in order to succeed, the reforms initiated must necessarily be complemented by others that are equally indispensable. For us, the transformation of this country is a complex and integral process which will have to be attacked from distinct fronts and with different plans of action. Because of this, the revolution has a program, and that program will be carried out methodically and in its totality.

The two strategies of the oligarchy move in unison, in perfect concert, from within and from without. The conspiratorial action of the adversaries of the revolution functions at these two levels. One of their principal instruments is the synchronized propaganda and twisting of the truth that operates through certain foreign news agencies, through some internationally circulated magazines, and through the majority of the newspapers printed in Peru, newspapers that represent and defend the interests of the Peruvian oligarchy and its foreign accomplices.

The vast majority of Peruvian newspapermen have little or nothing to do with this insidious campaign of lies because they are not responsible for the editorial policies adopted by the majority of newspaper owners. In general, that immense majority of newspapermen really sympathize with the revolution. But those who control and monopolize the ownership of the press are members of the oligarchy, enemies of the transformation we are realizing.

. . . The revolution will go forward until it achieves its objectives, without haste and without hesitancy, by its own route and with its own methodology. We have learned how to resist pressures. We will not be provoked, but we will be implacable in the defense of the revolution on whose success depends the future of Peru. Do not confuse tolerance with weakness. In the Peru of today, the lines are clearly drawn. This revolution will be defended whatever the price. Its adversaries, within and without, should understand this with no room for error. The armed forces will sustain it, and the people will daily defend it more because they will feel it to be theirs.

. . . Thus, if we feel our duty and commitment is to the revolution, we have to be vigilant that it always be an example of purity, honesty, efficiency, sacrifice, and generosity. We have to create an awareness of the immense task that a revolution entails. It will be necessary to correct, from day to day, the errors that are inevitably committed in the mundane operation of the revolution. We have the honesty, the humility, the wisdom, and the valor that others have never had to recognize our errors and correct them.

Far from weakening the revolution, this will strengthen it because it will give it added moral authority. But we will be supremely demanding of ourselves; we will aspire to be a bit better each day; and we will encourage the honest criticism which is an invaluable contribution in every creative effort. Above all, we will never forget the sacred duty of always being loyal to this revolution on which depends the future of our fatherland.

. . . I want to close by directing myself first to those who are not yet involved in the revolution and, second, to the campesinos of the country. To the first group I want to say, in the name of the Revolutionary Government, that in this national mission there is a place for every Peruvian who sincerely desires a profound change in our country. Only those who identify with the oligarchy or with the hated past against which we revolted will be excluded from the revolution. This is a minority in Peru. The great majority of the blue-collar and white-collar workers, the intellectuals, the industrialists, the students, and the professionals, that is to say, the true people of Peru, have no reason to identify with the past nor to defend the interests of the enemies of the revolution. It is for them and with them that we are making this revolution.

My final words this evening will be for the campesinos because the revolution has begun the agrarian reform, the agrarian reform that many dreamed of but very few believed would some day be realized in our country, the agrarian reform that is awakening the campesino and exciting the admiration and respect of the whole world. Nevertheless, as we predicted the day it was promulgated only three months ago, it is now the target of sabotage and obstructionism.

To those campesinos, for whom we effected the agrarian reform, today we say that you should not be deceived, that you should remember those who when in power dictated a reform law designed to defend the great landowners, that you should understand that the propaganda of those who seek to confound and create confusion cannot be sincere, and that you should be ready to defend with your own lives, if necessary, the lands and water that are and will be yours.

In great part, the future of the revolution depends upon the efforts and the responsibility of the campesinos to make the agrarian reform a success. There exist, and there will continue to exist, problems of implementation. But the campesinos should be alert to the enemies of this reform because they are the enemies of the revolution. The campesinos should never forget that this reform and this revolution are being carried out for all the people, for all the poor of Peru. The benefits of the agrarian reform will be felt in other sectors of our society that were equally exploited by the same oligarchy that submerged the peasantry in misery. The revolution began in the countryside, but it will not stop there. The horizon of the revolution is the same horizon of the fatherland.

If we are in power, we have to accept the responsibility for both triumphs and defeats. On us depends the future of the revolution, but it will succeed. We have on our side the might of right, but we also have the right of might.

Reprinted, translated, and edited from *Peru. Velasco: La Voz de la Revolución* (Lima; Ediciones Participación, 1972), 1: 89–108.

SPEECH BY FRANCISCO MORALES BERMÚDEZ, 1976

My dear countrymen:

There are many ways in which the chief of state can set forth the guidelines and policies of the Revolutionary Government of the Armed Forces which he represents.

During this second phase of the revolution, we have addressed you many times through statements, speech, press conferences, and direct dialogue with the people both at the palace and in the different regions of our country.

Today I want to avail myself of another means of communication— television and radio—in order to come into your homes for a while and deal in a most sincere manner with matters that concern our beloved country. . . .

Today's speech or talk, on this the last day of summer, has the purpose of outlining the main problem areas and situations that our country and the revolutionary process are experiencing. One hears repeatedly that the government's authority is weakened, thereby weakening authority at all levels.

This is a confused situation which should be fully clarified by calmly identifying the real causes. In the first place, we have to admit that there obviously has been a change in the methods and political management of the government, as we stated publicly on August 29. [On this day Morales Bermúdez replaced Juan Velasco Alvarado as president of Peru.]

We have opened the channels of dialogue and of freedom of expression which were very limited during the first phase of the revolution. This has enlarged the scope of political debate, a characteristic of the "Revolution with Freedom" that we practice. But we are also facing a typical situation wherein the intense propaganda of leftist and rightist opponents, who can now express their opinions, with the psychological fear of many of being considered "less than revolutionary," has led to a confusion between the need to establish authority and the need for repression and rightist fascism. The result is to endanger the revolutionary process, to which contribute, paradoxically, through their lack of lucidity and clear political vision, not only the opponents of the process but also its supporters who still do not comprehend the essence of revolutionary humanism.

. . . Another cause of this apparent weakening of governmental authority can also be identified. It has been barely seven months since we initiated the second phase of the revolution and assumed the responsibility of leading the country. We did so at the request of the armed forces in conjunction with the police forces, fully conscious of the great political and economic difficulties which this responsibility would entail. In the areas of economics and finance, my five years' experience as minister of economy and finance [1969 through 1973] and my assumption of the premiership in 1974, where I devoted most of my time to the economic affairs of the country, made it evident to me, as I announced publicly, that an economic crisis was approaching. . . .

As there was no hiatus between the first phase and the second phase of the revolution, because we followed a strict norm of revolutionary ethics, we have in fact absorbed all the virtues and defects of the revolution since its inception. The Revolutionary Government is now suffering a natural attrition after exercising power for over seven years, seven years of profound structural changes within a model that seeks to be original and unique and that has the problems of identification and attitude to which we referred above. But this phenomenon does not have its origin in the second phase, because credibility was already lost in the latter part of the first phase. We now have the obligation and the moral and patriotic duty to regain that credibility. We should acknowledge frankly and humbly the mistakes which undoubtedly have been made, for to err is human. Moreover, it would be impossible to hide them, for any period of time, just by denying them. . . .

I would now like to convey to you some reflections on the doctrinary and political-doctrinary aspects of the revolution. In order to leave no possible doubt, we ought to set forth the present and immediate political objectives. In short, these are: to consolidate the revolutionary process, avoiding its degeneration into communist statism or its return to already outdated forms of pre-revolutionary capitalism, and to complete the structural reforms in order to turn Peru, in time, into a humanist, socialist, Christian, solidary, pluralist society, truly democratic and fully participatory. That is to say, to attain the final objectives of a fully participatory social democracy. This objective runs parallel to the development of the country, to make it a great, strong, and prosperous nation. Therefore, the corresponding plan for the achievement of these goals will, without any shadow of a doubt, be conceived in such a manner as to merit the enthusiastic support of the majority of the Peruvian people. . . .

And when in order to eliminate all doubts we must practice self-criticism, we shall do so; and we shall begin doing so now in this speech. Since the first phase of the revolution, we have had the tendency of not stating in a clear, simple, and unmistakable fashion what we believe, what we seek, and what we stand for. In order to avoid being accused of not being sufficiently revolutionary, or of being petit bourgeois defenders of privilege, or of not wanting to free ourselves from the past, or of thinking with certain prejudices, we frequently adopted attitudes which consisted of either dressing up or toning down our real thoughts. We then hid these thoughts behind a certain type of jargon, which interested and committed propagandists, both foreign and domestic, termed *revolutionary*. However, if we are right, and we are; if our revolutionary objective is superior, and it is; from the moment we affirm the validity of our actions and from the moment we no longer fear to state in a clear and unequivocable manner, for example, that we disagree with certain measures that are considered "revolutionary" only because Marxists preach them, we will dispel this fear that has been imbued from within and abroad, and we will affirm ourselves and reaffirm our own superior ideology. In the end what will endure is not what is thought of us today, but rather what we finally achieve, and for that reason it is essential to define everything clearly.

. . . The principles of the Peruvian Revolution are humanistic and Christian. Nothing can be clearer than this or the consequences derived therefrom. The essence of both principles is that man is the end and not the means or the instrument of others. The human condition is a constant, and therefore no one has the right to manipulate or use human beings as objects for profit or power.

If we want to achieve justice, justly, and freedom, freely, we must . . . use proper methods. For this reason, our revolution cannot be imposed by blood and fire because that would mean the manipulation of the masses and the sacrifice of many people for the sake of an uncertain future. This fact reveals that in the realm of practical politics, the most acute problem which a movement such as ours has to face is how to carry out profound structural change while still guaranteeing personal freedom. The solution we have found is gradualism. Gradualism should not be confused with reformism because reformism places a limit on the amount of change and also because reformism, in reality, only demands palliatives to prevent the traditionally privileged groups from losing power. Gradualism does not mean stopping halfway down the path, but rather means advancing by stages, with each stage being characterized by effective solutions to the problems within the limits of existing resources. . . .

We want to make this perfectly clear because if we do not proceed in this manner the economic system will collapse and we will be left with only two alternatives: either the revolution will be truncated and [will] die, or an implacable socialist dictatorship will have to be imposed by violent means, which will preclude the people from having true participation in the collective decisions. If anyone knows of another way in which the problem of harmonizing structural transformation while maintaining people's freedom can be solved, please let us know, as we shall be very grateful indeed.

. . . My dear fellow countrymen: the armed forces, with the police forces, are and always will be bound to the revolutionary process and will defend this revolution to the end.

It should be remembered that this revolutionary process is the creation of the armed forces, who initiated the revolution on October 3, 1968 and who now direct the process in this second phase. The armed forces, guardians of the nation, are a permanent institution. The rulers are representatives of their institutions, but while men change, the institutions live on. There is no difference in either our principles or our objectives; what has changed are our methods and procedures of governing.

It was the armed forces that decided to change the political leadership last August 29. The armed forces understood long ago that the desire of our country to be free and sovereign abroad necessarily required that the people be free from all forms of domestic exploitation. The armed forces also understand that national dignity begins by acknowledging and respecting the dignity of each citizen.

Therefore, the progress of this revolutionary process is indissolubly and unshakeably linked to the armed forces. Its zealous efforts to avoid distortions and to frustrate attempts to thwart it are therefore understandable. Thus, the revolution is the very embodiment of our military conscience, and when its goals and objectives are achieved, it will make every officer, every soldier, every man in uniform feel satisfaction in having accomplished his mission and will maintain each one of them in constant vigil to prevent the original design from being distorted.

A revolution which thus exalts justice, freedom, work, participation, solidarity, creativity, honesty, and respect for human dignity is a revolution which deserves [our] living for, deserves defending and dying for. . . .

Reprinted, edited, and translated from *La Revolución Peruana: Consideraciones Políticas y Economicas del Momento Actual* (Lima: Empresa Editora Perú, 1976), pp. 3–43.

6
The Consequences of Military Rule

Policy Consequences of Military Rule, 1964-76

The "Brazilian model" which emerged after 1964 was followed by new military rulers throughout Latin America, including those in Argentina (1966–73, 1976–), Bolivia (1964–?), Chile (1973–?), and Peru (1968–?). In general, these military leaders made no pretense that their political roles would be limited to a temporary cleansing of the body politic, followed by a return to liberal democracy. (Although, as of May 1976, this was the initial position of the new military junta in Argentina.) Instead, an explicit commitment to modernization and development through military rule, which eliminated "politics," came to characterize the new military leadership.

This does not mean that no divisions existed within the military or that some officers did not favor either a return to an apolitical military or to some form of military populism. On the contrary, in every instance, most notably in Argentina and Bolivia, important ideological and personalistic cleavages divided the military establishments. Indeed, in Bolivia, military rule after 1964 often seemed less developmentalistic than an extension of the pattern of coup and countercoup so typical of Bolivian history.

Nevertheless, even when significant divisions existed within Latin American military establishments, there existed a common desire to direct national modernization and development, while preventing a return to what the officers viewed as corrupt and inept civilian politics. Officers holding a narrower conception of the military role lost influence compared to those intent upon military orchestration of national development.

The movement toward institutionalization of military rule in Latin America since 1964 raises numerous questions concerning the policy orientation and the impact of these military regimes. To raise such questions is to ask, at least implicitly, for appropriate criteria for evaluating the performance of military policy makers and of the political and economic programs for which they, with civilian technicians, have been responsible. Obviously, the sort of performance criteria chosen will heavily influence, not to say determine, the outcome of any evaluation of governmental performance, whether by civilian or military regimes.

It would seem appropriate, therefore, to begin any evaluation of the impact of

223

military rule since 1964 by examining performance in relation to those policy objectives which military leaders themselves have identified as matters of critical national significance. These can be found in their explanations for ousting civilian governments and in subsequent elaborations of their policy orientations (as seen in the speeches and writings reproduced in part 5 of this book).

Many policy measures and objectives of the military regimes have been responses to special historical or economic circumstances in each country, such as the tin mines in Bolivia, the vulnerability of the Chilean economy to fluctuating copper prices, and the traditional Andean land tenure system attacked by the Peruvian military after 1968. Yet, there have also been certain common commitments which seem to characterize the military rulers of the 1960s and 1970s. These include: (1) the establishment of a new state apparatus—"neither capitalist nor Marxist"—to replace the formal democratic institutions and practices of the past, and (2) economic recovery, modernization, and growth.

According to the military leadership, the old political institutions and practices gave rise to corruption, failed to solve pressing national problems, and allowed the advance of internal subversion. This subversion sometimes extended into the armed forces themselves. In Brazil and Chile, especially, the threat of leftist political penetration of the armed forces contributed significantly to the military's decision to assume control.

Despite the perceived need to create new political institutions, military leaders in Latin America have not created clearly defined or widely accepted political structures to replace the constitutional forms and symbols of the pre-1964 years. Everywhere "decree laws" or "institutional acts" have provided transitory movements in the direction of a new political order. These transitory measures have lacked any firm juridical base or source of legitimacy. New constitutions have been written (or are "in preparation") and innovative legislation implemented. But into the mid-1970s, military rule depended overwhelmingly upon military power rather than upon a successful end to the quest for a legal and institutional design through which the military could implement their vision of a harmonious, hierarchically ordered polity without "politics," without class conflict, and without the irritating ambiguity of ideological, social, and political pluralism.

While no juridical or institutional design made operational these military orientations, the commitment to ending "politics" meant that another common consequence of military rule has been serious erosion of civil liberties, freedom of the press and mass media, and organizational rights and autonomy of labor, political parties, and other interest groups. The "temporary suspension" or repression of autonomous interest groups and political movements often was predicated upon a fierce anti-Marxism (though in international affairs this did not prevent Peru, Bolivia, and Argentina from expanding relationships with the Socialist bloc), but it also extended to reformist and even traditional oligarchical groups (as with the principal landowner and industrial interest groups in Peru).

Opposition political movements or parties have often been outlawed, and the mass media have been censored, closed down, or simply taken over by the military governments. The process of curtailing civil liberties and imposing restrictions upon would-be opposition groups has taken many forms, including systematic arrests and torture (Brazil and Chile), the use of troops or police against strikers (Peru, Bolivia, Brazil), "banishment" (Peru, Bolivia), and "removal of political rights" for fixed periods (Brazil). As the selections on Argentina, Bolivia, Brazil, Chile, and Peru make clear, however, not even the harshest of repression has totally eliminated resistance or "politics."

In Argentina and Bolivia, military leaders found themselves continually enmeshed in alliances with civilian political groups in efforts to create some popular and organizational base for effective governance and to utilize civilian technical expertise. In Argentina, Brazil, and Chile, civilian economists and technicians have played important ministerial roles in military rule while conservative economic interests and politicians have sought to cooperate with government programs. This made clear that military antipolitics often served the interests of the economically powerful even better and more determinedly than previous civilian regimes.

And what of the corruption and venality of civilian politicians which the military intended to eliminate? What of the willingness of civilian politicians to take the part of foreign investors and profit from the denationalization of natural resources, industry, and commerce? The longer the military regimes maintain power, the more evidence accumulates to indicate that the morality, honesty, and selflessness of the military guardians of national honor are not immune to corrosion and temptation to personal enrichment or ambition. Scandals involving a variety of improprieties have tarnished the image of Argentine, Bolivian, Brazilian, and Peruvian officers. To 1977, no serious charges of corruption surfaced in Chile, though it is difficult to imagine that none of the Chilean officers will succumb to temptation as did their colleagues throughout the rest of Latin America.

The economic and social policies and the impact of the Latin American military regimes since 1964 have been more varied than their political orientations. This diversity corresponded to the unique economic problems and resources of an emergent international power like Brazil, the impoverished Andean economies of Bolivia and Peru, or the more industrialized and complex economies of Argentina and Chile. Yet, despite the diversity, certain basic economic objectives and strategies were shared by the military regimes. Priority was given to reducing inflation and to economic stabilization through programs heavily influenced by the neoliberal economics of civilian advisers (for example, Roberto Campos in Brazil, or the University of Chicago-oriented economists in Chile).

These stabilization programs typically relied upon wage restraints and re- laxation of price regulations, which led frequently to real income declines for the working classes. They also sought to reduce government expenditures, and end budget deficits. This, in turn, has been associated with significant un- employment problems, as well as a failure to expand sufficiently needed public services through government investments (health care, housing, education). In Chile, for example, very significant declines occurred in university enrollments as the military government terminated educational programs.

With the exception of Peru (the only country under consideration where quasifeudal land tenure institutions still prevailed at the time of the takeover), military governments slowed down and reoriented agrarian reform programs by emphasizing agricultural modernization rather than the sociopolitical and redis- tributionistic aspects of agrarian reform. Even in Peru, however, the effects on income and welfare of the military-directed land reform seem to have been neutral, at best, if not regressive, while accompanied by serious problems with agricultural production and productivity. In none of the five countries has military rule truly benefited the rural and urban working classes from the standpoint of improved real income levels or availability of public services.

In terms of economic growth, the consequences of the policies of these military regimes have varied considerably. The Brazilians achieved impressive economic growth rates, especially after 1967. They also reduced substantially the rate of inflation. The Argentines (1967–69) also managed to reduce briefly the inflation rate, but did not achieve the economic growth rate experienced in Brazil. Lack of firm political control, however, led to a resurgence of inflation and even to a restoration of civilian (Peronist) government (1973–76) before a renewed crisis brought a return of the military in 1976.

In Chile after 1973, inflation continued at very high, though declining rates (over 300 percent per year), while economic output actually declined. As the selection on Chile indicates, even the official government assessment of the economic results of military rule point to a considerable decline in output, the closing of numerous factories, high unemployment, and, in general, a serious economic depression. Military rule in Bolivia and Peru has also been associated with mediocre growth rates, increasing inflation, and undiminished difficulties with unemployment.

Another common economic strategy of military rule has been heavy reliance upon private enterprise and foreign investment, even when nationalization of certain basic industries occurred. In Argentina, Brazil, and Chile, military governments even sold off publicly owned firms to private (often foreign) interests in the name of reducing public expenditures or increasing economic efficiency.

Thus, despite their nationalist declarations, military rulers in Latin America since 1964 depended extensively upon inputs of foreign capital to modernize and develop their economies. This orientation included even the Peruvians who, despite nationalization of key foreign firms and adoption of more restrictive foreign investment regulations, continued to court foreign capital. In the cases of Brazil and Chile, newsletters distributed by their embassies and consulates in the United States proudly published long lists of new foreign investment attracted by the favorable policies of the military regimes. If Latin America's military rulers in the 1970s were economic nationalists, they were also quite pragmatic nationalists in regard to the role of foreign investment in the Latin American economies.

To evaluate the overall performance of these military regimes which dominated Latin America in the mid 1970s, it is necessary to consider the political, economic, and social welfare effects of military rule. Depending upon where priorities are placed, different analysts arrive at different overall assessments of the impact of these military regimes. Yet the selections which follow illustrate that whatever the economic impact of these military governments, they have shared in the politics of antipolitics. Whether in "rightist" Brazil and Chile or "leftist" Peru, labor and other mass organizations have been repressed, coopted, or destroyed. A tight rein on dissidents, control or closure of the mass media, and an emphasis upon unity and the collective good—as defined by the military—characterized Latin American military rule after 1964.

In these respects, the policy consequences of military rule have been relatively uniform. Periods of liberalization (*distensão* in Brazil) have been quickly followed by renewed repression when opposition groups acted as if the military leadership actually meant it when they said criticism would be allowed.

The selections which follow analyze the policy consequences of military rule in Argentina (1966–73), Bolivia (1964–76), Brazil (1964–76), Chile (1973–76), and Peru (1968–76). The focus of these authors ranges from description and analysis of economic programs and social welfare outcomes to political methods, including extensive use of torture in Brazil and Chile. The selections make clear the diversity of circumstances and contexts for military rule in Latin America in the 1960s and 1970s, but they also make clear the underlying unity of orientation, objectives, and methods.

Thus, while military rule brought land reform in Peru, an "economic miracle" in Brazil, and economic depression in Chile, it was the politics of antipolitics which emerged as a universal, if qualitatively variable, technique and consequence of military rule. Whatever the economic success or failure, whatever the rhetoric or legitimizing symbols, military rule brought about a

new type of elitism, authoritarianism, intolerance, and coercion to Latin
American politics in the years after 1964.

John Thompson

Argentine Economic Policy under the Onganía Regime

Argentina's economic progress has been retarded, largely by distortions stemming from the Perón era (1946–55) and its aftermath. Perón's advent marked a turning point in Argentine history and was, indeed, one of the few real social revolutions that have occurred in Latin America. Basing himself on the urban working classes and trade unions, Perón established a fiercely nationalistic and dictatorial regime that transformed Argentina from a pastoral country, dominated by wealthy cattle ranchers, into an industrialized nation. His policies aimed at industrial self-sufficiency and the elimination of foreign influence, regardless of cost, and hence led to a consistent misallocation of the country's rich endowment of human and natural resources.

Despite the country's comparative advantage in agriculture, an industrialization drive was set in motion behind a wall of protective tariffs. Foreign-owned railroads and utilities were taken over by the Argentine government, and the state established a foreign trade monopoly. Prices paid to agricultural producers were deliberately kept low. Consequently, agricultural output declined, and all incentive to invest in the agricultural sector was removed. As agricultural and private industry became increasingly unable to provide employment, the government absorbed surplus labor by overloading the payrolls of state-owned enterprises, particularly the railroads. Governments which followed Perón proved incapable of significantly altering this state of affairs. Of 200,000 railroad employees in 1966, it was established that 40,000 were superfluous. Similar situations prevailed elsewhere in the public sector which, due to extensive nationalizations, employed large portions of the labor force. In all, the state enterprises employed some 100,000 redundant workers. To further aggravate matters, rates for public service were held artificially low for political reasons, and state enterprises became dependent upon transfers from the central government to meet their operating deficits.

Since Perón relied heavily on the working class for his support, wages were allowed to rise much faster than productivity and prices. The entire system was underwritten by growing budget deficits, financed by the Central Bank. A seemingly endless inflationary-recessionary spiral set in. In some years, the economy spurted ahead rapidly, but in most, it stagnated or showed an absolute decline. At the same time, annual price increases averaged 27 percent.

229

After Perón's ouster by the armed forces, the majority of the working class looked back on the Perón era as the only time that the government cared about their welfare. Throughout the late 1950s and early 1960s the persistent electoral strength of the Peronists undermined the effectiveness of successive governments. The armed forces remained implacable foes of Peronism, and military reactions to Peronist victories at the polls were responsible for the series of coups which alternated with weak civilian regimes. The Onganía government thus inherited a situation in which for years there had been a net disinvestment in the country's infrastructure; Argentine industry was thoroughly uncompetitive; and class consciousness and discontent were strong. In addition, the peso had suffered massive depreciation and was chronically overvalued; consequently, the country experienced periodic foreign exchange crises and accumulated a large external debt.

The Stabilization Effort: 1967–68. The group of military men who installed [Juan Carlos] Onganía as president in June 1966 had no program of their own, merely a feeling that a drastic reordering of the country's affairs was needed. Unlike previous military regimes, however, they did not intend to serve as a caretaker government until new elections could be called, but intended to stay in power until all necessary changes had been made. General Onganía himself spoke in terms of remaining in power for ten years, envisaging a revolution proceeding through three stages—economic, social, and political. Then with the country thoroughly restructured, government would be returned to civilian hands.

The president's civilian advisers fell into two groups: "nationalists," those of a more authoritarian temperament, suspicious of foreign penetration and favorable to a "managed economy," and "liberals," those who were internationalist in outlook and believed more strongly in the workings of a market economy. For several months, the government appeared uncertain as to which course to follow, but the appointment of Dr. Adalbert Krieger Vasena, a liberal economist, as economics minister proved to be a turning point in favor of the liberal option.

In March 1967, he began a comprehensive stabilization program. The peso was devalued from 250 to 350 per U.S. dollar, and controls on capital movements were removed. This large adjustment, in sharp contrast to the piecemeal devaluations of earlier years, left the peso undervalued, and hence allowed a substantial leeway for price increases. In addition, it enabled the government to impose taxes on the country's principal export products, while still improving the export sector's competitive position. At the same time, the authorities obtained a package of loans and stand-by credits from the IMF [the International Monetary Fund], the United States Treasury, and foreign commercial banks, which helped to bolster official reserves and discourage speculation.

Domestically, the authorities began an all-out campaign against inflation. The original 1967 budget was replaced by a much tighter one. Expenditures were held at the 1966 level in real terms, as a result of which state-owned enterprises were forced to increase their rates to compensate for the smaller transfers. Revenues, on the other hand, rose sharply due mostly to the new taxes on agricultural exports. The planned deficit was reduced from 34 percent of expenditures in 1966 to 14 percent in 1967. Although the actual deficit turned out to be somewhat larger, Central Bank financing of the deficit was cut back sharply.

In their 1968 budget the authorities, while by no means relenting in their anti-inflationary efforts, also strove to encourage sustained growth. A strenuous effort was made to hold down current expenditures by further reducing transfers to state enterprises. "Rationalization" programs designed to increase the efficiency of such enterprises were introduced, and by the end of 1968 only the railroads showed excessive deficits.

In addition to extensive use of fiscal and monetary policy, the authorities took direct action against cost and demand inflation. Wages were allowed to rise by no more than 15 percent in 1967 and frozen throughout 1968. Strict controls were placed on unions, which drastically reduced the number of days lost through strikes. At the same time, a set of "voluntary" price guidelines was laid down for industry, and those industries which did not comply were threatened with the loss of government contracts and credits, as well as with import liberalizations.

While the cost of living rose by 27 percent in 1967 and GDP by only 2 percent, the 1967 effort was generally successful. Much of the increase in the cost of living was the direct result of higher prices introduced by the government itself and higher import costs brought on by the 40 percent devaluation. Furthermore, the rate of price increase slowed as the year progressed. Perhaps even more important, the authorities succeeded in showing their determination to carry out a strict austerity program, which helped to restore confidence in the country abroad as well as to combat the prevailing inflationary psychology at home.

The downward trend in the rate of price increases that began in late 1967 was continued and consolidated in 1968. Wholesale prices rose by only 3.9 percent, while the cost of living rose by 9.6 percent. At the same time, the economy came out of its 1967 slump, and GDP showed an increase of 4.8 percent, with the rate of activity accelerating as the year progressed.

In both years, the country ran large balance-of-payments surpluses. Large inflows of private capital followed the devaluation, and the country had a fairly large trade surplus. Overall, the 1967 balance of payments was in surplus by $348 million. The net reserve position of the monetary authorities improved by $433 million.

In 1968, the trade surplus was reduced, owing mostly to poor weather conditions and difficulties in exporting meat to traditional markets. However, the authorities managed to meet the increased foreign exchange costs of their development program by floating external bond issues in United States and European capital markets which, in addition, helped the country to obtain longer maturities on its foreign debt and to improve its credit rating abroad. Thus, the country achieved a large capital account surplus and the balance of payments was again in surplus, this time by $171 million.

With improvement evident in all sectors, 1968 seemed to be the year in which the government's stabilization policies were vindicated. In the light of the improved financial situation of the country, on August 14, 1968, Argentina accepted the obligations of Article VIII status in the IMF, by which it pledged not to maintain multiple exchange rates or place controls on current account transactions. Furthermore, with the peso appearing more stable, the authorities announced plans for a new peso (*peso fuerte*) worth 100 old pesos, with a parity of 3.5 per U.S. dollar—a step carried out on January 1, 1970.

As part of the "liberal" economic strategy, the authorities deliberately strove to attract capital inflows. By stabilizing the currency and stimulating higher levels of growth, they decided that Argentina would be better able to attract direct private investment. They relied heavily on borrowings from the IBRD [International Bank for Reconstruction and Development] and the IDB [InterAmerican Development Bank] for their capital projects and also turned to private capital markets in the United States and Europe for the first time in a generation. In addition, Dr. Krieger Vasena made several trips to Europe and the United States to confer directly with private investors in an effort to convince them of Argentina's determination to reverse the policies of previous years as well as to embark on a period of rapid growth in an atmosphere of stability. To further reinforce confidence in the peso, the Central Bank engaged in forward market operations not allowing the discount on the peso in the six-month futures' market to fall below 8 percent. In 1968, the intervention point was successively reduced to 7 percent and 6 percent.

In 1968, the value of both imports and exports fell. The 7 percent fall in exports occurred mostly in the first half of the year. It came as the result of both poor weather conditions and difficulties in exporting meat to Argentina's traditional markets in Europe. Increased protectionism in the EEC countries and, above all, the British ban on meat imports from countries where foot-and-mouth disease exists (which lasted from December 1967 to April 1968) denied Argentina access to its most important markets. In the end, however, the British meat ban may have been a blessing in disguise, since it forced Argentine policy makers to rethink their entire policy on meat shipments abroad. Even after the United Kingdom temporarily lifted its ban on meat imports, Argentina was reluctant to resume its former practice of shipping whole carcasses to the

U.K. market without any price guarantees. By the end of 1968, 45 percent of the meat exports consisted of "special cuts" which fetch higher prices and contain higher inputs of Argentine labor. Furthermore, through aggressive marketing techniques, the authorities were able to penetrate newer markets, and by the end of the year, Argentina was shipping meat to more than sixty-five countries.

Imports declined by 4 percent in 1968 due to low levels of consumer demand in the first half of the year and a reduced dependency on foreign sources of petroleum.

In spite of the shrinkage in foreign trade, confidence in the country grew. Foreign private investment in the country totalled $154 million, compared to a total of only $141 million over the previous three years. The government sought to encourage selected foreign investment in 1968 by introducing a program of rebates on import duties and income tax rebates for foreign investment undertaken in underdeveloped areas of the country—notably Patagonia. Official capital flows were aided by government placement of $75 million in bonds in the United States and Europe. The large inflows under errors and omissions, which followed the devaluation, were not repeated in 1968. In addition, the adoption of free convertibility of the currency in 1968 makes strict comparison of 1967 and 1968 figures difficult.

By November 1968, the position of the Central Bank had strengthened so that it turned from a net seller of foreign exchange to a net buyer. Moreover, the forward discount on the peso settled to less than 4 percent, and the Central Bank no longer needed to intervene in the futures' market. In fact, large amounts of capital, presumably Argentine capital which had taken refuge abroad, were returning to the country and further strengthening the country's external position.

After installing Onganía as president, the military was, for the most part, content to retreat to the shadows of politics and allow the president and his advisers a free hand in managing the country's affairs. However, the armed forces tend to see themselves as trustees of the nation's destiny and tend to react strongly against social disorder.

Since the days of Perón, the unions have been a powerful force in the nation's life. Class consciousness is high, both in terms of occupational status and between descendents of the country's earlier settlers and those of the immigrants of the nineteenth and twentieth centuries. Through the threat of strikes, they hold a veto power over the policies of most governments, and, until the Onganía regime, they were able to obtain substantial real wage gains despite their stagnant productivity. Although the unions were divided among themselves, from 1967 onward, they provided the main opposition to the government.

In January 1969, the government relaxed its wage freeze and allowed an across-the-board wage increase of 8 percent. In addition, employee social security contributions were further reduced so that the net increase in take-home pay was about 11 percent. Nevertheless, the workers felt that they were being asked to carry the greatest burden in the stabilization program. The average real wages of unskilled industrial workers declined roughly 3 percent in the period June 1966–June 1969, while per capita GDP rose by more than 3 percent. Therefore, there was some redistribution of real incomes at the expense of industrial wage earners.

TIME LOST THROUGH STRIKES IN THE FEDERAL CAPITAL	
Year	Thousands of man-days
1965	1,265
1966	1,913
1967	245
1968	24
1969	251

SOURCE: Minsterio de Economía y Trabajo, *Informe Económico*.

Aside from its incomes policy, the government also sought more direct control over labor. The main trade union grouping, the General Confederation of Labor (CGT), split into two major factions. The "Azopardo" group, under the leadership of Augusto Vandor, was willing to extend a limited degree of cooperation to the government. On the other hand, Raimundo Ongaro's followers, the "Paseo Colón" group, a collection of Peronists, Marxists, and left-wing Catholics decided on a policy of intransigent opposition to the government, with the ultimate objective of bringing it down. Unions in the latter category were "intervened," that is, they were not recognized as bargaining agents, and their funds were confiscated. As the above table indicates, controls on strikes proved almost completely effective.

While the regime was thoroughly authoritarian and puritanical, it did not engage in widespread acts of repression. Verbal opposition was tolerated, although no political parties were permitted. Freedom of the press and civil liberties in general were respected to a reasonable degree, although individual issues of publications sharply critical of the government were confiscated. Likewise, some opponents who became too critical were jailed, but only for short periods of time. Nonetheless, the government, and to a certain extent, President Onganía's personality conveyed the impression that it was convinced of the righteousness of its own course and would not be swayed by criticism. Therefore, the ordinary channels of dissent were choked, and the government appeared determined to follow its own course. In the end, this proved to be bitter medicine indeed to swallow for a labor movement long accustomed to getting its own way.

235

The Consequences of Military Rule

The government's long-run objective was to rebuild the labor movement around the "participationist" unions and return to a system of free collective bargaining as soon as possible. Labor-management negotiations for 1970 wage contracts were scheduled to begin in September 1969. However, the authorities' timetable was upset in May 1969 when, in the wake of clashes between the police and students and workers in Córdoba, latent working-class discontent came to the surface and local disturbances erupted into a nationwide general strike. Street battling between workers and security forces raged throughout the country, and several dozen people were killed. The level of violence in the May–June riots reached such intensity that the authorities were forced to declare martial law. They imprisoned Ongaro, along with several other opposition labor leaders, and in doing so succeeded in making him a symbol of opposition to the government's policies. For a time, it appeared that the government was in danger of being overthrown. The president, in an attempt to defuse social tensions, dismissed his entire cabinet, including Dr. Guillermo Borda, the nationalist minister of the interior who was closely associated with the suppression of students and workers. Dr. Krieger Vasena was replaced by Dr. José María Dagnino, an American-trained economist generally regarded as a disciple of Dr. Krieger Vasena. While he pledged to maintain his predecessor's policies, he promised a greater employers' share in the burden of future stabilization programs.

Undeniably, the government suffered severe setbacks, losing its image as a source of stability and order as well as its claim that its successes were based on "social consensus." The unions became militantly united in their opposition to the regime's policies, demanding wage increases of 40 percent, and staged three general strikes during the summer. The murder of Augusto Vandor late in June served to further heighten the climate of violence.

Reprinted and edited from *Inter-American Economic Affairs* 24, no. 1 (summer 1970), pp. 51–75.

David Rock

Military Politics in Argentina, 1966-73

The advent of the Onganía government marked an important political hiatus. For the first time a military government was in power rejecting the transitional and provisional role of its predecessors and declaring its intention to rule for an indefinite period. The responsibility for change, which had been previously left to the civilians, was now to be carried out by a military regime, if necessary by force and without the encumbrance of having to seek the support of public opinion. As soon as it took power the government moved quickly into an assault on the major institutions which had played an important part in politics in the immediate past. The political parties were abolished and the universities purged of their left-wing and centrist elements. Of the major civilian institutions, which before had been overtly involved in political activities, only the CGT escaped.

In 1967 the Onganía government was in a stronger position than any of its predecessors. The last barrier to its authority, the CGT, was broken. It was now free, it seemed, from the need to bargain with any of the major groups and could implement whatever policies it chose. It now appeared that the complex competing "horizontal" and "vertical" pressures from the past had been finally superseded by a united and purposeful military dictatorship. Simultaneously with the confrontation with the CGT, the government revealed its plans on the economic front. Onganía appointed as minister of the economy a leading member of the neoliberal school, Adalbert Krieger Vasena. He announced a program of diversifying and rationalizing Argentine industry through another major attempt to quicken the flow of foreign investment. It was hoped to overcome the balance-of-payments bottleneck by encouraging the export of industrial products. To prepare for these objectives, a new anti-inflation stabilization program was announced which included a strict incomes policy.

The Krieger Vasena plan posed a threat to two vital political groups. It was opposed first by the smaller domestic entrepreneurs and their leading association, the General Economic Confederation (CGE). There were fears that the stabilization program, as had happened under Frondizi, would trigger a major recession and widespread bankruptcy. Once again there was talk of a "takeover" of Argentine industry by "foreign monopolies."

236

The Krieger Vasena plan was also opposed by the unions, which saw it as a disguised attack on wages and an attempt to raise the level of domestic savings at the cost of working-class consumption. In 1968 another major division occurred in the ranks of the CGT. Vandor continued in the hope that he could eventually pressure the government into making concessions. He therefore maintained his contacts with members of the administration. He was opposed in this by a rebel CGT group led by a printers' leader, Raimundo Ongaro. Although at first this group had little following, it rapidly evolved into the most vocal source of opposition to the government.

The Onganía government had thus brought about several very significant changes. Added together, these threatened to disrupt and transform the essential pattern of politics, as it had evolved since 1955. In spite of its retention of certain superficial vertical features, the class-based horizontal structure, based on the conflict between Peronism and anti-Peronism, had been the central axis of politics since Perón's downfall. This was now threatened by the military regime which had put all the parties on an equal footing in the ranks of the opposition. In doing so it had abruptly cut the normal channels of communication through which sectional opinions were expressed and the horizontal pattern of politics maintained. For the first time ever Radicals and Peronists found themselves in the same camp. Secondly, the adoption of the Krieger Vasena plan, and its aggressive provisions for eliminating inflation and enhancing the flow of foreign capital, had a similar parallel effect on two key interest groups, the unions and the smaller employers. This not only meant the intensification of the gathering confrontation between "nationalist" and neoliberal groups, but also implied a new common interest between the former and the unions against the government. A third major factor was, in part, a by-product of the first. In suppressing conventional political activities, the Onganía government weakened the capacity of formal political vehicles like the parties and the CGT to act as articulating agents for the major socioeconomic groups. The protests of entrepreneurs tended less to be expressed through the parties, and those of the workers less through a CGT dominated by Vandor. A further stage in the growing atomization of formal political bodies before 1966 was the tendency afterward for new vehicles of political articulation and mobilization to emerge. Examples of this were the growing importance of the CGE, representing the entrepreneurs, and Ongaro's wing of the union movement, representing dissident segments of the working class.

For a little over two years the Krieger Vasena plan seemed highly successful. By 1969 the rate of inflation had fallen to a comparatively negligible amount. Wages were falling, but gradually and without the traumatic shocks of the past. There was no apparent sign of any dangerous buildup of working-class opposition. Fears that the plan would provoke a major recession proved largely unfounded. Unlike Frondizi's stabilization plan in 1959, Krieger's had the advantage of having been introduced during a period of depression. Cyclical forces encouraging economic recovery for a time proved stronger than the deflationary influence of government policy.

However, the *pax onganiana*, and the determined effort it marked to escape from the mould of stagnation which had begun in 1949, eventually failed. Suddenly in May 1969, there was a spate of student unrest in the interior cities of Resistencia, Corrientes, Rosario, and Córdoba. In Rosario and Córdoba these movements quickly and spontaneously evolved into major urban riots. The more significant was in Córdoba, where the students were joined by large numbers of striking auto workers. Only when the army was brought in in strength was the outbreak quashed.

These events destroyed the Krieger Vasena program and led directly to Onganía's downfall a year later. The army, which since 1966 had remained united behind the government, now divided between the adherents of repression like Onganía himself and other groups led by the army commander in chief, General Alejandro Lanusse, which supported a more conciliatory policy in the hope of curbing unrest. The *cordobazo*, as the rebellion in Córdoba became known, remains the central event in comtemporary Argentine history. It underlay the fundamental realignment of political forces which culminated in the restoration of Peronism in 1973.

The revolts in the universities were closely associated with pressures deriving from or complementing the central orientation of the Krieger Vasena plan. Since 1966 there had been an effort to "functionalize" the universities by emphasing technical and managerial training, and by restricting their intake in accordance with estimates of demand for different professional qualifications. The revolts of 1969 were triggered by dramatic changes in the food prices charged in university refectories as part of a campaign to rationalize costs. Reactions like this clearly relate to frustrated mobility aspirations among students and were culturally based responses to sudden, violent changes in disposable incomes. This illustrated the chronic political problems produced by twenty years of economic stagnation, combined with the government's praetorian zeal for efficiency.

Similar pressures were apparent among the Córdoba auto workers. Throughout the 1960s the auto industry had been subject to wide oscillations in output, and this made for great insecurity among the workforces. The flashpoint for the strike in 1969 was the sudden waiving of traditional privileges concerning Saturday afternoon working. But again, this can be a preliminary basis for any general explanation. Any simple Marxist argument along the lines of progressive pauperization cannot be applied literally in this context. As Krieger Vasena remarked soon after his resignation in June 1969, the Córdoba auto workers were among the best paid in the country. It was not that the auto workers were becoming any poorer in the literal sense. The source of their reaction is more explicable in terms of fluctuations in output and intensity of labor.

Further facilitating the links which developed in Córdoba between the students and the auto workers was that many of the students were themselves shift workers in the auto plants. A second point relates to the divisions in the national CGT between Vandor, Alonso, and Ongaro. In Córdoba, this had produced a chaotic situation among the groups in different plants claiming to represent the work force. When the spark came, the different factions proved unable to exercise any form of effective leadership and were simply carried along by events. These conditions of institutional fragmentation, which again relate to government policy and behavior since 1966, seem to have played some part in the central pattern of events.

Although the *cordobazo*, and the other lesser movements, were largely spontaneous and leaderless, it was not long before attempts were beginning to fashion their energies into a new popular opposition front against the government controlled by New Left groups. None of these was ever successful. At first it seemed that Ongaro's group would gain the upper hand. Within a short time a rough alliance had emerged between him and the most active of the Córdoba union leaders, Agustín Tosco of the light and power workers. In 1970, a new radical union, Sitrac-Sitram, emerged among the Córdoba auto workers. It too began to call for the formation of a popular liberation front.

Thus, 1969 saw the emergence of the threatened new popular force. If it lacked a unified leadership and a coherent, shared ideology, it had some of the vertical, cross-class features of the populist alliances of the past. Workers, students, and in some cases businessmen had united in a violent protest against the government. In doing so, they isolated the neoliberal groups which had supported the Onganía government and the Krieger Vasena plan. Onganía's destruction and repression of traditional political institutions in 1966 and the weakening of the unions in 1967 underlay the violence of the reaction in 1969 and its tendency to spawn new, organized groups like the radical Sitrac-Sitram.

This new movement was not Peronist. Neither Perón nor Vandor, who was murdered in mysterious circumstances a few weeks after the *cordobazo*, had played any significant part in its conception or execution. If the new movement sought inspiration in anyone, it was the mythical figure of Ernesto [Che] Guevara. For the first time in twenty years, the division between Peronists and anti-Peronists had been superseded. Instead of dividing society along class lines, the policies of the Onganía government had finally come to unite them.

In 1970 the dangers to the military government posed by the new alliance were increased with a sudden profusion of Marxist and Peronist guerrilla groups. This was a novel phenomenon, and it illustrated the point to which opposition to the military government had escalated. From the end of 1969 onward, the guerrilla groups made a series of spectacular raids on police stations, army outposts, and banks. There was also a spate of kidnappings. The most important was the abduction and execution of former president Aramburu by the Peronist Montoneros group. This event was the signal for an army coup led by General Lanusse against Onganía in June 1970, and his replacement by a former military attaché in Washington, General Roberto M. Levingston.

In 1970 and 1971 the economy again plunged into recession, and, as in the past, this gave a further impulse to unrest. There was a marked slowing of industrial production, coupled with a heavy deficit on the balance of payments. Soon after the abandonment of the Krieger Vasena plan, inflation had again swiftly developed. Unemployment also increased and by the middle of 1971 had reached the same level as in 1967 during the first phase of the Krieger Vasena plan.

On the political front, the most significant events occurred in March 1971. Following the resignation of a popular provincial governor, Bernardo Bas, there was another major uprising in Córdoba, again involving students, middle-class groups, and auto workers. The difference between this and the movement of 1969 was that in 1971 there was much greater control and coordination over it, led in particular by groups like Sitrac-Sitram. It was also widely reported that sections of the leading Marxist guerrilla group, the ERP, were closely involved. The feared links between Marxist guerrillas and popular uprisings appeared to be in an advanced form of gestation. Although this may have been exaggerated, it proved to be the spur to a radical change of policy by the army. Within a week of the movement in Córdoba Levingston's short rule was brought to an end, and Lanusse himself personally took control. The principal aim of his government, constantly reiterated by himself and other members of the administration, was to drive a wedge between "subversion" and the popular uprisings, to eliminate the former and to control the latter.

Lanusse immediately announced presidential elections for March 1973 and called upon the traditional political parties to join with the government in a "Great National Agreement" to save the country from revolutionary anarchy. By restoring the privileges and full legal status of the parties, the agreement marked the final abandonment of the practices followed by Onganía's "Argentine revolution" in 1966. The turnabout on the economic front, which had begun with the downfall of Krieger Vasena in 1969, was now followed in 1971 by a change of equal scope at the political level. These efforts at conciliation did not include the New Left groups. Ongaro, Tosco, and others were imprisoned. Militant unions like Sitrac-Sitram were dissolved by government decree. Under government promptings, the official CGT reacquired the privileges and bargaining power it had lost in 1967. Meanwhile, the war against the guerrillas continued without quarter. In August 1972 a number of imprisoned guerrillas who had been recaptured after an escape attempt were summarily shot in the naval garrison of Trelew. These were the central guidelines of government policy—the revival of the traditional political bodies to fill the institutional vacuum left by Onganía, accompanied by a root-and-branch campaign against the New Left groups.

However, Lanusse's boldest stroke, achieved in the face of bitter opposition among certain groups in the army, was to include the Peronists in his project of reviving the traditional structures and using them as a buffer between the government and the forces of popular unrest. In a further energetic attempt to shift popular attention away from the left, the government began a campaign to persuade the Peronists to join the ''Great National Agreement'' and then to speculate publicly on the possibility of Perón's return from exile. It was evident that if the old grudges against Perón were far from dead, the government felt that the situation was sufficiently desperate to justify a major change of attitude. In this way the sixteen-year ostracism of Perón suddenly ended.

Reprinted and edited from *Argentina in the Twentieth Century* (Pittsburgh, Pa.: University of Pittsburgh Press, 1975), pp. 207, 209–217.

Military Rule in Bolivia after 1964

On November 4, 1964, [Alfredo] Ovando and [René] Barrientos occupied the presidential palace and declared themselves copresidents. But as the crowd gathered outside the palace persisted in shouting their preference for Barrientos, Ovando allowed Barrientos to assume the formal title alone, while he occupied the post of commander in chief of the armed forces.

Barrientos insisted that his assumption of power was not to be regarded as a counterrevolutionary move. In fact, he pledged a restoration to "the true path" of the 1952 Revolution, from which he maintained the Paz government had greviously deviated. But he began his rule with the same ephemeral base of support—military and peasants—that had crumbled beneath Paz; furthermore, like Paz, he looked to the United States as his principal source of economic assistance and, in so doing, accepted the logic of the stabilization plan that called for the containment of the labor left. Although many of the peasants tended to identify with Barrientos because he had an Indian mother and spoke Quechua, he was actually dependent for immediate effective support on alliances with key peasant leaders whose competition among themselves inhibited attempts to mold the peasantry into a power bloc. The peasants failed to constitute an effective counterweight to miners and other workers, and Barrientos was dependent almost exclusively on his military supporters for the imposition of his economic game plan.

In early 1965 the Mining Corporation of Bolivia (Corporación Minera de Boliva—COMIBOL) was placed under the control of a military director. Control Obrero (workers' control), the provision of the nationalization decree empowering union leadership to veto management decisions, was nullified. Miners' pay was halved to the equivalent of about US $0.80 a day, and the COMIBOL work force was cut by 10 percent. The number of subsidized food items in company stores was also sharply reduced. When the miners responded in May 1965 by striking, the military moved into the mines and, after a violent clash, terminated the strike and disarmed the miners' militias. Leaders of the miners' unions were hustled into exile and were soon joined by leaders of other unions that protested the treatment of the miners. [Juan] Lechín was among those exiled, and the Bolivian Labor Central (Central Obrera Boliviana—COB) was effectively dismantled. In September 1965 the mines were placed under permanent military occupation, and the remnants of independent labor organization in most sectors were eliminated.

Meanwhile, with an eye to legitimizing his rule through elections in 1966, Barrientos attempted to construct a new civilian political organization. The organizing cadres for the Popular Christian movement (Movimiento Popular Cristiano—MPC) were to be drawn from right-wing anti-Paz factions of the MNR, and their target group was to be the peasant masses. The organizing campaign was not successful, however, and the MPC remained a phantom party.

Ultimately Barrientos decided on a broad-front tactic. Four small parties with nothing obvious in common—the MPC, PIR, PRA [Partido Revolucionario Auténtico], and the Social Democratic party—plus what the pro-Barrientos peasant leaders had designated the *bloque campesino* (peasant bloc) composed the heterogeneous Frente Barrientista (Barrientista Front). With the bulk of the peasant vote (but with relatively few city dwellers' votes), Barrientos won handily over five lesser-known opponents in the presidential elections of July 3, 1966.

In order not to lose his grip on the power base he had started with, Barrientos frequently increased the salaries and perquisites of the military and continued the process of granting land titles; but most attempts to expand that base beyond its original components proved futile. Cultivation of the urban middle class was difficult as the laissez faire drift of the Barrientos government, offering greater privileges to foreign investors, ran against the nationalistic grain, which was strong in that sector. Most labor organizations remained implacably opposed to his government, and students and teachers became increasingly alienated.

The killing of Ernesto "Che" Guevara in 1967 and the defeat of the guerrilla movement he had led might have consolidated support for Barrientos within the military, but an incident the following year aroused the ire even of a number of military officers. In August 1968 Antonio Argüedas, former minister of government and a close personal friend of Barrientos, announced that he had been an agent of the United States government and that agents of that government had penetrated all levels of the Bolivian government. The importance of the incident lay not so much in what was said (the rumor mill had been circulating the same information for a long time) as in who had said it because Argüedas had been the man in charge of the government's large-scale crackdown on labor, students, and other leftist groups. Nationalistic indignation was aroused, and a cloud of suspicion enveloped the government.

By 1969 Barrientos had dropped many of the formalities of constitutional government and was relying more and more on coercive measures to contain potential opposition. Moreover, as had not been uncommon in Bolivian political life, he was being publicly criticized by his own vice president, Luis Adolfo Siles Salines. Many Bolivians believed at that time that the tenure of Barrientos depended more on the military than on any other political base.

The tenure issue was eliminated rather than resolved when the president was killed in a helicopter crash on April 27, 1969. Ovando was in Washington at the time of the crash, and the vice president, Siles Salines, received permission from the army high command to assume his mandate.

Elections had been scheduled for July 1970, and it appeared for a few months that Ovando might wait for an electoral mandate and assume the presidency by constitutional means. The death of Barrientos, however, initiated a great deal of political activity and maneuvering among the various political parties and forces. The fluidity of the situation became particularly apparent in July when the popular mayor of La Paz, General Armando Escobar Uria, announced his candidacy for the presidency. On September 27, 1969, however, calling for national pacification and a true nationalist political program, Ovando dismissed Siles Salines and moved into the presidential palace. He installed a new ideologically eclectic and regionally diverse civil-military cabinet, which he described as representative of the national left, annulled the elections scheduled for 1970, and dismissed the Congress. Attempting to harness the political energy contained in the issue of economic nationalism in general and anti-Americanism in particular for the provision of immediate popular support for his new government, Ovando proceeded to nationalize the Bolivian Gulf Oil Company and to nullify the Petroleum Code. He also imposed restrictions on capital movement, gave the state mining bank a monopoly over mineral exports, withdrew the army from the mining camps, and publicly criticized what he viewed as the emphasis the United States placed on military assistance as opposed to economic assistance.

In adopting this populist-nationalist stance, Ovando had rejected his own past associations and allies, who had advocated the acceptance of international economic and military assistance, gambling that sponsorship of popular measures would provide him with a new and stronger power base. But the popularity of his policies did not translate into widespread political support for his presidency. Thus, lacking organized backing from the populist-leftist-nationalistic sector, he had to turn again to those advocating international cooperation in economic and military affairs. Lechín was again exiled for several months, and a miners' hunger march in December 1969 was denounced as subversive. In February 1970 United States military assistance, which had been temporarily suspended, was reinstated, and in September 1970 an agreement in principle was reached with the Bolivian Gulf Oil Company for financial compensation.

By mid-1970 failure to convert populist rhetoric into real benefits for the masses and concessions he had made to the right had chipped away much of the diffuse popular support Ovando had originally enjoyed. Thus, he was left in the untenable position of posing as a leftist whose base of support was the predominantly rightist military. Ambivalence and a power vacuum at the highest levels of government seemed to invite conspiracy from both right and left.

In October the situation deteriorated. The first move against the Ovando government came from the right. On October 4 General Rogelio Miranda led a revolt of the La Paz garrison, forcing Ovando's resignation and claiming the presidency for himself. He was, in turn, forced by some of the more moderate conservatives among his colleagues to step down in favor of a junta. The junta had hoped to unify the armed forces, but a group of younger, more nationalistic officers under the leadership of General Juan José Torres González had different ideas. This group, with some support from students and the Bolivian Labor Central (Central Obrera Boliviana—COB), plus the armed muscle of the air force, were enough to topple the junta and install Torres in power on October 7.

From the start Torres faced many of the same problems that had plagued Ovando, but, having been dismissed in July as commander in chief of the armed forces, he was not associated with some of the more damaging compromises of Ovando's last months in office, and he enjoyed more organized support from the nationalistic left. The Workers' Political Commando (Comando Político de los Trabajadores), for example, organized in October to back Torres, embraced the PRIN [Partido Revolucionario de la Izquierda Nacional], the POR [Partido Obrero Revolucionario], the Siles Suazo splinter of the MNR, and the Moscow-oriented wing of the PCB [Partido Comunista de Bolivia].

This support made it possible for Torres to weather the first attempt to unseat him. He had held office only three months when it took place. Participants in the abortive coup, led by Colonel Hugo Banzer Suárez, commander of the elite Colegio Militar in La Paz, were isolated within hours as a mass demonstration by workers and students suggested that Torres's faction of the military had strong popular support. Civilian demonstrators had urged Torres to distribute arms to them as a hedge against future coup attempts by right-wing military elements, but Torres, mindful that he had no control over these groups, refused.

Torres made a serious, but ultimately futile, attempt to win the full confidence of the left. He tolerated the organization in July 1971 of the People's Assembly. The majority of the delegates to this two-week session represented the trade unions, although peasant organizations and students were also represented and six leftist parties were allowed two delegates each. Neither the MNR, the largest political party, nor the military was represented. The assembly lacked the means to implement its program, and proposals to establish a people's militia and to reinstitute trade union control over COMIBOL, among others, served only to unite in opposition the disparate elements who saw their interests threatened by the assembly.

Even more provocative to opponents of the Torres government in general and to the military hierarchy in particular was the emergence of the Military Vanguard of the People (Vanguardia Militar del Pueblo—VMP). A manifesto published by this group in August 1971 noted that the lower ranks of the army were the proletarians in a class-stratified institution and proposed the replacement of the existing hierarchy with a popular army at the service of the people. The VMP, a secret society of junior officers organized on a cellular basis, was active only in La Paz. By publicizing its intentions while lacking a firm base, the VMP merely gave premature warning to its opponents.

In deference to his civilian supporters, Torres had purged a number of right-wing officers from the military, but he was apparently unwilling or unable to allow the predominance of the military among the country's institutions to be undermined. As he wavered between the irreconcilable pressures of the military and the unions, the minimal control he had exercised over each of these groups was eroded.

Meanwhile, Banzer and his principal collaborators, exiled following the abortive coup in January, had returned surreptitiously and were being harbored by military colleagues in Santa Cruz. By August, rumors had spread throughout the country that Banzer, supported by such diverse entities as Bolivian Gulf, the Brazilian government, and the FSB [Falange Socialista Boliviano], was plotting a coup. The government apparently placed credence in these rumors because on August 18, 1971, Banzer and a number of his colleagues were arrested by the police in Santa Cruz. The remaining conspirators proceeded to organize a demonstration and to occupy the town square, the major radio stations, the university, and the trade union headquarters. By nightfall, effective control of Santa Cruz was in the hands of the insurgents, and military garrisons all over the lowlands were declaring their support for the insurrection.

Within a couple of days the garrisons of the Altiplano were wavering in their support of the central government. Workers and students in La Paz organized a large demonstration in favor of Torres and demanded weapons to defend his government. Those supporting Torres had few weapons to distribute. Nevertheless, the violence and loss of life accompanying this change of government was greater than at any time since the 1952 Revolution. In the final confrontation only one military regiment, the Colorado Regiment, of La Paz, was willing to fight to preserve the government. Many workers, students, and other civilians, however, some with and some without weapons, attempted in vain to hold out against the insurgents. Street fighting in La Paz reportedly left some 200 dead and 500 to 700 wounded.

On August 21 Torres retreated to the Peruvian embassy, and Banzer emerged from imprisonment to assume the presidency. Before dawn on the morning of the following day tanks rolled through the streets of La Paz, their loudspeakers announcing that Bolivia had been saved from communism. The last of the serious fighting took place on August 23, when armored-car units and air force fighter planes attacked students at the Higher University of San Andrés, in La Paz. The Banzer government announced that 7 students had been killed; other sources maintained that casualties were several times that number. About 300 students were arrested. All of the country's universities were closed thereafter for more than a year while faculties and student bodies were purged of opponents of the government and a new university reform decree eliminating university autonomy was drawn up.

The power base of the new government consisted of an alliance of groups drawn together for the most part by their fear of Torres's radicalism and their commitment to order, anticommunism, and private enterprise. In addition to Banzer's military allies, the major components of the Nationalist Popular front (Frente Popular Nacionalista—FPN), as the new ruling coalition was called, were the FSB and the core of the MNR, under the leadership of Paz. Considering the family background (the landowning class of Santa Cruz) of the new president and his consistently conservative stance, the collaboration of the FSB with his government was not surprising. The involvement of the MNR has been seen in part as a consequence of the nearly total exclusion of that party from the government of Torres, particularly in its later days. Paz was invited to return from exile, but he did not assume a formal position in the government.

The two parties were allocated five ministries each, and at the departmental level one party was to nominate the prefect and the other, the mayor. The military retained the ministries of defense, government, and agriculture, and the ministries of industry and of hydrocarbons were filled with representatives of private enterprise. One of the most notable shifts in the power structure was that of regional base; almost half the cabinet members were natives of Santa Cruz.

The precariousness of the collaboration of such traditional foes as the FSB and the MNR was apparent from the start, as fistfights erupted between members of the two groups at the swearing-in ceremonies for the cabinet. Both parties suffered internal dissension as a consequence of their collaboration with each other and with the military. The MNR leaders were constrained by the military in their efforts to mobilize their traditional popular base, and the FSB had never had a mass base, so both parties were, to a degree, dependent on the pleasure of the military for their continued participation in government.

The new minister of government, Colonel Andrés Selich, head of the ranger unit that had been specially trained by United States military advisers to deal with guerrilla movements, launched a pacification program in which he enjoyed considerable autonomy of action. Predictably, public employees were among the first groups to be purged, both because they had served a government considered radical and because all available patronage was needed to undergird the new government. Other groups that were targets of the government ministry's campaign were labor and student leaders, worker-priests, and journalists. Within a month of the coup d'état, for example, more than 100 journalists had vanished from their former posts.

By early 1972 the visibility of the rangers and the zeal and apparent lack of discrimination with which Selich had pursued his campaign against those he considered communist subversives had provoked sharp protests from the church and appeared to have brought the shaky government coalition to the verge of disintegration. The presbyterial council of the diocese of La Paz called on the government ministry to end the repression, and the bishop of Corocoro expressed outrage over the unexplained invasion and search of his house by the police. MNR leaders in the government were antagonized by the arrests of many members of their rank and file; and the detention of former vice-president Nuflo Chávez Ortiz and of Paz's son, an international civil servant, aroused extreme indignation.

More importantly, the elite status and virtual autonomy of the rangers were resented by many in the upper echelons of the regular military hierarchy. The rangers were far better paid, fed, and equipped than other military units and wore a distinctive uniform. Moreover, many in the upper echelon of the regular military ranks perceived that close ties existed between Selich and the United States military assistance group. At a birthday celebration in December 1971 for a newly appointed commander in chief of the armed forces, the rangers were openly accused of being mercenaries under foreign control.

Banzer announced the dismissal of Selich that same month. Initially, Selich held out in the ministry and threatened to shoot anyone who tried to remove him. He was finally assigned to diplomatic exile in Paraguay and later was forcibly retired from the army. Nevertheless, rumors that he was plotting a coup persisted. The seriousness of such threats to the government could not be reliably ascertained. The majority of subversive plots that the government reported to have uncovered in the course of 1972, however, were attributed to leftist groups.

The semipublic bickering and dissembling within and between the parties in the governing coalition that continued throughout 1972 appeared to enhance the power of Banzer vis-á-vis the civilian leaders, but in July he acquiesced to MNR pressure and permitted the legalization of labor unions (though not of the major federations). The devaluation of the peso from about 12 to 20 to $1 (U.S.) in October, however, sparked a new crisis. A general strike shut down business activity in the capital, and demonstrations resulted in clashes between strikers and police and in large-scale arrests of labor leaders. On November 23, Banzer, stating that he had uncovered a leftist plot to overthrow the government, declared a state of siege.

In December Banzer announced that his government had uncovered another massive plot, in this case to assassinate him and ''Vietnamize'' Bolivia. The plotters were said to be components of a front group known as the Anti-Imperialist Revolutionary Front (Frente Revolucionaria Anti-imperialista— FRA). More than twenty Bolivian organizations, including virtually every party to the left of the MNR, were listed as components. Also listed among the plotters were about a dozen leftist organizations from other parts of the hemisphere, including three composed of Chile's Mapuche Indians. The plot was said to be funded by Cuba and supported by the People's Republic of China (PRC) and the Soviet Union and to include an attack by a 7,000-man guerrilla army that was in training in Chile.

A reinvigorated campaign to round up subversives followed this announcement. By January 1973 the number of political prisoners, many of whom were held in special camps in remote areas, was estimated by some sources at more than 1,500. As had been true in several other Latin American countries, the thoroughness of the antisubversive net was such that even personal libraries of suspects were examined for literature that might be considered subversive.

It was announced in January that the coalition of the Christian Democratic party (Partido Demócrata Cristiano—PDC), formerly the PSC, and the PRA had entered into an opposition pact with the Siles Suazo faction of the MNR, known as the Nationalist Revolutionary Movement of the Left (Movimiento Nacionalista Revolucionario de la Izquierda—MNRI). In early February the coalition appealed to the armed forces to restore constitutional order and guarantee free elections. The armed forces high command responded that ''when the social and economic objectives (of the government) are achieved, the political conditions necessary to enter into an institutionalization process will be studied.''

The reappearance in Bolivia of Colonel Selich in May 1973 set off a chain of events that resulted in the most severe crisis that the Banzer government had yet confronted. Suspected once again of masterminding a plot to overthrow the government, Selich was arrested on May 14. It was announced on the following day that Selich had died as a consequence of falling down a flight of stairs while attempting to escape. The original official version of the event met with considerable skepticism, and on May 18 a new official version was released. Government Minister Alfredo Arce Carpio announced at that time he had discovered that Selich had been beaten to death by overly zealous interrogators.

The announcement provoked outrage from both military and civilian sectors, and the FSB threatened to withdraw its support from the government if Arce were not removed from office. President Banzer discouraged precipitous action by his opponents by posting army vehicles and troops around the National Palace, while acquiescing to FSB demands and accepting Arce's resignation. The commander in chief of the armed forces, General Joaquim Zenteno Anaya, also resigned, claiming that Banzer's coalition was inoperative, and the president himself took charge temporarily of that vacated post. Meanwhile, President Banzer was reportedly sharing his power to a greater extent with other military officers.

Reprinted and edited from United States Government, *Area Handbook for Bolivia*, 2d ed. (1974), pp. 239–46.

Albert Fishlow

Brazil's Economic Miracle

The Brazilian "miracle" is no longer a transitory curiosity to be casually explained away. Rates of growth of national product of the order of 10 percent, and even more for industry, have resulted in about a 50 percent increase in Brazilian income per capita since 1967. Inflation rates are currently of the order of 15 percent. By comparison with recent global trends that statistic is all the more impressive. And monetary correction for the exchange rate and many financial assets compensates for the distortions induced by a rising price level. Exports have responded extremely well in recent years, and their value will easily exceed $5,000 m. this year with the aid of favorable terms of trade for agricultural products. Yet this last development should not slight the substantial gains in exports of manufactures. In response to attractive incentives, they now represent sales of more than $1,000 m. compared to a meagre $50 m. in 1964.

These accomplishments have not gone unnoticed. The Brazilian model has been viewed with eager interest by other developing countries both within and without Latin America. Certainly the Chilean military, before undertaking their own recent intervention, were highly conscious of these material successes of their Brazilian confreres. The phenomenon may even be more general. Other countries have also fashioned impressive records of economic growth by opting for frankly capitalist, international market-oriented, and politically authoritarian regimes. The cases of Spain, Portugal, and Greece come immediately to mind.

These circumstances make it all the more essential to probe more deeply into the Brazilian experience to answer three fundamental questions: (1) To what extent is the Brazilian miracle related to the technocratic efficiency and political stability made possible by successive military governments since 1964? (2) What groups within Brazil have especially benefited from this new style of development? (3) And ultimately, how viable is the Brazilian model—is the present growth likely to continue? The responses to these queries go far to illuminate the origins, consequences, and prospects of the Brazilian miracle.

251

Origins

The present Brazilian growth, impressive as it is, is not without precedent. From the mid-1950s to the early 1960s a comparable acceleration had taken place that already placed Brazil among the foremost industrialized developing countries. That experience was the acme of the import-substitution process, emphasizing internal markets and domestic production to replace dependence upon foreign supplies. It was self-limiting, owing, in part, to the deficiencies of the strategy, in part to international market conditions, in part to internal political crisis.

The most serious contradiction of the strategy was its inattention to the balance-of-payments problem. Import substitution did not literally mean domestic manufacture of former imports—that phase had already been surpassed in the 1930s; it meant production of newer goods, principally consumer durables, whose import had been limited in any event. Consequently, national plants implied new demands for equipment that more than offset any reduction in import requirements for final products. At the same time, exports were neglected. Today that seems sinful; then it appeared more rational in a world of declining terms of trade and inability to compete in industrial exports. When more favorable exchange rates were offered, as they were on more than one occasion, the response was disappointing and dashed faith in a more aggressive internationally oriented stance.

The resulting persistent pressure in the balance of payments was offset by substantial foreign investment. That was the principal paradox of the import-substitution strategy. In the guise of reducing foreign dependence, it considerably increased it. Subsidies, direct and indirect, proliferated to attract simultaneously the foreign exchange and technological competence required to establish modern industry. But inflow of capital necessarily sets in motion return repayments. And new net investment could not be attracted without limit. In fact, in the early 1960s it slowed down considerably. The uncertainties surrounding the sudden resignation of President Quadros, and the less favorable climate for private foreign enterprise, contributed. But so, too, did a more fundamental and underlying limitation of the import-substitution strategy. By bunching together the introduction of new goods, demand for which was initially high because they had not previously been available, policy had managed to recreate in a modern setting all of the predispositions towards a classic trade cycle. The investment boom of the late 1950s created the excess capacity of the early 1960s and an inevitable slowing down of capital formation. What structuralist critics of the time commented upon as stagnation was in reality an import-substitution trade cycle.

Against this background of slowing growth and accelerating inflation fed by inadequate and inappropriate policy response, the coup of March 1964 occurred. The recovery promised by the economic advisers of the new regime, led by Roberto Campos, was slow in coming. Granting the difficulty of the underlying problems, I am none the less inclined to stress the inefficiency of many of the policies followed. There was vacillation in monetary stringency such that the money supply increased by 75 percent in one year and 15 percent the next. It produced predictable continuation of inflation and accompanying recession. Overemphasis upon reducing governmental deficits in 1966 even after excess demand had been drained from the economy aggravated the situation. The spate of reforms introduced by innumerable decrees were confusing without really being effective; many could have been formulated more effectively over a longer time span. The governing consideration in economic policy-making was not to respond to the special characteristics of a developing economy in cyclical decline, but rather to seek to impose upon Brazil the conditions in which orthodox monetary and fiscal instruments could work effectively.

That strategy was ill rewarded. Its reversal by a more pragmatic Costa e Silva government led to much happier results. Under the guidance of Antônio Delfim Neto, expansionary monetary and fiscal policies were tried and proved successful in inducing recovery. A constantly devaluing exchange rate to compensate for differential inflation reinforced a much expanded battery of incentives for industrial exports. Such reforms, and many of the earlier ones which had scarcely been effective, took hold because the economy was in full recovery. An environment of growth is more conducive to structural change than the context of economic recession. The recovery in its first years was fed by expanded public demand. The deficit in 1967 actually increased as a proportion of national product. Because of the prior excess capacity, savings requirements initially were limited. With the initial momentum thus created, reinforced by demand for consumer durables, the Brazilian economy definitively escaped from the import-substitution cycle. More recent expansion has been accompanied by a further accumulation of capital; indeed, one can speak of a renewed investment boom in which foreign investment has come to figure prominently once again.

This view of recent events is at variance with an interpretation that stresses the distinctive rationality of economic policy after 1964 and the constructive role of technocratic guidance unemcumbered by an overt political process. In the first place, it emphasizes the continuity of current and previous growth. Indeed, the present emphasis upon rapid growth of exports in response to incentives bears a distinct affinity to the earlier policy of subsidized import substitution. There are important differences, of course, particularly in the balance of payments but also in implications for domestic efficiency. Yet both represent conscious market intervention to induce growth, and the export phase is a logical next step built upon the prior existence of national industrial capacity. Nor are the policy instruments after 1964 essentially novel. Exchange-rate reform was more thorough in 1961 than in 1964; and the tariff reductions in 1967 were less far-reaching than the nominal declines indicate, and were in some cases offset by subsequent increases and administrative decisions. The relative freedom from balance-of-payments difficulties after 1964 was purchased by slower income growth, as well as much more liberal treatment by creditors. These permitted a return to less divergent import and export rates rather than instituting them for the first time.

Secondly, it suggests that the tutelary role of the military in tolerating the disappointing economic results of the 1964–67 period because of excessive commitment to cabinet stability was counterproductive rather than essential to the growth that followed. Nor did foreign investment revive until well after economic growth was in full sway, despite the receptivity of the new regime to private capital inflow. Post hoc, propter hoc is a poor principle to invoke. One can even invert the logic. It is entirely likely that the limited expansion of the political process surrounding the presidential succession in 1967 permitted internal dissatisfactions to surface and provided the necessary context for the reversal in economic policies that emerged. Much the same may be happening now.

Consequences

This interpretation also helps to put into proper perspective the division of the gains of recent growth. There now seems to be agreement that the income distribution did worsen during the 1960s. The picture is not a pretty one. Every decile of the population except the first experienced a relative decline in income. Of the total gain in Brazilian income per capita over the decade, the richest 10 percent of the population appropriated almost three-fourths, the poorest 50 percent less than a tenth. Urban incomes, already higher, grew more rapidly than rural earnings. Those with university education experienced a rise in income of 52 percent, while the half of the population with some primary education in 1970 received incomes only 14 percent greater than those in 1960. Persons aged 40–49 obtained the largest gain of any age group; all below 30 suffered relative declines. Of the six regions, only the richest, the state of São Paulo, registered an above-average increase in income.

It is the official position that this process of income concentration was a necessary concomitant of accelerated growth. Rewards, in this view, were apportioned to scarce skills by a well-functioning market process; the appropriate response is to increase their supply by investment at the upper reaches of the educational system. Ultimately the benefits will trickle down. The evidence is more consistent with another explanation. Income concentration during the decade was a direct consequence of harsh and inequitable wage policy. Between 1964 and 1967 there was a loss of 20 percent in the real minimum wage and somewhat less in industrial wages. Under the guise of a new, "technocratic" wage adjustment scheme that incorporated expectation of future inflation, labor bore the brunt of the failure to attain stabilization targets. For the difference between expected inflation and actual price rises was directly translated into loss of real wages. After 1967 the decline halted as inflation was brought under effective control. But the gains of productivity increase were still denied to workers. The increase in real wages since 1967 stands much below what is consistent with the rapid growth in output per worker. From 1967 to 1971 real nonagricultural wages increased by 13 percent, less than half the recorded productivity gain. Even now the real minimum wage, despite all intervening wage supplements, is not far different from what it was in the mid-1950s. Two decades of growth have gone for naught for the poorest segment of the population.

It is policy rather than the requirements of growth that has enforced this shift in the functional distribution, and within that of wages alone. To be sure, modern technology does impose a demand for skilled workers and that bias is translated into a potential source of inequality. But the relative contribution to the realized deterioration of the Brazilian distribution arising from that source is, in fact, a comparatively small part of the story. Encouragement to savers, fiscal incentives for private accumulation of wealth, continuing high profits for financial intermediation, all reinforce the direct consequences of wage policy itself.

This result is predictable from a model of development that forecloses a broadly based political process. The priorities cannot be those of the mass of Brazilian poor, who require food and shelter now rather than far in the future. About a third of the Brazilian population is to be found in families unable to attain the equivalent of the minimum wage in the northeast—less than £200 for a family of five. The priorities cannot be to extend universal education to a minimum level to eradicate differentiation in the labor force and ensure access to schooling for the most deprived. In 1970 the census reported 37 percent of the 7–9 age group not attending school at all, and 32 percent of the 10–14 group similarly not enrolled; more than a quarter of children between 10 and 14 could not read or write. The priorities cannot be to move ahead with a serious program of agrarian reform to counteract the concentration of wealth and property income in the primary sector, where the burden of poverty is most pressing. The smallest (45 percent) of the farms in Brazil in 1960 possessed less than 3 percent of the land; that glaring disparity remained.

The priority has become growth for its own sake, growth as a panacea for all ills. Distributionism has become an enemy of the state, "a veritable confidence game which would end up leaving the nation dividing the misery more equally.'' Yet the actual resource transfer required to bring all Brazilian families up to a minimum poverty standard is of the order of 6 percent of the income of those above the line. Such a transfer would reduce inequality, but only modestly. Its principal merit would be to direct the gains of growth to those who need it most immediately, the very poorest. The problem of Brazilian inequality is not merely couched in relative incomes; what counts perhaps more are the implications for the standard of living.

These distributional consequences of the Brazilian model are as real as the product or trade statistics. And they are as intimately related to it. A market system oriented toward maximum growth, and unencumbered by popular wishes, will almost inevitably emphasize profits at the expense of wages, will almost inevitably tolerate monopoly gains and prevent labor from organizing, will almost inevitably subsidize investment and attract foreign capital to exploit especially favorable opportunities. In such circumstances, excesses occur, and have occurred. The miracle must also be judged by those who gain and lose.

Reprinted and edited from *The World Today* (November 1973), monthly journal of the Royal Institute of International Affairs, London, 29: 474–79.

Peter Flynn

The Brazilian Development Model. The Political Dimension

One conspicuous feature of most recent discussions of the "Brazilian development model" has been the neglect of its political dimension. There has been much analysis of devices for curbing inflation, stimulating exports, or attracting foreign investment, but little attention to the political costs of choosing such a model or the degree to which built-in political constraints may now make it difficult for the model followed in recent years to be modified by, for example, a new administration with perhaps rather different social or political priorities.

The general impression conveyed by apologists for the regime is that those directing Brazilian development have been working since the coup of April 1964 in some kind of political vacuum, that Brazil has become, in the title of a previous article, a "country without politics" (a phrase echoed more recently in statements from the new military ruler of Chile). This coyness with regard to politics is, however, itself part of the model under discussion. To paraphrase the notorious remark of the old *mineiro* politician, Artur Bernardes, who said in the 1920s that the social question was a matter for the police, one may say that since 1964 for the planners and *tecnicos* the political question has been a matter for the soldiers. The armed forces, who previously were perceived (as until recently in Chile) as holding the ring for democracy, have since 1964 held it for the technical planning experts behind the current development model. The careful insulation from political opposition or tensions has been designed deliberately to allow Delfim Neto and his colleagues to proceed smoothly with their development strategy and to reassure those foreign financiers so important to the model's success that Brazil is a safe, sound, and stable investment.

But this picture of a politically sanitarized or cauterized Brazil is dangerously misleading, both in terms of the relevance of this model for *other* developing societies and, more particularly, in relation to recent suggestions that the government of General Ernesto Geisel, due to take over next March, may make some substantial changes, especially with regard to greater distribution of wealth and resources and a more open political system. This immediately raises the question of the political costs which the model entails, of how these are intrinsically linked to its social and economic strategy, and of how far these political demands may produce a degree of inflexibility which makes any significant change of direction far more difficult than might at first appear.

Such questions are particularly worth asking at a time when there is some talk of a thaw in Brazilian politics. Any change of president always produces some excitement and uncertainty, and Ernesto Geisel is coming to office just as the political system is showing renewed signs of strain. What, then, are the *political* requirements of the Brazilian model, the stresses currently being felt, and the extent to which they are capable of being resolved by a new administration, which may want to introduce new development priorities?

The Model

Though the Brazilian model can be variously described, and though the economic strategy has changed over the last nine years (with, for example, much greater emphasis on an export-based economy instead of the previous pattern of import substitution), the essence of it is contained in its description by Professor Fishlow and others as "authoritarian capitalism." In this sense, it is an explicitly chosen development pattern in which the political authoritarianism directly serves a narrowly defined form of capitalist development, which since 1964 has been intimately bound up with international, above all United States, capitalism. The general lines of its development have been set out clearly in earlier articles in *The World Today*, but its central feature is a capital accumulation process which gives the highest priority to economic growth, at the expense of other factors, such as distribution. It is a model which explicitly recognizes that the promotion of this rapid growth will produce, at least in the short term, widening disparities in real income, and which imposes, in consequence, a tightly controlled political system designed to serve these purposes. The much abused term *model* is more than usually appropriate, as the Brazilian system since 1964 has been produced, in effect, on a drawing board. It is designed to perform certain functions, which it does well, but is, for that very reason, less readily adaptable for other purposes.

The theorists of the regime are absolutely clear about their choice of strategies which favor growth at the expense of a more equitable pattern of distribution, relying, if at all, on some form of "trickle-down" mechanism to satisfy distributive demands. For example, Dr. Mário Henrique Simonsen, director of MOBRAL, the Brazilian literacy movement, in a recent paper was unambiguously clear that the Brazilian development philosophy is one which "establishes as a basic priority the accelerated growth of the GNP, accepting as a short-term liability the corollary of an appreciable imbalance between individual rates of income. . . ." Speaking with evident satisfaction of an established, government-controlled system of wage adjustment, he explained that "in the first place, it has served to simplify and pacify wage-claim negotiations;

these are no longer resolved by rounds of strikes and other forms of collective pressure, but simply by rapid mathematical calculations. . . ."

The Political Corollary

The application of this model in a country of Brazil's level of development by 1964 has meant, in practice, the imposition of directly related political policies. The first logical requirement, in order to push through with all possible speed policies which by design favor certain groups or classes at the expense of others, is a monopoly of political power, with full control of the state apparatus, a monopoly which, as President Allende of Chile found to his cost, can scarcely be achieved in an open democratic system. Since the model implies, in particular, continuing, even increasing, disparities of income, at least in the short term and possibly longer, it will at once demand control of most of the popular political forces in a modern, industrialized society. This will affect, first and foremost, organized labor and the political bodies associated with it, since to achieve, for example, the mathematical simplicity of wage bargaining advocated by Simonsen requires a degree of control unacceptable to trade unions and other groups alert to working-class interests. By 1964, though trade-union development was still far from perfect, and notably less aggressive than elsewhere, the power of the *sindicatos*, both in and outside Congress, was already formidable. One of the first explicitly accepted costs directly stemming from this model has been the virtual extinction of any political force or party based on, or linked to, organized labor. Any attempt at reorganization has, on the contrary, been broadly categorized as political subversion, a term commonly used for any opposition to the model of political economy being followed by the regime.

This essential feature of the model was all the more readily acceptable because the forces behind the coup, especially the civilian groups, were those which had most consistently and fiercely opposed *trabalhismo*, the political movement linked to organized labor, first under Vargas and later under Goulart. The Institutional Act No. 1 of 19 April 1964 was largely the work of Francisco Campos, long known for his authoritarian sympathies, who in 1937 had been the chief author of the corporatist *Estado Novo* constitution. The civilian elements in the coup, leaders such as Carlos Lacerda, Magalhães Pinto, or the São Paulo newspaper owner, Júlio de Mesquita Filho, were mostly from those anti-Vargista groups associated with the National Democratic Union (UDN), so that the model to be adopted was immediately conceived in terms of the priorities and ideologies of the most conservative political forces in Brazil. This was reflected, too, in the *cassações* (loss of political rights) of the leaders and most prominent supporters of the political movements which, however confusedly, represented an enlarged political role for the working classes. From the start, therefore, the model was one which excluded these more popular forces, reflecting instead an elitist concept of political economy inimical to wider participation. It was never a model easily adaptable to participatory demands at a later date.

But the monopoly of power needed to make the Brazilian model work smoothly goes beyond the exclusion of popular forces working through Congress. It soon demanded, again logically in terms of its own premises, the virtual extinction of Congress itself and an end to effective party politics or even a "loyal opposition." The main break came in October 1965 with the Institutional Act No. 2, which gave sweeping new powers to the president to abrogate, for example, the mandates of federal deputies and suspend citizens' political rights, being immediately followed by the Complementary Act No. 4, which dissolved Brazil's political parties, replacing them with two artificial groupings, Aliança Renovadora Nacional (ARENA) and Movimento Democratico Brasileiro (MDB), the first broadly favoring the government, the second made up mostly of the old opposition parties.

These measures, important in all kinds of ways, showed in particular that the conservative politicians, who had worked with the soldiers to produce the coup, could not, when the test came, muster the necessary degree of political control. The further limitations to party politics imposed in October 1965 by the hard-line officers, when the civilian leaders had suffered a severe setback in gubernatorial elections the previous month, were designed to ensure the tighter control necessary for the development strategy to be followed within the context of "national security."

The new moves by the armed forces already revealed growing tensions between the civilian leaders in the coup, who had originally hoped the soldiers would soon withdraw in their favor, and their *dispositivo militar*, or military backing. The civilians' assumption—as apparently the assumption of right-wing civilian groups behind the recent Chilean coup—was that the soldiers would soon withdraw in their favor. But October 1965 showed that they had been mistaken, and now tensions increased between the conservative civilians, on the one hand, and an ever more coherent coalition of military leaders and *tecnicos* responsible for the Brazilian model, on the other. This process came to a head in the Institutional Act No. 5 of 13 December 1968, which, together with the simultaneous Complementary Act No. 38, dismissed Congress indefinitely, dissolved state and municipal assemblies, gave sweeping new powers to the president, and imposed a rigid censorship on the press and all other media.

The immediate reason for this "coup within the coup," which consolidated all power in the hands of the soldiers and *tecnicos*, was that the regime had once again not only been challenged, but had been *seen* to be challenged, this time in Congress by congressmen critical of government policy and, more seriously, by extraparliamentary opposition in the form of urban guerrilla groups. The significance of such a challenge, and of the swift and fierce reaction to it, needs again to be understood in terms of the regime's development model.

Reliance on Foreign Support

Right from the start the Brazilian development model was open to the well-aimed criticism that it was neither genuinely Brazilian nor genuinely developmental. The second point is examined later, but it is the reliance of the post-1964 development strategy on foreign, above all United States, support which is most relevant. It is still unclear how great a part the United States Government and its associated interests played in the coup of 1964, but there was no doubt where its sympathies lay. As in the more recent case of the Allende administration in Chile, there was ample evidence of deep hostility in United States business circles to the Goulart government and of close links between those elements hostile to Goulart and the men eventually responsible for the coup. General Vernon Walters, for example, recently revealed in the Watergate hearings as one of the most senior officers in the CIA, was in 1964 the United States military attaché in Brazil, closely associated with both Carlos Lacerda and Castello Branco, and the swift return of United States and other investment showed the widespread relief at Goulart's removal.

If the Brazilian development model was heavily dependent on foreign confidence and financial support from the very beginning, by the end of 1968 this dependence was even greater. By this time, as Simonsen and others have made clear, the current development model was already in full operation, involving, above all, a swing from that import-substitution industrialization which had been pursued since at least the mid-1930s to an economy which gave every priority to industrial production for exports. This change of strategy was such that some observers see current legislation, so generously favoring those who wish to produce in Brazil for *export*, as the exact mirror image of legislation which previously supported, for example, foreign investment favoring production for the *internal* market within the pattern of import substitution. The new strategy urgently required massive foreign investment to sustain the export expansion, which in turn was needed to allow Brazil to shoulder the very large foreign debts being incurred in that process. The much tighter political control, therefore, was not only needed to suppress opposition at home but, still more important, to convince observers abroad that the regime had sufficient determination and political muscle to justify and sustain the confidence of foreign investors.

It is worth noting that this was another reason not just for the repression at this time of the urban guerrillas and other opposition groups, but for the *way* in which they were suppressed. The extreme severity of the repression, with its associated features of violence and even the systematic use of terror, was again a reflection of the regime's need to be seen abroad, as well as at home, as being capable of staying in full control. The further significance of extraparliamentary opposition as a serious obstacle—in terms of the resulting outcry and polarization—to any future attempts at moves towards greater legitimacy based on participation are discussed later. It is more important at this point, however, to emphasize how the exclusion of the conservative political class from late 1968 onward was again contained in the logic of the model being followed, especially in its dependence on foreign interests.

Exclusion of Nationalist Critics

One of the most significant features of the ''coup within the coup'' of December 1968 was that it imposed further controls on the more nationalist elements of the bourgeoisie. The open-door strategy followed since 1964, and especially since 1967, had provided opportunities for foreign, particularly United States, investment, and for foreign penetration of the economy far beyond anything that would have been allowed previously by Brazilian nationalists, civilian or military. This was of the very essence of the model chosen but brought growing criticism from what may broadly be described as the spokesmen of the more nationalist bourgeoisie, especially in São Paulo. Such criticism could again raise alarm abroad and was, consequently, in part responsible for the purges in Congress and in other quarters after December 1968. On 30 December, following the Institutional Act No. 5 came the *cassações* of eleven deputies, and on 16 January 1969 the removal of two senators, thirty-five deputies, and other prominent figures, including judges of the Supreme Court and one from the Higher Military Tribunal. On 7 February a further move got rid of thirty-three members of Congress, eleven being from the government's own party, ARENA. All civilian elements considered at all critical of the government's policy were now being removed, and the same process was continued by increasingly severe censorship of the media, backed by sterner national security laws, all part of the necessary political control demanded by the development strategy.

However, the clearest example of the need and nature of such control came not with the attack on organized labor, the media, Congress, or even the more nationalist civilian elements who originally supported the coup, but with the fierce reaction of the now strongly established coalition of soldiers and *tecnicos* to growing criticism from *within* their ranks, from military officers who favored a more nationalistic and distributionist development model. This challenge from within the regime was, and remains, crucially important, since for any system such as that adopted by Brazil since 1964 the most serious opposition is always intra-elite: hence the speed and vigor with which it was suppressed.

Eclipse of Albuquerque Lima

The main spokesman for this nationalist criticism throughout 1967 and 1968 was General Afonso Augusto de Albuquerque Lima, representing a traditional form of military nationalism which can be traced back at least to the *tenentes* of the 1920s. One of the hard-line officers who in October 1965 had pushed the regime towards fuller control of Congress by abolishing the political parties, he was closely associated with Marshal Artur da Costa e Silva, who appointed him to the Ministry of the Interior after taking office as president in 1967. Albuquerque Lima was then a major general, aged fifty-seven, with substantial support among middle-ranking officers and many of the younger economists associated with the regime. While resolutely hard line in his views of maintaining tight political control, he strongly advocated more attention to the northeast and Amazonas and was very suspicious of growing foreign control of the economy. Together with some other members of the government, such as Jarbas Passarinho, the minister of labor, he was also concerned over the effect on wages, and the pattern of distribution generally, of policies aimed at reducing inflation and promoting growth. He became increasingly critical of the economic policies of Delfim Neto, the finance minister, and Hélio Beltrão, the minister of planning, demanding, both in meetings of the security council and in public speeches, more attention to national problems such as housing and agrarian reform, higher priorities for the northeast and Amazonas, and ''the real participation of people of all socioeconomic levels in the modern processes of economic development.''

However ill-defined, these demands brought immediate reaction from those determined to stand by the development model already being followed. In January 1969, Albuquerque Lima resigned from the Ministry of the Interior openly disagreeing with government policies, especially on regional development, the housing program, sanitation, and agrarian development. Some of his close associates, such as Brigadier Eules Bentes Monteiro, head of SUDENE, the agency for the development of the northeast, also left office. Albuquerque Lima was given a job in Rio de Janeiro, where he could be watched, and the growing criticism of the Costa e Silva government was damped down.

In the struggle for power among the army leaders during the crisis produced by Costa e Silva's stroke at the end of August 1969, the position of the hard-line nationalist officers at first seemed to be strengthened, although Albuquerque Lima, clearly the strongest candidate for president outside the rank of four-star generals, tried in September to lull fears that he was an extreme nationalist less sympathetic to foreign business interests. He had widespread support in all four armies but eventually was passed over in favor of the more senior General Garrastazú Médici. The group he represented was, however, still very strong, as was seen in the elections in the Military Club in May 1970, and it seemed that, if he were to be promoted to a four-star general, his personal position would be extremely powerful. But in the next promotions list the following November he was deliberately passed over, though second in seniority in the list of three-star generals. His support had proved too small at the top, and he was forced, in the usual manner, to retire from active service. With his departure, the whole nationalist group within the army leadership seemed at least temporarily defeated, with swift moves to replace any officers who openly criticized the government's overall strategy. For example, when the new director of the Escola Superior de Guerra, General Rodrigo Otávio Jordão Ramos, in June 1971 gave an inaugural speech with markedly populist overtones and began opening the college to wider debate, he was summarily removed.

The sharp curbing of these dissident officers, urging more nationalist priorities and greater attention to distribution rather than growth, was again all part of the model being followed. This, as argued above, demands complete control of the organized working class, of parliamentary opposition, of criticism from the media, and, above all, of any dissident groups within the armed forces which might alarm or offend those financial interests abroad whose support is indispensable to the Brazilian model.

New Strains

While the strength and coherence of the Brazilian model are impressive, as is the government's determination in carrying it through, the political costs are equally obvious and the vulnerability of its essential political underpinning is far greater than its apologists allow.

In broad terms, the continuing success of the model depends on much more than the readiness on the part of an incoming regime to maintain the rigid controls already described. There are more serious issues with regard, first, to the wider degree of legitimacy which the military-led government must seek to achieve eventually and, secondly, to the degrees of effectiveness which it is perceived to have, especially by those critical elements within the controlling elite which have been only temporarily repressed. Both these closely related questions have again become much more urgent since the start of the lively debate over the relation between growth and distribution. This had been rumbling for some time, but flared up after analyses of income distribution, based on the results of the 1970 census, showed that despite six years of the military government the pattern of distribution was, in important respects, worse than in the early 1960s: the rich, on the whole, had become richer and the poor, poorer, and there were similar growing disparities between the richer and poorer regions of the country. Such criticism has embarrassed the regime more than it admits, and its spokesmen have tried hard to give more favorable interpretations to the facts or justify the inequalities in terms of Brazil's present stage of development. The worsening pattern seems, however, undeniable and should scarcely be surprising in relation to the deliberate acceptance by the model, as Simonsen makes clear, of growing disparities in income for the sake of high levels of growth.

The regime was so sensitive to this issue of redistribution that it was for a time closed to public debate: but such discussion is only part of the wider-felt need to strengthen the basis of legitimacy of the government at a more popular level and to prevent the nationalist demand for a more genuinely Brazilian development, with more tangible benefits for the people and the country as a whole, from growing in volume. These issues appear to be at the root of renewed political strains and tensions, which are becoming more evident as the present administration comes to an end. Legitimacy and effectiveness are difficult issues for any military government, especially after some years in power. The problem of wider and more popular legitimacy is, however, particularly acute for the Brazilian regime in relation to increased speculation as to the possibility of moving, with the advent of General Geisel, to a strategy favoring far more than in the past greater attention to distribution and a return to a more open political system.

It is precisely at this point that some of the built-in political constraints begin to appear. Most of them have been touched on already, namely a broken labor movement, a ruined party system, an emasculated Congress, and a degree of political bitterness, caused by the fierceness of earlier repression and violence, which cannot be appeased merely by government fiat. In terms of a return to open politics the position is even worse than it was at the end of the *Estado Novo*, since in such a young population a whole generation has grown up with no experience of any political system other than military control, again a calculated political cost of the current model. Meanwhile, many *tecnicos* and a new class of military politicians are deeply entrenched in power, a situation which causes much concern to some more thoughtful elements of the civilians and soldiers. More insidious still, in terms of the construction of a more open political system, the regime has produced, if not always hostility, more frequently a passive indifference or bitter cynicism, as reflected in the behavior of the electorate in the congressional elections in 1970.

Popular Support?

The apologists of the current model not only brush aside such issues, but even claim that their strategy has widespread popular support. Hard evidence is not really available, since relevant research has been extremely difficult—again an aspect of the Brazilian model, and one of its lesser political costs; but what evidence there is suggests that these government claims are largely whistling in the dark. This was seen to some extent in the popular reaction to the attempts of the Médici government to win support by a massive propaganda exercise associated with the newly established AERP, the public relations department headed by Colonel Octávio Costa. This tried, for example, to exploit the euphoria of World Cup success to stimulate enthusiasm, producing rousing nationalist sambas and military marches, and enlisting the support of World Cup heroes in government campaigns. The media poured out slogans and jingles to the effect that no one could now hold back Brazil, that Brazilians should love Brazil or leave it (the latter, incidentally, a straight borrowing of a slogan from the United States). The observable public reaction was one of cynical amusement, with sharply barbed, sometimes obscene, new versions of the slogans rapidly spreading round the country.

Other, more skillful attempts have been made to win popular support and, in particular, to hand off criticisms concerning the neglect of distribution and the disregard of the real interest of Brazilians at the expense of foreign interests. These efforts, described as forms of *indirect* distribution by Simonsen and others, seem to have had slightly more success. In the prosperous center-south, for example, the upper working class acknowledge the benefits of the INPS, the social security system; and the BNH, the National Housing Bank, has helped, in particular, lower-middle-class groups with house buying. There is a general reflection in these areas of the economic boom, and some "trickle down" seems to be taking place. Moreover, MOBRAL, the campaign to promote literacy, can claim dramatic success in the numbers involved in its courses and in its undoubted potential as a form of development agency. It has now established links in every *municipio* [municipality] in Brazil, and its director has the imagination and enthusiasm to extend its range of activities much further.

But these successes in certain respects heighten the awareness of how much more could have been done if greater priority had been given to areas such as education, social medicine, and questions of distribution generally. Many working people tend to see other schemes as poor substitutes for higher wages and freer bargaining. There is considerable suspicion of projects such as the Social Security Guarantee Fund and the efforts launched in September 1970 under the headings of PIS (Program for Social Integration) and PIN (Project for National Integration). These seem to have done little to convince many working class people, especially in more depressed areas such as the northeast, that the government really cares about wider distribution of resources, while the more sophisticated workers frequently dismiss such initiatives as token sops in response to growing criticism. The same is said of initiatives such as PRO-RURAL (Program of Assistance to the Rural Worker), launched in May 1971, or PROTERRA (Program of Land Redistribution and of Stimulus to the Agrarian Economy of the North and Northeast), started in July 1971, which are frequently dismissed as avoiding the real issues of agrarian reform and as providing no real evidence of government concern for the northeast. Though official apologists claim much for these projects, both as development initiatives and as sources of more popular support—and hence legitimacy—for the regime, current evidence does not justify such claims, as the government seems to realize in practice by maintaining the rigid political controls already analyzed.

Built-in Inflexibility

The structural obstacles to a return to open politics or to a swing to distribution are, then, very serious. The Brazilian model implies a total social process in which the political dimension is intrinsically linked to the form of capital accumulation being pursued. This makes any partial change of policy favoring greater distribution at the expense of growth extremely difficult and, in particular, runs directly counter to any development strategy based on popular participation. Designed for certain purposes, it is a model of great inflexibility with severely limited capacity for change and adaptability to new demands. It is this very inflexibility which makes any proposals for significant shifts of policy under the incoming government much more difficult to realize than is apparently assumed; but which also makes renewed strains within the system all the more notable.

While it is not suggested that the system is about to fall apart, there is currently evidence of increasing political tensions, which could offer a serious challenge. As seen already, the most difficult pressures for such a system to withstand are those from *within* the groups who have control; and, once again, the challenge turns on the highly charged issues of nationalism and of who benefits from the current model.

One strongly critical group are the civilian politicians originally associated with the coup but ousted in the subsequent shifts of power. Their criticism is often couched in liberal form, demanding a return to democratic politics and civil liberties, but essentially they represent those interests, especially *Paulista*, which want a more nationalist model of capitalist development and, in particular, greater control over United States penetration of the economy. This criticism has been growing steadily since the end of 1968, with the daily *Estado de São Paulo*, for example, often criticizing the present regime in terms similar to those previously used against Vargas. The main weakness of this powerful political lobby has been its lack of an effective *dispositivo militar*—though now this support seems to be growing.

The current model has obviously produced very strong vested interests among the *tecnicos* and the military officers who have benefited from their part in its elaboration. These, in turn, are strongly supported by international forces deeply involved in the present system. Their degree of influence, and just how it works within the controlling groups of military officers and experts, is difficult to plot with accuracy, but the speed and force of the reaction to the earlier challenge from more nationalist officers was a measure of their power. Again Chile had provided a recent example of the influence which a multinational corporation such as ITT is willing to exert, and similar forces are extremely strong in Brazil, in a system which has since 1964 done everything to court them.

Nevertheless, there is continuing evidence not only of the existence of more nationalist criticism of the role of foreign, especially United States, interests, but of the growing confidence and coherence of such criticism. Partly this stems from the excitement and debate always generated by a change of president, but the tensions seem to go much deeper, relating yet again, through an interesting irony, to the nature of the development model. Its constant political requirement is, as emphasized, the need to be seen to be in control. This has led since 1964 to an overriding concern with security, especially *internal* security as elaborated in the meticulously refined theories of security and development produced in the Escola Superior de Guerra. Always one of the main strands in Brazilian military thinking, it has grown in recent years to such a degree that it has overshadowed the other major and closely related theme, that of nationalism. The concern for nationalism has always been there, even in the writings of some of the major theorists on security and geopolitics, but throughout the period of the Cold War, and especially again during the campaign against the urban guerrillas, the emphasis on nationalism was subordinated to that of security.

New Nationalist Challenge

With the guerrilla threat at least temporarily repressed, the theme of nationalism has reappeared more strongly, linked to and quickened by the debate on the need for greater distribution and, to some extent, by the example of a different form of military regime in Peru since October 1968. Some of Albuquerque Lima's supporters from the middle ranks of the army have now become more senior, as have many of the *tecnicos* who favored a more nationalist and distributionist strategy. They are part of that long tradition within the Brazilian army of genuine commitment to national development as they understand it. Their views of society are frankly capitalist and elitist but, above all, nationalist, and they are sincere in their concern for national progress. The controversy over distribution since 1970 and the growing revelations of the extent of foreign control have shocked many of them and bred doubts concerning both the legitimacy and effectiveness of a model which only now is being perceived as favoring a narrow socioeconomic group in close collaboration with interests outside Brazil. There has been, therefore, a revival of the call of *brasilidade* and the need to do things more *brasileiramente*, in a truly Brazilian way. . . .

But the model cannot, as argued here, be taken piecemeal or easily be modified in parts. Its political demands do not allow an opening of the system to wider participation. Its social priorities do not allow a turn to much greater distribution. Its dependence on foreign confidence, finance, and interpenetration does not allow strongly nationalist controls of external interests.

Far from being above politics, the Brazilian development model is highly vulnerable unless it commands a monopoly of political power. Having been supported in recent years by soldiers whose main job was to keep it outside the political arena, it will be ironical if it is now seriously called in question, again by soldiers, for being neither genuinely Brazilian nor genuinely developmental.

Reprinted and edited from *The World Today* (November 1973), monthly journal of the Royal Institute of International Affairs, London, 29: 481–94.

Thomas G. Sanders

Military Government in Chile

The Chilean military regime which assumed power on September 11, 1973, faced a number of problems common to authoritarian and military governments. They had to reorganize the political structure to provide for military control, develop an ideology to guide policy, carry out an economic program, repress any activity regarded as dangerous to the regime, and cultivate the support of various civilian groups. It was especially important for the regime to enlist civilian assistance in Chile, since the armed forces officers had not formulated a coherent view on national problems and very few had studied in universities. The present article discusses the principal characteristics of the regime that was established after the coup.

Military and Civilians: Formulating an Ideology

The military junta consolidated its power by completely transforming the political system, closing Congress, abolishing the Unidad Popular (UP) parties, and placing the other political parties in indefinite recess. The junta itself took over executive and legislative power and later assumed authority for formulating a new constitution. The judicial structure remained intact, apart from a purge of about twenty judges. The Supreme Court abdicated its constitutional role in supervising military tribunals, because the junta had decreed that Chile was in a state of internal war. The military tribunals themselves assumed responsibility for trying leaders of the previous government and other political enemies of the new regime.

Armed forces officers occupied all cabinet posts except those dealing with the economy (though in a cabinet shift of April 1975 civilians increased their posts from three to six). Civilian advisers and members of the bureaucracy who had not been active members of the UP parties held most of the second-level positions. Military officers also took over the direction of the various provinces, temporarily suspending mayors and municipal councilmen from their positions. The junta replaced UP activists with new appointments, but otherwise, former provincial officials were reconfirmed.

The junta itself was composed of armed forces Generals Pinochet, Leigh, and Merino, and General César Mendoza of the police. At the time of the coup Merino and Mendoza were promoted over their superiors to direct their institutions in the battle.

Although the armed forces acted alone in the coup, they were keenly aware of Allende's civilian opponents, some of whom had been in contact with some officers before the coup. After September 11, as they began to restructure the government and formulate an ideology, the military incorporated civilians into their regime.

The precoup activities of groups opposing Allende reveal much about the ideology that was to develop. Most military officers and many civilians shared a fierce hostility toward the Allende regime. Some, like the Christian Democrats, had expressed their opposition through Congress, but others had moved outside the normal political channels to demonstrate, strike, and in some cases to act violently. While most of the Christian Democratic leaders had hoped until the end to change the policies of the UP within the institutional framework, many other Chileans opposed to Allende had looked to a coup as the necessary solution.

Allende's opponents did not come only from the middle and upper classes, as is commonly assumed. The Christian Democrats had strong support among farmers, workers, and in certain unions; in 1973, they won control of national unions in steel, petroleum, copper, and at the head of the Central Labor Confederation (CUT), in Santiago. The UP, meanwhile, had begun losing support even in its natural bases: one of the most crippling blows to the precoup economy was a strike against the government by the traditionally Marxist copper miners at the El Teniente mine. When they marched on Santiago and fought a pitched battle with government supporters in front of the presidential palace, copper workers in other mines stopped work to express solidarity with them. The Christian Democrats had also recaptured control of the secondary school student movement in 1972, and probably would have done the same in the university student movement, but the UP-controlled directorate had refused to hold the elections scheduled for 1973.

The armed forces, however, were much more impressed with the opposition outside the political parties. This stemmed in part from their long-time antipolitical attitude and in part from the fact that the Christian Democrats tried until the end to work out an institutional arrangement with Allende to save the country. The legalism of the parties and their search for a compromise with the Marxists contrasted with the intense and totally uncompromising attitude with which the military acted on September 11. The military felt more sense of identity with civilian groups who acted outside the political process, such as the thousands of middle-class women who marched through the streets in December 1971, banging their empty pots in protest against food shortages. Other important antigovernment groups, all motivated by an absolutist anti-Marxism, were the shopkeepers, professional organizations, truckers, and Patria y Libertad, a "nationalistic" organization formed in 1970 and committed to violence against the government. All these groups were especially active in August–November 1972 and June–September 1973. In the latter period, they openly pleaded with the military to intervene, and some contacted certain military officers directly. According to later testimony by General Leigh:

> They sent us messages, "Act, because this country has no remedy. All of us trust in you." The women . . . went in front of the Defense Ministry to shout. They said that we were chickens. They left corn at the door of our houses. They said we were cowards. Whoever had been in my position on that day would have acted. There was no other way out.

One of the distinctive characteristics of Chile's new regime, in comparison with other Latin American military models, is the extremely narrow civilian base on which it has been organized. Having lost faith in the system, the armed forces associated themselves with civilians who also had lost faith in it. Although most of the Chilean population opposed Allende, the military selected collaborators only from the most conservative side of the political spectrum, rejecting the Christian Democrats, the country's largest party. The bulk of Christian Democrats welcomed the military intervention, but they would cooperate only as a party and within a political framework. The National party, representing about 20 percent of the electorate, disbanded with alacrity, and many of its members took government positions. Military spokesmen allege that they "invited" certain civilians to collaborate, but the chief criteria of acceptability, a militant anti-Marxism and abandonment of political affiliation, inevitably restricted the participants.

Although the military believed that the civilians they invited were nonpolitical, this was a delusion. Some of the collaborators had strong political convictions indeed. The armed forces leaders lacked clear ideas on how to govern Chile, and the civilian participants did not hesitate to give them advice.

One of the most important influences on the military government has been a Catholic integralist group whose leading theorist is Jaime Guzmán, a young law professor. The integralists date far back into Chilean history to the Catholic, traditional, hierarchical, Hispanophile thinking which is rooted in the colonial period. Through much of Chile's history as a republic, they found a home in the former Conservative party. The integralists were limited in recent years in Chile to a small, predominantly upper-class group. In the mid-1960s, however, they took a new lease on life when Guzmán, then a student, led a movement called the *gremialistas* to victory in student elections at the Catholic University in Santiago. Integralist groups organized subsequently in several Latin American countries, including Chile, into the Society for Defense of Tradition, Property, and Family (TPF) and began publishing a journal, *Fiducia*. In addition to gaining control of student government in the Catholic University on a program of student depolitization, they clashed with the hierarchy of the church over its support for agrarian reform, which the integralists condemned as confiscatory and socialist, and over Marxism, which they believed the church should oppose without reservation.

Enough has been said to suggest why the integralist position was attractive to the military officers, some of whom were sympathizers with those viewpoints before the coup. Its central themes articulated within a comprehensive, religiously oriented philosophical framework, corresponded closely to the gut feelings of the military: nationalism, anti-Marxism, traditionalism, authority, hierarchy, a sense of duty and morality, and opposition to political parties.

The integralists offered both an explanation for the deterioration of modern life (materialism and egoism) and a social solution based on corporatism, which could be easily adapted to the *gremios* (nonpolitical professional and interest groups) that led the fight against Allende and offered their assistance to the junta. Corporatist thinking in Chile was not new in the 1970s; it had been very strong in the 1920s and 1930s, when it influenced Ibáñez and other military officers. Writing over a year before the 1973 coup, Guzmán sketched the outlines of a new social order:

> We consider that important reforms should be introduced into our institutional regime in order to complete the strengthening of presidentialism initiated some time ago. The intermediate organisms in which men are grouped according to neighborhood, employment, or their function in society should be incorporated into national decisions, thus putting an end to the unjust monopoly the political parties maintain by virtue of the existing juridical system. . . . Particularly urgent is the modification of the prevailing mechanisms for settling labor disputes, whose inadequacy until now is possibly to blame for inflation and unfair wage anarchy.

The integralists, though small in number, had the clearest, most articulate social philosophy among the various groups composing the Chilean right, and as individuals they moved quickly into the areas where they could promote their interests most effectively. One of these was in drafting the Declaration of Principles, which was published by the junta in March 1974 and is the most serious attempt to define the new government's ideological orientation. It reflects the integralist position completely. Like comparable ideological positions in the 1920s and 1930s, it perceives Marxism as a mortal threat, but it also rejects the liberal, democratic, and capitalist Western societies for their "materialism," preoccupation with consumption, and debility caused by Marxist penetration.

The principles themselves are based on a Thomistic view of society, beginning with the natural rights of human beings, the end of the state as the common good, the priority of human associations over the state, and the prohibition of state interference in the intermediate associations (the principle of subsidiarity). A corollary is the initiative of individuals as the motive force of the economy, the right of private property, and limited interference by government in the economy.

The new Chile, according to the Declaration of Principles, will be based on an "eminently nationalist" ideology, and Chileans are invited to "overcome mediocrity and internal divisions, making of Chile a great nation." The government, it declares, will be authoritarian, impersonal, and just, subject to certain values, and respectful of human rights. Because of its value orientation, "Chile is not neutral toward Marxism, and the present government does not fear or hesitate to declare itself anti-Marxist."

The declaration also refers to a "new institutionality . . . cleansing our democratic system from the vices that facilitated its destruction." The key principle is decentralization of power, based on social organizations, though the armed forces continue to hold political power. Society is to be based on interest groups (labor, entrepreneurial, professional, student) which are autonomous from state control and "depolitization . . . so that the *gremios* and other intermediate organizations become authentic vehicles of social participation," with the state "harmonizing the reasonable aspirations of each sector with the national interest," all adding up to a system ("democracy") which "will be organic, social, and participatory."

The armed forces will remain in power for an indefinite period "because the task of reconstructing the country morally, institutionally, and materially requires a profound and prolonged action. . . . It is absolutely necessary to change the mentality of Chileans." When this stage is complete the armed forces will turn over power through "universal, free, secret, and informed suffrage," and assume "the role of specifically institutional participation that the new constitution assigns them . . . which will be . . . national security, in the broad sense that this concept has in the present epoch."

Though the perspective is often confused with fascism, it is best described as "organic statism," adopting the terminology of Alfred Stepan. Regimes with comparable views in the 1920s and 1930s also called themselves democratic, but in practice they never were. Rather, such corporate principles became instruments of revenge for those threatened by a movement to the left, as well as tools for the government and powerful economic groups to disenfranchise and control the rest of society. The Declaration of Principles has not been fully applied, but the first two years of military government in Chile do not contradict that pattern.

The same corporatist concepts have been reiterated by junta spokesmen when they refer to a new constitution, which was expected to be finished a few months after September 11 but has repeatedly been postponed. The committee drafting the new constitution is composed of respected and conservative legal scholars and includes an important integralist representative, Jaime Guzmán.

The integralists have concentrated on securing positions in three cultural and social sectors which are important in shaping Chilean thinking. One area is communications and public relations for the government, where integralists hold many of the top positions. A second is the National Secretariat for Women, and a third the National Secretariat of Youth. The Secretariats for Women and Youth are two parts of a tripartite organization of society which the new government has substituted for the old system of parties. The third part is based on the *gremios*, which are composed of business, professional, and labor organizations. While the armed forces provide overall political directions and technicians concern themselves with the economy, the integralists have established themselves firmly in key positions within the civic organizations.

Military and Civilians: Economic Policy

Just as the armed forces had no coherent ideology at the time of the coup, they also had no economic philosophy. In this area, too, they turned to advisers from the conservative, anti-Marxist side of the political spectrum who had opposed the steady increase of state control, not only under Allende, but under Frei as well. The advisers believed that private enterprise should provide the chief initiative in economic development and that foreign investment was indispensable, especially given the state of decapitalization that existed by September 1973. The remedy they proposed was not simply to halt, but to turn back the socializing and nationalizing processes that had predominated in Chile's economy for a decade.

The economic ministerial posts were assumed by persons long active in Chilean public life, such as Fernando Léniz (president of *El Mercurio*, the country's leading newspaper), Jorge Cauas (president of the Central Bank, under Frei), and Raúl Sáez (one of the so-called wise men who directed the Alliance for Progress); but economic orientation and planning became the task of a group of well-trained young economists called the "Chicago boys," who in the 1950s were awarded scholarships by the United States government to study economics chiefly at the University of Chicago and in some cases at the University of California in Berkeley.

At Chicago, these students from Chile's Catholic University were influenced by the monetary views of Professor Milton Friedman and returned to Chile with the free market orientation which was then characteristic of the University of Chicago's Department of Economics. Though they found jobs in business and in the schools of economics and agronomy of the Catholic University (which became known in the 1960s as centers of "Chicago thinking"), their position vis-à-vis public policy making under Frei and Allende was totally marginal. The chief economists in those administrations took their cues largely from the United Nations Economic Commission for Latin America and viewed with disdain the private enterprise orientation of the Chicago M.A.s and Ph.D.s. Like the ideologists, however, the Chicago economists had the clearest, most coherent economic program to propose, and their outside degrees gave them great prestige. They were closest to the military when the upper level of Allende economists was totally purged, and they moved into the vacuum. And like the ideologists, they found an open field to apply their views.

The economic situation in September 1973 could hardly have been worse, and any judgments about subsequent Chilean economic performance must take into consideration the catastrophe left by the UP. In the year from September 1972 to September 1973, prices on goods sold publicly increased 452 percent, but since many if not most products flowed through the black market, the inflation figure for all goods sold probably ran to at least 1,000 percent. Agricultural production for the harvest of 1972–73 was down 20 percent from the previous year, while mining had dropped 20 percent in comparison with 1970, industry 10 percent, and construction 40 percent. Foreign reserves fell from $350 million in 1970 to minus $600 million, while the foreign debt rose an additional $800 million. Nearly 60 percent of the government budget was financed by emissions of paper money. A substantial portion of the public deficit stemmed from subsidization to cover losses in more than 450 companies owned by the government.

The junta's policy to deal with these economic difficulties fell into two stages. The first was a period of adjustment to a market economy and "gradual" stabilization, under the direction of Fernando Léniz as minister of the economy, lasting from September 1973 to April 1975. The second was a period of "shock treatment," with Jorge Cauas as minister of the economy, designed to reduce by drastic means an inflationary rate which had remained high. This began in April 1975 and was scheduled to last through 1975.

Although the shift to a free market economy depended on establishing a new set of rules and a climate of confidence for domestic and foreign investment in 1973, the main prerequisite for investment—and the most immediate problem—was to reduce inflation. Since the entire price structure was distorted by controls on many items, declining production, shortages, and the black market, the policy at first adopted was to free all but a small number of items to seek new levels and to reallocate resources in a closer relation of supply to demand. This meant an initial accentuation of inflation in hopes of later achieving stabilization. When controls were lifted in the last quarter of 1973, prices zoomed, especially in food products. In October alone prices rose 87 percent, and the year ended with an inflation rate of 508 percent, though from March 1973 to March 1974 the increase was 814.1 percent.

Wage policy had two objectives in the last months of 1973: to keep adjustments lower than prices in order to dry up excess purchasing power and at the same time to make some adjustments so that real wages would not drop below the subsistence level. The Chilean salaried classes received five salary increases in three months, bonuses, and increases in family allowances. Family allowances of white-collar workers and laborers were equalized for the first time in Chilean history.

At the time of the coup, salaried workers' real purchasing power had been declining steadily and by October had reached less than half of what it had been in 1970. The compensatory increases in 1973 and especially a large *reajuste* (wage adjustment) early in 1974 were designed to cushion against the price rises and restore purchasing power to the 1973 average, which the government hoped to maintain during 1974 by automatic *reajustes* every three months.

A second measure against inflation was to reduce government expenses drastically. The government owned over 450 industries, some of which had been purchased legally, but most of which had been taken over illegally under the Allende regime. The new administration wanted to detach the state from production to reduce expenses as well as to reorient the philosophy of development. It gave some of the industries back to their original owners and put most of the rest up for sale. The sales went slowly, however, and the government owned and had to subsidize more than it wanted.

The government also reduced expenses by eliminating subsidies on various products and by dismissing certain workers from the UP regime. Public receipts were expected to be higher because of higher prices and greater vigilance in tax collection. As a result of these measures, the government planned on an inflation of 50 to 80 percent for 1974.

Industry and agriculture, the government hoped, would recover their growth by responding to the stimuli of free prices and the benevolent policy of government. To capture additional savings, the rate of interest on deposits and loans was freed. The exchange rate was unified, and the escudo was devalued to encourage exports and discourage imports. Foreign investors were offered completely equal treatment with Chileans, and the government pledged to try to change Decision 24 of the Andean Pact, which places restrictions on companies wishing to conduct business in the six-nation common market formed by the pact. Finally, to encourage an entrepreneurial attitude in farmers, the government began returning to their original owners lands that had been illegally occupied under the Allende regime, and dividing the cooperative *asentamientos* [land reform settlements] of the agrarian reform among their associates.

In the last quarter of 1973 and throughout most of 1974 the economy underwent a mild recovery. The economy as a whole grew 5 percent in 1974, agriculture 15 percent (still not recovering the levels of 1972), construction 10 percent, and industry 2 percent. The low industrial figure was due to lack of demand associated with reduced purchasing power. Externally, the balance-of-payments deficit was only $110 million, the smallest since 1970, largely because of an average copper price of $1.15 (U.S.) per pound in the first semester. An ominous sign for the future, however, was a drop in the price of copper, which represents 80 percent or more of exports, to an average of 70.3 cents a pound in the second semester. Though the new and higher price of petroleum imports was matched by copper sales in the first half of the year, a wide gap was apparent in the second.

The most serious problem, and one which undermined confidence in the whole recovery program, was the persistence of inflation, which was 350 percent in 1974. Prices rose more than expected in the early part of the year, which required salary *reajustes* greater than anticipated, which in turn drove the cost of living up still further, and so on. In the last quarter, the inflationary rate increased the most of all—to a rate of 370 percent annually—and in the first quarter of 1975 went up to 400 percent.

The government and the Christian Democrats gave divergent explanations for this unfortunate trend. The government blamed it on excess public spending, even though the fiscal deficit had been reduced from 19 to 6.8 percent of the gross domestic product between 1973 and 1974. The Christian Democrats pointed to the fact that monetary expansion had been only 200 percent and blamed two forms of inflationary expectations. One came from manufacturers and sellers, who wanted to recover their costs and set prices excessively high to compensate for inflation they anticipated in future months. The other form resulted from private savings and loan associations which issued certificates that were negotiable at any time and bore speculative interest rates higher than the expected inflation. Heavy deposits in the associations siphoned funds away from the banks and reduced the resources available to the government, and both banknotes and certificates of the associations circulated at an inordinately rapid velocity. Probing into more structural factors, critics contended that the government's economic model assumed that a free market would be competitive and would lead to reduced prices, but in Chile the private sector was monopolistic and speculative, preferring high prices and reduced sales to competition. The critics also expressed doubt that this model, designed for a state of relative equilibrium, should have been applied to Chile, with its distortions and disequilibria.

As 1975 opened, several other factors were added to the economic problems associated with the high inflationary rate. The price of copper skidded to less than 60 cents a pound, approximately the cost of producing it. Since petroleum prices remained high, the trade deficit predicted for 1975 jumped to $800 million. Industrial production, which had hardly held its own after September 1973, declined 12 percent between October 1974 and February 1975.

Purchasing power of salaried workers also had worsened during 1974. The government fell 5 percent short of its aim of holding 1974 salaries equal to the 1973 average. Critics demonstrated that the Consumer Price Index was based on the diversified purchases of the middle class, and since the highest price increases were in food, which comprises a larger proportion of lower-class purchases, the latter lost even more real income. According to one estimate, the loss of purchasing power for those living on basic items between September 1973 and September 1974 was 42 percent, and in the next six months, another 13.6 percent.

Unemployment, which the Allende regime had held at artificially low levels by simply creating jobs and paying for them with emissions of money, hovered around 10 percent in 1974 and rose to 13.3 percent in March 1975. Though in this first stage of their program, the economists chose gradual rather than abrupt stabilization—in part to avoid greater umeployment—some decline in employment was inevitable because of layoffs in the public sector to reduce expenditures and in the private sector to increase efficiency.

Albert Hirschman, in a study of Chilean inflation, refers to "The recurrent hope that somewhere there might be an 'expert' . . . who will know just the right prescription or perform just the right operation. For this reason the foreign expert and mission play an important part in the history of inflation in Chile." True to this pattern, no less than three outside experts, all similar in their economic approach, were invited to Chile in March 1975 for a debate on inflation. They were Milton Friedman and Arnold Harberger of the University of Chicago and Carlos Langoni of the Fundacão Getulio Vargas in Rio de Janeiro. All suggested the shock treatment, though they differed slightly in their judgment of how harsh it should be. After some discussion among the government economists, this approach was adopted; out went Léniz, and in came Jorge Cauas.

In a blunt statement on April 25 Cauas sketched out his program. The purpose was to cut inflation, "which is the principal preoccupation of all Chileans," and the chief means [would be by] reducing public expenditures and monetary emissions. Government expenses in escudos would be cut 15 percent and those in foreign exchange 25 percent, on top of an already planned reduction of 10 percent in 1975. Taxes would be increased, and the schedule of *reajustes* changed so that wage earners would lose the high percentage increases in May and June, reducing still further their purchasing power. Controls on savings and loan associations were announced, and businessmen were warned to cut prices and clean out their stocks because demand was going to decline significantly. General Leigh already had called businessmen on the carpet twice for "thinking only of themselves" and had told them to collaborate in the economic model or face the consequences.

The new Chilean government closed out its second year in power amid the consequences of the shock treatment. From June to August, stores in downtown

Santiago held sales to attract the last escudos before Chile shifts over to a new peso worth 1,000 escudos. Though figures for 1975 are not yet available, the country shows all the signs of the recession for which the government has opted. Industry continues its decline, with production in May 1975 down 24.6 percent from May 1974. Figures for copper production will drop 10 percent in 1975, in part to stimulate an increase in the price, which continues to be low. Construction is declining because the government, to save money, has paralyzed important public works. Agriculture, which had been impressive in 1974, faced a new set of factors discouraging increases: high fertilizer costs, high interest rates for credit, and especially, reduced public consumption because of the decline of the economy. In August the news magazine *Ercilla*, citing various institutions involved in agriculture, predicted serious drops in wheat, meat, wine, and fruit production. Total agricultural production may decline 7 to 8 percent this year, and the future is made more ominous by decapitalization through slaughter of livestock herds and eradication of fruit trees. Consumption of beef, eggs, and chickens is less than half what it was in 1970.

The working class has suffered more than anyone from the shock treatment. In mid-August, official figures estimated that unemployment in Greater Santiago was 15.9 percent, with industry leading the sectors at 22 percent. Critics argue that the figures are too low and point to especially high rates in the lower class. In some *poblaciones* [working-class neighborhoods] at least half the population is without work, and hunger and malnutrition are common. To alleviate what was called the "social cost" of the model, the government set up programs providing food supplements and National Minimum Employment. The latter provides jobs in public works at very low wages, without increments. Indeed, the wages are so low that many unemployed persons do not consider it worthwhile to participate because transportation costs absorb most of their earnings. Furthermore, the places available are far less than the number of unemployed, and work is not steady.

Decreased income and demand appear to be beginning to achieve their policy objectives: in July 1975, for example, the rate of inflation fell to 9.3 percent compared to 19.8 percent in June. Though no figures have been released for subsequent months, Pinochet, in his message to the nation on September 11, assured his audience that the "high rate of inflation which we suffered until the first half of this year has been defeated." He also pointed out that the deficit would be only 12 percent of the total budget. The effect of the shock treatment is "a return of the Chilean standard of living to what our present economic capacity can realistically provide." Government sources estimate that this will mean a 5 percent drop in production from 1974, but the Christian Democratic journal *Política y Espíritu* predicts a figure of 8 to 10 percent.

The hardships produced by the current economic model have been felt by practically all segments of society and have eroded the enthusiasm of the regime's civilian backers. Along with the integralists and the economists who had welcomed the coup as a means of carrying out their ideas, the new administration initially conformed to the interests of other groups that had struggled against Allende, such as professionals, truckers (who are small-scale entrepreneurs), and retail merchants. The leaders of the latter two *gremios*, Leon Vilarín and Rafael Cumsille, became two of the most important civilian spokesmen for the regime. Another important source of support was Patria y Libertad, which emerged from illegality to become a group of "nationalists" led by Pablo Rodríguez, a lawyer. Industrialists, who had not organized themselves effectively against Allende, and financiers, who had sent their money out of the country, also stood to benefit by the program, as did independent farmers. In addition, the government depended on support from the majority of the population who were relieved that the chaos of the last Allende months had finally ended.

During 1974, when the economy seemed to be recovering and inflation was expected to decline, the civilian coalition held together easily and unanimously, but as 1975 opened, it began to crack. In January Orlando Sáenz, former president of the Society of Industrial Development, called the anti-inflationary policy "one of the most resounding failures in our economic history" and gave the monopolistic character of Chilean industry and the "social cost" as the reasons for his judgment. He was soon joined in his criticisms by Cumsille of the retailers and Rodríguez of Patria y Libertad.

As the economy declined, everyone began to be hurt. Industrialists, farmers, and retailers were not doing well because the public had less money to spend. Various analysts began to recognize that those who clearly benefited most from the system were a group of financiers, dubbed the "*piranhas*," who had money to purchase former government-owned industries at cheap prices and who knew how to speculate in the volatile capital market. In spite of the fact that no one, least of all salaried workers and the unemployed, was content with the situation, the continuity of the government was not under serious challenge from the influential civilian groups. There were no other real options, only memories of Allende on one hand or a future of uncertain chaos on the other. Though many questioned the shock treatment, no easy alternative was at hand.

The armed forces leaders were also visibly concerned about the economic model, and sharp questions were raised about who was benefiting. It is important to reemphasize that most of the officers have no sense of identification with upper-class financiers and businessmen. Rather they are likely to react to an economic squeeze on the middle class, where they have relatives and friends. Junta spokesmen, especially Leigh, who is in charge of social programs, have repeatedly expressed their preoccupation with the "social cost." And they have asserted frankly that the upper classes have not borne their share of the sacrifices expected from society as a whole.

Despite the almost universal disaffection throughout Chile, the shock treatment seems certain to achieve its principal objective, a reduction of inflation, because the population has less and less to spend, and businessmen are on trial to compete for this shrinking money supply. Chileans will be appreciably poorer at the end of 1975 than they were in 1974, and if one takes population increase into consideration, poorer than in 1972.

Repressing the Opposition

With the overthrow of its democratic system, Chile became an "authoritarian" government, which by definition restricts the expression and activities of all or part of the political spectrum. Since its inception, the new government has attracted worldwide attention for the severity of repression, the sizable portion of the population affected, the arbitrariness of its procedures, the widespread use of torture, and the death of many persons.

The harshness of Chilean repression was perhaps predictable because of the political situation that prevailed when the armed forces intervened. The extent of political polarization supported predictions of a civil war, since the UP parties had received 43.4 percent of the vote in March 1973, and many of their followers were highly motivated and could be expected to resist. The brutality of the coup itself, in which thousands of persons died, in part reflected the conviction by armed forces leaders that a show of toughness would be an important safeguard against further resistance or a resurgence of the opposition. In addition to those who were killed resisting the coup, an even larger number was executed without trial throughout the closing months of 1973, the peak being in late September and early October. The principal victims were UP activists and foreign leftists who had entered the country during the Allende government.

Once the initial severity began to decline, Chilean repression settled into a twofold pattern: (1) suppression of suspected political dissidents through harassment, arrests, torture, imprisonment, and in some cases expulsion from the country; and (2) a series of restrictions on expression and activities by communications media, educational institutions, labor unions, and the non-Marxist political opposition.

In the first month after September 11, an estimated 45,000 persons were arrested and housed in temporary, crowded quarters such as the National Stadium, in Santiago. As October got under way, interrogations were conducted, often accompanied by torture, while prison camps were being set up. Although the authorities tried and imprisoned some of the detainees, they released most of them, but every day there were additional arrests. By March 1974 about 10,000 persons remained in confinement, and the current figure is estimated at around 5,000. In two years, the security authorities have detained more than 100,000 persons for at least twenty-four hours—1 out of every 100 Chileans.

Many thousands of Chileans have abandoned the country: more than 50,000 simply left, and about 10,000 received permission to go into political exile. Over 5,000 foreigners left with the assistance of various international refugee organizations.

Roundups of suspected dissidents have been facilitated by the declaration of a state of siege and by a curfew. In the first months of the new government, the armed forces and police intelligence units took charge of these activities, using regular troops because of the volume of detentions. Lack of coordination in this initial stage, however, led early in 1974 to a unification of security activities through the Dirección de Inteligencia Nacional (DINA). DINA grew out of army intelligence but also uses personnel from other armed forces branches. It includes civilians, some of whom are reputed to be members of Patria y Libertad. Like the security apparatus in Brazil, DINA has become a powerful force within the government. It is suspected of vetoing some liberalization efforts, and since it reports only to Pinochet, there are no means of institutional control over its activities.

DINA operates according to a now established pattern. Its agents, dressed in civilian clothes and driving unmarked cars, pick up persons at their home, at work, or on the street. In some cases, soldiers and police carry out mass roundups in *poblaciones* and factories. Interrogations take place in special buildings and are usually accompanied by torture. Following the interrogations, most are released. Other are summarily tried before military courts, and a certain number have disappeared. In mid-1975, between 50 and 100 persons were detained weekly in Santiago alone.

The principal institution dedicated to defending prisoners is the Committee for Peace in Chile, a joint effort by the major religious communities to provide counsel and assistance for prisoners and their families. The committee furnishes legal aid for those being tried by military courts, and it has submitted writs of habeas corpus to Appeals Courts and the Supreme Court for persons who are known to have been detained and who have disappeared. Thus far, these writs have failed almost universally, because the government denies knowing the whereabouts of the missing persons.

A second type of repression has been aimed at limiting political expression and activities. The regime, in attempting to establish national unity, expressly prohibits politics, though other kinds of opinion and criticism are permitted.

Government regulations compel communications media like newspapers, radio, and television to adopt a conformist line. At the time of the coup, media associated with the UP were closed down or taken over, and all others were placed under strict censorship. The only newspapers that continue to circulate are those formerly associated with the conservative side of Chile's once highly diversified and partisan press. Newspapers, radio, and television now censor themselves and consider severe criticism, political statements, and treatment of certain delicate topics out of bounds. Occasionally radio and television channels associated with the Christian Democrats have been suspended for brief periods for violating the norms. Such major magazines as *Ercilla, Mensaje* (edited by Jesuits), and *Política y Espíritu* (Christian Democratic) are critical of the government within the defined limits.

The change of government led to a drastic purge of the educational system, especially universities, including the dismissal and arrest of thousands of professors and students. In schools on all levels, teaching materials that were judged to be of Marxist or revolutionary inclination were eliminated. The new authorities reversed many of the educational reforms that had been occurring for nearly a decade.

In all the universities, military officers took over the rectorships. Existing student government was abolished, except for the gremialist organization in the Catholic University, and now student informers who sympathize with the regime guarantee an ideological conformity in what is taught. From time to time arrests of professors and students recur. In August 1975, for example, most of the political science department of the Catholic University was purged, and a number of professors in the pedagogical institute of the University of Chile were arrested and charged with political activities.

The new regime also purged labor unions of their leadership and abolished the Centra Unica de Trabajadores (CUT), which had been the national labor confederation. Of all social groups, workers and white-collar employees comprise the leading two categories among detentions. Hundreds of thousands of workers have lost their jobs. In individual unions elections were suspended, UP activists removed from their positions and replaced by persons chosen by seniority, while in non-UP-dominated unions, the former officers retained their positions. Junta decrees prohibited strikes and the right to present petitions. Occasional violations of these decrees have been vigorously repressed.

A degree of collaboration has nevertheless been established between the labor leaders and the government. In the first year after the coup, some labor spokesmen went abroad to defend the junta. Junta members often profess their concern for the condition of the salaried classes and invite union leaders to state their positions. On May 1, 1974, for example, the junta met with various labor leaders. The former secretary general of CUT in Santiago, Manuel Rodríguez, a Christian Democrat, called for an end to the restrictions on unions, which he said damaged the external image of Chile and deprived the workers of means for obtaining "that to which we have a right." Rodríguez also complained that restrictions against workers but not against owners were discriminatory. The unions have chafed under the limitations, and with the deterioration of the economy their members have been seriously affected by dismissals, reduced work schedules, and, at times, agreements to reduce wages to avoid dismissals.

The government's objective is to depoliticize the unions and make them more comprehensive within a corporatist framework (only about 30 percent of workers are union members). Nevertheless, the restrictions placed on their meetings and forms of expression are not encouraging signs for future labor autonomy. Previous "organic statist" models have also promoted comprehensive, corporatist labor structures and emphasized participation and protection of workers, but in practice they have served to defuse dissatisfaction and divert their interests into manipulable channels.

The military regime's policy in dealing with the former political parties has been twofold. The UP parties were abolished and the others placed in recess. Of the former UP components, only the Communist party continues to maintain a strong organization in Chile. Although its major leaders are outside the country, imprisoned, or dead, it still functions underground, occasionally publishing mimeographed declarations against the government. The Socialist party, which always lacked the discipline of the Communists, and the small far-left groups, which were cupolas without any base, have both disappeared from public view but probably have clandestine forms. The Movement of the Revolutionary Left (MIR) organized itself to resist, but a strong government countereffort leading to the death of its major leaders has effectively repressed it.

Although the Christian Democrats are in recess, they continue to symbolize continuity with Chile's democratic tradition. They also provide the principal internal criticism of the government's policies. During much of the past two and one-half years, government censorship prevented them from expressing their views. Late in 1974, Renán Fuentealba, the party's former president, was expelled from the country. Statements by party officials were rejected as a form of political expression no longer allowed.

In 1975 the Christian Democrats took advantage of the freedom to make economic criticisms. In May, former president Frei severely criticized the government's economic model and defended his 1964–70 administration against the interpretation that prevails among the armed forces and their civilian supporters. Recent issues of *Política y Espíritu*, the party magazine, include an alternative economic policy and critical discussions of the "social cost," human rights, and foreign policy. In general, the Christian Democrats doubt that the present economic model is workable and contend that until there is an improvement in Chilean human rights, one vital key to economic success—foreign investment—will not be forthcoming.

Conclusion

In spite of the country's disastrous economic situation and a growing discontent within the government, as well as outside, Chile's military will probably continue to control the country in the foreseeable future. The most obvious reason is the absence of any viable challenge to their domination. Other factors, however, contribute to their stability:

I.   The Allende regime was an unforgettable trauma to many Chileans. Things may be bad now, but many regard the disorder of the previous administration as even worse. This view is held by the armed forces and by the influential groups in the country.

II. That there could be an alternative to military government is equally uncertain, at least for the proximate future. A realignment of civilian support or alterations in the economic model are conceivable changes, but there is no alternative to the military as arbiters of power.

III. As in all repressive regimes (right or left), the security forces have now become an independent political force with a veto over any opening. The continued currency in Chile of the Marxist views the armed forces intervened to overcome gives the security forces ongoing justification for their role. They, as well as the armed forces which have spawned and protected them, will surely resist any change that might lead to an exposure of what they have done.

IV. The Chilean armed forces, in contrast to some other military systems, have maintained an extraordinary unity in their first two years. Minor speculation about a division among them focuses on General Leigh as a potential alternative leader, because of his obvious ambition and his populist (though corporatist and statist) comments. At the moment, however, the armed forces are united, and as commander of the air force, Leigh does not offer an alternative power base to the army.

V.   The junta has convinced itself (and probably most Chileans) of the following explanations for the country's difficulties. These explanations help defuse opposition, but the fact that they are not completely true may in time become more apparent to the armed forces and to a significant number of ordinary Chileans.

   A. The country's economic problems are solely a result of the Allende administration and the squeeze between high import costs and low export earnings from copper.

   B. Criticism of the regime's conduct concerning human rights results from a Marxist and communist campaign against Chile.

C. Though times are hard, the country has no alternative to the present economic shock treatment.

VI. The regime seems to have reasonable support, based on the first, second, and fifth factors. Gallup polls held in January and June 1975 revealed a surprisingly favorable attitude toward the junta. One may legitimately doubt that in the present climate of arbitrary arrest and fear, Chileans will give their real opinions. In the June poll, 71 percent considered the regime better than average or good; 54 percent (79 percent in January) preferred a strong and authoritarian government, 16 percent preferred a mild government of dialogue, while 30 percent did not answer; 66 percent thought that the government treats employers and employees equally; 20 percent favored elections with participation of the non-Marxist parties, 75 percent were opposed, and 5 percent did not answer.

The junta government is at a critical juncture and public debate is increasingly focused on economic policies. The economic shock treatment has been traumatic. With so much discontent, one must doubt whether it can continue for many months. The junta will have to decide whether or not to continue with the same economic team and perhaps even the same person at the head of the junta. If the shock treatment is successful in reducing inflation and a slow recovery begins, there may be no changes. If, on the other hand, inflation and stagnation continue, the armed forces may conclude that they have been ill served by their civilian advisers and look around for broader civilian support.

Any broadening, ideological or economic, will alter the structure described in this report and represent a more realistic response to the interests of the Chilean people. Chile's fundamental political difficulty stems from the tragic polarization that occurred between 1970 and 1973. To overcome the threat of one extreme, the armed forces took the simple way out, associating themselves with the other extreme. To maintain this tactic will institutionalize an authoritarianism that is unpleasantly reminiscent of those that were current in much of Europe and Latin America in the 1920s and 1930s and ensure continued international concern about Chile, not only from Marxists, but from others as well. The opportunity is there, on the other hand, for the armed forces to work toward a new and admittedly difficult political recomposition by initiating an authentic dialogue with the various social groups and political currents.

Reprinted and edited from Thomas G. Sanders, *Military Government in Chile, Part II: The New Regime* [TGS–9–'75], Fieldstaff Reports, West Coast South America Series 22, no. 2 (1975), pp. 1–12.

Abraham F. Lowenthal

Military Government in Peru, 1968-74

Peru's military regime has unquestionably put the country on the world political map. Washington, Moscow, Peking, and Havana have all expressed special interest in Peru's affairs. The Lima embassies of the latter three are now probably their biggest in South America, and the U.S. embassy has argued (with limited success) that Washington's policy toward Peru should be sympathetic, despite the political and legal difficulties posed for the U.S. government by Peru's treatment of certain American investments.

From several foreign perspectives, Peru's current process of military-directed change is regarded with hope. For many on the international left, Peru seems especially significant, particularly now that the "Chilean way" has been so abruptly closed. From this vantage point, Peru is contrasted with Brazil. In Brazil, leftist intellectuals have lost their jobs and rights, and some have suffered torture; many of their counterparts in Peru are advising the regime or are at least sympathetic to it (though a few have been interfered with, and some even deported). Bishops in Brazil condemn their regime; Peruvian bishops generally support theirs. The Brazilian regime promotes capitalist expansion, national and foreign, but the Peruvian government announces its aim to move away from capitalism. And while Brazil has tied itself ever more closely to the United States, Peru has acted to reduce its dependence on Washington.

Paradoxically, many international lenders and even some investors also regard Peru's experiment favorably. The military regime has earned plaudits for its prudent fiscal management and for its pragmatism in dealing with foreign companies. From this standpoint, Peru's regime is contrasted with Chile's under Allende and with Castro's. Whatever the short-term nuisance of re-negotiation contracts and absorbing nationalist rhetorical attacks, some foreign investors think the military regime is making Peru safe for them, now and for some time to come.

Within Peru, however, the military regime's program is not so widely acclaimed. Articulate observers from both sides of the political spectrum assail the government. Though the traditional (Moscow-line) Communist party openly supports the military regime, many on the left regard it as far from "revolutionary," but rather as an ally of international capitalism, exploiting the

288

Peruvian masses for the sake of dominant minorities. From the right, the military government's program is also viewed with deepening distrust. Even those businessmen who had adjusted themselves to the agrarian reform, a greatly extended state role in the economy, enforced profit-sharing and worker-management schemes, and countless other changes they might have resisted under other circumstances, found themselves alarmed by the sudden nationalization in 1973 of the entire fishmeal industry (Peru's main earner of foreign exchange) and by the repeated, escalating stress on social property.[1]

Despite its international stature, the Peruvian regime finds itself almost bereft of conspicuous support at home. No group is likely soon to displace or even seriously challenge the military, but the government encounters concerted opposition within several important sectors: labor, business, peasants, students, and professionals. One politically meaningful election after another reflects antiregime sentiment; opposition candidates have won the recent polls held by sugar workers' and teachers' cooperatives as well as the lawyers', doctors', and engineers' associations, and militantly antiregime student groups hold sway in practically all Peruvian universities. Some backing, particularly among the urban poor and among highland peasants who have benefited from the agrarian reform, is demonstrated from time to time, especially through mass meetings, but contrary evidence is even more striking. General strikes in several provincial areas, including Arequipa, Cuzco, and Puno, forced the regime to suspend constitutional guarantees temporarily in mid-1973 and again later that year, and major antigovernment demonstrations have occurred on several other occasions.[2]

The National System to Support Social Mobilization (SINAMOS), established in 1971 partly to organize support for the government, has instead been the object of intensifying attack from all sides, and even of some backbiting from within the regime. And though the army is surely Peru's preeminent middle-class institution, middle-class distress is increasingly perceptible. Housewives, bureaucrats, teachers, taxi drivers, secretaries: all are grumbling.

. . . The current [1975] Peruvian process cannot yet be easily labeled. Many of the regime's key activities remain ambiguous or apparently contradictory. In other areas, gaps have developed between rhetoric and practice, and it is hard to tell which, if either, will eventually be modified.

In the economic sphere, the regime's most obvious accomplishment has been to expand and fortify what had been one of South America's weakest states. The government has announced its intent to control all industries it defines as basic. It has already taken over, in addition to the fishmeal industry, a major share of mining and metal refining; all petroleum refining, most petroleum marketing, and some oil exploration; the railroad, telephone, and cable companies, and Peru's international air carrier; cement companies and a steadily increasing share of the electric utilities; 51 percent of every television station and at least

25 percent of each radio station; cotton, sugar, tobacco, and mineral exporting; importing and distributing of several key commodities; considerable food marketing; a majority of the banking system and of the insurance business; all reinsurance; even the operation of the airport's duty-free store and of a small chinchilla farm. Incipient government participation in pharmaceutical manufacturing and distribution may portend further expansion in this and other areas. All told, the state's share of national investment has jumped to almost 50 percent from 13 percent in 1965 (though this change reflects some decline in private capital formation as well as the expansion of government spending).

. . . But while the Peruvian state grows, the military regime repeatedly asserts it does not mean to end major private economic activity. When the fishmeal nationalization shocked the private sector (the official 1971–75 national plan had assured that the fishmeal industry would remain private), no fewer than seven cabinet ministers stressed within a week that the measure was exceptional and that complete abandonment of private enterprise was by no means contemplated. Reassurances to private business have not been limited to verbal expressions; generous tax incentives, tariff breaks, efforts to reorganize Lima's stock exchange, and other measures to stimulate private investment and reinvestment have accompanied the regime's moves in some sectors toward state ownership. Repeated government statements advocate "economic pluralism" and talk of four types of enterprise (state, social property, reformed private, and unreformed private for small-scale firms). No one explains convincingly, however, how such very different modes of economic organization can effectively coexist. Some Peruvians believe the private sector is doomed to extinction, therefore, and cite the measures taken against Empresas Eléctricas (universally considered a model firm) as further evidence that the regime means to finish off private enterprise. Others regard the social-property sector as an elaborate facade and point to cases like Bayer's acrylic fiber plant (accorded especially favorable treatment as a "strategic" industry) or the deal, highly favorable to the company, by which ITT transformed its assets in the telephone company into a hotel investment, as indicative of what is really happening. Not only Peruvian industrialists, but even the regime's own former minister of economy and finance, have had to call for clarification of the "rules of the game" under which Peru's economy is to operate.

In the political arena, the regime was similarly active, but again with ambiguous results. The government has vowed to destroy the traditional political system dominated by special interests and to replace it with one open equally to the influence of all citizens, a "social democracy of full participation." The task of destruction is being rapidly accomplished, but the second task is still far from realization.

The military regime systematically undercut almost all organizations politically influential in Peru before 1968 except the church and, of course, the armed forces. Established parties were severely hampered. Economic interest groups were crippled; the once powerful National Agrarian Society was dissolved, and the National Industries Society was stripped of its formal standing and forbidden to represent itself as national; its president was deported. The government weakened the labor unions by playing rivals (the CGTP and the CTP) off against each other and against a regime-blessed alternative (CTRP)[3].

Lima's newspapers, once influential, were first cowed into almost total blandness by a skillful combination of legislation, intimidation, and incentives and then taken over by the regime and entrusted, under conditions that amount to probation, to diverse political and social groups. The judicial system, perceived by the regime as a restraint, was "reorganized" and made much more responsive (to say the least) to government desires. Private universities, until 1969 governed individually, had their autonomy curtailed by the creation of a central national university system. Autonomous peasant federations, which gained some strength in the 1960s, were pushed toward atrophy and then effectively banned under a law establishing the National Agrarian Confederation. Individuals and families who only five years ago were among Peru's most powerful—Pedro Beltrán, the Prados, the Pardos, the Gildemeisters, and the Ayulos, to name just a few—had their influence, if not their wealth, very sharply reduced.

What is not clear, however, is whether the new political order is really to be anything different from a particularly efficient version of a traditional dictatorship, governed this time by a military-technocrat coalition. Despite all the regime's talk about full participation, very few Peruvians have a prescribed role in influencing government decisions, and few feel that the regime is responsive to their claims. It is no wonder that the regime lacks public support: citizens, particularly those whose views used to find expression through established political channels, resent an autocratic regime, completely military at the cabinet level, which can act arbitrarily without restraint.

The government's dealings with labor and peasant unions, professional and student organizations, business lobbies, and other groups suggest that the regime distrusts any autonomous organizations and wishes to deal only with units established or legitimized by the regime. The implicit—and sometimes explicit—concept for political organization is corporatist. The regime is steadily building up the apparatus by which one group after another is to be tied directly to the executive, which will attempt to harmonize all interests perceived by the regime as legitimate and expressed through channels considered appropriate. Political parties are not so regarded; persons with recent party responsibilities are specifically prohibited from becoming officials of various newly created participatory mechanisms: in the shantytowns, in educational units, in agricultural cooperatives, etc. Although repeatedly proclaiming its desire for participation and dialogue, the government evinces increasing impatience with those who question any of a number of central ideas. In short, the regime is authoritarian, and increasingly so.

Stable government without severe repression does set Peru apart from its immediate neighbors. (Brazil's regime is impressively stable but surely repressive, Chile's under Allende was unrepressive but unstable, and Chile's junta is so brutally repressive as probably ultimately to be unstable. Ecuador's government is neither stable nor repressive, but Bolivia suffers a regime that is both unstable and repressive.) Yet a closer look at contemporary Peru provides a somewhat murkier view. Protesting miners and peasants have been gunned down on occasion, as so often before in Peru's history. The press has been muzzled. Vague standards of "counterrevolutionary activities" have been intimated and sometimes applied—expressing opposition to the agrarian reform is prohibited, for instance. Leading antiregime personalities have been harassed, and a number deported. The regime repeatedly demonstrated—in dealing with students or with striking teachers, miners, and doctors, for example—that it prefers to quiet opposition by accommodation rather than by force. But when push comes to shove, the regime acts without regard for the niceties of constitutional doctrine. . . .

But one cannot dismiss the Peruvian military's talk of "full participation" as mere rhetoric. The regime's spokesmen may well be right in asserting that only harsh treatment of the previous power structure could facilitate eventual political participation by the Peruvian masses. Now that the preliminary job is mostly done, some efforts have been initiated, especially through SINAMOS and through the educational and industrial community mechanisms, to decentralize decision making and transfer it to the local level. At least a few of the top government leaders, especially in SINAMOS, and many of its operating personnel, seem sincerely committed to helping peasants, shantytown dwellers, parents of schoolchildren, and industrial workers organize to achieve effective power. While much of the regime's activity seemed aimed (successfully so) at demobilizing previously influential Peruvian groups, SINAMOS appeared to be politicizing and "raising consciousness" among several sectors which will eventually be in a position to pressure the army itself. . . .

In foreign policy, the Peruvian regime is widely acknowledged to be inventive and imaginative. Diplomatic relations have been established with the Soviet Union, China, and Cuba, and each of these ties opened up significant possibilities for trade diversification and eventual expansion. The USSR bought over 15 percent of Peru's sugar exports in 1973, China bought over 10 percent of Peru's copper, and both Cuba and China were important purchasers of Peru's fishmeal in 1972 (when Peru last had extra fishmeal to sell and badly needed a market). Substantial Eastern European investment and technical cooperation have been obtained. Major Japanese loans and investments have begun to come in, both for infrastructure and for industrial facilities.

All these steps, together with Peru's role in the Andean pact and other international organizations and its spirited championing of the two hundred-mile territorial sea limit, have been portrayed as reducing Peru's dependence, principally on the United States. Government spokesmen repeatedly claim—with considerable credibility in a country previously pushed around by Washington in connection with the International Petroleum Company (IPC) case, the refusal to sell supersonic military aircraft, and other issues—that Peru has now regained its dignity. And they suggest that important economic decisions affecting Peru, once made in New York and Washington, are now made in Lima.

The major growth sectors of the Peruvian economy—petroleum and mining—are still mostly premised on major foreign private investment, however. The military regime signed numerous contracts with foreign oil companies; and though the terms of these contracts are probably more favorable to Peru than those of previous contracts, they appear to be at least as generous to the foreign firms as are comparable arrangements made by other countries (like Indonesia) not noted for their revolutionary credentials. In the industrial area, even Brazil's avowedly pro-foreign-investment regime gets better terms, at least in some sectors, than Peru can command. It is hard to say, therefore, whether Peru's new foreign policy amounts to much more than a particularly flamboyant adjustment to the shifting realities of international power and to new fashions in international rhetoric. Making that adjustment intelligently is no negligible accomplishment, but it is not so fundamental a change as Peru's spokesmen herald.

The Peruvian military bases its claim to be revolutionary primarily on the structural reforms it has designed, promulgated, and begun to administer. Here, again, no easy label is appropriate.

The agrarian reform of 1969 brought a substantial redistribution of land in a country where the ownership of land has long been exceptionally concentrated. Within less than five years the regime took over virtually all Peru's large estates, beginning with the vast sugar plantations (which were not to be affected at all under the previous Peruvian agrarian reform legislation) and moved next to the highland areas. Land was expropriated and title redistributed at a pace faster than that of any recent Latin American reform but Cuba's, and perhaps Chile's under Allende. Legislation affecting access to water, without which land ownership may be useless, was sharply revised.

The industrial or enterprise reform provides workers a share not only in profits but also in management. [According to new legislation] workers within each firm employing six or more workers receive a fixed percentage of their company's profits, some distributed immediately in cash but more retained as commonly owned shares in the firm, which is eventually to be half-owned by the "labor community"—the collectivity of a firm's workers. The community's representatives have the right to participate in management decisions, to audit company books and records, and generally to assure that the workers' actual and prospective interests are being protected. Similar mechanisms exist in the mining, fishing, and telecommunications sectors.

. . . The social security system, built up piece by piece over a fifty-year period, was reorganized and rationalized. For those already covered it provided generous retirement, accident, and health benefits more equitable than before, and it extended coverage to a few new groups, including domestic servants and even artists. And labor legislation was revised to assure increased job security to the employed.

Each of these reforms transferred resources—present and especially future—from more to less privileged Peruvians. All represented considerable advances over the measures that previous Peruvian regimes had been willing or able to undertake. Substantial numbers of Peruvians, surely a majority of those groups whose members have voted in Peru's past national elections, were obtaining more, some significantly more, from the national system than they did prior to the military regime.

Viewed from another perspective, however, the reforms were at least as noteworthy for their limits as for their advance. The military regime's measures were carried out, if somewhat self-consciously, under the banner of Tupac Amaru, the mestizo leader who headed Peru's main Indian uprising against the Spanish conquerors. But the reforms seem unlikely to affect significantly the fundamental distribution of power and rewards in Peruvian society—that is, between those already participant in Peru's economy and politics and those (the Indians, generally speaking) still largely excluded from the system's benefits. As several scholars have shown, the income distribution resulting from the laws decreed so far—even if they are fully implemented—will occur almost exclusively within the top quarter of Peru's income recipients; three-quarters of Peru's population is unlikely to be much affected. The great majority of Peruvians will not obtain land, because there is not enough to go around. They will not become members of industrial communities, because they are not among the aristocracy of Peruvian laborers working in industrial firms of the requisite size. They will not get improved social security benefits, because they are not among the privileged minority covered by the "national" scheme, nor will they enjoy job security, because they have no steady job to begin with. And the benefits their children get from the educational reform will probably be strictly limited, for, on the past record, their children are likely to be among the majority of school attenders who drop out before the sixth grade.

. . . In short, the military regime [sought to] distribute resources and rewards in a more equitable way to those Peruvians already able to make their own demands heard and felt—by strikes, land invasions, votes, or other forms of organized expression. In this sense, the military government carried on the process of "segmentary incorporation" that Peru's elites managed for generations: to admit claimants with voice and power into the political and economic system, but on terms that protected its boundaries and prevented the minority within from being overwhelmed by a coalition of the majority without. The identity and relative influence of those on top had changed somewhat, and that is important. But the process of internal domination continues, and those on the bottom are pretty much the same as before.

Excerpts from Abraham F. Lowenthal, "Peru's Ambiguous Revolution," in *The Peruvian Experiment: Continuity and Change under Military Rule,* ed. Abraham F. Lowenthal (copyright © 1975 by Princeton University Press), pp. 4–17. Omission of footnotes. Reprinted by permission of Princeton University Press.

Notes

1. In 1976, the Peruvian regime partially reversed the nationalization of the fishmeal industry and deemphasized social property. [ED.]

2. Demonstrations and armed confrontations intensified at the end of 1976, despite the ouster of Velasco Alvarado. A general strike in the summer of 1977 again seriously threatened domestic order. [ED.]

3. CGTP is the Confederación General de Trabajadores del Perú, the Communist party labor organization. CTP is the APRA-affiliated Confederación de Trabajadores Peruanos. The regime-sponsored CTRP is the Confederación de Trabajadores de la Revolución Peruana. [ED.]

Julio Cotler

Concentration of Income and Political Authoritarianism in Peru

During the last few months, more than one observer of the political process has recognized the development of a seemingly paradoxical situation, a situation which in reality is the expression of the new character taken on by class conflict recently. This supposed paradox consists of the fact that while the Revolutionary Government of the Armed Forces moves forward with the reorganization of the state and of the productive apparatus, advocating a program initially antioligarchical—but whose development is more consistent with state capitalism in association with international corporations—the pressure and combativeness of the popular classes against the bourgeoisie and the government have actually increased. These pressures are aimed both at breaking out of the established limits of the reforms introduced by the government, which are enmeshed in the capitalist structure, and at achieving the political autonomy of the workers. The massive popular mobilization of workers which developed in May and June of 1973 in Moquegua, Arequipa, Chimbote, and Lima are indisputable signs of this situation.

Moreover, as a result of the growing state of emergency among the popular classes, a key element of this apparent paradox has been laid bare. This consists of the inoperativeness of the institutions of corporate hue that the government has introduced in order to contain and control social conflicts. SINAMOS,[1] the CTRP,[2] and the agrarian leagues can be relatively effective in recruiting demonstrators who will applaud official personages for the antioligarchical reforms carried out, but they are frankly incapable of fulfilling the corporativizing function for which they were intended. Fundamentally this is because the workers are discovering in the everyday reality of the class struggle the necessity of securing and preserving their autonomy and of defining politically their specific interests as a dominated class.

It is precisely due to this incapacity of the above-mentioned institutions—in spite of the fact that they enjoy the support of the authorities and their intermediaries the communications and propaganda media—that the government has had to resort to traditionally repressive methods in order to contain the popular pressures: firing, jailing, and deporting workers, union leaders, and politicians. That is to say, the Revolutionary Government of the Armed Forces

296

has openly revealed its political precariousness in the sense that the governmental institutions find themselves incapable of isolating, channeling, and diminishing the popular struggles.

Crudely stated, the paradox is this: the government claims that it "has done more for the Peruvian people than any other government," but it finds itself incapable of assembling the massive and organized support of the popular classes, thereby forcing it to make ever more frequent use of repressive methods.

How can we explain this apparent contradiction? The bureaucracy and its organs of information have readily accepted the "arguments" that most likely originate in the state security agencies. For them, this contradiction is only explainable in terms of the political "agitation" of the ultra-left, of APRA, and, depending upon individual sympathies and affiliations, of the Communist party. The existence of conflicts of class interest do not enter into these considerations since they are "undesirable" from the ideological perspective of the ruling group. In the last instance, popular mobilization is attributed to the perverse action of a few bad individuals who want to ruin everything for the vast majority. In this way the bureaucracy and its information agencies are ironically repeating the same arguments that *La Prensa* and *El Comercio*[3] have been using for decades to justify popular repression.

But these infantile arguments that divulge a demoniacal perception of the social reality encounter overwhelming difficulties. What magic, what omnipotent power do those miniscule groups have—as the official representatives or apologists of the government claim—when they do not possess the means for the massive diffusion of written propaganda, nor for speaking on television, nor of millionaire propaganda media? What power do they have, we repeat, to incite those sectors that according to the government will be precisely those who will benefit from the reforms?

Either these tiny groups have an overwhelming capacity for brainwashing the popular classes and convincing them that they are not beneficiaries of the reforms, or else, the Peruvian people are ungrateful, blind, and deaf to the actions that the government of the armed forces carry out on their behalf. It is neither one nor the other. On various occasions, the government has received massive demonstrations of support for carrying out measures that signified a popular victory after decades of desperate and violent struggle against the oligarchy and imperialism. We are not dealing, then, with an inability to acknowledge the actions of the government. Nor can the problem be explained in terms of the "Peruvian psychology" now so in vogue among some intelligent functionaries.

The explanation for this apparent paradox should be examined in light of the class nature of the reforms. In this sense, we maintain that the economic reforms, owing to the class nature of state capitalism that is evident in the country, have a very limited effect with respect to redistribution of income and wealth in favor of the popular classes. In the second place, these antioligarchical reforms have not been accompanied by a profound political democratization; on the contrary, the government is continuing to restrict the free expression and political articulation of the popular classes to the end of preventing them from constituting an autonomous power factor with the political capacity to intervene actively and directly in the conformation of a state that represents them.

That is to say, the new character of the class struggle in Peru consists of the popular classes being confronted in the economic sphere with very limited measures which do not satisfy even their immediate needs and in the political sphere with an apparatus that continues to prevent them from achieving an organization which would allow them to overcome said limitations: in sum, a class enemy that operates with new modes. We will treat each of these problems separately.

1. The Distributive Scope of the Economic Reforms

From the economic point of view, the reforms carried out by the Revolutionary Government of the Armed Forces, as we have stated elsewhere, are characterized by their segmentary orientation. That is to say, the benefits derived from them are not spread among the aggregate of the popular classes, but rather favor determined segments that are isolated from the whole. Moreover, when one analyzes quantitatively the scope of the most important measures, it is surprising to note that they have had a very limited impact. And this last point is due to the fact, as we have been arguing, that these reforms affect only tangentially the dominant nucleus of the capitalist-dependent structure, while on the other hand they attack in substantive form the areas and operational nature of the traditional agrarian structure of the country.

Two studies sustain these hypotheses. An examination of the distribution of per capita income allowed Richard Webb[4] to point out that in general terms the inequality and concentration of income in 1961 was more pronounced in Peru than in many of the so-called underdeveloped countries. According to Webb's calculations, the 10 percent of the population with the highest income possessed 50 percent of the national income, whereas the poorest 10 percent received only 1 percent of that national income—a difference of fifty times between the two groups.

If one accepts the hypothesis that these proportions did not vary significantly up to 1969, it is appropriate to ask in what way have the agrarian reform, the industrial reform, the mining reform, and the fishing reform—the most radical of the government's measures—affected the distributive pyramid.

DISTRIBUTION OF INCOME, 1961

Annual Per Capita Income	Percent of Population	Percent of National Income
Less Than 2,000-5,000 Soles (About $46-$115)	37	6
5,001-10,000 Soles (About $115-$230)	25	12
10,001-20,000 Soles (About $230-$461)	22	20
Over 20,000 Soles (About $461)	16	62

SOURCE: Based on the data compiled by Richard Webb. The dollar equivalents were prepared by Loveman and Davies and are based on 43.38 Soles to the dollar.

In the first place, these measures favor the redistribution of income *within* each economic sector of production in such a way that the areas of highest productivity, such as in the case of mining, for example, do not transfer benefits to the areas of least productivity such as agriculture. At the same time, with the exception of the mining and fishing industries, the redistribution within each sector is realized in turn within each production unit, thereby fixing a second phase of segmentation of the population and the fragmentation of the consciousness of the social interest groups.

With reference to the Agrarian Reform, Adolfo Figueroa states the following:

In fact, the redistribution of income that is generated as a result of the redistribution of property touches only the economic surplus previously appropriated by the hacendado: the implicit rent from the land and the net profit. Therefore, the transference of income represents 14 percent of the aggregate agrarian value. Fourteen percent of 7,859,000,000 Soles [about $182,000,000]—which is the value of the affected agrarian sector—gives us about 1,200,000,000 Soles [about $28,000,000], not quite 1 percent of the national income for 1961. This is what is redistributed overall by the Agrarian Reform. If this percentage were distributed equally, the Agrarian Reform would increase by one-half of 1 percent the income of the campesinos who constitute the poorest 25 percent of the country. But with the way the Agrarian Reform is being implemented, not even this effect is anticipated.

The explanation for this last assertion is based on the fact that "the Agrarian Reform does not simply redistribute income *within* each subsector. For a quarter—and perhaps half—of the rural population, the redistributive process is doubly slanted against them: they are made to participate in the redistribution in the sector of lowest productivity and within each sector, of the most backward subsector." From this the author argues: "the conclusion of this study is that the agrarian sector has been segmented by the strategy of income redistribution."

Now then, if one accepts the hypothesis that the "central problem of income redistribution in Peru is that the agrarian sector determines the distributive profile," the obvious conclusion is that the Agrarian Reform has had a very limited impact on the transformation of the country's income structure.

Moreover, as a study by H. van Wettering[5] has shown, on the basis of the existing system of affecting land, around one-fifth of the rural population of the country will receive three-fourths of the land, thus making it impossible for the great majority of the rural population to obtain land. In addition, this same study demonstrates that most of the meager income received by the campesinos will be transferred to the commercial and industrial sectors, that is to say where the nucleus of modern capitalism is concentrated.[6]

The General Industrial Law follows the same pattern seen in the Agrarian Reform. Figueroa notes this as follows: "The law affects the manufacturing sector that generates approximately 15 percent of the national income and occupies 5 percent of the labor force. Of this 15 percent, the law concentrates on the net profits of those firms which are estimated to generate 30 percent of the income of the industrial sector. That is to say, the law affects 4.5 percent of the national income and transfers to the workers 10 percent of this sum—0.5 percent of the national income—in cash form and 15 percent in the form of property accumulated in the name of the workers"—or about another 0.5 percent of the national income. But again, this participation is realized in a fragmentary fashion because "of the 10 percent of the net income that the law gives to the workers, only 5 percent is prorated equally while the other 5 percent is distributed in direct proportion to individual salaries."

Now the executives of these companies, who also form part of the industrial community, have average salaries seven times higher than those of the workers. Thus, "for 1971, it is estimated that participation in the 10 percent of the net income meant an annual average increase in income of 2,611 Soles [about $60] per worker; that is to say, a 4 percent raise. However, according to the law's provisions, this percentage was not distributed equally among all the companies' workers."

Finally, Figueroa is emphatic about the minimal redistributive impact of the mining and fishing reforms: "The mining and fishing laws affect 2 percent and 8 percent of the national income, respectively. If we assume that the net income is 50 percent of these percentages, then of this 1 percent and 4 percent, 8 percent and 4 percent are distributed as income to the workers. Thus, as one can see, the overall amount to be redistributed is practically nil." Thus, the fishermen received an average of somewhere near 2,500 Soles [about $58] for 1972 as income from the fishing communities.

Finally, it is necessary to remember that the industrial, mining, and fishing reforms benefit only a small fraction of the laboring population, less than 10 percent of the nation's labor force. Under these conditions, the unemployed and underemployed in the cities—according to official figures between 40 and 50 percent of the economically active population—are excluded from these reforms.

If to all these considerations one adds the fact that according to unofficial sources the inflation rate in the country this year will be 26 percent (if the rate for the first six months continues), one can conclude that the real benefits accruing to the popular classes as a result of the reorganization of the state are very limited. *That is to say, the income pyramid that we presented above has not been greatly affected.* Therefore Webb concludes that: "In reality the changes that need to be carried out are of such magnitude and so different from the present measures that their implementation would mean a revolution."

The limitations on income redistribution can be explained, we repeat, by the class nature of the measures adopted. These affect only tangentially the hegemonic nucleus of the economy composed more each day of capital controlled by the state and international concerns. By way of illustration: if the industrial communities received half of the property immediately, the rise in income of those workers affected would not be 4 percent but 25 percent, according to Webb's calculations. It is precisely this fact that invalidates the distributive impact of the antioligarchical reforms. In effect, these reforms, by erroneously falling on the traditional sectors, provide for a very narrow margin of income redistribution among the popular classes.

It is precisely because of this that the class struggle since 1969 has assumed a new character. Up to 1969, the popular pressures sought the eradication of the traditional and oligarchical forms of domination and thus had a strong populist streak that was manifested by the petit bourgeois leadership. Today, as a result of the process of modernization now being carried out, the popular pressures are attacking capitalism in its modern or modernized versions, thereby making clear their class orientation.

2. Political Authoritarianism

The aggregate of the antioligarchical reforms which are derived from the conformation of state capitalism have been juxtaposed to the development of aspirations and expectations among the popular sectors which, in turn, were fomented by the fiery vehemence of the articles, speeches, and official proclamations which assured us that the day of national and popular class liberation is at hand, here and now. The disparities evident between the limited real benefits received by the popular sectors and the propaganda about the possibilities opened up by the revolution of the armed forces without any doubt led to the development of a series of movements to make said possibilities a reality.

Precisely in order to contain this popular mobilization that in conscious or unconscious form, directly or indirectly, is attacking the restrictive redistributive policies of the regime, the government has felt compelled to act in a bureaucratic and authoritarian manner against the popular masses so as to prevent them from becoming a power center and from putting an end to the limitations to which they are subjected. To this end, the political strategy of the government is directed towards preventing the dominated classes from becoming masters of their own social existence, and instead they become objects to be cared for with paternal benevolence by the technocrats.

If the floodgates curbing the possibility of the *political* expression of the popular aspirations and needs were opened, it would unloose a process of political democratization which could, without any doubt, blow to bits all the organized programs and tactical plans elaborated by the Revolutionary Government of the Armed Forces.[7]

It is precisely because of this that the government has had to create an atmosphere characterized by state secrecy, seeking to control bureaucratically the workers' organizations. Undoubtedly, the "military" nature of the regime abets this situation in an important way, but it does not explain it. The explanation is to be found in the class interests which the regime serves.

Within this framework it is understandable why an enormous outpouring of reports, bulletins, and studies are stamped "secret," "confidential," "restricted circulation," or something equally suggestive. The politics of "national security," an ideology followed by this regime, adds to the monopoly of information, restricting political life to the "highest agencies" and specialized organs of the armed forces that offer the public the versions they consider expedient. Thus, the dictum of Manuel González Prada—"It is time to destroy the infamous pact of speaking in whispers"—was never more true than today.

A few months ago, a progovernment newspaperman wrote several articles proposing the creation of an "international data bank" for the purpose of studying world problems empirically. To make such a proposal when Peruvians have no possibility of knowing the contents of the secret reports produced by the different official agencies is the worst kind of irony. Why did he not propose instead the creation of a documents center where such reports would be deposited so that Peruvians, and particularly workers, could find out about, for example, the conclusions decided upon by the commission charged with examining the situation of the Cerro de Pasco Corporation?[8] Why did he not make public the state of negotiations with the Grace Corporation?[9] Why did he not make known the data and studies regarding the cooperatives and the SAIS,[10] and so on?

Is the Revolutionary Government of the Armed Forces afraid of the people's judgment about the direction of government policies, or does it perhaps consider the popular sectors to be potential enemies?

This same newspaperman subsequently made an equally cynical proposal: the establishment of a National Institute of Public Opinion that would study the population's opinions regarding the state of affairs in the country. In a situation where information about transcendental matters are state secrets, in a country where it is impossible to find out what is really occurring (unless you happen to be in one of the circles made up of the principal figures of the bureaucracy), in a country where the communications media practice self-censorship, to say the least, to the point of becoming mere echoes of *El Peruano*,[11] in such a country on what basis can you form an opinion? Moreover, in a situation where fear of [being deported] or of being accused of sabotage and taken to the police station is rampant, it is virtually an insult to call for the establishment of an agency dedicated to sounding out "public opinion."

It is in the atmosphere of secrecy, fear, and uncertainty that rumors and gossip of all kinds spring up with a heretofore unknown splendor—which is saying a lot for Lima—rumors which reflect badly on the nation's leaders themselves. In this way, the political culture of the oligarchy, in which only a few privileged individuals had knowledge about political events, lives on and is reinforced in this regime that has carried out antioligarchical reforms. In a word, even if the oligarchical faction of the bourgeoisie has been eliminated, its political style remains unaltered.

Finally, in a society governed by political secrecy, it is worth asking how a "social democracy of full participation" can be created. In a society governed by a bureaucratic group which has exclusive control over information and decision making, how do they intend to create the "new man"? In effect, the fundamental feature that characterizes political democracy is the *massive and public* diffusion of all information regarding every problem that affects the republic, particularly its exploited sectors; to the end of providing freedom of expression and participation in the progress of the political life of the country.

The monopolization of information is strictly tied to the bureaucratic character of the country's political life, that is to say, to the imposition by decree of the economic and social organization of the country, without even symbolic participation by popular organisms. The thesis that the pressure of the masses and their . . . confrontations are illegitimate and "undesirable," together with the military concept of life that the population should accept the orders imparted by their superiors "without question or muttering," necessarily contributes to the growing isolation between the government and the society.

Examples abound. Today in the heart of the bureaucracy, the conformation of "social property," which will be the priority sector of the country's economic structure, is being discussed by small committees. But these small committees have no input from the group to be most affected—the workers. The different ministers, on the other hand, have their advisory commissions composed of technocrats and businessmen in which the aspirations, preoccupations, and needs of the popular sectors are not even represented. Again, the judgment that the advisers should be "duly prepared" individuals does nothing more than to insist upon the technocratic character of politics. In this way, politics is being confused with administrative acts.

It is within this framework that one can understand the supposed paradox that was presented earlier. If this government continues to find itself increasingly incapable of dealing with the popular masses, this is not due simply to the fact that it is a "military government." Rather it is because there exists a structural contradiction—around which the class struggle develops—between the class nature of the economic reforms and political democratization. The principal leaders of the country are perfectly aware of this as can be seen in the repeated declarations of the minister of economy. The active participation of the popular classes in the political life of the country would endanger both the rhythm and the nature of the reforms. The political participation of the popular classes and the development of popular power—*and that is exactly what is being discussed*—would allow room for the "politicos" to modify the program of the Revolutionary Government of the Armed Forces.

In this respect, the Chilean case is illustrative. Thanks to the support of the popular classes, the Popular Unity government was able to develop the important measures that distinguished it. . . . There, precisely due to the fact that the government *was based on the political power of the popular classes*, the workers were able to say: "this government is a piece of shit, but it is *my* government." It would be very difficult to find popular sectors in Peru that could make that same assertion.

The technocratic belief that political change can be effected outside the development of the class struggle, as an administrative act, leads to the development of a repressive policy which leaves bare the political precariousness of the Peruvian government. . . .

Translated, reprinted, and edited from "Concentración del Ingresso y Autoritarismo Político en el Perú," *Sociedad y Política* 1, no. 4 (September, 1973), pp. 6–11. This article so enraged the Peruvian military government that it confiscated the issue in which the article appeared and deported Cotler and the magazine's editor, Aníbal Quijano.

Notes

1. The National System to Support Social Mobilization. See page 289 of the previous selection by Lowenthal. [ED.]

2. Confederation of Workers of the Peruvian Revolution. See page 291 of the previous selection by Lowenthal. [ED.]

3. *La Prensa* and *El Comercio* are Lima's two leading newspapers and both were formerly owned by members of the oligarchy. [ED.]

4. "Trends in Real Income in Peru, 1950–1966," Princeton University, Research Program in Economic Development, Discussion Paper No. 41, February 1974; and his "Government Policy and the Distribution of Income in Peru, 1963–1973," in Abraham F. Lowenthal, ed., *The Peruvian Experiment: Continuity and Change under Military Rule* (Princeton, N.J.: Princeton University Press, 1976), pp. 79–127; and Adolfo Figueroa, *El impacto de las reformas actuales sobre la distribución del ingreso en el Perú* (Lima: CISEPA, Universidad Católica, 1973). [ED.]

5. Hylke van de Wetering, *La Reforma Agraria: un enfoque dirigido a medir su impacto en la economia regional* (Lima: 1970).

6. It is necessary to offer a warning here to avoid misunderstandings. Not one of the authors cited, nor the author of this article, has developed these arguments with the intent of denying the importance of the Agrarian Reform, but rather to establish its limitations. If the Agrarian Reform is indeed a necessary condition for raising the standards of living of the campesinos, it is clear that it is insufficient by itself. This is because of the particular nature of the reform and the relation the countryside has to the overall economy. Thus, for example, Figueroa and Webb show how the policies of agricultural pricing and of food imports noticeably restrict in another way the benefits obtained by the campesino population who are on the periphery of export agriculture.

In effect, the fact that the bases of the capitalist system—the market—have not been affected leads necessarily to this situation. In this respect, look at the difference between the agrarian reforms in Cuba and in Mexico.

7. The proposition, expressed by ideologists and other public officials, that the land reform and the creation of labor communities constitute acts of "transference" of political power is pathetically simplistic. How would they explain then that in every opportunity when the workers (to whom they have supposedly transferred this power) do not accept the dictates of the authorities, they are deported, jailed, or submitted to military justice?

8. Once one of the most powerful foreign corporations in Peru (largely United States owned) with vast holdings in both mining and agriculture. [ED.]

9. Grace is a powerful multinational corporation which had massive holdings in Peru in such areas as agriculture, chemicals, and shipping. [ED.]

10. SAIS, Agrarian Social Interest Groups, are agrarian cooperatives which combine lands from Indian communities with those of nearby expropriated haciendas. [ED.]

11. Since independence, *El Peruano* has been an official government organ. [ED.]

Acknowledgments

Grateful acknowledgment is made to the publishers and authors for their permission to reprint the following selections in whole or in part:

"Politics and Professionalism: The South American Military," by Charles D. Corbett. *Orbis* 26 (Winter 1973): 927–51.

" An Overview of the European Military Missions in Latin America: The Origins and Nature of Professional Militarism in Argentina, Brazil, Chile, and Peru, 1890-1940," by Frederick M. Nunn. *Military Affairs* 29 (February 1975): 1–7.

"The Rise of Modern Militarism in Argentina," by Marvin Goldwert, Associate Professor of History at the New York Institute of Technology. *Hispanic American Historical Review* 48, no. 2 (May 1968): 189–205.

"The Influence of the German Armed Forces and War Industry, 1880-1914," by Warren Schiff. *Hispanic American Historical Review* 52, no. 3 (August 1972): 436–55.

"Emil Körner and the Prussianization of the Chilean Army," by Frederick M. Nunn. *Hispanic American Historical Review* 50, no. 2 (May 1970): 300–322.

"Military Professionalization in Peru," by Víctor Villanueva. Chapter 5 ("Los Militares Vuelven a Sus Cuarteles") of *Ejército peruano: del caudillaje anárquico al militarismo reformista* (Lima: Librería-Editorial Juan Mejía Baca, 1973), pp. 121–33.

"The Military and Argentine Politics," by Robert A. Potash. Adapted from Chapters 1, 2, 3, 4, and 8 of *The Army and Politics in Argentina, 1928-1945: Yrigoyen to Perón* (Stanford, Calif.: Stanford University Press, 1969).

308
Acknowledgments

"An Overview of the Bolivian Military in National Politics to 1952," by William H. Brill. *Military Intervention in Bolivia: The Overthrow of Paz Estenssoro and the MNR* (Washington: 1967 Institute for Comparative Study of Political Systems). pp. 5–9.

"The Military and Bolivian Politics after the Chaco War," originally published as "Germán Busch and the Era of 'Military Socialism' in Bolivia," by Herbert S. Klein. *Hispanic American Historical Review* 47, no. 2 (May 1967): 166–84.

"The Military and Brazilian Politics to World War II," by Ronald M. Schneider. *The Political System of Brazil: Emergence of a Modernizing Authoritarian Regime, 1964-1970* (New York: Columbia University Press, 1971), pp. 37–48.

"The Military in Chilean Politics, 1924–32," by Frederick M. Nunn. *The Americas* 27 (July 1970): 40–55.

"The Military in Peruvian Politics," by Víctor Villanueva. A translated version of chapters 3–5 of *El Militarismo en el Perú* (Lima: T. Scheuch, 1962), pp. 52–107.

"U.S. Army School of the Americas," by the staff of the U.S. Army School of the Americas. *Military Review* 50 (April 1970): 88–93.

"The Development Process and Stability Operations," by Raymond J. Barrett. *Military Review*, 52, no. 11 (November 1972): 58–68.

"A Latin American Perspective on the Latin American Military and Pax Americana," by John Saxe-Fernández. Reprinted from "The Central American Defense Council and Pax Americana," in Irving L. Horowitz et al., eds, *Latin American Radicalism: A Documentary Report on Left and Nationalist Movements* (New York: Random House, Vintage Books, 1969), pp. 75–101.

The Military-Campesino Pact, a speech by Juan José Torres. Reprinted from *Chile, Perú, Bolivia: Documentos de tres procesos latinamericanos* (Buenos Aires: Centro Editor de América Latina, S.A., 1972), pp. 17–21.

"Argentine Economic Policy under the Onganía Regime," by John Thompson. *Inter-American Economic Affairs* 24, no. 1 (Summer 1970): 51–75.

"Military Politics in Argentina, 1966–73," by David Rock. *Argentina in the Twentieth Century* ed. David Rock (Pittsburgh, Pa.: University of Pittsburgh Press, 1975), pp. 207, 209–217.

"Brazil's Economic Miracle," by Albert Fishlow. *The World Today*, Monthly Journal of the Royal Institute of International Affairs, London (November 1973), 29: 474–79.

"The Brazilian Developmental Model: The Political Dimension," by Peter Flynn. *The World Today* (November 1973), 29: 481–94.

Military Government in Chile, Part II: The New Regime, by Thomas G. Sanders. Fieldstaff Reports, West Coast South American Series 22, no. 2 (1975): 1–12.

"Military Government in Peru, 1968–74," by Abraham F. Lowenthal. Excerpts from "Peru's Ambiguous Revolution," in *The Peruvian Experiment: Continuity and Change under Military Rule*, ed. Abraham F. Lowenthal (Princeton, N.J.: Princeton University Press, 1975), pp. 4–17.

"Concentration of Income and Political Authoritarianism in Peru," by Julio Cotler. Translated from "Concentración del Ingresso y Autoritarismo Político en el Perú, *Sociedad y Política* 1, no. 4 (September 1973): 6–11.